Coping with Poverty

Adaptive Strategies in a Caribbean Village

About the Book and Author

This ethnography of Leeward Village, a large coastal community on the little-known Caribbean island of St. Vincent, illustrates how people in one of the poorest countries in the Western Hemisphere pull together in positive and creative ways to adjust to the many adversities they face. Like their Black counterparts elsewhere in the Americas, Leeward Villagers are the rural members of a stratified, state-level society; they have been inculcated with society-wide norms and ideals but not given the skills and opportunities to achieve them. Dr. Rubenstein's contribution to the Afro-American anthropological literature is in going beyond the standard account of the manner in which poverty is reflected in family organization, lifestyle, or religious expression. He offers a more encompassing analysis that includes a serious effort to examine the multiple ways poor Black Vincentians cope with the economic difficulties they face.

Hymie Rubenstein is associate professor of anthropology at The University of Manitoba.

Coping with Poverty

Adaptive Strategies
in a Caribbean Village

Hymie Rubenstein

Westview Press / Boulder and London

Westview Special Studies in Social, Political, and Economic Development

Published in 1987 in the United States of America by Westview Press, Inc.; Frederick A. Praeger, Publisher; 5500 Central Avenue, Boulder, Colorado 80301

Library of Congress Cataloging-in-Publication Data
Rubenstein, Hymie.
   Coping with poverty.
   (Westview special studies in social, political,
and economic development)
   Includes index.
   1. Blacks—Saint Vincent and the Grenadines—Social
life and customs. 2. Blacks—Saint Vincent and the
Grenadines—Economic conditions. 3. Saint Vincent and
the Grenadines—Social conditions. 4. Saint Vincent
and the Grenadines—Economic conditions. I. Title.
II. Title: Coping with poverty. III. Series.
F2106.R83   1987   972.98′4400496   86-32530
ISBN 0-8133-7387-5

Composition for this book was provided by the author.
This book was produced without formal editing by the publisher.

Printed and bound in the United States of America

(∞) The paper used in this publication meets the requirements of the American National
     Standard for Permanence of Paper for Printed Library Materials Z39.48-1984.

6   5   4   3   2   1

HAIROUN[1]

Hairoun! home of the wretched,
A Sceptred isle set in a western sea,
An Antillean gem of poverty and greed,
Where few men thrive and many suffer,
Where women bear children by the hour.
A land with no industries so ever
A land of small farmers without farms
A land of huge farms without any farmers.

You may think there will be trouble soon;
I can almost hear Cuba! Zanzibar! now Hairoun!
But let me hasten to reassure
That politicians debate the budget still,
And all this talk about the people's will
Is sacrificed, of course, at the right price.

Hairoun, AWAKE! and earn once more your Carib name.
Cast out all grudge and hate
And if you try to lay the blame
Remember none is guiltless in this state.
Rid yourself once and forever
Of all traces of colour and favour
Which still persist despite your clamour,
And bend your back to the task ahead,
To cleanse your shores of poverty and greed.

K. M. Coombs,
Flambeau, volume 1, 1965.

[1]The aboriginal Carib name for St. Vincent

Table of Contents

TABLES

xiv

FIGURES

Preface

Black poverty has been a much studied phenomenon. As a social problem it has been the subject of countless investigations by welfare agencies, government departments, and research institutes. As a scholarly concern it has attracted the attention of scores of social scientists, including many anthropologists. The manner in which economic deprivation is reflected in family organization, style of life, and religious and ceremonial expression have all been reported upon. Still the picture is far from complete and several substantive areas, including the basic one of how poor Black people manage to make a living, have received less attention than they deserve. Many theoretical and empirical controversies, such as the role of African survivals and the applicability of the culture and poverty model, keep resurfacing. Most accounts also suffer from a piecemeal approach, as if to suggest an aversion to holistic description where the topic of poverty is concerned. As a result, the tendency has been to look at several features of poverty in a given institutional setting--the family has been a favorite arena for this-- or to concentrate on a single process such as the formation of social networks in several different spheres. Little effort has been made to deal with the multiple responses to poverty in diverse areas of life.

This book addresses these two limitations in Afro-American anthropology by describing how the members of a large coastal village on the little-known southeastern Caribbean island of St. Vincent deal with economic adversity and social stratification. Most Leeward Villagers are the poor, lower-class descendants of slaves and my aim is to describe how they manage to cope with the many historically-rooted environmental, economic, and social constraints they face. The study concentrates on three areas of adaptation to material deprivation and status inequality. These are the economic sphere where the problem of gaining a livelihood is the central concern for most people; the arena of family and household where kin and affines are enlisted for survival; and the realm of non-familial social life where friends, neighbors, and patrons are tapped or appealed to for social and economic aid. Like their Black counterparts elsewhere in the Americas, Leeward Villagers are the rural members of a class-stratified state. This means that they have been inculcated with many society-wide Vincentian norms and ideals. But their social and economic position in the society also means that they have not been granted the skills and opportunities for acting out many of these norms and ideals. Villagers have reacted to this blockage in many ways. In the economic arena a myriad of occupations are pursued and combined in an intricate manner. Dyadic and polyadic exchange relationships are struck with peers, and patrons are sought out in times of need. Those who cannot make a living in the community leave for shorter or longer periods of time to search for work, sending money home to support their families. Prevented from acting out the social forms associated with mainstream norms of kinship and household organization, villagers have also responded by arranging their conjugal behavior, domestic personnel, and household activities in such a way as to ensure their economic well-being.

This is not to say that an optimal solution to the problem of surviving in one of the poorest countries in the Western Hemisphere has been worked out. Villagers recognize that they are poor and frequently state that life is hard in the community. Still, they exhibit a remarkable capacity to adjust in positive and creative ways to the many adversities they face. Coping with poverty is the basis of their survival.

Acknowledgments

Almost all the fieldwork upon which this study is based was made possible by fellowships and research grants from the Province of Ontario (1970), the Canada Council (1970, 1971), the Centre for International Studies at the University of Toronto (1969), and the Social Sciences and Humanities Research Council of Canada (1980, 1985). I thank each of these bodies for their generous support over the years.

Stuart Philpott first sparked my interest in the West Indies. As my thesis supervisor at the University of Toronto he saw me through all the stages of my doctoral program and devoted a good part of a long delayed sabbatical to reading and improving several drafts of my Ph.D. thesis, a work which has influenced parts of this book. He has always been my most demanding critic and for this I can only be grateful. Many thanks are also due to W. Peter Carstens who was Chairman of the Anthropology graduate program during most of my graduate training. His sound advice and encouragement saw me through many difficult periods.

Colleagues at the University of Manitoba have also helped me over the years. Whenever I needed help in reading a draft chapter or simply sounding out an idea, Brian Schwimmer, Raymond Wiest, and H. Christoph Wolfart could always be relied upon for help. For technical assistance I am also grateful to Michael Kelly, Arden Ogg, and Roxie Wilde.

I wish I could thank individually all those Vincentians who made this study possible. The people of Leeward Village have always received me with much warmth and have showed much tolerance of my constant intrusion into their lives. Although many of those who were most kind to me would not object to my using their names here, I have decided to employ pseudonyms for all villagers and for the community in which I have lived and worked for over two and one-half years.

My last visit to the village during July and August 1986 was as personally and intellectually rewarding as my first in September 1969 when I hesitantly entered as a novice anthropologist. I have been back to Leeward Village three times since 1969. I am married to an islander and was proud to have been granted Vincentian citizenship in 1980. This book is dedicated to my wife, 'Tomsie,' whose help in the field and patient encouragement at home can never be repaid.

Hymie Rubenstein,
Winnipeg, Manitoba,
May 11, 1987

Chapter 1

Introduction

THE PROBLEM

To the casual observer, the societies of the Caribbean Sea present a very Western appearance. English, French, Dutch, and Spanish are the official languages. The national political and legal infrastructures include legislatures, formal courts of law, and full-blown civil service bureaucracies. Branches of multi-national banks and insurance companies, well-stocked department stores and supermarkets, movie houses featuring the latest films, and fashionable boutiques have long been part of the urban landscape. The established religious denominations are the Anglican, Roman Catholic, and Methodist churches. Primary and high schools, post-secondary institutions, including several universities, and white-collar vocational aspirations mark the national educational systems. Baseball stadiums, cricket grounds, soccer fields, and race tracks are examples of everyday sports and recreational life. All these features are overt testimony to the regional suzerainty of late 20th century European and North American institutions, conventions, and values. Because of the apparent domination of Western lifeways, many anthropologists, as students of cultural variation, have shown little interest in the region. Several years ago Michael Horowitz (1967a:1) introduced his study of a peasant village in Martinique with the observation that:

> At first glance it is curious that any anthropological work has been done in the West Indies at all, for there are almost no indigenous people, the *sine qua non* of traditional ethnological inquiry.

Never high on the anthropological research agenda (Mintz 1970: 14), the region has attracted fewer scholars than other more 'exotic' areas--Africa, native North America, and the Pacific--and studies carried out there have had little theoretical impact on the discipline as a whole (Wilson 1973:1).

But there is more to West Indian society and culture than the conspicuous duplication of Western elements. Not far below the Euro-American veneer lies what researchers have variously termed "creolized culture," "neoteric society," "contra-culture," "bicultura-tion," "cultural pluralism," "lower-class value stretch," "normative dualism," "plural acculturation," "duality of cultural patterning," and "a moral system within a moral system" (Bryce-Laporte 1970; Crowley 1957; Gonzalez 1969:10-11; Lowenthal 1972:32-33; Reisman 1970:133; Rodman 1963, 1971:194-195; Rubenstein 1976; M.G. Smith 1965, 1966:xxx-xxxi; R.T. Smith 1956:149; Whitten and Szwed 1970:38). Each of these concepts implies that West Indian culture is a complex amalgam of features of European and non-European provenience. These notions also highlight the role played in the West Indies by its most important non-Western immigrants: the millions of Africans who were violently uprooted from their homelands and unwillingly transported to the region during the era of large-scale plantation agriculture. From the historic perspective of colonial society, most of the descendants of these slaves are peoples:

> . . . whose traditional culture has been forcibily changed
> or dissolved through the intervention of forces from the
> Western world. . . . Such groups have characteristics
> different from those of the larger society within which
> they are living, yet they cannot be termed primitive,
> peasant, folk, or any other such designation which implies
> a traditional basis for the society (Gonzalez 1969:10-11).

Gonzalez calls these societies "neoteric," meaning recent in origin, to distinguish them from more "traditional" types of societies. Their members are neither economically, socially, nor culturally self-sufficient but must adjust to the institutions characteristic of the dominant or mainstream portions of the polities in which they are living. Neoteric peoples are habitually poor and politically powerless and they nearly always belong to racial or ethnic groups which are different from those of the elite members of their societies.

Stripped of much of their African heritage by the conditions of slave society (Mintz 1974:11-12; M.G. Smith 1957), encouraged to internalize Western cultural traditions, yet prevented by one means or another from "acting White," low-income Black West Indians are a neoteric people. A good deal of work has been carried out over the years regarding the ingredients of the Black neoteric way of life. Still, some of the most fundamental questions about the origin, functioning, and normative status of forms of behavior and belief Afro-Americans do not share with other members of their societies remain unresolved. Are the distinctively Black phenomena part of the African heritage or did they develop in response to the conditions of slave society (see Abrahams and Szwed 1975; Frazier 1957, 1960, 1966; Herskovits 1937, 1958, 1966; Herskovits and Herskovits 1947; Whitten and Szwed 1970)? Do they represent signs of a unique and separate cultural tradition among poor Blacks or are they merely situational, *ad hoc* responses to material deprivation (see Liebow 1967; M.G. Smith 1965; Valentine 1972)? Are they the product of class-based lifestyle differences, a creative ethnic response, or deviant versions of mainstream ways of behaving (see Blake 1961; Blauner 1970; Frazier 1966; Goode 1966; Henriques 1953; Moynihan 1965; Valentine 1972)?

As too often happens in these cases, some researchers have tried to answer these questions from an inadequate data base. The result has been that much of the theoretical disputation has been inconclusive simply because the various positions have lacked sufficient documentation. Moreover, if the West Indian "contra-culture," like its Black American counterpart, represents a complex blend of elements from several different sources--the African background, slave society, post-Emancipation plantation life, the peasant adjustment, the conditions of poverty, Euro-American institutions and values, and adaptation to racial and ethnic dis-crimination (Blauner 1970)--there may be too much preoccupation with narrowly-based descriptive and theoretical frameworks. In other words, the possibility of such multiple sources of present-day Afro-Caribbean society and culture may call for the use of broader, more eclectic conceptual models.

This book tries to deal with these theoretical and empirical issues by describing the causes and consequences of poverty in Leeward Village, a large rural community in the southeastern Caribbean island of St. Vincent. My central concern is how poor villagers deal with the problem of securing a livelihood--of getting enough food, clothing, shelter, and other life-sustaining necessities. I contend that if the full implications of poverty in Leeward Village--and, by implication, Black communities like it elsewhere in the New World--are to be appreciated, it is important that the descriptive material not be prematurely tied to a preselected

4

theoretical position. In particular, inferences about the historical antecedents or normative status of behavior and beliefs should be avoided until enough data to make methodologically defensible judgments has been collected. This can be done by employing a research strategy which can simultaneously, though parsimoniously, incorporate the multiplicity of factors, historical and contemporary, internal as well as external, that may be affecting the way of life of low income Blacks. Such a methodology is provided by cultural ecology.

Cultural ecology provides an inclusive framework for identifying the network of linkages between a population and its habitat, mode of production, social organization, and ideology. Often treated as a research strategy rather than a separate discipline or theoretical perspective (Anderson 1973:183; Heider 1972:208; Netting 1971:1, 4; Steward 1955), cultural ecology is particularly suited to the task of integrating disparate descriptive materials. This integrative capacity is partly the result of the subscription of cultural ecology to both the holistic axiom and functionalist thinking in anthropology (see Anderson 1973:180, 183, 185; Friedman 1974; Geertz 1963:1; Heider 1972:208; Helm 1962:631-632; Netting 1968:11-12, 21-23; Steward 1955:37, 42; Vayda and Rappaport 1968). But following a cultural-ecological research design does not require the systematic tracing out of all the possible links between ecology, social organization, and ideology. Such a task would be as unscientific as it would be impractical: research must be bounded, focused, and problem-oriented if it is to be productive. In cultural ecology the boundaries, focus, and problem-orientation concern the causal interconnections between the manner in which different peoples exploit their surroundings to gain a livelihood--the material provisioning of society--or otherwise ensure their well-being and particular features of their social organization and supporting belief systems. Central to this concern, yet antithetical to an interpretation of holism which insists that everything in nature and culture is equally connected to everything else (Geertz 1963:6; Steward 1955:37), is the notion that some features of a people's behavior and belief systems are both more interdependent than others, and more closely related to ecological issues (see Anderson 1973:187; Geertz 1963:6-9; Harris 1968:4, 1979; Helm 1962:638-639; Steward 1955:37).

Tempering this ecological focus has been an extension in another direction. There has been increased recognition that the term 'environment' has too often been restricted uncritically to the climatic, edaphic, biotic, and other non-human components of nature. That the *social environment* plays a fundamental role in ecological processes is now well established (Anderson 1973:194; Barlett 1980:551-553; Bennett 1969:11-12; Helm 1962:633; Netting 1968:15; Sahlins 1968:368; Service 1962:7, 113; Vanstone 1974:3; Vayda and Rappaport 1968:488). Ranging from the "intercultural environment" (Netting 1968:15)--the influence of neighboring societies--to inter-personal and demographic constraints within the local group itself (Anderson 1973:194), the social environment often presents the same sorts of problems and requires similar kinds of responses as those of the physical environment. It matters little, for example, whether the environmental influence happens to be a prolonged drought or an intensification of intervillage warfare if the consequence is that the adversely affected group is forced to migrate to a new area to survive. Although ecological analysis can handle both sorts of environmental influence--an important consideration in the Caribbean where overseas exogenous constraints of various sorts have been at least as important as those posed by the local physical and social milieu--the presence of external factors greatly complicates matters (see Bennett 1969:12). There is also the danger that in expanding the environment concept to include social, cultural, and other human influences "ecology" becomes almost synonymous with the whole field of anthropological inquiry (Anderson 1973:181-182; Netting 1968:15). Conversely, this could also produce a serious weakening of the ecological mode of reasoning by inappropriately labeling any study involving relations between people and some aspect of their envi-ronment 'ecological' (Anderson 1973:182, 186). Both sorts of prob-lems--the difficulty in reconciling physical and social environmental variables and the need to distinguish between ecological and non-ecological concerns--may be solved by heeding Netting's (1968:13) admonition to concentrate on issues involving human survival:

> Neither the total habitat nor the whole of culture is considered. The critical features of the environment are those which directly affect man's subsistence quest or threaten his physical well-being. *What is relevant in the environment depends on man's devices for coping with it* (see also Moran 1979:20; Vayda and McCay 1975:293).

In concentrating on environmentally relevant concerns, cultural ecologists have found it useful to employ the concept of *adaptation*. Probably the central notion in cultural ecology (see Alland 1975; Anderson 1973:187; Bennett 1969:9-19; Helm 1962; Keesing 1976:205-225; Netting 1971:4; Sahlins 1968; Steward 1955:39), adaptation defines the relation between people and their social and natural environments as dynamic and creative. Graves and Graves (1974:117) concisely describe these qualities as follows:

> The image of man as a relatively passive pawn of inter-personal cultural forces, which has pervaded anthropo-logical theory in the past, is now giving way to a view of man as a more active agent in shaping his destiny . . . . "Adaptation" nicely captures a growing consensus among anthropologists that the nature of man is best described as neither totally active nor passive but interactive. Operating within the many constraints which his physical and social environments impose, he seeks to overcome the problems confronting him by choosing among perceived available options. Through the aggregation of such choices man modifies and is modified by the world around him in a mutually evolving system.

Like all too many scientific concepts, adaptation has held different meanings for different researchers, some defining it in terms of the maximization of well-being (e.g., Sahlins 1968:368), others taking it simply to refer to the ability to survive and reproduce (e.g., Cohen 1971:3; Hunter and Whitten 1976:71, 125-126). A core idea unites most usages, however: the presence of coping mechanisms which enable a population to establish a viable *equilibrium* with its environment (Alland and McCay 1973:143; Anderson 1973:198-199; Bennett 1969:11, 1976; Helm 1962:634-635; Keesing 1976:207; Moran 1979:7; Rappaport 1968, 1977; Vayda and Rappaport 1968:493). Although equilibrium means that some balance has been struck with environmental forces it does not imply that the solutions that have been worked out are the best of all possible worlds, that the population in question is thriving or even well-off using measurable criteria. Adaptations need only be "good enough" (Rappaport 1977:152). Even Sahlins (1968:369) who argues that "Adaptation implies maximizing social life chances" agrees that:

> [M]aximization is always a compromise, a vector of the internal structure of culture and the external pressure of environment. Every culture carried the penalty of a past within the frame of which, barring total disorganization, it must work out its future. . . . [A]daptive responses can have disadvantageous side effects, as the modification of one constellation of custom sets off untoward consequen-ces elsewhere in the system. To adapt then is not to do

perfectly from some objective standpoint, or even necessarily to improve performance: it is to do as well as possible under the circumstances, which may turn out not very well at all.

It should also be borne in mind that although adaptation is a dynamic process this does not mean that it necessarily involves either continuous structural transformation--the constant evolution of society--or the generation of highly specialized mechanisms for dealing with natural or social constraints. Cultural systems are "conservative" and fundamental changes in form and function tend to occur only with as much frequency as is necessary to ensure survival. Indeed, the chance for long-term viability is likely enhanced by maintaining a flexible, highly generalized relationship with the environment. As Rappaport states (1977:171):

> The *probable* effect of structural change in response to *specific problems* is the reduction of long-term flexibility. There is likely to be a trade-off, then, in adaptive response sequences, of long-term systemic flexibility for immediate efficiency (or other advantage). In an unpredictably changing universe it is good evolutionary strategy . . . to give up as little flexibility as possible, to change no more than is necessary. (To put the matter in more familiar terms, structural change in response to particular stresses is likely to lead to increased specialization and increased specialization to earlier loss in the existential game, a game in which even the rules change from time to time.)

A cultural ecological research strategy is used in this study to explore the response to livelihood constraints in Leeward Village. In analyzing the local-level adaptive mechanisms for coping with poverty from an ecological point of view I am reacting against two sets of limitations which characterize Afro-Caribbean anthropology. The first set has to do with a preoccupation with theory-building in the literature. Models as diverse as those dealing with the African heritage (Herkovits 1937), the organization of slave society (Freilich 1961), the influence of 17th and 18th century European culture (Greenfield 1966), the culture of poverty (Rodman 1971), wage-labor migration (Solien de Gonzalez 1969), cultural pluralism (M.G. Smith 1965), social pathology (Blake 1961), local-level community organization (Clarke 1966), and national class stratification (R.T. Smith 1956)

8

have tried to win over the same body of descriptive material, a literature characterized by large empirical gaps and many unexplored research areas. Too much theory has been running after too little data. In this regard the concept of adaptation has considerable heuristic utility for it allows the setting aside of detailed discussions of such thorny issues as the origin and normative status of particular Afro-American traits and complexes until enough data has been collected to make scientifically defensible judgments. Rather than asking, for example, whether Afro-Americans carry a unique cultural tradition, adaptation directs attention in an entirely different direction. As Bennett (1976:847) has suggested:

> This concept [adaptation] appears to introduce a new level of generalization. Instead of abstractions from behavior, like culture, or the reductive formulas of psychology or genetics, it focuses on human actors who try to realize objectives, satisfy needs, or find peace while coping with present conditions.

To be sure, this does not mean that questions about the origin and meaning of Black social forms and belief systems should be ignored; only that attempts to address such issues should be postponed until there is certainty about what the facts really are.

In Leeward Village many of these facts have to do with the effects of the social environment in the adaptive process. As elsewhere in the Caribbean, the colonial period in St. Vincent saw such a massive and deliberate alteration of the local flora and fauna as to produce the appearance of immunity from indigenous natural environmental forces. Except for the nearly inaccessible interior, most of the pre-Columbian landscape has been transformed into living sites, farmland, and pasture. A whole variety of alien species of plants and animals also have been introduced from other regions. Few visitors to the island (or natives, for that matter) realize that such typically Vincentian food items as bananas, breadfruit, and mangoes are not indigenous to the island. Of all the crops that have at one time or other been major overseas exports--tobacco, cotton, sugarcane, bananas, and arrowroot--only the last may be a regional cultigen. St. Vincent is a dramatic, but not atypical, example of the human ability to deliberately reshape nature to meet species-specific material and social needs. Although it would be absurd to view Vincentians as somehow free from the constraints of the physical milieu, there is reason to pay less attention to the natural landscape and more to the social environment, especially the world outside the island, than if St. Vincent were, say, an isolated non-Western tribal society.

The second set of limitations characterizing Afro-American research which this study addresses are of a substantive rather than theoretical nature. Over the past several years many researchers have studied how Afro-Americans cope with low incomes and associated economic and social problems (e.g., Brana-Shute 1976; Lieber 1981; Stack 1974; Valentine 1972; Whitten 1967; Whitten and Szwed 1970). But although the broad outlines of the responses to poverty have been traced, the picture is far from complete. For one thing, our knowledge of Black adaptation is lopsided, particularly in Caribbean research, because of a long-standing preoccupation with lower-class family organization (see Blake 1961; Clarke 1966; Greenfield 1966; Henriques 1953; Roberts and Sinclair 1978; Rodman 1971; Slater 1977; M.G. Smith 1962b; R.T. Smith 1956). For another, there has been a tendency either to study adaptive behavior within a single domain such as the family (e.g., Rodman 1971; Gonzalez 1969) or to take several different arenas and look for examples of the same kind of process (e.g., Wilson 1973). Again, this has resulted in a piecemeal picture of Black adaptive strategies.

An ecological research strategy is particularly appropriate in this situation. As elsewhere in the Caribbean, much behavior in Leeward Village seems oriented to choice and flexibility--core concepts in cultural ecology--with folk statements being unreliable guides for predicting action. Expressed ideals often contradict accepted norms and both sometimes bear little resemblance to observed behavior. Informants often supply information which they think the investigator would like to hear or which they feel will place their behavior in a more favorable light. Moreover, as M.G. Smith (1962b:12) has argued:

> In such culturally heterogeneous societies as the West Indies, we cannot expect informants to provide reliable generalizations about family forms or relations . . . . Individual variability seems at first glance the rule rather than the exception. Whether this rule itself reflects some systematic principles of organization, the layman can hardly tell us, nor can the analyst unless his data is complete.

Such a situation calls for an examination which *a priori* does not assume unthinking conformity to cultural rules or moral precepts and which would, therefore, conclude that behavior is deviant, or, at best, characterized by normlessness when explicit prescriptive (or proscriptive) statements are absent, difficult to elicit, or not often followed.

But a sweeping denunciation of previous work is not my intention. Much excellent scholarship yielding valuable insight into the nature of Caribbean society and culture has been carried out in the region. What I wish to suggest is the orientation studies should now be taking because of the limitations present in extant accounts and suggestions about new directions in Caribbean and Afro-American research (Valentine 1972; Whitten and Szwed 1970; Wilson 1973).

OUTLINE OF THE STUDY

Economic and social organization in Leeward Village is the product of a complex set of internal and external spatial and temporal forces. The historical baselines and present-day setting of Leeward Village adaptation to poverty are the subject of Part I, *Historical Background and Contemporary Scene*. The European expropriation of the island, the subjugation and exile of the native population, the estate cultivation of sugar cane by African slaves-- all within the context of over 300 years of colonial domination-- have left their inexorable imprint on village life. These and other historical issues are examined in Chapter 2, *St. Vincent: The Island Background*.

It is also essential to place the reaction of villagers to the conditions under which they are obliged to live within the context present-day societal events and processes. Chapter 3, *St. Vincent: The Contemporary Scene*, examines the manner in which a deteriorating economic situation, volatile and nepotic political system, and restrictive color-class social hierarchy have placed severe limits on the social and economic well-being of most islanders.

It is important as well to root the manner in which poor Vincentians have responded to these conditions within a local-level historical and geographical framework. Chapter 4, *Leeward Village: Past and Present*, reconstructs village history from its earliest European settlement in the 18th century. The discussion focuses on the factors which have generated contemporary population size and composition, the size and layout of the community, and the pattern of local land distribution. Also described are the "type" of community Leeward Village is, local social and economic organization, and the nature of community solidarity and integration. The chapter also describes the articulation between village social differentiation and island-wide class stratification.

The three chapters in Part II, *The Organization of Economic Life*, show how villagers subsist under the constraints of local-level and island economic underdevelopment and social stratification.

Chapter 5, *Work, Wealth, and Class*, describes the level of material life of villagers, local wealth and lifestyle differentiation, and the organization of village occupations. Village occupational complexity, in which a large but limited and shifting range of economic opportunities are manipulated, is shown to affect both the sexual division of labor and the nature of vocational aspirations. The manner in which individuals and families adjust to sporadic and unpredictable economic resources through household economic cooperation and joint consumption is also documented.

The size, distribution, tenure, transmission, and exploitation of village agricultural land are treated in Chapter 6, *Land Tenure and Use*. The first three of these features are a product of the local economic and historical events described in Chapter 4. The tenure and transmission of holdings are also affected by strategic decision-making behavior and by an interplay between societal and local modes of the ownership and transfer of property. In turn, the size, distribution, and tenure of farmland, together with the pattern of plot allocation, are a few of a host of factors determining the use of village lands.

The most conspicuous adaptive strategy that has developed among villagers for dealing with poverty and the lack of local opportunities is the topic of Chapter 7, *Labor Migration*. Removal from the village has a long history and has involved a host of migratory destinations. Several kinds of movement have taken place, some comprising only men, others both sexes. Migration is an institutionalized feature of village life and has had deep and lasting social, ideological, and economic consequences for the community and its members.

Part III, *Kinship and Social Organization*, views the problems of making a living in Leeward Village from the perspective of inter-personal relations, network ties, and social groupings. Three chapters describe the way kinship relationships, sexual and conjugal behavior, domestic-group life, and friendship ties are responses to limited and unpredictable material and social resources.

Chapter 8, *Kindred Organization*, examines the role played by kin in the lives of villagers. The kindred, an ego-centered network of relatives, has received less attention in the literature on Carib-bean family organization than it deserves. Since the kindred is the category from which most household members are recruited but

12

among most of whose members marriage is prohibited, a discussion of its structure and functions is essential for an understanding of community domestic organization and conjugal behavior.

The features of conjugal and quasi-conjugal relations are described in Chapter 9, *Sex, Mating, and Marriage*. The temporal distribution of conjugal forms, the meaning attached to sexuality, the organization of reproductive activity, the distinction between local and societal forms of mating, and the types of unions available to different community members are shown to be influenced by material poverty, normative variability, and behavioral flexibility. Chapter 10, *The Household*, details the manner in which consanguineal and household ties are used to secure individual and collective welfare. Malleability is the rule in this area of social life. It is illustrated in the configuration of domestic groups, household leadership, the recruitment of household members, the organization of domestic group functions, and the developmental cycle of the household.

Villagers are also surrounded by non-kin whom they turn to for social support, emotional gratification, and material aid. Chapter 11, *Friendship*, describes the way in which the arena of voluntarily entered friendship relations is used to ensure social and economic well being by examining labor and food exchange, patronage, and female-based dyadic ties.

The empirical findings of the study are examined within the framework of Afro-American and Caribbean anthropology in Chapter 12, *Black Adaptive Strategies*. This is done by viewing the results of the cultural ecological research strategy used in this study within the framework of some of the traditional models of Black society and culture.

METHODOLOGICAL CONSIDERATIONS

I have visited St. Vincent four times since I began my first field research in August 1969 as a doctoral candidate at the University of Toronto. In all, I have spent 32 months on the island, most of them in Leeward Village. My last field trip took place during July and August 1986 and I plan to return to the island for a whole year in the summer of 1987. I first decided to go to St. Vincent to do an anthropological study of poverty. St. Vincent has long been known as one of the poorest territories in the Caribbean, having suffered over the years from repeated natural disasters and economic difficulties (see Chernick 1978; O'Loughlin 1968:46-49;

Starbird 1979). I also selected the island because, except for an unpublished account of a Baptist religious cult (Henney 1968), no anthropological work had been reported on. In a discipline noted for the "territorial imperative" among its practitioners this was a consideration of some importance. In 1969 St. Vincent was also one of the few remaining English-speaking Caribbean territories, and the only Windward Island, a group which also includes Dominica, St. Lucia, and Grenada, that was still a full-fledged British Crown colony, and I suspected that continued political subordination might be a significant factor in the island's economic marginality.

I selected Leeward Village as the locale to carry out fieldwork largely because of its demographic and economic features. The 1960 *Eastern Caribbean Population Census* (1963) reported a largely Black, occupationally heterogeneous village of over 2,000 inhabitants. Little West Indian ethnographic research has been carried out in villages this large and complex and I suspected that its sheer size would influence both internal stratification and economic diversity. This was borne out by first visits to the community where striking differences in house size, design, and condition suggested life-style differentiation at least by wealth and income.

A perusal of island census reports also indicated that the community was marked by low marriage rates, high levels of non-marital conjugality, considerable unemployment and underemployment, and a large ratio of women to men. Each of these features have at one time or another been linked to material poverty and low levels of living.

Fieldwork in the Caribbean is unlike research in many other regions. The physical dangers and personal hardships often associated with work in isolated, non-Western societies are absent; so is the problem of establishing rapport in urban fieldwork in highly indus-trialized societies. To be sure, I was considered an outsider in Leeward Village, a *stranger* whose physical appearance, nationality, education, speech, and level of living was met at first by formal and deferential treatment. It was during the early period of research that I was cast in a role that had never had any real meaning to me before: being a White man. As time passed, however, it became clear to villagers that my behavior did not fit the social position they had assigned to me. I visited the homes of and associated with the poorest of villagers, I attended religious services of the low-ranking Baptist cult, I drank in the rum shops, I accepted cooked food from low-status persons, I helped pull fishing nets ashore, and I attemp-ted to speak in the local dialect. Although the contradiction between what was expected of me and what I actually did proved somewhat distressing to several members of the village elite, I believe that I gained the respect and affection of many poorer villagers among whom I formed several close and lasting friendships.

The effectiveness of my fieldwork techniques and the adequacy of the material that I gathered are best evaluated by the results obtained and are only briefly summarized. The time-worn practice in Caribbean ethnographic research of collecting domestic group composition data via a house-to-house census was followed. This was supplemented by the gathering of detailed genealogies from a small number of individuals. The four-month return visit to the community in 1972 made it possible to conduct another survey of household personnel--this time based on lengthy sessions with knowledgeable informants living in various parts of the village--to study changes in membership between 1970 and 1972. Other censuses and surveys included a study of land holdings and use, a survey of household economic activities and organization, a detailed investigation of income and consumption patterns among a small number of house-holds, a questionnaire on occupational and educational preferences among senior schoolchildren, a questionnaire administered to a small number of informants on their beliefs and practices about sexuality and marriage, and a survey of migration and remittances among a large sample of households.

Although it may lack some of the physical and emotional demands of research in other parts of the world, Caribbean ethnography has the following essential methodological requirement:

> [E]very community study projected for the area . . . must employ research methods which take cognizance of the centuries of struggle among Western powers for political and economic dominance of almost every island, with few exceptions. This, of course, involves the examination and analysis of written records, of documents, and of archival and library materials--in short, a host of sources which are ordinarily meagre or non-existent for the student of isolated primitive tribes (Manners 1960:82).

I spent much time transcribing material from often barely legible government ledgers. For example, a study of marriage patterns in the village and an investigation of the transmission of arable land required weeks of perusal of marriage registries, deed record books, and other government documents covering a period of over 200 years.

Still, most of my time was spent with selected informants working on a variety of particular topics--fishing technology, the marketing of agricultural produce, reciprocal exchange relations, friendship associations, etc.--and engaging in that *sine qua non* of anthropological research, participant-observation.

My most recent visits to the island in 1980 and 1986 enabled me to update some of my data, particularly on local-level and national economic and political change since 1972. It also gave me the opportunity to study the economic implications of community political coalitions and patron-client ties and the way these articulate with national power networks--topics whose importance I failed to appreciate during previous field trips. Some of the descriptive gaps in my understanding of land use, friendship ties, marriage ceremonial, and other areas were filled in as well during these two field trips. Nonetheless, except where I indicate otherwise through the use of statistical and other data, the bulk of the present study is about events that took place and material that was gathered during the main phases of island residence, 1969-1972.

PART I

HISTORICAL BACKGROUND
AND CONTEMPORARY SCENE

Chapter 2

St. Vincent: The Island Background

THE PHYSICAL SETTING

The little known island of St. Vincent lies in the southeastern part of the Caribbean, 97 miles west of Barbados and 170 miles north of Trinidad (Map 2.1). It is a small, hilly, vividly green island, 18 miles long and 11 miles wide, with an area of 133 square miles (85,120 acres) and a 1984 estimated population of slightly over 100,000 (St. Vincent 1985:6). A north-south mountain range bisects the island into eastern (or windward) and western (or leeward) halves. Wide valleys and rolling coastal plains are formed from the chain's gently sloping lateral extensions on the windward side of the island. In sharp contrast, the terrain on the leeward half is rugged and deeply rigged, its long, narrow valleys squeezed between the spurs of hills which branch off from the central range.

St. Vincent's popular appellation, "Gem of the Antilles," is richly deserved, its physical beauty long recognized by visitors and residents alike (Carmichael 1833:3-4; Colthurst 1977:150-151; Henney 1980:162; Shephard 1831:1-2). John Colthurst (1977:150-151), a magistrate assigned to St. Vincent in 1838, described the beauty of the island in the following terms:

> My late tour through the district has given me the opportunity of seeing the country, which is picturesque in the highest degree, and has tempted me to call it little Switzerland, upon a small scale to be sure, but completely so in miniature. I am so delighted with some things which I have seen that I will leave one of these pages here and there [in my journal] for rough sketches, for in truth, in

20

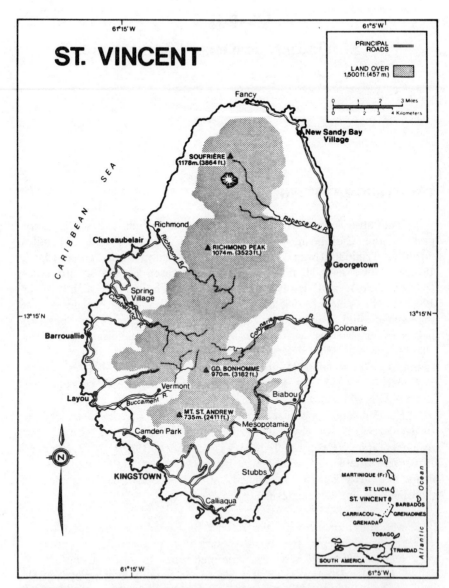

FIGURE 2.1   ST. VINCENT IN THE WEST INDIES

all my wanderings I never saw such a field for the
landscape painter of the picturesque.

One hundred years later a visiting anthropologist made a comparable
observation of the place and the people.

Vincentians take considerable pride and pleasure in the
natural beauty of the island. Some of the local folk
theorists, in good geographical deterministic tradition,
even attribute the islanders' warmth and friendliness (for
which they have a well-deserved reputation) to the fact
that they live in such an attractive, bountiful, and con-
genial setting (Henney 1980:162).

Tropical fruit trees of every imaginable kind--coconut, mango,
avocado, orange and grapefruit, cocoa, sugar apple, soursop, guava,
banana--dot its lush and varied landscape. Natural and human-
imposed features lend a romantic flavor and aura of mystery to the
island. The former include high, cloud shrouded mountain peaks,
silvery-gray sand beaches, a nearly impenetrable virgin forest
interior, and an active 4,000 foot volcano. These are complimented
by ancient native stone-alters and deeply etched petroglyphs,
scattered ruins of 18th century sugar factories, a lofty fort protect-
ing sea access to Kingstown, the island's capital, the Gothic-like
Roman Catholic presbytery with its imposing towers and arches, and
the oldest and one of the most beautiful botanical gardens in the
West Indies. Among its scores of tropical plants, trees, and flowers
lies a gnarled direct descendant of one of the breadfruit trees
brought to the island in 1793 by Captain Bligh of Bounty fame.

The climate is tropical and nearly perfect. Annual rainfall
averages 100 inches, about 70 percent falling from May through
November, conveniently leaving the tourist season dry and sunny.
Even during the rainy season, precipitation generally occurs in short
heavy downpours, followed by clear skies and clean, fresh air. The
temperature seldom exceeds 85 degrees fahrenheit during the day
and the prevailing trade-winds often cool the night air to below 70
degrees. The official hurricane season is from mid-July to mid-
October, but most storms pass north of the island.

Hurricanes rarely touch the St. Vincent Grenadines, a chain of
small islands, islets, cays, and rocks strung between the mainland
and neighboring Grenada, 68 miles to the south. With its shimmering
blue-green waters, protective coral reefs, land-locked bays, picturesque coves, and miles of powdery-white, almost deserted beaches

the Grenadines are considered among the most spectacular cruising grounds in the Western Hemisphere (McCarry 1980; Starbird 1979). They also boast some of the most luxurious and expensive resort facilities in the Caribbean. Britain's Princess Margaret maintains a beach house on 1,400 acre Mustique, a privately-owned islet where residential lots currently sell for $100,000.

The natural beauty of the Grenadines is complimented by the human-made charm of Kingstown, the island's capital. A far cry from such tourist emporiums as Nassau or booming commercial centers as Port-of-Spain, Kingstown with a 1984 population of 18,400 (St. Vincent 1985:6) is more a large town than a major urban center. Brightly painted buses with open sides and wooden benches bounce down its narrow streets, country passengers and agricultural cargo alike churned up as drivers maneuver between open drains and potholes. Each vehicle bears some name or expression: *Easy Dancing, Sweet Music, Brother B, Mister Danny, Ebony Love, Soon Come.* Despite its sometimes hurried ambiance and unkempt appearance, there are no highrise hotels, casinos, duty free shops, or McDonald franchises. Instead, there is a rural-like atmosphere with country market vendors hawking small caches of home-grown fruits and vegetables spread out at their feet, picture-post card scenes of fishermen casting their nets in the harbor, and the sounds of cocks crowing at dawn.

Vincentians appear to be a warm and easygoing people and there is little overt sign of the kind of racial strain and tourist antipathy that frightened so many white people away from other islands during the Black Power 1970s. Even the beggars are inconspicuous, lacking the predatory skills of their more aggressive peers in the larger territories.

For the visitor in search of a lazy sojourn in a tranquil setting St. Vincent and its Grenadines dependencies offers an ideal combination of equable climate, glorious scenery, unparalleled sailing, casual living, uncrowded beaches, and friendly people.

This sybaritic vision of physical splendor, carefree existence, and natural bounty, is one which St. Vincent doubtless shares with many other tropical islands. And like those projected by its counterparts, this image screens out less visible--and generally less agreeable--features of island existence; features most tourists never see and many locals choose to ignore.

The undisturbed, easy-going pace of life and the island's sojourner, are nonetheless symptomatic of serious natural limitations and economic ills. A rugged topography and inaccessible interior, for example, mean that only 30 percent of the island is suitable for crops and pasture. Similarly, the fructiferous plenty is partly the product of the surrender of land which could be more intensively cultivated to natural forces and less profitable tree crops because of a depressed agricultural economy. The small rate of urban growth is a reflection of commercial stagnation and industrial underdevelopment. So are the empty beaches in the Grenadines whose troubled tourist industry has seen five hotels close in recent years. Even the shimmering Caribbean deflects attention from the inability of local waters to supply enough fish to meet island needs. The fishing techniques, quaint and colorful to the outsider, are also inefficient, unremunerative, and dangerous: more than one crew has been lost in St. Vincent's wind-swept seas.

Economic stagnation at the national level translates into human misery at the individual level. Unemployment and underemployment rates are among the highest in the region. Malnutrition and intestinal disease among children under the age of five account for 57 percent of all deaths (University of the West Indies Development Mission 1969:4-5). Even the agreeable seaside warmth of the Caribbean sun translates into oppressive heat for the ill-paid laborer who must spend a lifetime bent over a hoe.

St. Vincent has also had more than its share of natural disasters. The majestic Soufrière volcano, so long silent, erupted violently in 1979, covering half the island with volcanic ash. Property, livestock, and much of the banana crop--the island's chief agricultural export--were lost as 20,000 people, or nearly one-quarter of the island population, were forced to spend several months in hastily arranged and badly provisioned refugee camps. In 1902, the same volcano was responsible for the death of 2,000 people and the permanent relocation of thousands more.

Volcanic eruptions have not been the only physical calamities Vincentians have had to face. Its peripheral location in the hurricane belt did not spare the island in August 1979 from what turned out to be the Caribbean's worst tropical storm this century. Hurricane Allen's 115 mile per hour winds leveled 95 percent of the bearing banana trees--the lifeblood of the agricultural sector. It also destroyed an ambitious multi-million dollar Kingstown land reclamation scheme and other waterfront facilities. Hundred's of homes and commercial establishments were damaged beyond repair and without benefit of insurance coverage. Breadfruit and mango trees by the hundreds, their fruit an important part of the diet of the poor, were uprooted or saw the loss of their half-grown produce. The total loss to the economy was unofficially estimated to be over $50 million.

THE SOCIAL SETTING

But it is at the level of human-produced phenomena that adversity is most strongly felt. Even the innocuous tourist impression of the texture of island social relations--the overt friendliness of the people and the depiction of St. Vincent as a "safe" place to visit even during the height of the Caribbean's brief flirt with American-style Black Power rhetoric in the early 1970s--obscures both deep-rooted tensions and overt racial bias. Simply stated, most tourists are White and in St. Vincent a light complexion is still a primary determinant of social placement and personal evaluation (Brana-Shute and Brana-Shute 1980:6; John 1966). Together with other criteria of rank, it serves to perpetuate the division of society into categories based on differential access to social, medical and other services, livelihood pursuits, power and influence, and prestige and respectability.

Discriminatory access to local resources, particularly those controlled by the government, is exacerbated by the low quality provided. At first glance this is belied by a tabulation of what is available. Indeed, given the small size of the country and the coastal concentration of much of the population, the number and variety of social and allied services gives the impression of adequacy if not abundance. In the early 1970s, three hospitals--a general center in Kingstown, and two smaller facilities, one on the central windward coast and one in the Grenadines--served the needs of a population of 90,000. By the early 1980s a privately-owned hospital in Kingstown was added to the list. These medical units were supported by a system of 24 regional clinics, staffed by resident nurses and state-employed district physicians. There was also a home for the aged poor and a mental hospital in the southern part of the island. The central library in Kingstown had 12 regional branches in the early 1970s and the main post office operated 37 rural depots. There were also 37 government primary schools, 22 denominational elementary schools, two government high schools, a government vocational institute, five private church and secular secondary institutions, two public junior highs, and an extra-mural branch of the University of the West Indies. Two prisons, one for men and one for women, and a network of over 20 police stations completed the list of main government and private services. At one time there was a reform school for delinquent boys but it was not rebuilt after it was burnt to the ground for the second time by its residents in the early 1960s.

Notwithstanding this appearance of abundance, the adequacy of public service has often been questioned. In a government-commissioned report--later suppressed by the central administration--of the country's social and economic prospects by a team of development experts from the University of the West Indies one conclusion reached was that:

> It is perhaps the most outstanding economic feature of this island-state that most things are being done, in most places, most inadequately; and given the limited absolute quantity of resources, with little hope for real improvement (University of the West Indies Development Mission 1969:66).

The basis for such pessimism lies in the current Vincentian social and economic situation. In turn, present island conditions are the legacy of over 250 years of historical events and processes, the end product of which has been the creation of a poverty-ridden, underdeveloped society. Since the various adaptive mechanisms found among Leeward Villagers are responses to poverty, island economic stagnation, and related life-chance constraints, cultural ecological analysis requires consideration of the historical baselines from which these constraints have been generated (see Netting 1968:21-23; Orlove 1980; Richardson 1975; Sacks 1979). For example, in his stimulating discussion of the problems involved in studying Caribbean community organization, Manners (1960:82) argues that:

> [E]very community study in the area, whether diachronic or synchronic, whether problem-centered or presumptively microscopic, will in some measure have to take notice of the past effects and cultural end-results of the vagaries of sugar production, or coffee, or cacao, or cotton, or indigo; of the production and sale of rum; of the shifting periods of mercantilist and modern capitalist forms of exploitation; . . . For all of these, and many more events and elements in the Caribbean tradition since the earliest period of contact, have had their impact upon present culture in greater or lesser degree.

The main formative events and processes whose legacy has been inherited by the contemporary Vincentian society have been: (1) European territorial expropriation and political incorporation; (2) subjugation and elimination of the indigenous inhabitants; (3) transfer of cultivable land to European colonists; (4) monocrop, capitalist estate production of sugar cane for overseas consumption;

(5) importation of slave and indentured agricultural laborers; (6) maximization of overseas profits combined with minimal colonial reinvestment; (7) pervasive external social, economic, and cultural dependence; (8) severe agricultural depression following a brief early period of economic prosperity; (9) formation of a color-class system of stratification; (10) generation among the slaves of mechanisms for coping with their servitude; (11) creation of a large peasantry and rural agricultural proletariat during the post-Emancipation period; and (12) development of wage-labor migration as a response to economic stagnation.

THE FORMATIVE YEARS

The sighting and naming of St. Vincent by Christopher Columbus in 1498 did not lead to its early colonization. Though simultaneously annexed by both Britain and France, each of several expeditions sent to the island between the late 16th and early 18th century was turned back by the native Carib inhabitants (Burns 1954:36, 354; Coke 1808: 181). It was not until 1719 that French small-holders from Martinique were allowed to buy lands on the leeward coast of the island (Coke 1808:181; Shephard 1831:23-25). Though production was limited in scale--few farms were over 100 acres--the cocoa, tobacco, and coffee grown were shipped to Europe even at this early stage of colonization (Shephard 1831:lix-lxvii).

The signing of the Treaty of Paris in 1763 transferred control of St. Vincent to Britain and witnessed the displacement of the French planters by English colonists from North America and other Caribbean islands (Burns 1954:505). As if to make up for lost time, by 1771, over 20,000 acres of arable land expropriated from the Caribs by a treaty they had been forced to sign two years earlier was already in the hands of these settlers. But the colonists yearned for more. As the head of the royal commission sent in 1764 to administer the sale of agricultural land noted:

> The soil of St. Vincent's has been some time known to be the richest and most fertile of the Carribbee islands, and the country which the Charaibs possessed to be the most fertile of St. Vincent's (W. Young 1795:62).

Encouraged by their London sugar buyers ". . . the new settlers . . . aimed at nothing less than Possession of the whole territory of the Isle" (Shephard 1831:27-28; Coke 1808:186), and ignored the Crown's instructions ". . . not to molest them [the Caribs] in their Possessions . . . nor to attempt any survey of their Country, without previous or express orders from Home" (Shephard 1831:28). The Caribs resisted encroachment on their territory and this was used as a pretext to request British military help (Shephard 1831:28-29). Defeated in 1773, the Indians lost much of the land "granted" to them in the 1769 treaty.

But the Caribs continued to resist. With the advise of French emissaries from Guadeloupe and assisted by many of the Frenchmen still left on the island, they carried out several successful military operations against the English between 1793 and 1796, even forcing the local militia to retreat to the capital in 1795 (Shepherd 1831:63-70). They were crushed the next year, however, after a large British force was sent to St. Vincent. To prevent any further insurrection, it was decided that the Indians should be banished and in 1797 5,080 Caribs--the bulk of the island native population--were transported to a small, inhospitable island off the coast of Honduras. Their lands, some 11,000 acres, were granted or sold to various individuals, including those who had helped defeat the Indians. The few Caribs allowed to stay behind were given 233 acres of land upon which they were prohibited from growing sugar cane.

The juridical and administrative means for this "final solution" to the Carib problem had been put in place several years before. Initially grouped with nearby islands into a political unit called the "Southern Caribee Islands," St. Vincent and the Grenadines were made into a single colony in 1776 (Burns 1954:505). The colonial government was a miniature replica of the British Parliament: corresponding to the King, House of Lords, and Commons were a Crown-appointed Governor, a 12-member nominated Executive Council, and a 19-member elected Legislative Assembly (Burns 1954:280; Shephard 1831:195-196). High property qualifications for holding office ensured that both Council and Assembly consisted of owners of large estates and urban merchants and lawyers. Electoral eligibility was also based on property considerations, a condition which was not removed until 1951.

British Common Law and legislation passed in Westminster generally applied to the Colony, along with acts concerned with overseas colonial matters. The island political bodies controlled some local issues, including those relating to slavery. The "Old Representative System," as this form of government has been called (Ayearst 1960: 17), remained unchanged in the island for the next 100 years. An oligarchy of White planters, businessmen, and attorneys successfully kept control despite periodic conflict with the Governor and the Colonial Office in London (Ayearst 1960:17-126).

SUGAR, SLAVERY, AND PLANTATION SOCIETY

British expropriation and colonization of St. Vincent, the subjugation and banishment of the indigenous inhabitants, and the political machinery set up to run the island were all motivated by a desire to profitably exploit its agricultural potential.

The period from British settlement in 1763 to Emancipation in 1838 turned out to be the most prosperous in the island's history despite the comparatively late start to large-scale cultivation and the over 30 years of conflict with the Caribs. Although St. Vincent was discovered earlier than some of the other Caribbean islands, it had been settled later than most. Neighboring Barbados, for example, remained unsighted until 1536, but was colonized by the English in 1625, and began producing sugar for export in the 1640s (Greenfield 1966:33-38); St. Vincent, discovered in 1498, was settled by the French in 1719, and started shipping sugar overseas only after 1775 (Deerr 1949:200).

At first, however, the English settlers produced the same crops as the French on farms not much larger than their predecessors (Shephard 1831:lix-lxvii). But the real wealth of St. Vincent lay in the later cultivation of sugar-cane on large plantations. By 1827, at the height of cane production, there were 108 sugar estates in the Colony averaging 372 acres each. The consolidation of estates and the processing of cane products--sugar, molasses, and rum--in expensive estate-owned factories drove out most small-scale cultivators. It also resulted in a dramatic growth in sugar production: a 74-fold increase between 1766 and 1775; a 300 percent increase between 1775 and 1800; and a 59 percent increase between 1800 and 1825 (Deerr 1949:200).

Large holding size and intensive cultivation, combined with 18th century technological know-how, demanded a correspondingly large labor force (Williams 1970:121-124). This demand was met by African slave labor (see Lowenthal 1972:26-28; Williams 1964, 1970:111-155). Increases in sugar production were paralleled by increases in the Colony's slave population: from 3,420 in 1763, the year the English took over the island; to 11,533 by 1787; to 16,500 by 1805; and to 24,920 by 1812 (Burns 1954:629; Coke 1808:184; Deerr 1949:178; Shephard 1831:iv-v; West Indian Census 1946 1950). The reverse held for the White population which fell from 2,104 in 1764 to 1,053 by 1812 as small proprietors continued to leave the country during the period of rationalization of production and amalgamation of holdings. Those Whites who remained or entered at the time, dependent though they were on British banking interests to help finance their operations, were generally well to do to begin with. One commentator has described the West Indian estate owner level of living as follows:

> The late eighteenth century and early nineteenth century was the period of the planter aristocracy. Beautiful gardens and stately royal palms framed the great house, sometimes imposing enough to stand comparison with the noble mansions of England. . . . Despite the wealth of the planters, however, there is contemporary evidence of the cultural poverty of the colonies. The upper classes seemed to be interested in money-making and little else beyond eating and drinking. Almost no art, music or literature was produced in this society (Ayearst 1960:22).

A description by Mrs. A. C. Carmichael (1833:33-39), a plantation owner who lived in the island during the 1820s, of a typical estate dinner party--an event she calls the "only media of intercourse" among the elite--confirms this view of "cultural poverty" amid material luxury.

> Dinner being announced about six . . . we sat down, in number between thirty and forty--the gentlemen greatly predominating; there was very little general conversation during dinner, and, so far as I could see, not much even between those who sat next to each other. . . . The dinner was very much like all West Indian dinners--a load of substantials, so apparently ponderous, that I instinctively drew my feet under the table, in case it should be borne to the ground.
> Turtle and vegetable soups, with fish, roast mutton . . . and turtle dressed in the shell, with boiled turkey, boiled fowls, a ham, mutton and pigeon pies, and stewed ducks, concluded the first course. Ducks and guinea birds, with a few ill-made puddings and tarts, &c. formed the second course. . . . A great deal of wine was drank during dinner. . . .
> The ladies did not remain long at table, but soon retired to the drawing-room; but there, nothing like conversation took place,--indeed the constant domestic drudgery of a female's life in the West Indies . . . leaves them no time for improving the mind,--and in society, the ladies are too generally found distinguished for that list-

lessness, and meagreness of conversation, which arises from an uninformed mind.

To ease this burden of "constant domestic drudgery" and to help support dinner parties of such scale, an average Vincentian planter household employed at least 15 slave-servants: a butler, a head maid, several housemaids, a cook, waiters and waitresses, a scullion, a nanny, a chambermaid, and a laundress (Carmichael 1833:113-121).

The economic boom supporting such opulence was short-lived. The rapid expansion in sugar production during the last third of the 18th century gave way to stable outputs and declining profits during the first third of the 19th. Overproduction of British West Indian sugar (Williams 1970:280-290) combined with competition from cheaper sources in the region (Lowenthal 1972:54-55), produced both a glut in the English market and a growing metropolitan unwillingness to maintain the artificial colonial tariff and trade preferences which has been put in place during the early days of the industry. According to Mrs. Carmichael (1833:16-17, 63), declining sugar revenues soon brought economic hardship to the Vincentian planter:

[T]he affluence which once in some degree existed, is to be found no more; and it would be now more correct to say, that with very exceptions, they, although nominally proprietors, are really nothing else than the farmer for the British merchant, who receives their annual produce
. . . . West Indian produce for several years has gradually been decreasing in value, while the expenses of every article requisite upon an estate has not at all decreased; and such is the desperate state of affairs, that upon a small estate, it requires the whole produce to pay the current expenses, and not a farthing remains for the proprietor or his family.
There are few West Indian estates that are altogether out of debt, and some it is to be feared are involved beyond their real value.

The fate of the planter class in St. Vincent was intimately tied to the growth of European mercantilism and its eventual transformation into industrial capitalism. Indeed, the West Indian case is one of history's best documented examples of the relation between metropolitan centers and peripheral colonial regions, on the one hand, and development and underdevelopment, on the other. Generated by the differential exchange of commodities, capital, and labor among three economically-linked areas--Western Europe, the Caribbean, and West Africa--these two modes of production were instrumental in the economic advancement of Western Europe and the economic impoverishment of the West Indies (Frank 1969).

Mercantile colonial expansion based on monocrop sugar production transformed the region into ". . . an appendage or satellite of European imperialism, its resources being drained away from domestic development to metropolitan aggrandisement . . ." (Williams 1970:47; see also Mintz 1974:44). Profitable sugar-cane cultivation required a large capital outlay for land, machinery, labor, and administration. For this reason, most planters were obliged to rely on the financial backing of European banking and merchant concerns (Lowenthal 1972:27-28), and control and even ownership of plantations soon passed into the hands of mercantile houses ". . . . which advanced loans to build the factories and to operate the estates, monopolized traffic in slaves and supplies, and gleaned most of the profits" (Lowenthal 1972:28).

Founded only for capital accumulation in the metropolis, prohibited by parliamentary edict from developing any indigenous commerce, trade, or manufacture which would compete with established home enterprises, St. Vincent, like her sister colonies, was no more than a one-industry branch-plant, dependent on the mother country for most of its foodstuffs, financial capital, shipping, work force, and manufactured items (Williams 1964:51-57). The result was economic collapse when the industrialization the island helped finance began to displace mercantilism as the dominant mode of British capitalistic production.

But the Vincentian estate owner was no mere pawn of British capital. Many properties were controlled not by resident proprietors but by persons who had inherited their estates without ever having set foot on the island. Other holdings were in the hands of British merchant houses. In both instances nearly all the profits from the sale of plantation produce were kept in the metropole rather than reinvested in colonial economic improvement or expansion (Lowenthal 1972:33-34). Moreover, since the aim of most resident planters was to make enough money to establish a comfortable existence in England or North America, little attention was paid in the island to the provision of medical care, social aid or even education.

> There is no public or private establishment for the relief
> of the aged or sick poor White and free inhabitants, nor
> even an hospital for casual accidents . . . ; the infirm, or

sick White, or free person, has no resource but individual support and charity, and this in a country [St. Vincent] where so few ties of relationship exist, must necessarily be precarious (Shephard 1831:210).

[T]here are few children who remain in the island after ten or at most twelve years of age, for there is no possibility of procuring either public or private teachers, beyond merely in reading and writing, and those of very ordinary attainment. . . . Some few families have tried a governess, but it has been found not to answer; for they almost invariably marry soon after coming out--so that at present there is really no alternative, excepting that of sending children to Europe, or leaving them to grow up totally ignorant. As for boys, there is no possibility of educating them in the West Indies (Carmichael 1833:25-26).

Of those sent abroad for study, many never returned. Lacking teachers, students, and intellectuals, the island was home only to those who could not leave or whose economic interests demanded their presence.

Actual or dreamed-of absenteeism and a concomitant preoccupation with short-term profits also discouraged any interest in such estate matters as soil conservation, advanced planting and sugar-manufacturing techniques, and labor and cost-saving devices (Doorhan 1971:57-58). An absentee orientation even made it difficult to attract suitably qualified candidates for nominated and elected office. In turn, a deteriorating political and economic climate and inadequate social and cultural amenities inevitably encouraged further emigration.

SOCIAL STRATIFICATION

These myriad of problems, though they may have affected the lives of individual planters and the economic viability of the Colony, did little to alter the social structure of the local society. Basic slave institutions and patterns of organization had been worked out soon after British settlement and did not change appreciably until the slaves were set free. Indeed, so firmly entrenched did many of these institutional arrangements become during the short 75-year period between British colonization in 1763 and Emancipation in 1838 that their outlines can still be seen in contemporary class stratification and peasant social organization.

The Free Population

According to Mrs. Carmichael (1833:18), a pro-slavery propagandist, an elaborate system of social differentiation had developed in St. Vincent by the 1790s based on an earlier division between Whites, Colored persons or Mulattoes, and Black slaves. The "superior category of Whites" consisted of estate owners, senior government officials, lawyers, merchants, doctors, clergymen, and locally stationed naval officers. Whites of "secondary rank" were socially segregated from elite Whites and included estate managers and overseers, junior government officials, and small-time merchants. Below the elite and secondary White strata lay the Colored or Mulatto population, the children and descendants of unions between White men and non-White women. It too was composed of two sections, free persons and slaves. The free Colored group, in turn, contained two membership categories based on differences in occupation, education, wealth, and general evaluations of respectability. The "superior" group of Colored males included salaried shop attendants, law clerks, accountants, dry goods and rum shop proprietors, and self-employed masons and carpenters. The superior Colored women were dressmakers, owned small shops, or peddled dry goods through the countryside. The "lower classes" of Mulattoes, male and female alike, generally were employed as domestic servants in the homes of wealthy Whites.

The free people of color held an intermediate social, economic, and legal position in society. The ambivalence this created lead to their preoccupation with social standing, especially when dealing with slaves.

> [T]hey are so tenacious of rank, and quarrel so unnecessarily with the negroes, whom they treat, generally speaking, with so much contempt and disdain, that there is no possibility of pleasing both parties. . . .
>
> The first property they are anxious to possess is a slave, and they certainly keep their slave to his duty under a very different discipline from that practised by white people; and to be sold to a coloured owner, is considered by a negro to be an extreme misfortune. . . (Carmichael 1833:70, 75).

In turn, Black slaves exhibited ". . . a most decided dislike to the coloured population" (Carmichael 1833:18) and refused to work under the direction of non-White overseers.

The Slaves

At the bottom of the social hierarchy lay the bulk of the colonial population, the slaves. Although most were Black sugar-cane workers, like the other sectors of the population, they were internally differentiated by color (Black or Mulatto), birth place (local-born or African), and occupation ("head person" or "common field laborer"). Colored slaves were nearly all Creoles, or native born West Indians, and tended to be used as household staff, estate artisans, and peddlers.

Rank differences were at least as keenly observed among head slaves as they were among the free members of society.

> [T]here are an abundance of nominal ladies and gentlemen among slaves. Drivers (that is, black overseers), head boilermen, head coopers, carpenters or masons, head servants, these are all Mr. so and so: a field negro, if asked to go and tell a boilerman to come to his master, returns and says--Massa, Mr. ___ will be here directly. They say, "Ma'am," to a domestic servant; . . . [W]hen they go to their grounds [allotted plots of farmland], these head-people hire negroes, sometimes belonging to the estate and sometimes not, to work for them, while they work very little themselves, and merely superintend (Carmichael 1833:282-283).

Social differentiation also extended to nationality and assimilation to Western European culture.

> [N]ative Africans do not at all like it to be supposed that they retain the customs of their country; and consider themselves wonderfully civilized by their being transplanted from Africa to the West Indies. Creole negroes invariably consider themselves superior people, and lord it over the native Africans (Carmichael 1833:251-252).

Not all Africanisms disappeared. Slave religious belief and practice, for example, show a combination of African elements and Christianity. *Obeah* (witchcraft) and a belief in *jumbies* (spirits of the dead) occurred on all estates and represent good evidence of the pervasiveness of aboriginal ideology. At the same time, all slaves were baptized and most were familiar with the basic tenets of Christianity (Carmichael 1833:253-256, 220).

Christian belief and practice did not absolve them from the onerous task of estate cultivation. Praedial slaves formed the bulk of the estate population and they toiled in the fields from dawn to dusk six days a week. Survival for the slave population required obtaining enough food to sustain themselves under a system of forced labor which demanded nearly all their time and energy. Food was always a scarce resource for plantation workers and there is much evidence of hunger, malnutrition, dietary deficiency diseases, starvation, high mortality rates, and low levels of fertility throughout the Caribbean during the slavery period (Dirks 1978). Unlike their counterparts in some of the other islands, Vincentian slaves were forced to supply nearly all their own foodstuffs. This attempt by planters to minimize their costs of production placed an additional burden on the slaves. But it also generated a "proto-peasantry" (Mintz 1974:151-152) during the pre-Emancipation period. The economic activities which the slaves were obliged to carry out to feed themselves--the unsupervised cultivation of crops, the processing of certain foodstuffs, the market sale or barter of fruits and vegetables, the rearing of stock, etc.--were the basis for the establishment of a fully-developed and semi-independent peasantry after the abolition of slavery (Mintz 1974:152). It is the development of such a peasantry that represents the earliest and clearest example of the process of New World Afro-American culture building.

The only food regularly given to the slaves was a weekly ration of two pounds of salted cod-fish per adult and one and one-half pounds per child under 12. At Christmas this was supplemented by a small distribution of pork, flour, sugar, rum, and sewing material (Carmichael 1833:192). With seeds and plants supplied by the estate the slaves grew produce in small plots behind their houses and in larger "provision-grounds" on land not suitable for commercial cultivation. Except during crop time when they were obliged to work seven days a week, the slaves were permitted to cultivate their gardens on Sundays and every other Saturday (Carmichael 1833:174). The house gardens contained a variety of subsistence and cash crops, most of which are still grown by peasants today: watermelons, beans, peas, cabbages, turnips, carrots, tomatoes, pumpkins, christophines, cucumbers, herbs and spices, and such starchy tubers as cassava, tannias, and arrowroot (Carmichael 1833:136-137, 162-178).

The more distant provision gardens contained the main subsistence crops, plantains and bananas, as well as yams, eddoes, tannias, and maize. Some of vegetables were cultivated only for market sale, although even food staples might be sold if there were a surplus.

Most slaves also raised stock--chickens, ducks, pigs, and goats --for home use and market sale and many even sold fish caught in the streams that passed through their estates (Carmichael 1833:177-179). Those living on plantations close to Kingstown sold animal feed, wood, and English vegetables to residents of the capital. Even though the slave codes prohibited it, some slaves made and sold charcoal (Carmichael 1833:196). Others gained access to cash by hiring themselves out to head people on their own or neighboring estates; some also worked as agricultural laborers for other Whites during their free time and were paid in cash or produce (Carmichael 1833:283).

The processing and sale of agricultural crops was an additional source of cash revenue for many slaves. These included farine, a kiln dried oatmeal made from cassava, laundry starch, also made from cassava, and arrowroot starch (Carmichael 1833:165-166, 177-178).

Surplus garden produce, processed food, meat, and fish were sold in special slave markets held in Kingstown every Sunday. The disposal of produce took the form of market exchange and barter, the latter involving the swapping of slave goods for ". . . bread, salt pork, salt beef, mackerel, corned fish, cakes or other nice things" (Carmichael 1833:176).

The illegal sale of charcoal did not represent the only inter-dicted activity that slaves employed to deal with the oppressive system of slavery. Other coping mechanisms included the theft of estate produce, dereliction of duty, lying, and running away. Escape was probably the least successful strategy owing to the small size of the island and the absence of established communities of runaways which could harbor fugitives. Stealing, the feigning of illness, and various sorts of deception were everyday occurrences. Slaves stole sugar cane, provision crops, milk, eggs, alcohol, and household items belonging to their owner's family (Carmichael 1833:103-104, 259-264). These items would either be consumed or exchanged for other goods or foodstuff. So skilled were the slaves in larceny--"Negro methods of theft defy the watchful eye" (Carmichael 1833: 260)--that the planters attributed it to deliberate enculturation.

The elder negroes teach theft to their children as the most necessary of accomplishments; and to steal cleverly,

is as much esteemed by them as it was by the Spartans of
old (Carmichael 1833:264).

Evading work was also a common mechanism for reducing the burden
of estate labor.

Employment is their abhorrence--idleness their delight;
and it is from having so minutely watched their dispo-
sitions, habits, and method of work, that I have come to
the conclusion,--that *to overwork a negro slave is impossible* (Carmichael 1833:96; emphasis in original).

Feigning illness was especially common among field slaves and
formed part of a larger process of deceit:

Negroes have more imaginary diseases than any set of
people I ever was amongst: they are fond of quackery . .
. . Monday morning is always a great day for the sick; all
lazy or ill-disposed negroes come into the hospital at least
once a week, and sometimes oftener (Carmichael 1833:204).

The first defect of character which struck me as very
marked among negroes was a love of deceit. The day I
landed in the West Indies, I was shocked to see many of
our servants so badly clothed, particularly as they
informed me that they had no other clothes, not having
even a change; and they declared they had not received
any for some years. Of course they were soon well
clothed; . . . Shortly afterwards it was ascertained that
they had recently received clothing; yet they firmly
denied it, . . . (Carmichael 1833:257).

All these economic and social activities--the proto-peasant production and sale of agricultural produce, stealing, lying, etc.--testify to
the "innovative resiliency and creative integrity of the slaves"
(Mintz 1974:14), the ability to deal in positive ways with the daily
challenges of one of history's most oppressive forms of human
exploitation.

The slaves also exhibited creativity and innovation in working
out their sexual and family lives within the constraints of the slave
productive regimen.

As soon as a negro girl attains the age of sixteen or
seventeen, she probably gets a husband; and the male

children perhaps a year or two later, get wives, when of course they have houses of their own; negroes, therefore, never have many children living within them. On occasion of a marriage, it is often necessary to build a house, and there is then usually a merry making; the master or the manager deals out rum and sugar to those who have helped build it, and the new comer frequently gives supper on the night he takes possession (Carmichael 1833:131).

Despite the encouragement of the 1825 St. Vincent Slave Act (Shephard 1831:xlv), there is no evidence to suggest that such arrangements were actually based on legal, Christian marriage. In fact, Carmichael loosely employs the terms "husband" and "wife" to refer to all types of slave union. Still, the formation of a separate household suggests that a common form of domestic arrangement was the nuclear family made up of a slave couple and their children. In such unions the woman was responsible for the cooking and laundering while both partners, assisted by their children, worked together in their estate-provided gardens (Carmichael 1833:180). Many of these arrangements were short lived. Coke (1805:289), a missionary and historian who visited the island during the late 1780s, argues that:

The common practice is, for either men and women, when their partners are afflicted, to consider all obligations cancelled,--to leave them to get other husbands and wives.

Carmichael (1838:298) also tells us that "Many negro men . . . have two or more wives," although coresidence was maintained with only one of them. Cases of multiple paternity also underscore both conjugal instability and a matrilateral emphasis in kinship affiliation:

The negro cares little for his father; but many are a loss upon this subject, for there are not a few females who are sufficiently cunning to obtain presents for their children from two or more men, who they separately claim as the fathers of their children (Carmichael 1833:297).

Household forms other than the nuclear family one also occurred. Old slaves no longer capable of working, for example, rarely lived by themselves (Carmichael 1833:191). Presumably, they became the dependent members of households containing their younger kin. The process of child rearing also suggests that Carmichael, in her apologetic zeal, overemphasized the presence of stable nuclear families. When they were about one year old, infants were placed under the care of slave "nurses" who looked after them during the day so their mothers could work in the fields. Allowed to return home at night, children remained under this day-care arrangement until the age of eight when they were simultaneously turned over to their families and placed in a children's sugar-cane weeding gang.

To sum up: Carmichael (1833) distinguishes between six different social strata in St. Vincent during the heyday of sugar and slavery: primary Whites, secondary Whites, superior free Coloreds, a lower class of free Colored people, Colored head slaves, and Black field slaves. Although the precise number in each category is unknown, a crude estimate is possible based on extrapolations from several sources (Colthurst 1977:238; Deerr 1949:178; Shephard 1831: iv-v; West Indian Census 1946 1950) and this is presented in Table 2.1.

TABLE 2.1 POPULATION OF ST. VINCENT
AND THE GRENADINES, 1834

Population Category	Number	Percent
Primary Whites	650	2.4
Secondary Whites	650	2.4
Superior Free Coloreds	1,500	5.7
Lower Class of Free Coloreds	1,500	5.7
Colored Head Slaves	3,000	11.3
Black Field Slaves	19,266	72.5
Total	26,566	100.0

The existence of such an elaborate, multi-variable system for defining social position should not be allowed to obscure the fact that the most fundamental distinctions were those based on race and legal standing. Slavery and racial stratification were the foundations upon which all else rested and social interaction between Whites and non-Whites, regardless of whether the latter were free or not, was both legally defined (Shephard 1831:xlv-xlviii) and circumscribed by the social etiquette of race relations. The result was a birth-ascribed caste system of stratification for the allocation of rewards, privileges, rights, and responsibilities (Berreman 1972).

THE POST-EMANCIPATION PERIOD: 1838-1899

Economic and Political Change

Following a four-year apprenticeship period, the "peculiar institution" as Stampp (1956) so aptly called it, ended in St. Vincent with the freeing of its 22,266 slaves in 1838. Opinions vary about the reaction of the slaves to their newly-acquired status. Colthurst (1977:226, 230), a Special Magistrate sent from England to adjudicate disputes arising over the transition from slavery to Emancipation, notes that on most estates in his Leeward coast district, an area which included Leeward Village, the slaves willingly signed contracts promising to work for their master for a one-year period following Emancipation, at a rate of 1s.6d.

> Considering all things and the difficulty in arranging a free system of labour after so many ages of slavery, I feel great satisfaction in being able to say that at this moment [2 September 1838] the labourers throughout my district upon the various estates, with the exception of one, are fully at work and receiving a fair remuneration for their labour (Colthurst 1977:230).

Anderson (1938:35), a Vincentian historian, has argued that, on the contrary, for several weeks the ex-slaves refused to work on their estates for the wages offered by their former masters. Regardless of the immediate effects of this transformation from slave to proletariat status, estate labor held little appeal for the former bondsmen. Experiments with both task-work and a daily wage proved unsuccessful and between 1838 and 1841, the number of plantation workers decreased from about 15,000 to 8,586 (Mathieson 1967:184-85). By 1845 there were 4,500 free laborers--three-quarters less than 20 years earlier--engaged in estate sugar-cane cultivation (Davy 1971:183).

Like her British West Indian neighbors, St. Vincent turned to other sources of labor to make up for the local shortage, and between 1841 and 1882 over 6,000 West Africans, Portuguese, East Indians, and poor Whites from Barbados were brought to the Colony as free and indentured workers (Anderson 1938; Burns 1954:662; Byrne 1969:159; Curtin 1969:82; Roberts 1955:245-288; Wright 1929: 244). But the entry of these three groups only delayed the inevitable. Sugar production continued to fall, and by 1895 was one-quarter of what it had been in 1834 (Deerr 1949:200). A failure to modernize manufacturing techniques, increasing competition from cane grown more economically elsewhere in the region, steadily declining sugar prices throughout the 1800s, the removal of British tariff protection, and the production of cheaper European beet sugar spelled the end of the reign of King Sugar in St. Vincent by the second half of the 19th century (Burns 1954:658-662; Williams 1964, 1970:361-390). For example, in his introduction to Colthurst's journal, Marshall (1977:22) notes that:

> [Colthurst] discovered that most of these professional agriculturalists, in both Barbados and St. Vincent, were "both ignorant and positive" as far as the principles of scientific farming were concerned. They neither read books nor discussed "improvements in the system of agriculture." They opposed all suggestions for innovation because they were prisoners of habit; and in the Agricultural Society, the one topic of conversation was the state of the market for their staples.

As the sugar industry was slowly dying, a new crop, arrowroot, was beginning to take its place. A herbaceous perennial yielding a high quality starch, it was grown by estate slaves for domestic sale from at least the early part of the 19th century (Carmichael 1833: 177-178). By 1830 it was already being shipped overseas (Wright 1929:254), and by 1847 ranked second to sugar in commercial value (Davy 1971:187). It continued to be an important peasant and plantation crop until 1888 when production for export ceased when decreases in the quality of the starch brought falling prices and declining markets (Wright 1929:254).

The problem of product quality which affected the arrowroot industry again highlights that, as in earlier times, the Vincentian planter contributed to his own demise by neglecting his enterprise. In 1848, for example, only 12 of 100 estate owners were living in the country. A perennial sign of a lack of interest in the island, absenteeism also meant that most plantations were administered by urban-based businessmen and attorneys. Unfamiliar with the day-to-day running of a sugar plantation, motivated solely by a desire for short-term gain, often responsible for several scattered estates, and faced with a shortage of experienced local personnel, these agents were forced to appoint managers and overseers who lacked both the training and inclination to improve planting or productive techniques (Davy 1971:184; Doorhan 1971:56). Many estates were forced into bankruptcy during the post-Emancipation era and were taken over by the British merchant consignees who had advanced credit to the planters and disposed of their crops. Increased overseas control was soon matched by external political administration. The system of partial self-rule which had remained almost unchanged for over 100 years was suddenly and voluntarily surrendered in 1876 when St. Vincent, following the lead of nearly every other British West Indian island, requested Britain ". . . to erect such forms of government as your Majesty may deem desirable for the welfare of the Colony" (Burns 1954:655). Radical though it may have been in appearance, this request was motivated by reactionary concerns:

> After the Emancipation Act (1838) quite a few of the ex-slaves bought out mountain lands and by their industry and resource began to qualify for the franchise. It was this prospect of eventual government by the free Blacks placed against the backdrop of the Haitian revolution and Morant Bay Rebellion in Jamaica which prompted the White overlords [in St. Vincent] to surrender the constitution and opt for pure Crown Colony rule (John 1973:82).

The prospect that Blacks might someday rule the Caribbean was equally repugnant to the Crown. "Fear of the negro masses and the conviction that negroes could never look after themselves" (Doorhan 1971:115; see also Ayearst 1960:17-18, 30 and Lowenthal 1972:64), together with a steadily worsening colonial economic situation, the difficulty in finding capable candidates for elected positions, a paucity of eligible voters--there were only 193 in 1854 (Burns 1954:653)--and the near depletion of the island treasury prompted Britain to introduce full Crown Colony Government one year after St. Vincent's plea for help. Composed entirely of nominated members who could be relied upon to carry out overseas policy, the new system gave unrestrained operation to bureaucratic nepotism and delayed the political participation of Black people for decades. In particular:

> Crown Colony Government was not on the side of the ordinary people but continued to favour vested interests, invariably white. White colonists were usually supported by the governor and were the real makers of government policy. Where the association of non-whites was tolerated, it was usually because they shared the views of the white ruling elite (Doorhan 1971:117).

Post-Emancipation Black Adaptive Strategies

As elsewhere in the English-speaking Caribbean, the continued support of traditional vested interests meant that little effort was made to introduce social measures or economic schemes to improve the life chances of the mass of Black people (Doorhan 1971:118; Lowenthal 1972:66). Even those reforms which happened to benefit the Black population were, in reality, meant to remedy colonial fiscal ills. For example, the steady decline in sugar-cane cultivation which resulted in the accumulation of dozens of idle estates in the hands of a few British merchant houses merely prompted a Royal Commission of inquiry sent to the region in 1882 to conclude that peasant cultivators should be encouraged to take up the slack by growing a greater variety of crops for export (Augier *et al* 1960: 237). A second Royal Commission in 1897 specifically singled out St. Vincent, belatedly recommending that:

> . . . suitable portions of thousands of acres of uncultivated fertile lands on the seacoast in the hands of private owners be acquired by the State and made available for settlement in small lots (Wright 1929:241).

Fearing a shortage of estate labor, the plantocracy opposed agricultural land reform. The program went ahead without their support and proved a social and financial success when several plantations totaling 5,600 acres were subdivided into holdings ranging from one to seven acres (Wright 1929:241).

But this scheme came too late and did too little; it also showed little awareness of the ambition and determination of the very people to whom it was directed. Immediately following Emancipation, two economic strategies were simultaneously being pursued by the former slaves: peasant cultivation and wage-labor migration. Both strategies were aimed at economic self-determination and both were antithetical to planter interests. Ironically, the foundation of the peasant option had been laid during slavery when the bondsmen were obliged to feed themselves from their own gardens (Carmichael 1833:135-137), a custom which continued during the apprenticeship period (Colthurst 1977:170-171). This practice was transformed into the rental and purchase of small plots from planters who had decided to reduce or abandon cultivation. In one case:

> An entire estate was bought by a few black people who afterwards subdivided it, making villages and gardens and

44

in every way endeavouring to render themselves independent (Anderson 1938:35).

Between 1845 and 1847 alone, some 12,000 acres, or at least 30
percent of the country's cultivable land, were being worked by
small-scale peasant freeholders and renters (Davy 1971:183; Williams
1970:338).

The second strategy witnessed the beginning of an exodus from
the island that is still taking place today. As in several of the other
British colonies, a variety of factors--low agricultural wages at
home, higher rates of pay and better working conditions in other
islands, competition from indentured labor, the seasonality of
employment on sugar estates, the efforts of many planters to
restrict the sale of land (including idle estate property) to potential
peasant cultivators, the small size and marginality of those plots
that were made available, and the presence of limited non-agricul-
tural opportunities--prompted large numbers of ex-bondsmen to
migrate almost as soon as they had gained their freedom (see Augier
et al 1960:196; Hill 1977:209, 220; Lowenthal 1972:59-60, 213-214;
Marshall 1982:6; Midgett 1975:58; Philpott 1973:19; Richardson 1983;
Rubenstein 1982a; Williams 1970:359, 448).

The potential exodus of workers had not gone unanticipated. In
his tour of the island two weeks before Emancipation on August 1,
1838 the Lieutenant-Governor warned the slaves of the dangers of
leaving the island.

When you become free, I have no doubt . . . that attempts
will be made to persuade [you] to quit this island by the
promise of greater wages elsewhere. You will certainly
have an undoubted right to go where you please and hire
yourselves but let me caution you about leaving this island
for any other. In the first place, there is a law which
prohibits any person quitting this colony who has anyone
here dependent upon him or her for support without
giving security that the party so left shall not become a
burden to the parish. In the second place, if you do go,
you must recollect you go to a strange country, you will
have new masters to please and perhaps different laws to
govern you; and above all, if you should be beyond
protection of the British government, you would run the
chance of being carried into foreign settlements, and
there sold as slaves. There have been, unhappily, numerous
instances of this horrid system of late. Therefore take my

advice, think well and often of these things before you consent to quit St. Vincent (Colthurst 1977:220-221).

Such admonitions together with supporting legislation (Colthurst 1977:221) had little affect. Many estate laborers, actively recruited by agents sent to attract workers by offering free transportation, double the normal sugar estate wages, improved employee benefits, and land for subsistence cultivation began migrating to worker starved Trinidad and Guyana (Byrne 1969:165; Marshall 1982:6; Mathieson 1967:85; University of the West Indies Development Mission 1969:12; Thomas-Hope 1978:66). Migration accelerated during the last third of the 19th century when seasonal and other short-term unskilled construction and plantation work became available in South America and the Hispanic Caribbean. For example, the first French effort to build a Panama canal during the 1880s attracted many Vincentians laborers (Proudfoot 1950:14). Although exact figures are not available, large numbers of workers must have been involved in these different movements: between 1881 and 1891, the number of persons in 15-44 year old age cohort--the one most sensitive to migration opportunities--decreased from 18,080 to 17,190 (Byrne 1969:156-157).

Migration undoubtedly raised the life-chances of many poor Vincentians. But it did little to improve national economic prospects. In 1886, Britain was obliged, for the first time, to assume full control of the island's treasury by providing annual Grants-in-Aid, a practice which continued until 1908 (Duncan 1970:42, 62).

Chapter 3
St. Vincent: The Contemporary Scene

THE TWENTIETH CENTURY

St. Vincent entered this century still burdened with the problems of the last. The sugar industry, near death by 1900, was only resuscitated by the high prices brought about by the First World War (Wright 1929:246, 257). The industry limped along in third place in export earnings behind cotton and arrowroot--most of its production used to satisfy the domestic market--until 1950 when there was a large increase in output with the completion of a new central sugar mill. But output soon began to fall again and cultivation ceased entirely when the island's single factory closed in 1962 as a result of a combination of high manufacturing costs, depressed prices, and industrial disputes caused by low wages and poor working conditions (Duncan 1970:70; O'Loughlin 1968:47-48).

The industry was once more resurrected in 1981 with production earmarked solely for local needs. Used factory equipment was purchased from Trinidad and the quality of the product was so poor that islanders soon resorted to smuggling to circumvent the prohibition on the import of foreign sugar. The high manufacturing costs, limited scale, and labor disputes that doomed production in the early 1960s were exacerbated by the recurrent breakdown of the old equipment. Production stopped in 1985 and the country again imports its sugar from neighboring Barbados.

Cotton, which had not been grown since the early 1800s, was reintroduced in 1903 as both an estate and peasant crop (Wright 1929). Its markets and output were subjected to repeated ups and downs and competition from cheaper strains and synthetics in other countries. Production came to an end in the mid-1960s when off-island processing proved too costly after the island's only ginnery was destroyed by fire.

Arrowroot also experienced a revival early in the century. Prices began to pick up during World War I and production expanded with the penetration of the United States market in mid-1920s (Wright 1929:255). The crop soon became the island's chief export and mainstay of the peasant cash-economy. But disaster stuck this industry too in the early 1960s when a cheap synthetic substitute was developed in the United States, the main consumer country (O'Loughlin 1968:48). Production resumed in the early 1970s because of a renewed demand for the natural form of the starch, although its export earnings are less than three percent of those of the island's chief current cash crop, bananas (St. Vincent 1985:56).

Production of bananas began in 1953. By the late 1970s there were some 5,000 acres, or nearly one-fifth of the country's arable land, devoted to the crop. About 70 percent of this acreage is cultivated by small-holders. In 1984, bananas accounted for 38 percent of all primary agricultural export earnings, followed by starchy tubers (eddoes, dasheens, tannias, sweet potatoes, and yams)--nearly all them peasant produced--at 52 percent, and arrowroot at less than 1.5 percent (St. Vincent 1985:56). Like all the other cash crops that preceded it, the future of the banana industry is clouded with uncertainty. Low per acre yields in comparison to other producing countries, poor quality control, cheaper sources in nearby Central and South American countries, and market domination by a single overseas buyer, Geest Industries of Britain, all give reason for concern (O'Loughlin 1968:109-110; World Bank 1979:9).

Another old crop has also made a reappearance. Beginning in the mid-1970s tobacco, a plant not seen for over 200 years, began to be cultivated on a modest scale on mid- to large-size holdings. In good mercantilist tradition, all the crop is shipped to Trinidad for manufacture into cigarettes while St. Vincent imports all the raw tobacco for its own small cigarette factory from the United States.

This brief survey of 20th century agriculture, when viewed in long-term historical perspective, presents a picture of a series of minor booms and major busts. One crop after another has been introduced--or reintroduced for a second or third time--in yet another attempt to stimulate an economy which experienced its brief flirt with prosperity for a few decades during the 18th century. As both cause and consequence of a general pattern of economic decline there has been a steady decrease in estate cultivation as more and more planters left the island or turned to more lucrative urban-based enterprises.

Concomitantly, the peasant sector has grown tremendously. The 108 plantations which averaged 372 acres in 1827 were transformed, by 1966, into 10,465 plots of land averaging less than four acres (Table 3.1). Agricultural production, whether for subsistence, local markets, regional trade, or overseas shipment, increasingly is becoming synonymous with peasant cultivation. Still, the plantocracy, though diminished, cannot be ignored. In fact, there has even been an increase, since the slavery-based plantation era, of holdings over 500 acres. As well, although 96 percent of plots are held in parcels of less than 10 acres, these represent only 40.4 percent of the total of farmland in the state. Looked at the other way round, although only 32--or less than one-half of one percent--of the 10,465 plots of land in the country are 100 acres or larger, these make up 40.2 percent of all Vincentian farmland; the eight holdings over 500 acres form nearly one-quarter of all arable land in St. Vincent (Table 3.1). Translated into human terms, one percent of the population owns nearly 50 percent of the land (Hourihan 1975:30), and four families alone control over 12,000 acres, or nearly one-quarter of the farmland in the country.

TABLE 3.1 DISTRIBUTION OF AGRICULTURAL HOLDINGS
IN ST. VINCENT AND THE GRENADINES, 1966

Size of Holding (acres)	Number of Holdings			Area of Holdings		
	No.	%	Total %	No. of Acres	%	Total %
0 - 1	4,453	42.6	42.6	1,3625	3.5	3.5
1 - 5	4,762	45.5	88.1	9,521	24.1	27.6
5 - 10	828	7.9	96.0	5,071	12.8	40.4
10 - 25	320	3.1	99.0	4,611	11.7	52.1
25 - 50	52	0.5	99.5	1,789	4.5	56.6
50 - 100	18	0.2	99.7	1,250	3.2	59.8
100 - 200	8	0.1	99.8	1,105	2.8	62.6
200 - 500	16	0.2	99.9	5,195	13.2	75.8
500 +	8	0.1	100.0	9,571	24.2	100.0
Total	10,465	100.0		39,475	100.0	

The concentration of so much land in so few hands has aggravated the country's economic problems since estates are generally far less intensively cultivated than peasant plots, a trait that has been marked since Emancipation (Wright 1929:239-240). But many peasants also underuse their lands, and both tendencies represent a serious problem given the country's small body of arable land. Of the 39,475 acres of farmland in the state, only 26,000 acres, or 66 percent, are really suitable for crops and pasture. Of this 26,000 acres, 6,300, or 24 percent, are idle or seriously underused, a situation the World Bank (1979:14) recently called ". . . a luxury the country can ill afford." From 1961 to 1972 alone, land devoted to agriculture declined by nearly 20 percent (Brana-Shute and Brana-Shute 1980:23). Chapter 6 discusses the complex and generally ignored set of factors which have created the underuse of land in Leeward Village. Its consequences, however, are simple and readily observed. Less food produced at home means more food imported from abroad; and low agricultural productivity combined with dependency on imported food enlarges St. Vincent's ever-growing trade imbalance. Even during the 1820s when St. Vincent was already in economic decline and all raw materials and considerable foodstuff had to be imported, the value of exports consistently tripled the value of imports (Shephard 1831:xxxiii). In sharp contrast, for many years now the value of imports has been between two and six times the value of exports (St. Vincent 1985:50).

For an agricultural country, St. Vincent is surprisingly dependent upon imported food. In 1984, food amounted to 25 percent of the value of imports (St. Vincent 1985:51). Even the three staples of the diet of the poorer members of the society--wheat and flour products, rice, and sugar--are brought to the island along with most or all locally consumed dairy and poultry produce, grains and cereals, and fertilizer. St. Vincent also imports nearly all locally consumed building materials, petroleum products, hardware and machinery, and clothing and textiles, a fact which lead the World Bank (1979:20) to comment as follows on the country's prospects for industrial development:

> The dependence on non-food imports underscores the limited scope for industrial development. The potential for industrial development [in St. Vincent] is constrained by the small domestic market and the limited scale of agricultural output suitable for processing, particularly secondary processing. For only a few industries can minimally viable production units be sustained. Even regional markets are modest in scale; competing production in other islands and transport costs limit the potential to supply them. . . . The shortage of entrepreneurial

and management talent, inadequate transport facilities and the limited availability of financing, particularly for working capital, constrain the development of both export and import substitution industries.

The total industrial labor force of 1,300-1,400 persons represents less than five percent of the total work force and contributes only 9 percent of the Gross Domestic Product (World Bank 1979:20). As in the past, ". . . almost all significant export-oriented enterprises have been set up by foreign businessmen . . ." (World Bank 1979:20).

Agricultural depression and the absence of an industrial alternative have also adversely affected the ability of the government to provide social and other services. With the fastest growing population in the region (Byrne 1969), public expenditures have been impossible to meet from local revenue and Britain was obliged to resume treasury control in 1952. From 1960 to the mid-1970s direct aid from the United Kingdom ranged from 20-70 percent of total local revenue (University of the West Indies Development Mission 1969:55; St. Vincent 1963b, 1965, 1967a, 1970, 1976:21).

Public expenditure, whether from foreign sources or local revenue, has done little for the section of the economy which deserves the most support, the agrarian component. Despite former Prime Minister Cato's statement in the 1980 Budget Address (St. Vincent 1980:4) that: ". . . agriculture will remain for some time the most important sector of the economy, and my Government will spare no effort in ensuring that this sector will remain viable" only three percent of the 1979-1980 budget was devoted to it (St. Vincent 1979:25a). Not surprisingly, the agricultural program has been faulted on several grounds: contact between the handful of extension workers and the country's 10,000 cultivators is infrequent; the field staff is poorly trained; applied and research equipment is limited; experimental activities are inadequate in scope; and little credit aid in the farm loan scheme is distributed to small farmers (World Bank 1979:12-13).

THE CONTEMPORARY POLITICAL SCENE

Much of the blame for the current economic situation has been directed at the government (University of the West Indies Development Mission 1969:104).

A modern, efficiently run society requires a high valuation of impartiality, assessment on the basis of merit, impersonality in certain areas of behaviour, and a willingness to accept change. There are considerable obstacles to the emergence of such values in St. Vincent. In a society of such size social relations are inevitably influenced by personal contacts; the temptations to place [government] job applicants and to promote employees on the basis of who they are rather than on what they have achieved are often great; nepotism is likely to be rife; the bureaucracy will find it difficult to remain neutral; political competition is likely to be fraught with great bitterness and intensity. If St. Vincent is to modernize successfully it must somehow overcome the worst aspects of such tendencies.

Rooted in the paternalism, restricted access to positions of power and privilege, and resistance to innovation characteristic of the old Representative System and Crown Colony rule, "such tendencies" simply mimic tradition. Crown-Colony Government remained unaltered in St. Vincent from 1877 to 1924 when the nationalistic sentiments that were emerging throughout the British West Indies resulted in a new Vincentian constitution in which three of the nine members in the Legislative Council were elected (Ayearst 1960:33-34). This change did little to alter the existing political status quo. Both the right to vote and candidacy for office continued to be based on high property qualifications. With only three elected members and a restricted electorate, political parties were irrelevant and the election went uncontested (Ayearst 1960:31, 35). The Executive Council remained entirely composed of Crown appointees and the same kind of wealthy conservative men continued in office. Additional constitutional changes in 1935 increased the number of elected members to five in a new eleven-person Council and witnessed the beginnings of party politics with the election of four representatives from the political arm of the island's first trade union (Hourihan 1975:39). Again, real structural change did not accompany these developments. As one observer of the Vincentian political scene has argued (Hourihan 1975:40).

[T]he minority of elected members could easily be overruled by the majority of nominated and official members and/or Administrator [the Crown-appointed chief executive officer]. Moreover, it must be remembered that the legislators had been elected entirely by the small group of middle and upper class persons who could meet the voting qualifications, and this group was not about to jeopardize their own positions in favor of the poorer, uneducated, lower-class. It is obvious that the interests of the masses were not yet championed.

The interests of the Vincentian poor, the category forming the bulk of the populace, were not officially recognized until 1951 when a new constitution established an enlarged legislature. The new body consisted of 14 members: an Administrator, or deputy-Governor, as local chief executive authority and head of government; two government officials; three Crown nominees; and eight elected members. Property restrictions for voting and holding office were removed and three of the elected members were allowed to sit on a six-person Executive Council. In the election that followed all eight seats were won by the 8th Army of Liberation, the political-party wing of a national labor union (Hourihan 1975:47). Yet final decision-making and governance continued to be entrenched in the Executive Council: real power still rested with the Crown.

Indirect rule remained even after the introduction of ministerial government in 1958 and the modification of the Executive Council to include a majority of elected members. The Administrator continued to direct the most powerful government sectors--the judiciary, the police, finance, and the public service--and he could, and sometimes did, veto Administrative and Executive decisions. Additional constitutional changes in 1960, reducing the nominated portion of the Executive Council to one member and bestowing the post of Chief Minister on the person who controlled the majority of members of the Administrative Council, did not alter this situation.

It was not until 1969--206 years after it became a British possession--that St. Vincent finally dropped its colonial status and was transformed into a "State in Association with Great Britain." Introducing full internal self-government for the first time, the transitional period of Associate Statehood was soon followed by full sovereignty in 1979 when St. Vincent and the Grenadines became the smallest independent nation in the Western Hemisphere. The legislative body now has 13 elected members, 7 of whom form a Cabinet consisting of a Prime Minister and six Ministers, plus 6 senators, the latter appointed by the largely ceremonial Governor-General on the advice of the Prime Minister and Leader of the Opposition.

The rapid series of constitutional changes which began in the 1950s were accompanied by the development of a full-blown, albeit highly unstable, system of party politics. Starting from the efforts of charismatic labor leaders who championed the plight of the "down-trodden masses" (Hourihan 1975:47), intense, sometimes violent, partisanship has come to characterize the Vincentian political scene.

The first of these magnetic personalities was Ebenezer T. Joshua. A former schoolteacher and union organizer, Joshua, a fiery platform orator, and fellow labor leader, George Charles, directed the peasant- and worker-supported 8th Army of Liberation's 1951 election victory (Hourihan 1975:47). Once in office, its members quickly learned that under colonial rule they could do little to influence government policy. The Party soon disintegrated. Four of its members, led by Charles, joined forces with the nominated members of the Administrative Council hoping that this would give them at least some voice in decision-making (Hourihan 1975:48-49). The other four, under Joshua's headship, proved more intransigent and founded a new organization, the People's Political Party (PPP), in 1952.

The prospect of adult franchise stimulated the formation of still another party. Headed by lawyers and professionals, the New Era Party (NEP) also contained representatives of the plantocracy, and, in response to the expanded electorate, several spokesmen for the "downtrodden masses." The formation of the 8th Army of Liberation in 1951 caused this last contingent to defect and the NEP soon dissolved for lack of grass-roots support. The remaining members regrouped in 1955 under the direction of two barristers, Robert Milton Cato and Rupert John (later Sir Rupert, first Governor-General of St. Vincent), and formed the St. Vincent Labour Party (SVLP). They were soon joined by three disgruntled members of Joshua's PPP, two of whom had earlier crossed over from the NEP to the 8th Army.

Between 1956 and 1972, the PPP and SVLP dominated Vincentian party politics, engaging in four fiercely contested campaigns. Political opposition has not been matched by ideological variance. Formed by like-minded professionals, businessmen, labor leaders, and school teachers and faced with social and economic problems which have proved intractable, the two parties have been nearly indistinguishable in political philosophy and election promises (see Hourihan 1975:54-55; St. Vincent Labour Party 1979; New Democratic Party 1979).

With political philosophies and party platforms so much alike, several close elections and a small legislature in which the actions of one or two members can change the balance of power has prompted countless shifts in allegiance over the years.

It is of more than passing interest to note that five

members of the present [1966] legislature--Joshua, Young, Slater, Tannis and Lathum--have survived four elections under varying labels. After the old 8 Army came tumbling down like the pack of cards it was, Mr. Joshua formed his PPP in whose saddle he has since remained unchallenged. Young went over to PPP in 1954, joined the Labour Party in 1955, departed to lead the PLM [Peoples' Liberation Movement] in 1957, and defected to become a top brass in the PPP in 1964. Slater has been fairly constant. After a short honeymoon with the 8 Army he remained an independent until 1957 when he went over to the PPP to whom he has ever remained faithful. After the demise of the 8 Army Tannis also remained fiercely independent until 1958 when he joined forces with Labour, only to go over to the PPP during the '59 political crisis. Mr. Lathum, too, was an Independent member of the House who joined the PPP in 1956, quarrelled with the leadership, and enlisted in the ranks of the Labour Party in 1958. Added to these are George Charles and Afflick Haynes who also share colourful political careers. Charles led the 8 Army in 1951, ran as an independent in 1954, contested under the PLM banner in 1957, ran on a Labour ticket in 1961, and appears to be a PPPite at the present time. Haynes, on the other hand, was a independent in 1954, a member of the PPP from 1956-62, a Labourite from 1962-64, and seems to be a PPP supporter at the moment of writing (John 1973:89).

Mr. J.L. Eustace ran on the SVLP ticket in 1967, defected from the SVLP government in 1970-71, ran as an Independent in 1972, and, following his defeat in that election became Speaker of the House under the present [1972-1974] PPP dominated coalition government. Mr. R. F. Marksman ran on the PPP ticket in 1967, defected to the SVLP in 1970 (and was rewarded with a Ministry), and subsequently lost as a SVLP candidate in 1972. Mr. James F. "Son" Mitchell, the present Premier, contested as a SVLP candidate in 1967, became an Independent just before the 1972 election, ran as an Independent in that election and formed a coalition government (with six PPP members) with himself as Premier. And, of course, Mr. Slater had run as a PPP candidate in 1966, defected in 1967 [in the process bringing down the government], ran on the SVLP ticket in the election of 1967 (and received a Ministry), and lost as a SVLP candidate in 1972 (Hourihan 1975:197- 198).

The coalition between Mitchell and the six PPP members lasted until 1974 when Joshua and his wife, also an elected member of the 13-seat House of Assembly, resigned from Government and, together with long-time PPP supporter Clive Tannis, joined forces with his old opponent Cato and the SVLP. The three remaining PPP members sided with Mitchell and joined his fledgling New Democratic Party [NDP]. To reduce Mitchell's chances of success in the election caused by their floor-crossing, and having been privately assured by the SVLP that they would be brought into a new government, the Joshuas and Tannis ran a three-person slate in the 1974 election. This strategy paid off. Confusion among the electorate produced a SVLP sweep when 10 of its 13 candidates were returned. Both Joshuas were elected and Mitchell was returned as the sole NDP representative. Premier Cato awarded Mr. Joshua with an important portfolio in an alliance between individuals who had been bitter political adversaries for nearly 25 years.

Less than three years later Joshua resigned from Government after differing with Cato over the independence issue. Running nearly a full slate of candidates in the 1979 campaign, his PPP polled less that 15 percent of the popular vote and did not return a single candidate (The Vincentian 1979:4). Joshua's nearly 30 years in elected office were over and he surrendered party leadership to Clive Tannis. The victorious SVLP returned 11 of its 13 candidates, the NDP 2. Mitchell, who had chosen to run against Joshua, lost instead to the SVLP candidate. By pre-election agreement one of the two NDP Assemblymen gave up his seat, allowing Mitchell, the party leader, to gain entry into the House in an easily won 1980 by-election. The other NDP House member, less faithful than his colleague, but true to Vincentian political tradition, renounced his association with Mitchell and formed his own Working People's Party. Recognized as the official Leader of the Opposition, he named two Senators to the House. One of these was a former member of Joshua's PPP.

In 1981 Randolph Russell, the Minister of Health, resigned his post and left the SVLP, claiming the government was to blame for the country's economic difficulties. The government's attempt to bring in what was generally considered to be repressive public order and labor-relations regulations led to unprecedented organized bipartisan public opposition in the form of large demonstrations and a partially successful general strike in June of the same year.

In June 1984 Cato called an early and unexpected general election, hoping to capitalize on a divided opposition. Scandals involving the misuse of public funds by at least two government ministers, opposition to new taxation policies, and the memory of government's 1981 attempt to introduce undemocratic legislation helped to produce an NDP victory the next month. The NDP took nine of the 13 elective seats in the House of Assembly, and the party's leader James Mitchell became Prime Minister for a second time. Five SVLP ministers lost their bids for re-election and Cato resigned his seat and retired from a 34-year career in politics. Two of his former ministers are still facing charges of misappropriation of public funds.

Appealing to the same basic constituency for support--the numerically-dominant rural and urban lower class--in a situation where the social and material benefits of holding office are great, these "incredible political gymnastics," as one local observer called them (John 1973:86), are inextricably tied to contemporary island economic organization and social stratification.

> The country is a poor agricultural community divided between the small group of "haves" and a large undifferentiated mass of the "have nots."   Since any serious minded party must minister to the needs of this large category of working (and unworking) people all parties will necessarily use the same basic approach. And since the parties stand for more or less the same thing, and since gainful employment is so hard to come by, it is not surprising (though we might find it distasteful) to find men jumping from one side to the other to get a salary and, incidentally, to get something done for their constituency (John 1973:88).

CONTEMPORARY SOCIAL STRATIFICATION

Less rigid and compartmentalized than the legally-prescribed slave society system that preceded it, contemporary Vincentian stratification continues to be based on distinctions of race and color, income and property, occupation and education, prestige and respectability, and power. To be sure, St. Vincent is now a sovereign state with a fully-enfranchised Black electorate. The government, including elected politicians and senior civil servants, consists almost entirely of Black and Colored people. Many professionals--lawyers, physicians, accountants, clergymen, and others--come from poor peasant backgrounds. Numerous large and medium sized businesses, such as automobile dealerships, bakeries, boutiques, department stores, pharmacies, restaurants, and supermarkets are owned by Black or Colored people. Still, much of the traditional racial hierarchy endures. Notwithstanding the continual exodus of the European elite as island prospects kept deteriorating, major economic resources and positions of influence and social esteem remain in the hands of a small local group of wealthy White estate owners, professionals, and businessmen (Fraser 1975). De facto racial segregation, both social and residential, persists and interracial marriages are rare.

There are, of course, many examples of Black people rising from near the bottom to near the top of the class hierarchy. But this has blurred rather than obliterated the main social and economic boundaries. Most sources of locally sustained wealth and income-- the largest land holdings and the major wholesale and retail enterprises--continue to be transmitted along family lines. Branches of foreign banks, insurance companies, shipping agencies, telecommunication and public utility companies, and manufacturing concerns testify to continuing overseas economic control. As always, phenotypical differences are taken to connote differential inherent worth, and political decisions, overtly made by Blacks for Blacks, still favor long-standing vested economic interests. The result is continued restricted access to social and economic opportunities, rewards, and honors.

Although race and pigmentation are only two of several elements defining social placement in St. Vincent, status differences are largely expressed by the short-hand idiom of racial designation (cf. Lowenthal 1972:93-100, 134-135). *Black* is a term of derision referring to actual skin color, not racial or ethnic group membership, and there is a preference, especially among men, for marrying lighter-complexioned partners so as to ". . . have nice straight-haired children" (John 1966:14; cf. Braithwaite 1975; Henriques 1953:44-63; Philpott 1973:62-63; R.T. Smith 1956:191-200). Phenotype and its evaluation are not just a matter of skin shade alone; a narrow nose, thin lips, and straight hair--features associated with Western European physiognomy--are also part of what constitutes *nice looks*. Some Vincentian mothers, like their Guyanese counterparts (R.T. Smith 1956:212), even pull and squeeze their infants' noses hoping to make them *pointed*. Mulattoes returning to the island for vacations are admonished to keep themselves and their children out of the sun to retain their sallow complexions.

Even behavior, beliefs, and certain personality traits are attributed to racial inheritance (cf. Lowenthal 1972:95-96). Black people are variously described as boisterous and libidinous, prodigal and pious, quarrelsome and derisive, and covetous and unreliable; Whites are seen as inhibited and remote, yet dependable, business-like, and trustworthy; East Indians are felt to be clannish, par-simonious, devious, and unkempt.

Racial and ethnic stereotypes are sustained by social distance and deferential behavior. Interaction between members of different strata normally is limited to contexts which underscore disparities in wealth, power, and status. Poor people, for example, meet physicians, lawyers, police inspectors, magistrates, senior civil servants, clergymen, and other officials and professionals mainly in formal settings--hospitals and clinics, legal chambers, police stations, court rooms, government offices, and vestries. Differences in speech, dress, and demeanor--standard English, expensive attire or a uniform, and aloofness by the high-ranking person; the local creole dialect, poor clothing, and obsequiousness by the low-ranking one-- formalize the encounter and highlight social and economic inequities. Steeply sloped, rooted in the traditions of slavery-based plantation society, perpetuated by inherited differences in property and wealth, and rationalized by racial and ethnic prejudices, the Vincentian social hierarchy still permits some upward movement. The abolition of slavery and its codified birth-ascribed ranking criteria, the creation of a racially, socially, and economically intermediate Colored population, the steady exodus of high-ranking Whites, the increasing availability to Mulattoes of government and other ad-ministrative positions formerly filled by British expatriates (Harold and John 1966:7-8), the establishment of universal adult suffrage and the opening it presented to aspiring Black leaders, and growing opportunities for well-paid overseas employment and professional training have all resulted in the formation of new non-White elite and near elite groups. Folk stereotypes to the contrary, there is no simple bipolar distinction between Black and White in St. Vincent. Graduated differences in color, wealth, and status make it par-ticularly difficult to establish boundaries between the non-elite strata (Harold and John 1966:7-8). But hierachical differentiation in St. Vincent is no featureless continuum. Despite the increasing emphasis on non-birth ascribed criteria for individuals and groups and the presence of large numbers persons of intermediate com-plexion, wealth, and social standing the gap between rich and poor, powerful and powerless, exalted and lowly is as great as ever. Those who are rich or influential are few in number. Their identities are widely known and their pedigrees often stretch back to slave-owning ancestors. The elite and near-elite White population in 1970 numbered between 500-600 persons, less than one-half the total White population of 1,248, and represents a net decrease of 50 percent since 1844 (West Indian Census 1946:1950). Meanwhile the total Vincentian population tripled between 1844 and 1970, most of this increase represented by people with meager resources, little power, and low social standing.

Still, St. Vincent is no longer a caste society, and although racial, ethnic, and cultural factors affect social placement, the current system of social inequality is fundamentally based on class, i.e., on ". . . economic interests in the possession of goods and opportunities for income . . ." (Weber 1966:21). Differentiation by objective wealth-derived "economic situation" is reinforced by subjective judgments of "status situation" (Weber 1966:24) in which Vincentians rank each other by race and skin color, parentage and pedigree, ethnic affiliation, and style of life. A third dimension of hierarchical differentiation--political power or "party" (Weber 1966:270)--seems, at first glance, to enhance the close association between class position and status situation with the SVLP pictured as the camp of the rich and near rich and the PPP as the faction of the masses. A closer look at both overt and surreptitious political support shows otherwise.

> There is a lot of talk in St. Vincent that the parties are divided on class lines. This is sheer nonsense. In terms of educational qualification, shade gradation, or economic indices, the country is about 80 percent lower-class. And since both parties share the country evenly it is obvious that both are supported by a substantial portion of the working class. . . . Equally, on the other hand, because politics in a country as poor as St. Vincent is a relatively costly business, even the supposedly lower-class party [PPP] has had to compromise itself and seek support from certain middle-class businessmen who welcome the opportunity to exploit the political situation for their own economic ends. In any event the Planter class always looms in the background to hand out sufficient funds to either side to curry favour, safeguard their interests, and ensure that neither party has an overwhelming mandate to effect any real radical scheme (John 1973:80-90).

With wealth and income differences paralleled by evaluations of social worth and with authority wielded from the top down by the political elite and their wealthy supporters regardless of which party is in control, it is possible to deal simultaneously with the economic, status, and power dimensions of island ranking under the single rubric of social class. Except for elected politicians, nearly all who are phenotypically Black, this correlation between wealth, evaluations of social worth, and decision-making results in a system of stratification which resembles the color-class pyramids that have been reported for Martinique (Horowitz 1967:4), Montserrat (Philpott 1973:62-65), Trinidad (Braithwaite 1975:41-47), Jamaica (Henriques 1953:42-63), Guyana (R.T. Smith 1956:191-200), and Grenada (M.G. Smith 1965b:158-168). As in these other countries, the correlation between race, color, income, power, and prestige is far from exact. Many Whites are poor, large numbers of non-Whites--Mulattoes, Blacks, East Indians, etc.--are found at all ranks, and some of the most important and symbolically conspicuous positions held by the former White colonial elite--Governor-General, Bishop, Chief Medical Officer, Crown Attorney--are now in the hands of Black people.

The folk model of stratification--the perceptions, beliefs, and values of Vincentians about the ranking of individuals, positions, and groups--also displays internal 'contradictions' among the criteria of race, wealth, and style of life and this requires the occasional 'adjustment' of phenotypical ascription to match extant notions of social class (cf. Lowenthal 1972:99-100). When several hundred poor White agricultural laborers from Barbados migrated to St. Vincent during the 1860s (Roberts 1955:245-288), doubling overnight the local White population and challenging the association between color and class, the newcomers where ethnically designated as non-Whites to distinguish them from their elite racial peers. Termed *Bajans* because neither their resources nor style of life permitted them to be classified as *White* they settled mainly in the hills behind Kingstown. Yet although they shared the same class situation as poor Blacks, race and ethnicity proved determinative and most of them have remained in social, residential, and endogamous isolation from the larger Black population.

The Upper Class

Comprising no more than two percent of the national population, or less than 2,000 people, the upper class stands at the apex of the stratification pyramid. Its members include most islanders who are considered *White* by a combination of physical appearance, behavior, style of life, and structural position within the class hierarchy (cf. M.G. Smith 1955:51-57). This means that most *Bajans*, or poor Whites, are excluded since they lack the material resources, cultural traditions, and social standing associated with assignment to the elite category. Conversely, an ever growing number of Colored and Black people may be described as upper class because of their wealth, prestigious occupational standing, or high political office.

Like their colonial-society predecessors, members of the upper class have a near monopoly on the country's most important institutions and resources. These include estate agriculture, the import-export trade, large-scale manufacturing, wholesaling and retailing, the chartered banks, real estate agencies and insurance companies, the political and legal apparatus, the educational, medical, and social welfare systems, the traditional Christian denominations, and the small tourist industry. Consequently, their occupational roles include plantation owner, large retail merchant, business executive, industrialist, senior civil servant, lawyer, physician, and Anglican or Roman Catholic priest.

As in colonial times, the upper-class includes both creoles and immigrants. The senior management of foreign-based companies, British government officials, foreign-born physicians, civil servants recruited from other islands, and North American and West Indian clergymen make up most of the expatriate elite population. Upper-class creoles are divided between professionals and non-professionals. Most of the latter are members of the traditional White elite who own the largest estates and Kingstown businesses (cf. Fraser 1975). Creole professionals, on the other hand, are relative newcomers to the elite stratum. They represent the growing number of university-educated Colored and Black islanders--doctors, lawyers, top government employees, accountants--who achieved upper-class membership through movement from the middle class (and, in a few cases, even from the lower class). By contrast, elite White creoles who lack highly-trained occupational standing entered the stratum simply through birth-ascription; they are testimony to the continuing control of many island material resources and positions of high standing by individuals and families who trace direct descent from slave-owning ancestors. The entrepreneurial foundation of their wealth and position has shifted, however. Although three of the four largest estate-owning families are White, many members of the traditional elite have given up cultivation to enter the more lucrative fields of manufacturing, sales, and real estate. The island's biggest industrial concerns, supermarkets, hardware stores, hotels, clothing and textile emporiums, bakeries, jewelry and gift shops, furniture and appliance stores, real estate agencies, travel and shipping firms, lumber yards and building supply companies, and book and stationary stores are owned by White creoles. Those who still have a large land base are profiting from the continual sale of small blocks of cultivable land and house spots to peasant cultivators and overseas migrants.

Though no longer involved in direct island governance, the political influence of the traditional elite is still considerable.

In St. Vincent, both parties [SVLP and PPP] have had to reply on monetary backing from various members of the middle and upper-classes. This is so because no people's party could exist on the basis of financial support from the rank and file members. The population is simply too poor. Furthermore, this fact has played into the hands of the planter class. . . . [W]ith the introduction of universal adult suffrage . . . the planters had to devise new methods of maintaining their position as the socio-economic elite. Principal among these has been the adroit use of the dollar, for the members of the upper-class grant financial support to elements of both parties in order to protect their own interests (Hourihan 1975:57-58; see also Fraser 1975:205; Harold and John 1966; John 1973).

But it is their style of living and patterns of belief and behavior rather than their covert political role which distinguishes the upper class, White and Black, creole and expatriate, from other segments of society. Called *big shots*, *big boys*, or *first class people* by lower-class islanders, nearly all members of the elite reside in spacious, well-furnished homes in quiet, fashionable neighborhoods in the capital or in bedroom enclaves on the picturesque southern coast. Although many members of the elite are, by measurable material standards, no better off than lower-middle class people in the United States or Canada (cf. Philpott 1973:47), they still manage to employ one or more live-in domestic servants. Many also belong to exclusive clubs and all send their children to private schools, sometimes in neighboring islands or overseas. In other ways, however, they resemble their status counterparts in England and North America. Standard English is the language of everyday use (although many also speak or understand the lower-class creole dialect) and legal, Christian marriage is the basic of their domestic

64

conjugal life (although many of their men have *outside children* with lower-class women [cf. Philpott 1973:46]).

The Middle class

The middle class contains between 10,000 and 12,000 persons, or some 10 percent of the national population. Urban in lifestyle and residence, its members resemble the upper class in several areas of social and economic life. The same sorts of occupations are pursued, albeit on a much smaller scale. Its ranks contain owners of medium-sized Kingstown businesses, proprietors of small country estates, middle-level civil servants, headmasters and senior teachers, building contractors, nurses, pharmacists, middle-managers in commercial enterprises, bank clerks, police inspectors, highly skilled technicians, and overseers of large plantations.

Racial, color, and ethnic heterogeneity are pronounced. There are now more Black than Colored people among its members and many East Indians, Portuguese, and *Bajans* have also achieved middle-class status over the past few years.

Both birth-ascription and upward mobility are the routes for attaining membership in the stratum. As the list of middle-class occupations suggests, membership via achievement has grown in importance as educational opportunities and specialized vocational positions have expanded. Although secondary school training, local capital accumulation, and the investment of funds acquired through overseas migration have allowed many people to move into the middle class, inheritance and pedigree still play important roles in perpetuating membership. Indeed, many middle-class persons maintain their position more through family reputation, the status of their close associates, and the manipulation of symbols of 'respectability' --Christian marriage, church attendance, elevated diction, a quiet, dignified bearing, and so on--than they do through educational attainment, well-paying occupations, or the conspicuous display of wealth. Alternately, there are many self-made people who, despite all the financial and material requisites of middle-class standing, are confined to its lowest rung because of their rustic manners, lack of education, *broad* [course] speech usage, and bad reputation of their companions.

As a consequence, income, education, style of life, and social behavior are varied within the middle class. Many of its members are better educated and more 'worldly' than large numbers of upper-class people; others have barely completed a public school education and are in the stratum mainly through their achieved wealth. Because of this variability, there is little evidence of group solidarity or even consciousness of kind among its members. Yet most middle-class people share one fundamental feature: a compulsion to validate, if not raise, their soc;·l position by trying, on the one hand, to differentiate themselves from members of the lower class and, on the other, to emulate certain upper-class standards of behavior and belief. For several features of life style--standard English diction, European and North American recreational activities, fashionable dress, Christian modes of family life and religious affiliation--it is possible for many to at least approximate the upper-class model. Obtaining the requisite material possessions, especially a large, well-appointed house in a choice neighborhood is much more difficult, particularly for those employed in government service where earnings are much below those in the private sector. Still, nearly all manage to acquire the three island symbols of middle-class status: an automobile, a full-time domestic servant, and a telephone.

Except for government employees who are constrained by statute from overt political involvement, members of the stratum are keen players or vocal partisan spectators in the political arena. Except for the last election, a majority have tended to support the SVLP since the mid-1960s, and were instrumental in its several consecutive victories by swaying opinion and recruiting support among lower-class voters. One anthropological observer of the Vincentian political scene (Hourihan 1975:60-61) found that:

> [P]olitical leaders in St. Vincent generate support for themselves by the offering of inducements, or the establishment of transactions, which involve the exchange of support for an actual or promised allocation of such scarce resources as jobs, money, food, clothing, or building materials to their followers. . . . [S]upport is generated through a network of intervening individuals who act as local *agents* for the political leaders. . . . [T]hese agents are members of the rural middle-class, such as schoolteachers, rum-shop owners, or lorry drivers (Fraser 1974), who make implicit or explicit contracts or transactions with the potential voters in the name of one of the political parties or its leader. . . .

These agents, as Hourihan calls them, also include middle-class urbanites, who, like their rural peers, are rewarded with patronage for their lobbying efforts.

> [I]t is the Government supporters who receive government
> contracts, construction permits, or pioneer status and the
> resultant tax breaks for establishing new enterprises. And,
> at the village level, the agents also benefit. For example,
> schoolteachers may be appointed to headmaster or be
> transferred to more desirable locations; lorry drivers will
> receive government contracts for hauling materials or for
> transporting party followers to political meetings; rum-
> shop owners will receive a steady business from the local
> party followers, and will host party officials when they
> visit a given village (and benefit from the money spent in
> the shop)(Hourihan 1975:65).

Notwithstanding their often close political association, preoccupation with status validation forces many middle-class persons,
especially women, to stress social and ideological distance from the
lower class (cf. Philpott 1973:49-50; see also Lowenthal 1972:123-143).
A desire to rise even higher, insecurity about their lower-class
origins, and ambivalence about the appropriate behavior to exhibit in
certain situations all contribute to an emphasis on 'respectability'
and a concomitant condemnation of lower-class speech, manners,
sexual behavior, and religious belief.

The Lower Class

St. Vincent is a rural society and 80 percent of the population
lives in the scores of coastal and valley communities outside
Kingstown. Although poor islanders have been moving to Kingstown
since Emancipation and now make up about half of its 18,000
population, this number represents less than 10 percent of the nearly
95,000 island lower-class population (St. Vincent 1985:6). Consequently, most poor islanders are country residents and vice versa.
Totaling some 85 percent of the national population, the lower class
forms the largest segment of the stratification hierarchy. Membership is acquired by birth into a poor family and is perpetuated by
limited opportunities for upward mobility. Societal economic constraints and elite and middle class resource monopolization mean
that lower-class people also dominate certain positions in society:
the bottom ranks of the civil service, petty retailing and shopkeeping, peasant farming and inshore fishing, unskilled and semi-skilled

construction labor, agricultural wage-work, domestic service, and dressmaking. Characterized by low earnings and little prestige, these activities not only rarely allow life style enhancement, they often fail to satisfy even minimal individual and family subsistence needs.

Lower-class wage-labor activities are especially marked by seasonality of employment, frequent layoffs, insecurity of tenure, arbitrary dismissal, poor and tedious working conditions, few social benefits, and little chance for social and economic advancement. Yet as unremunerative and low in esteem as they are, the demand for jobs far exceeds their supply. The result is a high rate of unemployment--and an even higher rate of underemployment--particularly among adult women and young people of both sexes.

The same is true for self-employed activities. Peasant farming, fishing, the running of a small shop, dressmaking, and other lower-class occupations are marked by low profits and economic uncertainty. Dependence on uncontrollable market conditions and the marginal and unreliable purchasing power of a largely poor clientele also results in frequent abandonment of cultivation, the sale of fishing nets and sewing machines, and the closing down of shops.

Differences in life-chances most distinguish the upper and middle class from the lower class. On the basis of well established comparative indices of poverty and underdevelopment--low levels of per capita income; deficiencies of food, clothing, and housing; high infant mortality rates and levels of child malnutrition; a high proportion of the working population in the lowest paid occupations; and inadequate educational and health care delivery systems (Chernick 1978:87; Stavenhagen 1975:3-4; Todaro 1981:23-47)--members of the Vincentian lower class are not only badly off by island standards, they are worse off than most of their counterparts in other parts of the Caribbean (Chernick 1978:6-7, 269-272; University of the West Indies Development Mission 1969; World Bank 1979, 1980:430-442, 448-453). The University of the West Indies Development Mission report (1969:4-7, 117-118), for example, made the following observations: (1) the 1967 per capita income of WI$290 (US$145)--15 percent of which represented direct British aid--". . . is probably the lowest in the Western Hemisphere, with the exception of Haiti;" (2) the 114 lb. average annual consumption of protein--barely half that recommended for a normally active person--is a sign of a serious protein-calorie malnutrition; (3) the annual infant mortality rate which ranges between 92 per 1,000 to 132 per 1,000 is the highest in the West Indies and its dominant causes are various forms of malnutrition and gastro-enteritis; (4) health service ". . . are in such extreme neglect that it can now be described as primitive;" (5)

most villages have no pipe-borne water; and (6) ". . . about 80 percent of teachers are unqualified and about half hardly more than literate." The report concluded that:

> [M]ost of the people on the island are living in a way which, in terms of material and environmental conditions, could scarcely be far removed from the situation as it was under slavery (University of the West Indies Development Mission 1969:8-9).

Ten years later, a World Bank study (1979:25-29) cited nearly the same litany of problems as still plaguing the country:

> Although the island's population increased during 1970-78, water supply services deteriorated during the same period . . . . The number of teachers with specialized training is extremely low. . . . Moreover, many of the all-age primary schools are poorly equipped, badly dilapidated and without teaching materials. . . . [I]nfant mortality continues to be the highest in the English-speaking Caribbean. . . . The health care delivery system is seriously hampered by the shortage of funds, the dearth of trained personnel, and the dilapidated condition of existing facilities. The Central Hospital in Kingstown is poorly equipped, inadequately staffed and in serious disrepair. . . . The housing shortage is serious particularly with regard to low income groups. . . . Less than 30% of the existing housing stock was considered minimally adequate in 1970; the remainder required major improvement or replacement.

Another World Bank study of the Commonwealth Caribbean (Chernick 1978:87) reported that ". . . St. Vincent and St. Kitts seem to suffer from the most acute cases of extreme poverty in the region." More recently, a report commissioned by the U.S. Agency for International Development claimed that with an unemployment rate conservatively estimated to be at least 25 percent, "The situation in St. Vincent is the worst in the Eastern Caribbean" (Brana-Shute and Brana-Shute 1980:61). For example, in 1980 it took an average of five years for a school leaver to find employment, up from an average of three years in 1973 (Brana-Shute and Brana-Shute 1980:61). Technically speaking, most islanders are not even classified as "school leavers": of the total non-school population in 1970, 87 percent had less than a primary school education (Census

Research Programme 1973:374-378).

With a per capita gross national product of $330 in 1977, the second lowest in the entire region (World Bank 1980:xx), it is not surprising that the island is sometimes called as the "Third World's third world" (Starbird 1979:402).

Given these social and material conditions, the lower class appears as an undifferentiated mass of poor Black people. Most lower-class people are phenotypically and socially black--and vice versa--conspicuously separated from other segments of the society by differences in race, wealth, power, and status. But not all poor people are black and differences other than the most obvious class-linked ones differentiate the lowest stratum from the rest. Racial, color, and ethnic diversity renders the lower class just as hetero-geneous as the middle. Included in its membership is nearly all the racially-mixed Carib population, most *Bajans*, large numbers of East Indians and Portuguese, and hundreds of Colored persons. The lower class is heterogeneous in other ways as well. As the material from Leeward Village will show, income levels, life chances, patterns of behavior and interaction, family life, and ideology show considerable variability among people who are all too easily lumped into an undifferentiated category called "the poor" (cf. Philpott 1973:50).

Faced with a host of livelihood adversities and a history of political subordination, it is not surprising that there was an appeal to the government for help when universal franchise was finally granted in 1951. Public interest in politics is high among all classes in St. Vincent despite the near identity in party policy and program and the confusion and cynicism created by constant floor-crossing and party switching. Voter turnout up to 1972 averaged 80 percent of the electorate (The Vincentian 1979:4), and political events and personalities are an intense topic of conversation among all segments of society. Adult franchise was an especially important event among the lower class.

> The flood-gates of pent-up frustrations were unlocked and the people channelled all their released emotions into politico-economic movements. Everyone had to be a party man and a unionist in a fashion bordering on the fanatic. . . . Precisely because they had been denied a place in the political process the people got themselves to believe that politics held the key to all problems and offered the panacea to every ill (John 1973:85-86).

If Hourihan's (1975:59-65) findings are any indication, for many poor electors, participation in politics does indeed hold the key to economic well-being, if not the "panacea to every ill."

> [T]he scarcity of jobs, the high unemployment, and the meagerness of the economy have made patronage, and its counterpart, victimization, the very foundations of the economic and political life of the vast majority of Vincentians. In short, political support has become synonymous with patronage and affects the very means of subsistence and survival for most Vincentians. . . . [O]n the recommendation of the appropriate [middle-class] agents, those voters who elected the party in power are those who will be hired to work on road crews, land reclamation schemes, or other Community Development and Works projects. . . . In like manner, party supporters may determine which peasants or agricultural workers will be employed on the large estates, have free or low-rent housing, or be granted a small plot of land from the Government for growing subsistence vegetables.

Such patronage should not be treated in isolation. Political perquisites are only part, albeit a major part, of the nepotism that defines most hierarchical island relations.

> In St. Vincent many young people who are either unemployed or in such unremunerative and low status jobs as unskilled laborers, estate workers, porters, and errand-runners regularly point out that access to even a minor position requires the intervention and endorsement of a patron who will "arrange" matters. . . . The term "godfather" was often used to describe such an intermediary. The patron-client relationship is a personal one and takes into consideration such factors as the client's family relationships, voting record and political party support, and record of favors given and promised. . . . Observers often note, and Caribbean citizens will confirm, that politics is treated as a life and death issue; when you consider the importance of patronage jobs to those desperate for income, it is easier to understand why. Competition for the few positions available is intense and based on merit, or lack of it, that may have nothing to do with the job description (Brana-Shute and Brana-Shute 1980:77).

With limited island resources it is impossible to reward more than a handful of supporters in this way. "Generalized" and "indirect" forms of compensation often make up for this by substantially increasing the number of beneficiaries.

> [T]he reward may be in the form of a payment made to a village in a generalized sense, and at an unspecified time, but still be something that will benefit each individual. For example, the geographical pattern of voting can determine the location of new schools, post offices, or medical clinics; which roads will be repaired or extended (a very important factor in the transportation of home-grown produce to the various markets in mountainous St. Vincent); the locale of low-rent housing projects and land redistribution schemes; the distribution of surplus materials or gifts of foreign origin; and the installation or extension of electricity or water lines. . . . [O]ne member of a group of close relatives may be granted some reward (e.g., a job in Kingstown), the profits of which presumably can be distributed to the other members of that group, thereby reducing the need to grant another reward to the particular kin group from that particular economic category (Hourihan 1975:64-66).

A fluid political situation and the unstable nature of many hierarchical relationships has also meant that those rewards that are distributed or promised--casual government wage labor, jobs in the private sector, low interest loans, cash gratuities, gifts of used clothing, low income housing--may vanish overnight.

For lower-class Vincentians, then, political and class-based economic benefits, like other resources, are scarce, differentially distributed, unpredictably available, and ephemeral. The consequence is that, except for a handful of the closest lower-class clients of certain politicians, party involvement has not resulted in dramatic or permanent alterations in life styles or social standing; nor has political change brought a radical transformation in the 'shape' of Vincentian society. Stated otherwise, Vincentian social stratification has remained fundamentally unaltered regardless of which party or personality has been in power and regardless of whether the form of rule has been the Old Representative system, Crown Colony administration, or full parliamentary self-government.

The response of the rural poor has always been the same: exodus from the island. Faced with limited economic prospects at home and the uncertainties generated by constantly changing political scenarios, Vincentians have continued to seek relief in other places. Indeed, so important is migration as a strategy for coping with poverty that it is possible to speak of a "migration culture" (Richardson 1983:24) to describe the constellation of adaptive behaviors and beliefs associated with it.

The first wave of migration during this century took place between 1904 and 1914 when many unskilled Vincentians joined thousands of other West Indians employed in the American completion of the Panama Canal project. Cuba, the Dominican Republic, and the surrounding Hispanic mainland, especially Panama and Costa Rica, also continued to attract agricultural laborers from St. Vincent during the early part of the century. Employed on sugar-cane and banana plantations, islanders kept migrating to these destinations on a seasonal basis until restrictive immigration policies were enacted and migrant workers expelled during the 1930s (Proudfoot 1950:14-15, 19).

A worldwide slump in sugar prices in 1921 and the Great Depression eliminated many of the traditional migration outlets during the 1920s and 1930s (Marshall 1982). Nevertheless, work in the oil fields of Venezuela from 1916 and in the petroleum refineries of neighboring Aruba and Curacao after 1925, attracted many workers from St. Vincent. In 1929, however, the Venezuelan government prohibited the further entry of foreign-born Black people (Marshall 1982:9; Proudfoot 1950:15; Thomas-Hope 1978:68). This was followed by the dismissal and expulsion of 70 percent of the unskilled migrant labor force in Curacao two years later (Marshall 1982:9).

A renewed flow from the island to the southern Caribbean resumed during the early years of World War II. Nearby Trinidad was a particularly popular destination. Employed in the oil refineries and U.S. military and naval bases during the War, hundreds of Vincentians are still working and living in the island today. The renewed movement to Aruba and Curacao, however, was short lived. Automation in the early 1950s resulted in mass layoffs, enforced early retirement, and foreign worker repatriation (Marshall 1982:9; Proudfoot 1950:16). Still, many Vincentians returned home after having worked for 20 years or more in one of the two islands.

Removal from St. Vincent has also involved extra-Caribbean destinations. From about 1900, islanders began to migrate to the northeastern United States where they formed tiny immigrant enclaves in New York and Washington. Although much of this migration was of a permanent sort and tended to involve better-off

Black islanders, poor Vincentians also participated and many of these returned to their home communities after several years overseas (cf. Richardson 1983:133). Many were also forced home by racially-restrictive immigrant legislation passed in 1924 (Proudfoot 1950:14). A new migratory flow to these same two cities resumed after a more liberal immigration act came into force in 1965.

Along with those destined for urban areas, removal to the United States has for some three decades also seen hundreds of agricultural contract workers, recruited for six or more months at a time, picking fruit along the eastern seaboard and cutting cane in southern Florida. During the 1981-82 season, 450 Vincentian workers were recruited for the program after being nominated by government ministers (McCoy and Wood 1982:14). Political patronage was said to be the basis for selection (Brana-Shute 1980:73). The average cane cutter spent 20 weeks in Florida and grossed nearly $4,000, or some eight times the island per capita GNP (McCoy and Wood 1982:46, 66). A compulsory savings plan sent 23 percent of gross earnings back to the island to be deposited into a bank account claimed by the worker after his return (see Table 3.2, Column 9). Compulsory remittances form only a portion of the total capital flowback. Voluntary mailed remittances, consumer goods purchased in Florida and taken back to the island, and cash taken back at the end of the season represent 34 percent of gross earnings. Including the compulsory savings plan, $1.4 million in cash and goods was sent back to St. Vincent during 1981-82.

Seasonal agricultural work is not confined to the United States. Vincentians migrated to neighboring Barbados to cut cane for at least 20 years (400 made the trip in 1979 [Brana-Shute and Brana-Shute 1980:74]) and over 100 fruit pickers are now traveling to Canada each year.

But the largest and most important flow of Vincentians has involved removal outside the Hemisphere. Attracted by industrial labor shortages at the cheap, unskilled end of the occupational ladder and encouraged by the British Nationality Act of 1948 which gave Commonwealth Caribbean residents the right to claim full citizenship, over 10,000 Vincentians found their way to England starting in the mid-1950s (Davison 1962; HMSO 1967; St. Vincent 1963c, 1969, 1971). Despite the small relative size of the immigrant West Indian population--less than one percent of the entire British-born population--considerable racial antipathy and violence accompanied the flow there and resulted in passage of the exclusionary Commonwealth Immigrants Act of 1963 (G. Freeman 1982:30; Lowenthal 1972:223-225).

TABLE 3.2 REMITTANCES THROUGH THE POST OFFICE
AND SPECIAL FARM WORKERS SCHEME, 1955-1982

	Money Orders								
Year	West Indies	U.K.	U.S.	Can-ada	Other	Total M.O.	Postal Orders	Spec'l Scheme	Total
1955	54[a]	5	94	14	13	180	48	40	268
1956	63	37	87	16	14	217	171	26	414
1957	58	33	77	19	13	200	293	23	516
1958	57	37	71	25	9	199	394	28	621
1959	63	39	82	29	4	217	424	34	675
1960	63	60	85	28	3	239	797	NK[b]	1,036
1961	53	78	88	35	2	256	1,368	NK	1,624
1962	47	86	85	29	1	248	1,187	NK	1,435
1963	46	62	64	33	--	205	1,145	45	1,395
1964	42	66	69	33	--	210	1,263	43	1,516
1965	34	81	61	34	--	210	1,241	49	1,500
1966	35	71	63	41	--	210	1,197	37	1,444
1967	36	53	68	53	--	210	1,122	34	1,366
1968	38	56	71	61	--	226	1,118	63	1,407
1969	41	65	140	57	--	303	1,141	141	1,585
1970	47	59	131	59	--	296	1,119	203	1,618
1971	43	67	102	34	--	246	1,058	226	1,530
1972	48	69	94	37	--	248	1,259	116	1,623
1973	42	98	108	43	--	291	1,824	188	2,303
1974	39	26	49	51	--	165	2,140	281	2,586
1975	42	7	26	69	--	144	2,497	820	3,461
1976	36	3	19	103	--	161	2,523	569	3,253
1977	41	3	36	101	--	181	2,698	NK	NK
1978	NK	6	39	94	--	NK	2,918	NK	NK
1979	54	10	45	119	--	228	2,639	532	3,399
1980	62	1	64	93	--	220	2,312	1,070	3,602
1981	89	1	77	97	--	264	1,859	465	2,588
1982	82	--	72	82	--	236	1,397	117	1,750

Source: Reubens n.d.; St. Vincent 1963b, 1970, 1984
[a]($000)   [b]NK : not known

These various migration streams have removed thousands of lower-class Vincentians. Between 1921 and 1931, the annual net migration loss was 581 persons; between 1931 and 1946 it was 390; between 1946 and 1960 it was 740; and between 1960 and 1970 it was 1,256 (Byrne 1969:166; Davison 1962; HMSO 1967; Reubens n.d.; St. Vincent 1963c, 1969, 1971). The net migration loss during the 1960-1970 period alone was 14,250 people, an amount equivalent to 58 percent of the natural increase during the decade; without migration, the 1970 population of St. Vincent would have been 14 percent higher than it really was.

Most of these migrations occurred in a sequential or overlapping fashion, not so much because of local conditions--which generally have always been poor--or because of the inherent migratory disposition of individuals--Vincentians have always left in massive numbers whenever the opportunity to do so has presented itself--but in response to economic needs in the receiving country (see Marshall 1982; Thomas-Hope 1978). In turn, each stream was dammed up by restrictive legislation in the host country prompted by economic recession, automation, agitation by domestic laborers, and racial xenophobia.

But even if they are reacting to external forces over which they have no control, the social and economic effects of these movements on the lives of individual migrants and their families has been profound. Savings and remittances have enhanced both econo-mic well-being and style of living. Funds have been invested in new housing, consumer goods, agricultural land, small businesses, and the education of family members. Repatriated earnings have financed the migration of close kin, creating chains of sponsorship and fostering life-chance improvements.

At the community and national levels, however, migration has been a mixed blessing at most. The removal of 'surplus' people may have provided some relief to the unemployment problem and reduced the pressure on the provision of social resources and public services. The millions of dollars remitted over the years also has helped reduce the country's balance of payments deficits. Indeed, the data in Table 3.2 grossly underestimates the amount of capital sent to the island as a result of migration. Just as the compulsory savings of seasonal Florida cane cutters represents only four percent of the value of money and goods remitted by the workers (McCoy and Wood 1982), so also the total of money and postal orders forms a small part of the funds and items which are annually sent to Vincentians by relatives living overseas. Not included in the table are money orders cashed in the commercial banks--and these probably exceed those exchanged in the post offices by several times--cash sent by registered mail, goods shipped home by migrants, and cash and goods brought back by returned migrants and temporary visitors (cf. Richardson 1983:6). Although no figures are available, the total of these probably exceeds the remittances listed in Table 3.2 by a ratio of at least 10:1.

The gain in monetary resources must be balanced against the loss in human resources. A study of the types of migrants that have left and the disposition of the money they have sent back home soon indicates that emigration is far from a panacea for the nation's economic problems. Never a random phenomenon, migration has tended to remove many of the island's most ambitious, industrious, and intelligent adults at the prime of their working careers. Indeed, it has been said of Vincentian migration that:

> Apart from the dedicated few, those who remain are either those with vested interests, or dependents, or the apathetic (University of the West Indies Development Mission 1969:106).

The exodus of the younger, healthier, better trained, and more enterprising workers is not simply a matter of self-selection. Employers of Vincentian sugar cane cutters in Florida, for example, are permitted by their collective agreement to pre-select 60 percent of the labor force from individuals ". . . who have demonstrated their reliability and productivity during previous seasons" (McCoy and Wood 1982:8-9). The remaining workers are chosen ". . . on the basis of their physical appearance, work history, and attitude" (McCoy and Wood 1982:11).

There is also an ideological price to be paid for mass migration. A "migration-oriented society" (Philpott 1968: 466) such as St. Vincent may also develop a 'migration mentality':

> Perhaps the greatest danger posed by the present migratory trend is that it may eventually become institutionalized, if this has not already happened. In such a situation of institutionalized migration people come to see migration as the only means of achieving anything. The young grow up to think that this is the only way to make anything of themselves. When a society reaches this stage it is pretty well lost. No amount of planning and ingenuity can save it then. For it will have lost the heart and faith of its people--a faith which is the essence of societal

survival (University of the West Indies Development Mission 1969:106).

Migration from St. Vincent has also brought with it a denigration of local society and culture.

As in most (ex-)colonial societies, a negative valance attaches to local products; whether these are ideas, material items, or in this case, human resources. Imported ideas are considered superior, especially education and training. Thus, even the temporary sojourner who returns to St. Vincent with a skill or craft is credited with a legitimacy and competence that someone locally (with the same or superior expertise) would not enjoy, solely because it was learned abroad. This behavior only fuels the idea that merit or progress is irrational and not controllable (Brana-Shute and Brana-Shute 1980:78).

As elsewhere in the Caribbean (see Rubenstein 1982a, 1983) the bulk of monies remitted by migrants are neither placed in savings nor invested in productive ventures, but simply used to secure the basic necessities of life. Funds used to buy imported foodstuffs, clothing, household furnishings, and other consumer items or to finance chain migration result in reverse cash flows (canceling out much of the foreign exchange benefit of remittances in the process), strengthen external economic dependence, undermine the demand for indigenous products, and enhance local social and economic disparities.

Mixed blessing or not, migration has been the main means by which many families have been able to maintain or improve their level of living. Removal from the island indeed has become an institutionalized feature of lower-class life and it is the ambition of the overwhelming number of young people to leave St. Vincent, either temporarily or permanently (Brana-Shute and Brana-Shute 1980:72). Realization of this ambition is becoming increasingly difficult. Migration to such customary Caribbean destinations as Barbados and Trinidad is ever more difficult as regional governments, faced with economic problems of their own, make entry more difficult. The probability of renewed large-scale migration to England, the United States, or Canada, the destinations currently favored by would-be migrants, is not high as each of these countries continues to pass more exclusionary immigration laws. Indeed, the heyday of Vincentian emigration has been over for several years now and a counterflow of people is the order of the day; between 1971 and 1978, nearly 10,000 more people entered than left the country (St. Vincent 1976, 1979). Migration has proven to be just as illusive a resource as any other.

Chapter 4
Leeward Village: Past and Present

INTRODUCTION

The lives of Leeward Villagers have been inexorably affected by the adversities faced by all lower-class islanders. National economic underdevelopment, rural-urban disparities, a color/class system of stratification, and local-level ecological and other conditions have made the community one of the poorest on the island. Unemployment and underemployment are both high and there are many signs of material poverty and neglect. Dozens of houses are in a dilapidated condition, the school is badly equipped, and the nurse's dispensary dispenses precious little for lack of supply. Indeed, only the combined Police Station/Courthouse delivers the social services associated with it. But these conditions have not destroyed the will to cope with hardship, the desire to make the most of limited human and non-human resources.

Such resistance to adversity, as Mintz (1974:131-132) has noted, can take a multitude of forms:

> We need now to expand out view of such resistance by considering the most important structural alignments by which Caribbean peoples could establish their own perspectives, their own styles of life, vis-à-vis the outside world.

One such type of "structural alignment" is the rural community itself, the residential aggregate where 80 percent of the Vincentian population still lives. As a reaction to European capitalism and its concomitants--colonialism, slavery, the plantocracy, and overseas social and cultural hegemony--the rural community may be considered a "mode of resistance," a creative attempt to form a new way of life (Mintz 1974:131-145). If this suggestion is valid, it is surprising that so little attention has been paid to the origin, development, and organization of rural settlements in Caribbean studies. 'Non-community' themes have dominated rural research and the local group has often been dismissed as a unit of little ontological importance (cf. Wilson 1969:80). Anthropological studies of the Caribbean countryside have been characterized by two main research interests: (1) general ethnographic accounts (e.g., Herskovits 1937; Herskovits and Herskovits 1947; Hill 1977; Horowitz 1967a; M.G. Smith 1962b); and (2) descriptions and analyses of particular institutions such as kinship organization or social differentiation (e.g., Betley 1976; Clarke 1966; Greenfield 1966; Henriques 1953; Otterbein 1966; Rodman 1971; Slater 1977; R.T. Smith 1956; Wilson 1973). This has meant that most rural studies have been concerned with the community ". . . as a field or sample" rather than ". . . as an object or thing" (Arensberg and Kimball 1968:694). In short, they are studies *in* villages and only incidentally studies *of* villages.

Even when the community *qua* community has been examined, the attention paid to it has been incidental to other topics such as kinship and marriage, social stratification, economic organization, and religion and folklore. Territorial bonds and social forms are pushed to the background and the local spatial distribution of people--the territorial referent of social organization--is viewed as contingent on the more central issues under discussion. In short, the local spatial unit is not given a separate 'sociological reality.'

There are several reasons for this relative neglect of the local group in Caribbean studies. Caribbean communities do not 'stand out' from the surrounding landscape like their equivalents in other parts of the world. There are no public squares or central market places, and no communal lands, except that held by the church or central government. Many 'villages' are not even compact settlements with identifiable boundaries but dispersed homesteads and hamlets which overlap one another (M.G. Smith 1956).

Unlike many of their European counterparts, some of which can be traced back hundreds of years, Caribbean communities lack deep historical roots or a romantic past based on a rich body of oral and written tradition. This is because ". . . the peasantry everywhere in the Antilles is a relatively recent social product, a population reconstituted into a new economic form during the decline and fall of the slave-based plantation system" (Mintz 1974:157).

A shared religious system based on a single church affiliation, as is found in many Latin American and European communities, which functions to integrate and govern belief and behavior, is also uncommon in the Caribbean. Likewise, a blurring of boundaries and a concomitant 'openness' is the result of the ease in gaining membership by outsiders. Similarly, as Mintz (1971:38) has noted:

> Many research workers in Caribbean societies have been struck by the relative absence of community-based activity in daily life; such institutional centers as the church, the school, the social club, and the political party office are likely to be entirely absent or at least very unimportant in rural community life.

All these consideration suggest that Caribbean communities are not autonomous, corporate units: that they have no collective goals or a specialized set of functions apart from coresidence itself and that they consist of people who are generally linked by ties which are not rooted in institutional or group affiliation. Since so much research in Caribbean communities has employed a synchronic structural-functional paradigm in which identifiable, bounded groups and part-whole relations have been stressed (viz. Braithwaite 1975; Greenfield 1966; Henriques 1953; Otterbein 1966; Philpott 1973; R.T. Smith 1956), the result has been that so-called "loosely structured" social formations have ". . . at best been reported incidentally and at worst quite ignored" (Wilson 1973:3; see also Abrahams 1983; Barrow 1976; Dirks 1972; Mintz 1971:38-42). For example, in his introduction to a study of family organization in three Guyanese villages, R.T. Smith (1956:4) has argued that:

> This books deals primarily with certain aspects of the social structure of three village communities in the coastal area of British Guiana, but in attempting to arrive at an adequate understanding of these relatively small sections of the population we are obliged to consider features of the total society of British Guiana, so interdependent and functionally related are the local communities and the total society of which they are a part (see also Steward 1956:5; Manners 1960:81).

The neglect of the Caribbean community *qua* community can also be attributed to the way it has been defined. Several Caribbeanists have employed Murdock's (1965:79) definition of the community as ". . . the maximal group of persons who normally reside in face-to-face association" (e.g., Otterbein 1966:18; Philpott 1973:74; M.G. Smith 1956:295; Steward 1956:8). For Murdock (1965:79-84) the community is an intimate social group characterized by mutual aid and sharing, group solidarity and loyalty, concerted action, conformity to group norms, antagonism towards outsiders, and possession of a common culture. With reality presenting a different picture, it is not surprising that the community has been treated in such a cavalier fashion in Caribbean ethnology. The most common assertions have been that in the region there is ". . . a weak sense of community cohesion, and local communities are but loosely organized" (Wagley 1960:8) and ". . . only minor or fragmentary community-wide organization, with few institutional devises or traditions to express group sentiment or community will" (Mintz 1968:317). The following kinds of statements about the nature of local organization in particular Caribbean communities are commonly found in the literature:

Enterprise Hall [a small village in Barbados] . . . is not a complete community in the sociological sense. . . . [T]he inhabitants of Enterprise Hall do not form an integrated sociological community . . . (Greenfield 1966:80-81).

Socially, Rocky Roads [a peasant village in Jamaica] almost defies designation as a community, for the connotations of reciprocity, cohesiveness, and "togetherness" implicit in the word "community" are absent in the geographical area known as Rocky Roads (Cohen 1954:131).

These small [Belize] villages tend to be no more than clusters of households bound together by very weak threads of contiguity and kinship ties. Aside from lip-service for the community of origin, most of the features and values that typically characterize a structured community solidarity are absent (Ashcraft 1968:64).

[T]he residential community [in Providencia] is rarely an active structured entity or even a sentimental one. Only political considerations originating from outside ever treat communities as social entities--when baseball teams were organized or when schools taking the name of the community compete in drills on Independence Day (Wilson 1973:145).

But the absence of community spirit or a full-blown community life as integrative forces does not necessarily mean that integration as such is lacking; nor does it mean that cohesiveness cannot be provided except by structured groupings such as the church, the school or the social club. Indeed, as Wilson (1969:80) points out:

> [T]hroughout the Caribbean, the church, the school and the political party are institutions *external* to the village and not therefore organically part of the social system of the village. Frequently their personnel are alien, and certainly their rules are [cf. M.G. Smith 1956:303].

The implicit assumption in the negative characterizations of the Caribbean community is that people are living in a particular locale only because they happen to have been born there. Ignored are those social forces and cultural principles which *are* "organically part of the social system of the village" and function to bind its members together. The criteria for community membership, the factors involved in the formation, maintenance, and transformation of the community, the quality of community life, the nature of informal social relationships--friendship, neigborhoodship, kindred ties, etc.--linking people, and the meaning and effect of collective living on the lives of members receive little if any attention.

Defining the Community

Like all too many social science concepts--social structure, culture, peasant, tribe, class, etc.--"community" has proven to be an illusive concept. Hundreds of definitions have been offered over the years, some stressing territoriality, others social interaction or the localized intersection of social institutions, and still others the notion of "communis"--a community of feeling or sense of belonging to a group--regardless of whether propinquity is also involved. In an often cited sociological analysis of a sample of 94 definitions of the term, Hillery (1955:111) found that no less than 16 different concepts were employed ". . . and at least two authors could always be found who have presented conflicting definitions." Most usages, however, agreed that a community exhibits three elements--social interaction, area, and common ties--and these may be employed to define the community as a unit which ". . . consists of persons in social interaction within a geographical area and having one or more additional ties" (Hillery 1955:111). Although too general for comparative purposes this usage nonetheless permits the study of the nature of community organization without any preconceptions about the nature of local corporate groups, the role played by external societal institutions, or the level of *esprit de corps*.

Caribbean communities are structured and integrated by some of the same forces and patterns that interrelate people in all small local groups: temporal continuity; territorial association; social interaction; culture sharing and transmission; common interests; collective notions about honor, shame, reputation, and respectability; and a sentimental attachment to 'home.' An accurate portrayal of community organization and the manner in which it affects the life-chances of its members requires an analysis of each of these features.

HISTORICAL BACKGROUND

To those not used to West Indian country roads, the half-hour trip from Kingstown to Leeward Village can be an unsettling experience. The only land access to the village is via the Leeward Public Highway (see Map 4.1), a narrow, twisting route whose deep ruts and blind corners are a test of driver skill and passenger nerve. After yet another climb up a steep hill followed by a hairpin turn around an unbanked cliffside niche Leeward Village suddenly appears spread out in all directions along the foot and lower slopes of the Leeward Valley. Leeward Village is a compact settlement which contained 2,245 people in the spring of 1970. From the number of additional dwellings that were present by the summer of 1986 the population has increased to at least 2,500. Most houses are closely spaced along the main street and secondary roads, paths, and tracks leading off from it. The village occupies an area of about 140 acres and is hemmed in by the sea, by the narrow, rock-strewn Leeward River, by the agricultural holdings of villagers and the remains of the Leeward Valley Estate, and by perpendicular valley sides. The valley itself extends back slightly over three miles from Leeward Bay, one of a host of inlets that indent the Caribbean coast of the island, and is less than 1,000 yards at its widest point. Together with the factors that affected the settlement of the island as a whole these local geographical features--leeward coast, valley, bayside, river--account for the origin of the village and make it a viable ecological entity.

The leeward coast of St. Vincent was the part of the island first occupied by both the French and the British, and Leeward Village may

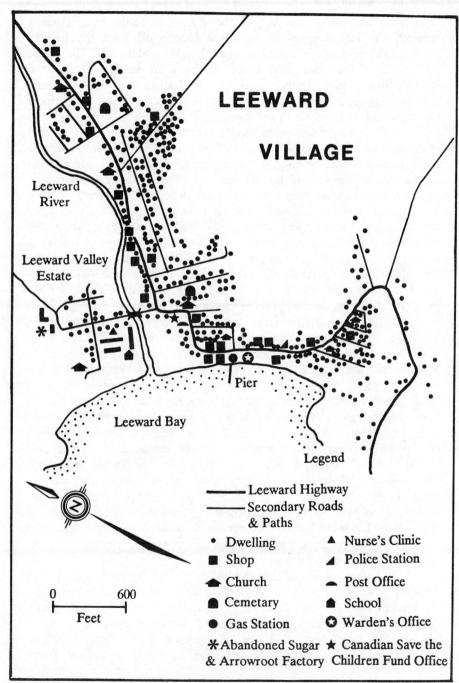

LEEWARD

VILLAGE

Leeward
River

Leeward Valley
Estate

Pier

Leeward Bay

Legend

———— Leeward Highway
———— Secondary Roads
        & Paths

•   Dwelling   ▲ Nurse's Clinic
■   Shop   ◢ Police Station
⬗   Church   ◖ Post Office
⬟   Cemetary   ⬠ School
●   Gas Station   ✪ Warden's Office

✶ Abandoned Sugar   ★ Canadian Save the
& Arrowroot Factory Children Fund Office

0   600
Feet

FIGURE 4.1   SKETCH-MAP OF LEEWARD VILLAGE
                SETTLEMENT PATTERN, 1970

have been among the earliest of the European settlements. Formed between the lateral spurs of hills that branch off from the island's north-south mountain range, the coastal valleys along the Caribbean side of the island contained some of the most fertile soils on the island. Steep side walls restricted cultivation to valley floors, however, while a wet and rugged interior circumscribed the inland extension of large-scale plantation agriculture. The difficulty and expense of cutting roads over ridges, around deep ravines, and into steep seaside cliffs meant that all shipping and most passenger traffic was by boat, giving additional incentive for the settlement of coastal areas first. Travel by sea also required sheltered harbors and an extensive bayside area for the construction of elaborate loading and storage facilities. A swift flowing stream to provide fresh water for drinking, bathing, and cooking as well as power to drive the sugar-cane processing machinery in the factory located on each estate was needed as well. Leeward Village met each of these conditions and a perusal of early French maps in the island indicated that Leeward Village was settled soon after the French arrived in 1719. In sum, agricultural production, particularly estate cultivation for distant markets, must have made the Leeward Valley an attractive site for entrepreneurial exploitation. But this factor alone does not account for the generation of a concentrated residential enclave of over 2,000 people by the mid-20th century from a dispersed valley population of only a few hundred people living in small centers and scattered hamlets less than a 100 years earlier. Such contemporary village features as population composition and size, settlement pattern and neighborhood divisions, the organization of occupations, migration patterns, and land tenure and use are also the product of historical events and processes that unfolded in both the valley itself and the larger island-society. Since the various mechanisms for coping with poverty found among villagers are responses to these events and processes, ecological analysis requires that their historical roots be examined. Indeed, specific historical events may be as important as particular ecological circumstances in shaping present-day social organization.

Like other areas of community organization, rural social and economic history has been neglected in Caribbean ethnology (see Rubenstein 1977). The slighting of historical antecedents is partly the result of the paucity of documented historical material on rural life and the unreliability and lack of temporal depth of the recollections of aged informants. As a consequence, rarely is account taken of local community history, particularly of events before Emancipation, for an understanding of present-day community life. Instead, the broad outlines of certain features of regional chronicle are mentioned either in passing (e.g., Greenfield 1966; Horowitz 1967a) or, as in Raymond Smith's (1956:8) influential study of family life in three Guyanese villages, merely ". . . as a descriptive background to what has been recorded during the period of field-work" (cf. Wilson 1973:28-43).

Other Caribbeanists have taken a different position, arguing that rural historical reconstruction is not only possible but necessary for an understanding of the present (Berleant-Schiller 1981; Manners 1960:82-83; Mintz 1974). For example, Manners (1960:82) asserts that:

> [E]very community study projected for the area . . . must employ research methods which take cognizance of the centuries of struggle among Western powers for political and economic dominance of almost every island, with a few exceptions. This, of course, involves the examination and analysis of written records, of documents, and of archival and library materials--in short, of a host of sources which are ordinarily meagre or non-existent for the student of isolated primitive tribes . . . . Moreover, every community study in the area, whether diachronic or synchronic, whether problem-centred or presumptively microscopic, will in some measure have to take notice of the past effects and cultural end-results of the vagaries of sugar production, or coffee, or cocao, or cotton, or indigo; of the production and sale of rum; of the shifting periods of mercantilist and modern capitalist forms of exploitation; . . . For all of these, and many more events and elements in the Caribbean tradition since the earliest period of contact, have had their impact upon present culture in greater or lesser degree.

As the Leeward Village material will show, local circumstances and events are equally important in what Mintz (1974:179) has aptly termed ". . . the teasing out of the history of particular Caribbean peasantries . . . ." Moreover, the efforts of valley residents themselves to improve their life chances and raise their social position have been instrumental in transforming Leeward Village from a series of small, scattered villages and hamlets during the mid-19th century to a compact village of 2,500 people by the last decades of the 20th.

The Estate System

French cultivators from Martinique first settled on the leeward coast of St. Vincent where they grew tobacco, cocoa, coffee, and other food crops and spices on farms averaging well under 100 acres purchased from the native Caribs (Coke 1808:181; Shephard 1831:liv-lxvii, 25). Even by 1776, 13 years into the British occupation, the mean size of the 29 separate holdings in the Leeward Valley and immediately adjacent areas was 42 acres (Shephard 1831:lix-lxvi).

After British settlers began occupying the valley in 1763 many of the French farmers left the island and most of the holdings of those who remained were sold in auction to English farmers. The French who chose to stay behind were obliged to either repurchase their holdings or rent land from the British colonists or the Crown (Shephard 1831:27-28, lxiv-lxvi). The 29 holdings into which the valley was divided by 1776 totaled 1,209 acres and were held by seven owners, nineteen renters, and an unknown number of "poor settlers" (Shephard 1831:lix-lxvi).

The period between British occupation of the valley and Emancipation in 1838 was marked by the consolidation of most of the small holdings into a few large ones, the continuing exodus of the French, the conversion from mixed farming to monocrop sugar cultivation, and the beginning of financial troubles for many of the estates.

The growing importance of sugar-cane cultivation was the driving force behind the amalgamation of farms. Each estate processed its own sugar products and the valley shows the remains of eight separate sugar-mill sites. By 1829 the consolidation of smaller holdings was complete. The valley now contained only five holdings, one of which was a comparatively inconsequential farm of 34 acres. The other four totaled 1,174 acres for a average of nearly 300 acres per estate (Shephard 1831:lix-lxvi).

Yet even during this period of major island sugar production at least two of the valley estates were already in serious financial trouble. The 740-acre Leeward Valley Estate, which is still the largest plantation in the valley, is a good illustration of the process of plantation indebtedness. Produced through the amalgamation of 20 contiguous holdings, the estate was acquired by Peter Pembroke in 1769-70. By 1780, its 224 acres, buildings, equipment, and slaves were valued at $105,600. The estate was willed to Pembroke's two eldest sons, the younger of whom, John, purchased his brother's interest in it in 1787. John Pembroke did not live in St. Vincent and, like many estates owned by absentee proprietors, Leeward

Valley Estate gradually began accumulating debts during the last part of the 18th and early part of 19th centuries. By 1813, $110,000 was owed to a London merchant company and Pembroke was obliged to mortgage the estate, its slaves, and all its sugar output to the company as security for payment of the debt. Most of the loan still remained outstanding when the first company sold the mortgage to another merchant house in 1813 for $96,000, the amount still owed to them by the estate. At Pembroke's death in 1819 the plantation was inherited by his eldest son, David.

Estate indebtedness did not directly affect sugar cultivation. Its production continued during the post-Emancipation period when it was joined by the cultivation of arrowroot, as indicated by the remains of several old arrowroot factories scattered throughout the valley. Smaller holdings also began to make their reappearance during the post-slavery era. But although the number of holdings more than doubled from five to twelve between 1829 and 1899, the four largest holdings totaled nearly 1,200 acres, or more than 90 percent of valley acreage (St. Vincent 1899).

Plantation agriculture during the post-Emancipation era continued to be marked by absenteeism and indebtedness. By 1847, the monies owed by Leeward Valley Estate had still not been repaid and the plantation was sold in auction in 1849 to yet another London merchant house for $43,000. The estate was again sold in 1885 by an heir of the firm to a local Vincentian planter, Albert Jones, the first island resident to own it in more than a century. Despite its debts, the estate had steadily increased in size since 1829 as a result of the ongoing purchase of small adjacent holdings and Crown lands and totaled 850 acres when acquired by Jones. Nonetheless, the growing unprofitability of estate cultivation is evident in the low price of $13,440 paid for such a large holding.

Another of the major estates in the valley suffered a similar history. Heavily in debt by the early 1800s, it was sold in auction three times between 1825 and 1863.

By the terms of the Albert Jones's will, Leeward Valley Estate was auctioned off to two Vincentian planters for $12,240 in 1901. It was promptly resold to the Crown the next year for nearly $13,000 to provide agricultural land and house-spots for some of the refugees who had been dispossessed by the eruption of the Soufrière volcano two months earlier. A block of 450 acres at the remote upper end of the estate was set aside for the refugees and established valley residents interested in purchasing land of their own. The remaining 400 acres--prime agricultural land located on the gently sloping seaward part of the estate--were sold for $7,680 to

William Murdock, a island planter whose father's estate had been destroyed by the eruption.

The Soufrière land grants and other peasant acquisitions have resulted in a dramatic increase in the number of valley agricultural holdings during this century. By 1971 these parcels totaled 289, a 24-fold increase since 1899. Estate cultivation, nevertheless, continued to be important, especially during the first few decades of the century, and even today the four largest properties account for nearly 40 percent of all valley acreage.

Crops grown on valley estates during the early years of the 20th century were nearly the same as those grown during the latter part of the 19th. On Leeward Valley Estate, still the largest property in the valley, despite its reduction to 400 acres, sugar cane continued to be the most important export crop, followed by arrowroot and cotton, the latter introduced in 1902. By 1930, arrowroot and cotton had changed places as revenue earners. Sugar cane was still predominant in both acreage and earnings until 1943 when its cultivation on Leeward Valley Estate was halted. Cotton and arrowroot were the chief estate crops from then until they were surpassed by bananas in the mid-1950s. Introduced in 1954, the export hegemony of bananas was the shortest of any estate crop. Its cultivation ended in the mid-1960s after the destruction of the entire planting by high winds. The abandonment of arrowroot soon followed and the entire estate was planted in coconuts in 1969. The trees began bearing in the mid-1970s and today represent the only source of estate crop revenue.

Leeward Valley Estate has been reduced in size throughout the present century and now has an area of less than 250 acres. Murdock began selling plots of land in the 1930s and between 1942 and 1945 alone, 21 parcels ranging in size from less than two acres to over ten acres were sold to villagers. By the late 1930s the estate began to meet financial and other problems from which it has never recovered. Low market prices for its produce, difficulties in securing cheap labor during periods of high extra-valley emigration, and poor management after Murdock's death in the late 1940s have been instrumental in the continuous sale of estate lands. Indeed, none of the four joint family owners live in the valley, although two are island residents, and only the choicest parts of the estate have not been put up for sale.

The Origin of a Reconstituted Peasantry

Leeward Villagers are a good example of what Mintz (1974:146-156) has called "reconstituted peasantries." Of the four types of such peasants he identifies, two have been present in the Leeward Valley: "early yeomen" and "proto-peasants." The first is represented by the French colonists from Martinique who settled the valley in 1719 cultivating their crops of cacao, coffee, and other food items and spices on small plots obtained from the Caribs. By 1776 at least 25 of these smallholders were still in the valley, although only 30 percent of them were able to repurchase their lands from the British, the remainder renting their plots from the Crown. The average size of holdings was 40 acres and only one exceeded 100 acres (Shephard 1831:lix-lxvii).

The French yeoman cultivators were displaced by the consolidation of valley holdings with the rapid conversion to monocrop sugarcane cultivation. But a new category of peasants was concomitantly being established on the estates themselves. Obliged to produce most of their own food, permitted to exchange agricultural surpluses in specially established Sunday markets, estate bondsmen represent a "proto-peasantry," ". . . slaves who later became peasant freedmen" (Mintz 1974:152). During the four-year apprenticeship period which preceded full Emancipation in 1838 the slaves retained both their home gardens and provision plots and continued to grow crops and rear domesticated animals for subsistence use and market sale (Colthurst 1977:170-171). Although data is unavailable, it may be assumed that the island practice of providing a house and provision garden of an acre and a quarter to the ex-slaves who continued to work on the estates as salaried laborers was followed in Leeward Valley (Mathieson 1967:83-85).

Between 1838 and 1900 a few small-scale cultivators became freeholders. In 1899, two-thirds of valley farms were in parcels of less than 100 acres: one holding was 4.5 acres, one was 5 acres, another was 13 acres, three were 20 acres, one was 25 acres, and one was 40 acres (St. Vincent 1899). But these eight pieces of land totaled less than 150 acres, or 8.2 percent of valley acreage. Moreover, four of these holdings, the forty-acre and the three twenty-acre farms, had only been acquired in 1896 when their Mulatto owner, Elsie Hopewell, bequeathed her 100-acre estate to a nephew, a Colored god-daughter, a bookkeeper, and a fourth individual. It is unlikely that any of these people were peasant cultivators.

It was only during this century that a full-blown, land-owning peasantry came into being. The 1902 volcanic eruption resulted in the resettlement of several hundred people in Leeward Village. Each family was granted a piece of provision land ranging in size from one-half to slightly over three acres depending on household size and whether any land had been owned in the devastated area. In addition, many refugees and established villagers bought additional holdings after the first distribution had been completed. In all, 145 holdings were portioned out between 1902 and 1907.

Later peasant land acquisitions have depended on individual initiative and declining valley estate prospects. Some of these involved the buying of plots from Leeward Valley and adjacent estates; others were the result of the sub-division of granted lands. By 1937, for example, there were 201 registered pieces of land in the valley, an increase of over 20 percent since 1907. Villagers were also successful in purchasing 26 pieces of land averaging five acres each from an estate in a neighboring valley during the mid-1940s. Land acquisitions are still taking place today although they have not resulted in a significant increase in the total peasant land base. The high price of holdings has tended to restrict purchases to tiny housebuilding lots close to the village.

Except for house-spots within the village or close to its boundaries, the bulk off peasant acquisitions have been towards the head of the valley--*the mountain* in local usage--and on top the long, flat ridge overlooking its southern portion. The grants and purchases between 1902 and 1907 were in the most remote parts of the valley far from access roads and sources of water. Many of these parcels are steeply graded, poorly drained, or stony and represent portions of the Leeward Valley Estate which were always agriculturally marginal or were never cultivated except, perhaps, as provision grounds for estate workers during and after slavery. Yet as small and unproductive as many of these holdings are, they have been of vital importance to many of those who have owned them. They have helped meet day-to-day subsistence needs and their surpluses have provided the means for the purchase of household necessities.

Except for sugar cane which requires an extensive land base, village farmers have grown many of the same cash crops as the estates. Cotton and arrowroot were still being cultivated by valley peasants long after they were discontinued on Leeward Valley Estate. Starchy tubers--sweet potatoes, yams, tannias, dasheens, eddoes, and manioc--have always been grown for both home con-sumption and market sale by smallholders, regardless of external market conditions.

Today the agricultural stagnation characteristic of the large valley estates also marks a large number of peasant holdings, and many of them are either idle or underused.

The Growth and Consolidation of Leeward Village

Leeward Village has not always been a large compactly settled community. Its 14 named neighborhoods (Map 4.2) are a product of various valley population movements and demographic perturbations. These changes are attributable to fluctuations in estate cultivation, the transformation of estate lands into peasant holdings, perceptions by dispersed valley residents of the benefits of village residence, and opportunities for extra-valley wage-labor migration. In turn, estate and peasant production as well as movement into and out of the valley have been affected by island-wide socio-economic conditions and overseas agricultural and wage-labor markets.

During the slavery era each valley estate contained its own body of resident slaves who were housed in small two-roomed wattle-and-daub dwellings "resembling a village of huts" (Carmichael 1833:124). Furnishings were not provided by the estate and even the initial construction of a house was the responsibility of the slave occupants themselves. Table 4.1 traces the changes in the growth and concentration of the main valley population centers between 1780 and 1970. The large Leeward Valley Estate contained two communities during the post-Emancipation period, Belair and Leeward Village, and these may have originated during the slavery period. On the other hand, one of the other four large valley estates, a 200-acre plantation at the extreme head of the valley, is not listed as having a distinct community associated with it on any of the island censuses. In addition, four other population enclaves not listed in the table or lumped with one or another of the centers for census purposes also existed during the early years of this century.

Changes in the distribution of the valley population between 1780 and 1970 are a product of the removal of dispersed valley residents to Leeward Village. The several estate communities scattered throughout the valley during the 18th and 19th centuries were represented in 1970 by only 19 households situated outside the village boundaries. Since 1834 at least eight distinct valley communities disappeared as their residents abruptly or gradually moved into Leeward Village. In most cases, migration to the village was a product of a combination of decreased estate employment and a desire to share in the social and economic benefits of residence in

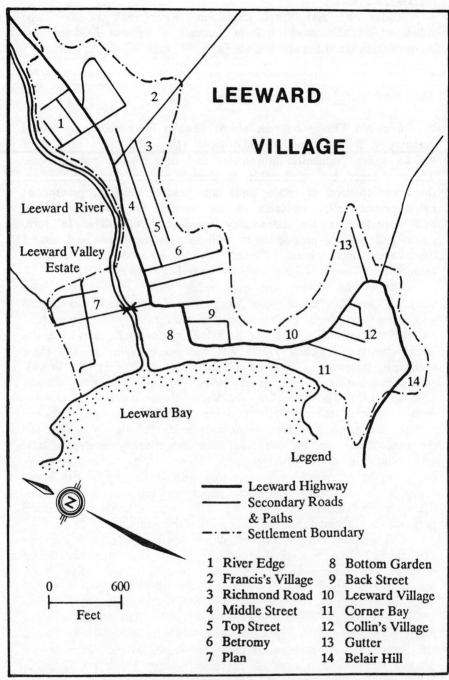

LEEWARD

VILLAGE

Leeward River

Leeward Valley
Estate

Leeward Bay

Legend

━━━━ Leeward Highway
───── Secondary Roads
          & Paths
─ ∙ ─ ∙ ─ Settlement Boundary

1 River Edge   8 Bottom Garden
2 Francis's Village   9 Back Street
3 Richmond Road   10 Leeward Village
4 Middle Street   11 Corner Bay
5 Top Street   12 Collin's Village
6 Betromy   13 Gutter
7 Plan   14 Belair Hill

0   600
    Feet

FIGURE 4.2   SKETCH-MAP OF LEEWARD VILLAGE
               NEIGHBORHOODS, 1970

or near the village center. Leeward Village's present size, settlement pattern, and division into neighborhoods are a product of the various movements among the valley population.

TABLE 4.1 POPULATION OF LEEWARD VALLEY, 1780-1970

Year	Leeward Village	Collin's Village	Belair Hill	Leeward Valley Estate	Palm Park Estate	Total
1780	NA	--	25	150	75	250
1827	NA	--	40	275	135	450
1871	166	308	26	233	20	753
1881	203	279	75	142	41	740
1891	490[a]	--[a]	63	150	25	734
1911	441	NA	NA	NA	NA	NA
1921	332	NA	NA	NA	NA	NA
1931	342	NA	NA	NA	NA	NA
1940	964	195	172	330	70	1,731
1960	1,149	345[b]	--[b]	150	--	2,207
1970[c]	1,151	329[b]	--[b]	755	--	2,235

Source: Eastern Caribbean Population Census 1963; Gibbs 1947; St. Vincent 1871, 1881, 1891, 1912, 1970; Shephard 1831; West Indian Census 1946 1950.
[a]Collin's Village is included in the Leeward Village population.
[b]Belair Hill is included in the Leeward Village population.
[c]Refers to the Eastern Population Census conducted that year rather than to my census data.
NA: not available

Map 4.3 illustrates the growth of Leeward Village between 1763 and 1970. The exact origin of the village is unknown although early French maps perused in the island show a small settlement located along Leeward Bay beginning just south of Leeward Village during the latter part of the French occupation.

Changes in the size and shape of the village between 1763 and 1902 seem to have involved mainly natural increase to the village population and the formation of a settlement at Collin's Village (Table 4.1 and Maps 4.2 and 4.3) at the southern part of the village, the latter resulting from the expansion of the Leeward Village population and the in-migration of residents from at least two different valley estates.

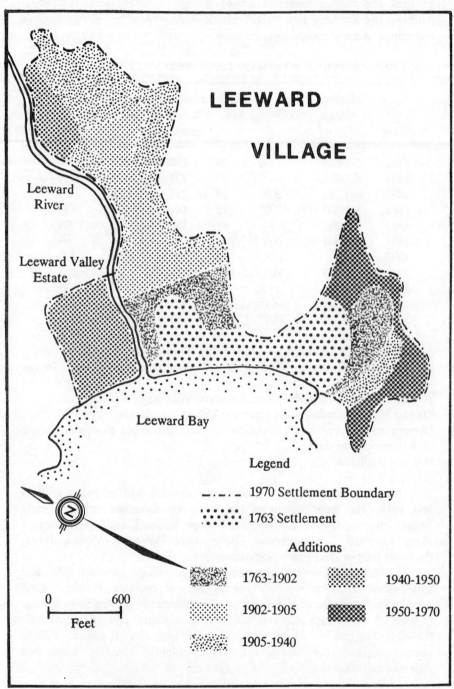

FIGURE 4.3   SKETCH-MAP OF THE GROWTH OF LEEWARD
VILLAGE, 1763-1970

The most dramatic change in village population and settlement pattern occurred between 1902 and 1906 when the new neighborhoods of Richmond Road and Betromy were created in the northeastern part of the village adjacent to the Leeward Public Highway (Map 4.2) to house some 500 islanders left homeless by the 1902 volcanic eruption. In all, 103 houses and house-spots were distributed along with the *mountain land* already mentioned.

Changes between 1905 and 1940 while smaller in scope also altered the shape and makeup of the village. Part of the population of a plantation adjoining Leeward Valley Estate moved to Collin's Village, Palm Park Estate residents slowly began migrating to various part of the village, and house spots in the new neighborhood of Francis's Village east and north of the area reserved for the eruption refugees were rented from the Leeward Valley Estate. The estate also began to sell house spots to villagers starting in the early 1920s when a block of land bordered by the Leeward Public Highway and the Leeward River was sold.

The sale of house lots by the estate continued during the 1940s and resulted in the formation of two new neighborhoods, River Edge, between the highway and the river in the extreme northern part of the village, and Plan in the far western part of the village (Maps 4.2 and 4.3).

Beginning in the late 1940s and continuing through the 1950s, villagers also began to lease and buy house-spots in Collin's Village and the adjacent neighborhood of Belair Hill from the owners of the estate overlooking the eastern portion of the village (Maps 4.2 and 4.3).

The bulk of acquisitions during the 1970s occurred well outside the village boundaries in the area northeast of the junction of the Leeward River and the highway or along the secondary road leading into the heart of the valley. In both areas land is more plentiful, prices are lower, and privacy greater (a consideration of some importance to many returned migrants) than within the village or along its ever expanding perimeter. The most recent expansion of the village began in the early 1980s with the subdivision of estate lands northeast of Plan. The price of house lots at nearly $2.00 per square foot rivals prices in the most expensive areas on the south coast of the island.

Village size and demography are also a product of extra-valley migration. More than any other process or institution migration has enabled villagers to increase both their life-chances and community social standing by allowing the accumulation of greater wealth than is possible within the village. Migration from Leeward Village probably began shortly after Emancipation with villagers participating in the general exodus of poorer Vincentians to other islands where the rewards for wage-labor were much higher. Migration from the village has continued up to the present and villagers have taken advantage of removal from St. Vincent whenever they have been able to do so. The total village population, its sex and age distribution, the expansion of village boundaries as new homes are constructed, the formation of residential hamlets outside the village, the removal of farmland from productive cultivation, and the establishment of new shops and other local businesses, all have been a product of extra-valley removal. These and other implications of migration are dealt with in later chapters.

CONTEMPORARY SETTING

Settlement Pattern

Ethnographic research in the Caribbean has focused mainly on either small villages or neighborhood segments of larger units such as towns and cities (e.g., Brana-Shute 1979; Clarke 1966; Greenfield 1966; Horowitz 1967a; Laguerre 1982; Philpott 1973; Rodman 1971; R.T. Smith 1956). Alternately, for small islands, Carriacou and Providencia, for example, (see Hill 1977; M.G. Smith 1962a; Wilson 1973), the entire society rather than the village-community has been the center of attention. Except for a recent study of Port-of-Spain, Trinidad (Lieber 1981), there has been a neglect of larger, more complex villages, towns, and cities, local groups which are very much a part of the West Indian landscape.

Although commercial and shipping activity account for the origin of Leeward Village, there is no central plaza or marketplace (cf. Philpott 1973:74). Instead, most shops, churches, and government offices are spread out, in ribbon-like fashion, along the Leeward Public Highway. In 1980, there were 36 retail outlets of different kinds in the village, an increase of four since 1971. These included a self-serve grocery, 17 smaller food stores, 9 rum shops, most of which also sold some foodstuff, a tailor shop, a shoe repair shop, 3 bakeries, a gas station, a tiny government-run market house, a tannery, and a handicrafts shop. The largest of these retail establishments or those specializing in a particular product are patronized by the entire population while the small shops, especially those selling food, serve only the immediate area. Together with the local fruits and vegetables sold by mobile vendors, the goods available in the food and rum shops satisfy nearly all day-to-day needs. These include sugar, flour, rice, baking powder, salt, cooking oil, margarine, bread, biscuits, and other bakery products, tinned and powdered milk, fruit juices and soft drinks, canned and salted fish and meat, bananas and plantains, rum and beer, candy, cigarettes, matches, kerosene, school supplies, yard goods, some clothing, buttons and thread, soap and washing products, toiletries, patent medicine, costume jewelry, hardware supplies, and funeral goods. Of course, no single outlet supplies all these and the small-scale of most operations together with the periodic though perrenial shortage of many goods usually makes it necessary to visit several shops to buy even such basic items as sugar, bread, and dairy products.

Leeward Village also provides its inhabitants with several non-commercial services. The largest structure in the village is the two-storied combination police station/courthouse. Down the street is the headquarters of local government, the Warden's Office, where village records are stored, local taxes paid, and 'Poor Relief' dispensed. The same building contains a tiny, poorly stocked library staffed by a part-time clerk. Further along the Leeward Public Highway there is a joint Post Office/Savings' Bank housed in rented quarters on the lower story of a private dwelling. Across the river from the main village area is the government primary school, a three-building complex reported to be the largest elementary institution in the country. Adjacent to it is a small medical facility. Staffed by a full-time resident nurse, the clinic receives perfunctory weekly visits from the district doctor.

Bordering the main road at the upper end of the village is the unkempt village cemetery. Much larger than the Anglican graveyard which is reserved for communicants, its unruly appearance is transformed when villagers tend their relatives' plots preceding the celebration of All Souls' Day.

Past the cemetery on the northeastern periphery of the village lies the little-used agricultural experimental station and stud-service facility. Adjacent to it is a small government handicraft training unit built in 1985 by the newly elected NDP government. Few if any classes were held in the center during July and August 1986. On the estate side of the road below the stud center is the more popular soccer field leased by the government from the owners of Leeward Valley Estate.

Two public bath houses, one in disrepair, complete the list of locally-provided state services.

The spiritual, social, and recreational needs of villagers are met by nine Christian congregations (Anglican, Methodist, Roman Catholic, Seventh Day Adventist, Spiritual Baptist, Pilgrim Holiness, Evangelical, and Brethren), two burial societies, several youth groups and sports clubs, and a variety of church-based women's groups. The village is also served by a branch of the Canadian Save the Children's Fund.

There were more than 450 dwellings in the village in 1986. They vary in size, design, construction materials, exterior finish, and state of repair and are the most visible sign of local wealth and life-style differences. The main building materials are concrete blocks, wooden boards, stone slabs, and wattle and plaster. The most popular type of dwelling is the prestigious *wall house*, a structure constructed from concrete blocks or stone slabs set on a stone foundation. A brightly painted plaster overlay, partially enclosed porch, glass windows, and galvanized roof result in a dwelling reminiscent of working class housing in much of the Third World. Most of the older wattle-and-daub thatch roofed houses were replaced by tiny government-financed pine-board dwellings early in 1970. House size varies considerably. Some homes are one-room units measuring 8 feet by 10 feet; others are two-story structures measuring 35 feet on each side. The typical house, however, is a single-floor unit measuring 12 feet by 16 feet which is partitioned into three rooms, a rectangular *drawing room* which opens off from the front entrance and two adjoining bedrooms of nearly equal size.

The village also contains many unoccupied, abandoned, and partially completed dwellings. Most of these are a product of migration. Empty dwellings or those left to deteriorate are usually owned by overseas migrants. Half-built houses or those which consist of only a foundation await the remittance of funds necessary to resume construction.

Most new houses, especially those built by migrants, are constructed with contemporary design features and up-to-date household amenities in mind. Modernity does not necessarily bring with it comfort and the low-pitched roofs, enclosed ceilings, and tight-fitting concrete construction of the new-style dwellings makes many of them unpleasantly hot from mid-morning until early night. The old-fashioned *board house* with its steep roof, open beam ceiling, unglazed shuttered windows, and floor elevated on wooden or concrete corner posts is much cooler by comparison. But it lacks the amenities most sought after in a new house: running water, a flush toilet, a shower, and an indoor kitchen. Such features are still found in a minority of homes. Most villagers obtain their water from roadside public stand pipes or from a single outlet in their yards and dispose of body wastes in a crudely built privy located as far away from the house as possible. Cooking also takes place in a small detached kitchen or lean to. This separation of food preparation from the main dwelling, although old fashioned by village standards, serves to keep vermin out of the house, a constant problem for those occupying modern houses.

Over 70 percent of dwellings are the property of one or more of their occupants. The remainder are either leased from the owner (20 percent of all dwellings) or occupied on a rent-free basis (9 percent of all dwellings). Rent-free occupation is usually connected with migration, the owner leaving a resident caretaker, usually a close relative, to look after the house.

A compact village settlement pattern means that there is little cultivable land surrounding most houses. Only the largest lots, those exceeding 1,000 square feet, contain several fruit trees and small vegetable gardens. The rest are bare patches of earth only slightly larger than the house they contain. Still, this does not prevent many of their owners from raising a few chickens.

A smaller proportion of house-spots than houses--52 percent as compare to 71 percent--are the property of the dwelling owner. This is because houses are less expensive to buy than the lots upon which they sit; a small wood-framed house could be built for $1,000 during the early 1970s while its associated lot might cost several times that amount.

Although most valley residents were living in the village proper by the late 1960s, 111 people or five percent of the valley population were found on isolated homesteads or small hamlet clusters in the heart of the agricultural area toward the head of the valley in a census of village population conducted early in 1970. By 1986 about 50 more people were living in *the Mountain*. Residential isolation does not connote social separation and most are linked to the village by ties of kinship and sociability.

Population Composition

Because of its history, most villagers are the Black descendants of slaves, and less than five percent are Colored, East Indian, *Bajans*, or White people. Leeward Village has a young population with 54 percent of residents under the age of 15. Adult females also outnumber adult males: there are 181 women per 100 men over the age of 20. Both the youthfulness of the population and the sexual imbalance are partly a product of migration. Movement out of the village removes proportionately more adults than children and more men than women. The imbalance among elderly villagers--there are 67 women and 22 men over the age of 70--may also be a product of greater female longevity (see Kunstadter 1963).

Local Government

Leeward Village possesses a modicum of self-government in the form of an unpaid Town Board consisting of four elected and two nominated members. The Board mirrors the national political scene both in form and function. Members are elected for their support of the ruling party and the central government appoints the two nominated members. Elections are vigorously contested with members of the national parties, including the Premier and members of the Cabinet, attending village political rallies. Leeward Villagers have nearly always supported the Labour Party at both the national and local levels and the victory of the NDP candidate, a native-born villager, in the 1984 general election ended 20 years of local SVLP rule. As an appendage of the central government, the Board plays an important role in village economic life. Its duties include the collection of house tax, the leasing of public lands, and the maintenance of village secondary roads and public buildings. The Board hires a Warden to carry out its administrative duties. The Warden recruits villagers to clean the school, bath houses, and other public buildings, to sweep the streets, and to make minor road repairs. Nearly all appointments are made because of support of the governing party and the 1984 NDP electoral victory brought wholesale changes in the personnel employed by the Town Board.

COMMUNITY ORGANIZATION

Community Type

For those who insist that small-scale independent cultivation defines the peasant way of life (e.g., Lewis 1961; Wolf 1955), Leeward Village is not a peasant village. Only 20 percent of the working population are primarily small-scale cultivators while only one-third of village households own any *mountain* land. Conversely, many cultivators are not, in an occupational sense, peasants since their large-scale productive efforts are market and profit oriented (see Foster 1967:7; Wolf 1955:454). Even with a less restrictive usage which includes self-employed individuals such as fisherman, shop-keepers, artisans, etc. (see Firth 1946; Foster 1967:6), the peasant label is only partially appropriate since nearly one-half of the adult working population are primarily wage earners of some kind. Indeed, many of these salaried workers cannot even be termed proletarians (as opposed to peasants) given their occupations as teachers, clericals, and civil servants.

Still, several peasant-like features characterize the community. As a rural settlement where the single most important livelihood source is small-scale cultivation in which the proprietors ". . . exchange a part of what they produce for items they cannot themselves make, in a market setting transcending local transaction . . ." (Foster 1967:6), Leeward Village fits a main criteria of a peasant village. As well, from a structural point of view--from the perspective of the relation between the village and the state--most villagers, whether they work land or not, are poor and relatively powerless but still maintain a measure of control over arrangements of production and distribution. They also have low social standing vis-à-vis the national system of ranking based not only on their material poverty but because they manifest certain behavioral features--a "little tradition" (Redfield 1956)--which are different from those of members of the urban elite. Each of these traits-- rural residence, subsistence-orientation within the framework of market exchange, external jural domination, some control over production and exchange, low socio-economic standing, and social and cultural discontinuity--has at one time or another been used to describe the peasant community (Fitchen 1962; Foster 1967; Kroeber 1948; Redfield 1956; Wolf 1955).

The Open Community

Further complicating the nature of community organization in Leeward Village is the problem of describing the village in terms of formal or institutional closure except by reference to geographical boundaries, a difficulty rooted in the history of the village and perpetuated by contemporary local and societal conditions. By Caribbean (Horowitz 1960) and Latin American (Wolf 1955) standards, Leeward Village is a relatively "open" community. The sheer size of the village--2,245 in 1970--places it well beyond the maximum for face-to-face association (see Foster 1961:177-178). Together with occupational complexity and continuous interaction with the outside world in the form of labor migration, and the presence of imported goods, services, and ideas this has produced considerable variability in level and style of living. Life-style differentiation and the imitation of middle-class behavior by those seeking to elevate their status have contributed to the social and economic 'individualism' that is expressed in an unboundedness of social relationships and the absence of corporateness in most areas of village life. Consequently, nearly all village and valley lands are privately owned and may be alienated to outsiders; there is little communal activity; many important social relations are maintained with persons in other parts of the island; there is complete freedom of community entry and exit along with a high rate of village exogamy; there are few formal social leveling mechanisms or means for controlling locally-defined deviant or anti-social behavior; *esprit de corps* is hardly evident; and there are several competing political and religious associations. Openness is especially evident in the relation between the village and the capital. Many villagers are employed full-time in Kingstown; others either find work there from time time or are obliged to go there to receive payment for government wage-work back in the village. Many cultivators sell most of their surplus in Kingstown while most better-off villagers purchase much of their food there. Attendance at secondary school, medical treatment, and the payment of land tax also draw villagers to the capital.

Complicating these features of openness is the intricate manner in which they are intertwined. In his study of Balinese village organization, Geertz (1959:991-992) discovered that the complexity among villages could be described ". . . in terms of the intersection of theoretically separable planes of social organization" such as shared obligations to worship at a given temple, common residence, ownership of rice land, and so forth. Although Vincentian villages do not exhibit the tremendous diversity discovered by Geertz in Bali, many, including Leeward Village, are cross-cut in a complex manner by both internal and external processes and institutions. Among the intersecting components which complicate Leeward Village social organization are settlement pattern, neighborhood divisions, Christian denominations, burial societies, kinship and marriage, friendship patterns, employment, political affiliation, and social and government services. Each of these is either independent or semi-independent of the rest, and suggests that Leeward Village is a 'composite unit' which is both internally divided and externally connected to other communities and to the total Vincentian society. Settlement pattern and neighborhood divisions, for example, simultaneously unite Leeward Village into a larger geographical unit and divide it into sub-village social segments. The larger unit is the entire valley community made up of the 95 percent of the local population residing within the village boundaries and the 5 percent who live outside the village but nonetheless maintain strong ties with it. The sub-village segment is the neighborhood, a unit which meets the traditional usage of the community as the maximal unit of face-to-face association. *De facto* residential endogamy and family house lot subdivision tend to keep kin together in the same neighborhood. Neighborhoods also are a focus of identity and ties between neighbors often form the basis for close and lasting friendships. But the neighborhood is neither closed nor corporate. Membership is obtained merely by changing residence, and there are no common rights or obligations connected with it like those associated with the Latin American *barrio*.

Christian sects also sub-divide the village while uniting it with other communities. The Evangelical, Brethren, Methodist, Anglican, Pilgrim Holiness, and Spiritual Baptist congregations draw their members from the valley population alone. Along with the other church groups, they segment the community on the basis of ideological solidarity, friendship ties, and communal activity. The Roman Catholic and Seventh Day Adventist congregations, in turn, include members from neighboring villages who regularly attend church services and participate actively in its social functions. Membership in the same congregation also unites villagers with their coreligionists in other parts of the island. The Seventh Day Adventist and Spiritual Baptist sects often hold joint services with other congregations and travel extensively to participate in church events in other parts of the island.

Ties of kinship, marriage, and friendship extend well beyond the village boundaries uniting Leeward Villagers with people in other communities, in other Caribbean islands, and in England and North America. Most people who were born in the village are now living somewhere else, and although kinship unites many villagers, Leeward Village is not a bounded kinship entity. Neither is it a marriage community: a study of courthouse records showed that 45 percent of marriages between 1945 and 1971 involved unions between villagers and outsiders.

A similar situation exists for the other features of village structural complexity--burial society membership, friendship ties, place of employment, social stratification, political party support, and social and government services--and points to the applicability of the traditional view that Caribbean communities have little cohesion and are loosely organized (Wagley 1960:8). Yet this does not mean that the community should be dismissed as an insignificant social unit. Indeed, its 'non-community' qualities reveal the operation of processes fundamental to its organization and the welfare of its inhabitants.

These processes are historically-rooted. Given the manner in which Leeward Village came into being and the social and economic difficulties with which its members have had to deal, a closed, corporate community organization could hardly be expected. A complex and varied history in which, unlike many colonized people, increased rural self-sufficiency followed rather than preceded proletarianization, and in which the colonized people were themselves 'immigrants,' form the basis of the Leeward Village experience. Most Leeward Villagers are the descendants of people who have gone through the sequence freeman-slave-freedman-proletarian-peasant. In each of these stages, save perhaps the first which involved the pre-Caribbean African past, there has been an intimate involvement in the institutions and forces of a larger state-level capitalist society. This involvement has left its indelible imprint on village life. Leeward Villagers have always been dependent on the larger island-society for employment, markets, goods and services, social mobility, and ideas. It is the total society--and the world outside--that brought Leeward Village into being, and it is these arenas that continue to sustain Leeward Village by satisfying, albeit inadequately, many of the material and ideational needs of its inhabitants. Leeward Village has never been isolated from the larger Vincentian society and its residents are the descendants of a rural, capitalist, agrarian proletariat rather than a pre-industrial folk. But as later chapters will show, contemporary and historical forces alone do not account for community organization for its members have played an important role in shaping the present as well.

Community Sentiment

The view that Leeward Village is the product of an unintegrated set of features--that local-level and external institutions and processes are centrifugal forces which weaken the village's coherence and integrity--is only part of the picture of community organization. The other part is about the presence of consolidating mechanisms, the "communis" that belonging to any social group brings with it. People live in Leeward Village or return there after a lengthy absence (sometimes of 20 years or more in the case of migrants) because this is the place where most of their kin and close friends are residing. Here too is the place they can most easily validate their status, obtain support, sympathy, and a sense of social worth. Here is where they grew up, where they experienced so much joy and sorrow. This is where their *old parents* [ancestors] are buried and where their umbilical cord lies marked by a mango or coconut tree. Leeward Village is home.

Attitudes towards Leeward Village are of two kinds, those directed towards the community and those directed towards fellow villagers.

Life is viewed as *hard* [full of adversity] in Leeward Village. The state of the local economy, prospects for development, and the level of social services are all felt to be limited. Some people blame the government for the depressed state of the village economy, others point to the alleged laziness of their peers, and still others single out the absence of local industry. A large-scale handicraft or other commercial concern, a hotel or two, or some other non-farming activity are felt to be the best means of achieving local prosperity. This belief is reinforced by the underdeveloped state of local agriculture and the experience of migrants who have come back from living in industrialized countries. Although considerable pride is taken in the Canadian-financed potable water system that was installed in the mid-1960s, indifference or disappointment is expressed about the school, the police, and other public services. There is even little notice taken of the physical surroundings, of the shimmering green-blue bay, the coconut rimmed silvery-sand beach, and the verdant hilly interior (cf. Wilson 1973:44-45). Adolescents and teenagers, for example, feel that the village offers little social or recreational life. This is coupled with a belief that things are *brighter* [livelier] elsewhere: in the capital, in other islands, and overseas. They are right, of course. There is no community center or organized recreational life and dances are held at the primary school only on major holidays. Not surprisingly, most young people would like to leave Leeward Village for one of these brighter spots and often express regret about their blocked migration aspirations.

Attitudes of villagers towards each other are much more equivocal. Relationships of kinship and friendship (or 'enemyship'), the relative social standing of those involved, and the social context of the evaluation all affect what people say about each other in private and public settings. Generally, however, it is difficult not to be struck by the amount of criticism, suspicion, mutual distrust, and malicious gossip that informs daily conversation and the interpretation of behavior (cf. Wilson 1973:161-165). A variety of village expressions summarize this characterization:

"Leeward Village people no damn good."
"Leeward Village people too bad."
"Leeward Village people na fit."
"You know what those [Leeward Village] people *can give* [are capable of]."
"These people too friggin' tief."

There is also a colorful vocabulary for describing gossip, scandal, and conflict: *bad behavior*, *getting on ignorant*, *fast* [presumptuous or thievish, depending on the context], *playing the fool/ass*, *moles* [harass], *melée*, *commess* [gossip], *macoe* [pry into someone else's affairs], *nigger business* [low status or disreputable behavior], *nastiness* [corrupt or deviant activity, especially of a sexual nature], *boderation* [interpersonal conflict], *bacchanal*, *street scene* [public altercation], *cut eye* [stare down at], *harass*, *scamp*, *Bad John* [disreputable character]. The aphorism "You see how these people behave" typically ends descriptions of village scandals, *street scenes*, and other *tupidness* [foolishness].

Well-off villagers interpret the inability of the poor "to better their position" to laziness, a lack of ambition, and a general preoccupation with living *now-for-now* [in and for the present]. This is often combined with a negative evaluation of negritude ("Nigger people are no good").

But there are too many exceptions to these generalizations for them to have any real utility as a guide for social interaction. Friends, good neighbors, close kin, village patrons and clients, *respectable* villagers, and even fleeting acquaintances who present a favorable first impression are exempt from such negative stereotyping. Attitudes to people in other communities also temper adverse local sentiment. Members of several other villages are often collectively characterized as *rude*, *selfish*, *quarrely*, or *nasty*. Particular communities are singled out for special treatment by the reputed presence of some undesirable trait. The men in one village, for example, are said to be *dangerous* because of their alleged propensity to resort to violence at the slightest provocation while all the people in another village are labeled *nasty* because it is believed that they have an aversion to bathing. When directed at some other community negative attitudes often take the form of a comparison in which it is concluded that behavior in Leeward Village, bad as it is, is far less reprehensible than it is elsewhere. Still, positive rejoinders to negative folk generalizations are seldom heard and a silent nod of ascent usually follows moralistic statements about the poor quality of village social behavior.

Reputation and Respectability

In his study of family life among rural Black peasants in Guyana, R.T. Smith (1956:211) argued that "the main village group" composed of lower-class black people:

> . . . forms a localized sub-system of the total social system, but it is itself differentiated internally, without however producing any significant social stratification within itself.

From the perspective of the society-wide system of social differentiation most Leeward Villagers are also members of the lower-class. But from the perspective of the folk system of differentiation used by villagers to rank each other, there is considerable intra-community diversity. Part of this diversity is about the evaluation of behavior in terms of a duality between societal and lower-class-specific systems of social ranking. There is, to borrow a phrase from R.T. Smith (1956:149), ". . . a moral system within a moral system so to speak," a mode of social placement and moral interpretation of behavior based on village-level beliefs and values. This dichotomy has been recognized elsewhere in the Caribbean and has been summarized by a distinction between "reputation" and "respectability" (Wilson 1969, 1973).

Respectability refers to an ideological complex based on adherence to the values of the middle- and upper-classes, a moral order upheld by the colonial church and whose origin lies in the European metropole. Accordingly, it is defined by such attributes as Christian monogamous marriage, respect for formal authority, sobriety, a preoccupation with upward mobility, and attention to elite norms of social nicety, decorum, and manners (Wilson 1973:99-104). Household "manners" include communication in standard English (as opposed to the local Creole dialect), avoidance of public altercations, and an emulation of the North American or Western European middle-class style of life: a large, well-furnished home; high educational aspirations for one's children; and a "modern" or "cosmopolitan" world view.

Wealth and color ranking reinforce differentiation on the basis of respectability (Wilson 1973:105). Since wealth in St. Vincent is often the result of inheritance and since race is an ascriptive trait, social inequality becomes a matter of birthright.

Leeward Village contains only a handful of upper- and middle-class people. The Anglican priest and his family, the Roman Catholic prelate, and three Peace Corps teachers were the only Whites in the village during the early 1970s. Although the latter were college educated and engaged in respectable occupations, their youth, temporary residence, and unknown family background made it difficult for villagers to categorize the Americans within the island-wide color-class system of stratification. The two clergymen were also foreigners. But as representatives of the church they were the ultimate spokesmen for respectability. The sexual morality of villagers was a major preoccupation of the Anglican priest who arrived in St. Vincent with no prior knowledge of lower-class Black West Indian family life. Few of his sermons failed to condemn the "promiscuity" of villagers and, unlike any of his predecessors, he refused to baptize illegitimate children. This swelled the membership of the Catholic church whose pastor took a less doctrinal stance on village reproductive behavior.

Since the owners of Leeward Valley Estate left the area in the 1940s few White people have lived in the valley for more than a year or two at a time and by the mid-1970s all the White ex-patriates were gone.

Their departure left no real vacuum for local and outside Black and Colored people have long composed the bulk of the village elite. These included four Black West Indian Catholic nuns, the village nurse, several middle-ranking civil servants, and a handful of the most prosperous shopkeepers and farmers. The traditional local elite only lacked one of its most important resident members, the village school headmaster, a middle-aged man who, unlike most of his predecessors, commuted to the village each day from his home near the capital. The locally-born elite number less than two percent of the village population. But as the wealthiest people in the community and as the main lay exemplars of respectability their influence more than compensates for their numerical insignificance. Large, well-furnished homes are the most conspicuous index of their prosperity. Most own a car, employ a full-time domestic servant, buy large quantities of imported food, live in nuclear family households, find at least their female members regularly attending church, appear neatly dressed in public, and send their children to secondary school. Most inherited some land or other property from their parents.

Not all wealthy villagers belong to this elite group and not all respectable people are also respected. Reputation is the counterpoint of respectability. It connotes a value complex rooted in the local community as opposed to the larger society; it counterposes the fundamental equality of people to the hierarchy of social classes;

and it is a judgment which applies to the individual *qua* individual in contrast to the person as a member of an identifiable social category such as upper class, lower class, black, white, rich, or poor. Unlike many of the symbols of respectability--a formal education, an elaborate church wedding, expensive housing, a 'good' family background--reputation can neither be purchased nor inherited. Since it is based on the notion of the innate equality of people, it posits no limit on the number of persons who can earn respect through the manifestation of appropriate behavior. Consequently, it ranks individuals by qualities which, in varying degrees, they all possess.

Just as respectability is a quality which is especially associated with the domestic world of women, reputation is largely part of the domain of men (Wilson 1969, 1973). It is earned by doing well anything that is culturally-defined as manly. In Leeward Village the activities through which men gain public recognition and a sense of personal worth include the ability to *control* [have affairs with] many women, the fathering of several children, *good talks* [oratorical skills], athletic prowess, physical strength, generosity, flamboyance in dress and demeanor (which, by itself or when combined with sexual prowess, evokes the enviable title *saga boy*), toleration of large amounts of alcohol, and knowledge of the world (as opposed to formal education)(cf. Wilson 1973:138).

These attributes of reputation are discussed, enacted, embellished, and evaluated in social settings dominated by males. These include the rum shops, certain street corners, the jetty, and other locales where men gather to talk, joke, argue, and drink. None of these settings involve closed, corporate groups, formal membership criteria, or ceremonial initiation (cf. Wilson 1973:165-166).

Many of the values and activities associated with reputation are the antipode of those associated with respectability. A respectably married man cannot simultaneously be identified as a *saga boy*. Nor can a God-fearing church elder be seen carrying on in the rum shop or idling at the crossroads. Indeed, moralistic condemnations of reputation-seeking behavior--drinking, womanizing, *liming* [idling] on street corners--is a near obsession among elite village women, the nonpareils of local respectability. But reputation and respectability can also complement each other. As he matures, a man may gradually shift his value-orientation by marrying his *keeper* [common-law wife], staying away from the rum shop, attending church from time to time, and assuming other respectable traits. Some men are so adept that they are even able to simultaneously manipulate features of both systems. An educated villager who is also a gifted orator or cricket player gains status in both arenas of social evaluation and becomes a *great* [highly esteemed] man. Certain values and behaviors making up the two value systems are also alternatives which may be situationally selected. In addressing a respected superior, for example, a lower-class villager will exhibit a deferential and modest demeanor and will communicate in standard English or some approximation to it. In the company of peers, the same person will be loud and boisterous, bragging about his accomplishments or abilities in Creole dialect.

A handful of men are so talented in one or more of the traits associated with reputation that they are able to gain fame that transcends the local community. Most are not so gifted and must be content to receive their personal fulfillment--their identity as a real man--in their home area. For these men social interaction at the village level is the basis for the values surrounding reputation, and underscores the long-known, but often ignored, assertion that in the Caribbean:

> [The] primacy of social factors and relations in the differentiation of rural communities simply reflects the fact that communities are essentially social units constituted, defined and distinguished in terms of social relations (M.G. Smith 1956:303).

Thus while respectability obliges villagers to confront the modes of evaluation represented by the larger society, reputation turns them inward, to informal settings within the home community, for their existential support. Community weakness from the point of view of externally-based formal institutions--the church, the school, the political party office--is countered by community integration from the perspective of kindred networks, neighborhood ties, rum shop gatherings, streetcorner assemblies, gossip networks, temporary agricultural task groups, and the other so-called "loosely-structured" social forms that will be discussed in later chapters (see Dirks 1972; Mintz 1971:40; M.G. Smith 1956; Wilson 1969).

The concern of villagers with respectability and reputation also counterbalances community openness in other arenas. Even the most *worthless* [disreputable] villager would agree that the values of respectability are those that everyone should subscribe to. Alternately, nearly all villagers are keenly interested in village happenings, and they know a great deal about each other even though the community is not a tightly-knit social unit. Nor need respectable villagers enter the shameful world of the streetcorner or rum shop to receive *commess* [gossip] for it will be conveyed to them in the privacy of their homes by their lower-class clients. Indeed, it is in the world of gossip, scandal, and conflict that the village achieves much of its 'closure' as a social entity, its moral separation from other villages.

Solidarity and Effigy Hanging

The form of behavior that most arouses community moral concern is the breach of the incest taboo. The worst violation of the taboo is intercourse among nuclear family kin. Mating between step-parents and step-children and between parents and informally adopted children is also considered *nasty*, although less so than among actual blood relatives. When incest is believed to have occurred, it brings a community-wide reaction which involves a mock trial and ritual execution of the guilty parties (Rubenstein 1976). *Hangings*, the term used by villagers to describe their treatment of what is considered an outrageous breach of family and community morality, is a feature of lower-class West Indian culture which has received no attention in the literature. In traditional social functionalist terms, *hangings* may be explained as ritualized forms of social control through which villagers act out their collective aversion to incest by symbolically punishing the guilty parties. But *hangings* are also a forum for the expression of community values, and they defy ready explanation solely in terms of their most obvious functional significance.

The problem is to account for the presence of *hangings* within the context of a fully developed, accessible island juridical system which defines incest as a criminal act and to which villagers readily turn to gain *satisfaction* [redress] in other situations. St. Vincent has been operating under British jurisprudence since 1763, and Leeward Villagers make use of its services when sexual transgressions such as rape, unlawful carnal knowledge, and bestiality take place. Larceny and physical assault are also quickly reported to the police, and slander often results in the filing of a civil suit. The village Police Station is manned by a sergeant and four constables and weekly hearings take place in the courthouse located on the upper story of the station.

A more complete explanation of *hangings* lies in describing them as a symbolic expression of the relation between the local community and the external society. In particular, they represent a local-level, lower-class response to exclusion from full access to and equal participation in the social institutions and cultural traditions of the larger island-society. The validity of this proposition may be examined by describing the manner in which *hangings* express community belief and practice about slander, family life, gossip, prestige, and societal institutions.

Two cases of incestuous mating in Leeward Village which were dealt with by conducting a mock trial and ritually hanging effigies of the participants are described, the second in the words of an informant indirectly involved in the events leading up to it.

> *Case No. 1.* By the time John McIntyre began to live with Meatrice Lewis, all her children, except her youngest daughter, Pauline, had moved out on their own. When Pauline was about 14 years old, she and John began a clandestine affair resulting in her pregnancy three years later. Meatrice soon discovered her daughter's condition-- like many mothers in the village she regularly checked her daughter's *towels* [cloth menstrual pads] for signs of pregnancy--and forced the girl to admit John's respon- sibility for it. As Pauline's pregnancy became public knowledge and in the absence of any other suitor, Meatrice's neighbors began taunting her about the fact that her own *keeper* [common-law husband], John, was the father of her daughter's unborn child. They were par- ticularly scandalized by Meatrice's not having acted in the appropriate manner by throwing John out of the house and giving Pauline a severe beating for allowing her *father-in-law* [stepfather] to have sex with her. Meatrice indignantly replied that John was not Pauline's real father, that he was supporting the girl, and that even if their accusations were true, it was none of their concern. Villagers believed that it was indeed their concern and concluded that Meatrice, John, and Pauline ought to be *hanged*.

> *Case No. 2.* "I was *friendin' with* [having an affair with] Walker's daughter, Linda, and I uses to, when she come on the beach and buy fishes, follow her up the road and we'd go through the fields and have our fun. Well, her father got to know and he keep telling her that he had to *bust his tail*, which means he had to work hard, to support her and she just lovin' man when she should a be lovin' him. Well, his daughter keep *turnin'* [shuffling from

one foot to another with her head downcast] and ask him what do he mean by that and he turn around and said, 'You don't know what I mean by that? You have man carryin' you up the road every morning and me who *mindin'* [supporting] you, I can't see you.' Well, this goes on for a period of time just talkin' and talkin' towards me and her being *friendly*. "Well, one day she had to carry his lunch [to him]. He's a farmer, and while she carry his lunch he bring up the same conversation towards me, and so on, and ask her out of me and him who does she love more, and she told him, 'Well, I have to love you more; you is my father. You caused me to be here in the world and I have to love you more. But the things Bill [the boyfriend] can do to me you can't do.' And he began to fuss about it. He said, 'Why? I'm the same man like Bill,' and so on, and he tried to hold on to her and have sex with her. When she was *shame* [ashamed] about it she tried to cry and tug away from him, and so on. He cut her with a *cutlass* [machete], lash her with a *cutlass* and cut her on the hand. And I'm not sure really but I don't think they make any children but they used to have sex. I find out by the girl telling me. She told me what was going on. And they had the *hanging*, the same *hanging* I was talking about, towards it."

In neither case was the violation of the mating prohibition ever reported to the police. Since *hangings* are conspicuous public ceremonial events, the village constables were undoubtedly aware of what was going on but took no action since no formal complaint was lodged. Being members of the Black lower class themselves, they would almost certainly have condoned the manner in which villagers handled the breach of the incest taboo.

A *hanging* is made up of two interrelated activities, a stylized jury trial which follows the form and content of mainstream criminal proceedings, and a ritual hanging of full-scale life-like images constructed by village carpenters to resemble the accused parties. The events begin after it has been established, to the satisfaction of most villagers, that an incestuous act has taken place. Several village men of outgoing personality, administrative ability, and good reputation organize and sponsor *hangings* for personal amusement, to punish the offending parties by publicly humiliating them in a dramatic fashion, to enhance their own community standing by demonstrating the skill needed to conduct such an elaborate enterprise, and for personal financial benefit. There are small fees charged for attending each court sitting and for previewing the effigies between the end of the trial and the actual 'execution.' Dances are also held after the verdict is handed down and require an entrance fee.

The sponsors select different villagers to play the various roles in the trial. These include a judge, policemen, jury members, a bailiff, a prosecuting attorney, a defense attorney, the accused parties, witnesses, and members of the family of the defendants. An effort is made fill the positions with persons who are articulate in Standard English, the respectable speech form in St. Vincent (cf. Abrahams and Bauman 1971). For this reason some of the organizers themselves play several the positions in the drama. An exceptionally eloquent villager--a respectable person of high reputation--is chosen to act as judge. The Crown witnesses are chosen by their familiarity with the facts of the case. Ideal witnesses are those with firsthand knowledge of the transgression. Most of the actors, including the jury, are given farcical pseudonyms for both comic relief and to 'obscure' their true identities. The most hilarious of these are reserved for the defendants and are selected to emphasize either some physical peculiarity (e.g., "Mr. Bandy-legs" was assigned to a bowlegged male defendant) or the breach of sexual morality associated with case (e.g., "Miss Upholder" was given to the mother who failed to show outrage when she discovered that her daughter was carrying her common-law-husband's child).

The trial is conducted either in a burial society meeting hall or a Leeward Valley Estate storage building. Deliberations are held two or three times a week over a two-month period. At the opening session the judge, who is dressed in a black suit and wig, requests the facts of the case. The prosecutor reads out the charge that on given a date the male defendant had sexual relations with his daughter. Although the hearings deliberately follow societal jural process, the multi-purpose nature of *hangings* encourages spontaneous departure from mainstream procedures. This includes uproarious verbal duels between competing attorneys, hilarious testimonies from the witnesses and other players, and constant interjections from the audience. At the final sitting, the jury, composed of six or seven villagers of both sexes, hands down the written verdict of guilty as charged. The judge announces the sentence--"The defendants shall be hung by the neck until they are dead. May God have mercy over their souls"--and signs the death ban. This acts as a signal for those who have acted as members of the family of the accused to express their grief with loud wailing and crying.

The end of the trial marks the beginning of a two-week period during which the *images* [effigies], whose faces have been carved out of coconut husks, are available for private viewing. Nightly dances are also held at this time.

The hanging of the effigies takes place either on the grounds of the village primary school or in an open pasture on the outskirts of the village during the first full moon following the handing down of the verdict. A village steel band leads a procession composed of several hundred people to the site and plays throughout the evening. Bamboo poles some 20 feet long are employed as gallows, and the *images* are pulled by ropes to their tops. This is followed by several hours of dancing to the music of the steel band while the gallows are continuously paraded through the assembled crowd, the *images* manipulated in a comical fashion. Finally, the ropes are sharply jerked, breaking the necks of the mannequins, while a village marksman fires at them with a rifle. Again, a public dance follows. No fee is charged for attending the effigy hanging, and most villagers try to attend, for it is a rare and enjoyable occasion.

Also in attendance at their own hanging are some of the actual individuals who were found guilty at the trial.

As collective forms of ritual punishment *hangings* represent a reaction to a serious breach of family and community morality. They also serve as a medium for the expression of beliefs and values which are distinctive to rural lower-class Black Vincentians, a feature which suggests that they are far more than a consequence of community moral outrage.

Slander. Villagers do not hesitate to appeal to the police and courts when they believe that they have been *advantaged* [taken advantage of]. But they nonetheless show the general fear among lower-class Vincentians of being *actioned* [taken to court] or *complained* [reported to the police] for slanderous assault. Since accusations of incest are almost never supported by the public testimony of the participants, there is no proof that it has really occurred. Villagers resolve the dilemma of their felt need to condemn incestuous behavior and the fear of being *actioned* by the parties concerned by obscuring their identities by using pseudonyms. Though this hardly has the desired effect--indeed, if no one knew who was being referred to, the purpose of the whole exercise would be in vain-- villagers believe that if they do not use the actual names of the parties, they cannot be sued for slander.

Family Business. Villagers succinctly express the lower-class conviction that *family business* is private business as follows: "When *family and family* [members of the same nuclear or extended family, especially those residing in the same household] have *boderation* [a quarrel], no outsider have no right to *come inside there* [involve themselves in the matter]." In one case, for example:

> Ronald Wilson learned that his niece, Dorothy, had assaulted her grandmother by kicking her in the stomach during a domestic quarrel and he rushed home from his job in Kingstown to punish the teenage girl. Dorothy's brothers and sisters, all of whom were living in the same home and being raised by their grandmother, came to the girl's defense. Suddenly the entire household erupted in cursing, fighting, and stone-throwing. A policeman who happened to be making his rounds at the time burst into the yard and began separating the combatants. His actions were loudly and swiftly condemned by the sizable crowd that had gathered to witness the altercation. The consensus was that what was taking place was clearly *family business* over which the police had no jurisdiction.

Villagers are, therefore, faced with the dilemma of wanting to punish the violation of the incest taboo and the high value they place on family privacy. Hangings offer a neat solution to this contradiction. They are a locally acceptable form of punishment which is purposely confined to a unit, the village community, which though it is larger than the one defined by *family business* is still composed of individuals of whom it is said "all suck from the same *bubbie*" [breast]. In other words, even if *family business* has been taken out of the family, the arena into which it has been thrust is still one which is qualitatively different from that represented by the island police and courts.

Commess. In a detailed discussion of *commess* [gossip] in St. Vincent, Abrahams (1970:291) argued that it is not only an important speech form among island peasants but that there is ". . . a great of talk about talk, and because of this, much judgment passed on communicative behaviour." One of these evaluations--that *commess* is without merit--is based on the recognition that it is often a source of *boderation* among kin, friends, and neighbors. It is also stated that habitual gossip-mongering is a sign of ignorance and laziness, that the *macoe* [person who spies on or otherwise pries into the affairs of others] and *melée-man* [person of either sex who constantly gets into trouble or who relishes the trouble others have gotten themselves into] are disreputable characters whose behavior is *worthless* [contemptible]. Even the recognition that *commess* is a pervasive feature of village life does not affect the judgment that it is alien to respectability, to mainstream morality and behavioral propriety.

Again villagers are faced with a contradiction between needing to act out their disapproval of deviant sexual activity and their belief that *commess* is antithetical to good manners and a commitment to mainstream moral and behavioral norms. The contradiction is resolved through its manipulation so as to obscure that it is *commess*. There are two ways in which this can be done: either by presenting *news* (a euphemism for *commess*) in a matter-of-fact way as part of the general flow of a conversation or by embellishing and dramatizing it. Presentation of *commess* in an unceremonious, impromptu manner directs attention away from the speaker, who becomes simply its medium; when flaunted ostentatiously, the *news* becomes secondary, and the event is the focus of attention.

In *hangings*, *commess* about the behavior of others is delivered within the highly stylized, theatrical framework of the trial. Within this dramatic, ceremonial milieu *commess* is elevated above its cruder, more mundane varieties. What is denigrated in everyday behavior is transformed into an exciting and artistic social event supported by ritual, paraphernalia, and the positive sanction of replication of a mainstream jural process. What is the activity of *low-caste* people in other situations becomes a community-wide moral statement, an attempt to cope with the baser parts of the human condition.

Prestige. Why are some of the actual defendants so *bare-faced* [shameless] as to attend the hanging of their own effigies, among the most jovial participants at the ceremony, and outwardly indifferent to the humiliating treatment they have received from their fellow villagers? Part of the answer lies in Abrahams' (1970:292-293) explanation of the ambivalence felt among Vincentian peasants who have been subjected to derisive gossip:

> Though there is fear of having one's name used in scandal-pieces, there is a contrary notion that prestige may result from having one's name used (and therefore known) by so many people. In some cases, because one becomes known (albeit notoriously), community scorn is

accepted and taken advantage of by individuals. Here the implication is that people would rather be feared as deviants than ignored.

This is especially true of *hangings*, because their sponsors include some of the *great* men in the community. To be singled out by such renowned (and respectable) people for such elaborate treatment detracts from the outrage and shame that might otherwise be felt.

A second reason the guilty parties attend their own hanging is to show that they are unaffected by community scorn and punishment. A village expression--"Me na live wit dem people"--summarizes the reaction to all types of negative evaluation of one's behavior by others and implies that the worst possible response is to appear to be affected by community ridicule. In other words, attendance by the guilty parties at effigy hangings is a face-saving mechanism intended to demonstrate strength, independence, and resilience when faced with contempt and derision.

Mainstream Institutions. Villagers are generally ambivalent when it comes to most government bodies. One the one hand, state institutions are respected because clearly they are the main sources of island power and authority, because they symbolize in a formalized manner some of the most prestigious norms of the society, and because they may prove personally useful, even profitable, from time to time. On the other hand, these same bodies are feared because their operation is imperfectly understood, because they are politically nepotic (a distinct disadvantage when one's party is out of power), and because of past experience of unsatisfactory dealings with them. In particular, the police and courts are respected for offering the best way to gain *satisfaction* in such cases as theft, assault, and direct verbal abuse. But they are feared because of the possibility of becoming the victim of their unpredictability or perceived favoritism and because of the confusion which invariably results because of a lack of understanding of the formal rules governing their operation.

Hangings nicely resolve this dialectic between respect and fear. Although much of their form is patterned along mainstream court procedure, that *hangings* take place at all and the comical way in which they are carried out is symptomatic of a marked dissatisfaction with societal jurisprudence. The arbitrariness of the government courts is emphasized, for example, by the defendants always being found guilty, and their aloofness and formality are parodied in the farcical and disorganized conduct of the trial. More important, perhaps, the very fact that these mainstream institutions are singled out for hilarious treatment places them, if only temporarily and ritually, under the control of that unit which controls them least, the rural peasant community.

As important as they may be from the perspective of folk symbolism, such controls have little effect on the day to day lives of community members. Most Leeward Villagers are poor. For many, a steady supply of necessities, including the provision of food, is a perpetual problem, sometimes a daily problem. This difficulty in *making a bread* [securing a livelihood] is reflected in the class, wealth, and occupational differences between villagers, in the pattern of valley land tenure and use, and in wage-labor migration. These issues are the topic of Part II, *The Organization of Economic Life*.

PART II

THE ORGANIZATION OF
ECONOMIC LIFE

Chapter 5
Work, Wealth, and Class

THE CLASS STRUCTURE

Not all villagers are poor and there is considerable variation in local wealth and lifestyle even among those who are nominally lower-class from the point of view of island-wide stratification (cf. Philpott 1973:50). The presence of representatives of the middle- and upper-class--the clergy, a few middle-ranked government employees, a nurse, a trade-union executive, and a few owners of small estates and large shops--has already been mentioned. Though numerically insignificant in composing less than two percent of the village population, they are the main exemplars of respectability and exert an economic effect far beyond their numerical strength. They own the best land in the valley; they are the major employers of agricultural labor; they influence the price of imported goods and the granting of credit through their retailing activities; they are the main moneylenders; and they act as the local intermediaries in the national system of political patronage.

Still, from the perspective of the island system of economic differentiation the bulk of villagers are members of the lower class (cf. R.T. Smith 1956). Even within the context of the local economy itself most villagers occupy the bottom portion of the class hierarchy and earn less than $5.00 per day in wage-labor or self employed work. Villagers operate almost entirely within a cash economy and the high cost of overseas items aggravates local economic difficulties. Agriculture may serve as an example. Even those smallholders who consume all they produce must buy imported seeds and other planting material, fertilizer, and tools. And they must sell some of what they grow or engage in some other economic activity to buy additional food and other items. Nearly 90 percent of valley land holdings are under five acres and over one-half are less than two acres. The possession of a small holding inevitably results in a combination of part-time work and a low economic return. On the one hand, it is impossible to farm a small plot full time; on the other, the return from the effort that is expended cannot support all but the smallest households.

The village lower-class may be divided into three sub-strata on the basis of income, property, and material style of life. Even members of the upper stratum consider themselves poor although in terms of their consumption of food, clothing, and shelter they are far better off than the majority of villagers, the 80 percent or so who occupy the lower-lower class.

The Upper Lower Class

This segment of the village lower class contains about five percent of the adult population. Commercial farming, often in combination with shopkeeping, is the most common sub-class occupation. Its membership also contains the village's most successful masons and carpenters, larger shop owners, representatives of the lowest ranks of the island civil service (uncertified teachers, postmistresses, Town Board Warden, minor customs officer), Kingstown shop clerks, and seine net owners. Varying occupations are reflected in a wide range in incomes. In 1970, farmers and shopkeepers earned between $750 and $1,250 per annum, tradesmen between $1,000 and $1,200, and civil servants and clerks between $700 and $1,800.

Nearly all its members own large, well-built and furnished single-storied concrete block or two-storied wood-framed homes. All homes are electrified and contain indoor plumbing and sewage disposal. The refrigerator is often conspicuously displayed in the living room but is usually stocked with only a few dairy products, leftover cooked food, and several bottles of water. About three-quarters of members of the stratum own one or more pieces of agricultural land. Only a handful have a car although most employ a full or part-time household servant.

Dress, diet, level of education, and associated behavioral traits distinguish sub-class members from both elite islanders and the other segments of the lower class. Those in minor civil service and clerical positions, activities which usually require some secondary school, dress and act in accordance with the expectations associated with their positions. A white shirt and dark trousers for men and a neat, fashionable dress or skirt and blouse for women are the normal mode of attire. Their patterns of speech and associated behavior approximate those of middle-class Vincentians.

The other members are far less middle-class in education, dress, and speech. This sub-class bifurcation extends to age as well. Most clerks and civil servants are under 30 years of age and acquired their status through post-primary school education; farmers, shopkeepers, artisans, and other uneducated members are mainly over 40 and achieved their position mainly through the investment of money earned during one or more periods of labor migration. At the same time, many of the public servants and clerks are the children of middle-aged sub-class members who were able to educate them by earnings from their trades, shopkeeping, or farming.

Except for speech usage. among its less educated members (who prefer to speak to their peers in a creolized version of Standard English) and sexual behavior among several of its males, many of the features of middle- and upper-class respectability are observed. Most adults are or have been married and nuclear family households are the most common domestic arrangement. Sub-class women nearly always appear well groomed and dressed in public and they always wear shoes. Female social life revolves around the home; rarely can they be seen idling in public or engaging in roadside gossip. But though they may give the appearance of disassociation from mundane street *happenings* [events], they take an active interests in village affairs. As among their elite counterparts, *commess* and *boderation* are brought to them in the privacy of their homes by their peers and social subordinates.

Many male members of the stratum also avoid *liming* on the roadside and streetcorner, preferring like their wives to hear *news* in a less public setting. Those who drink rum do so at home with friends or in back rooms of rum shops where they are less visible to passers-by. A concern with elite mores does not touch all their behavior, however. Because they are men and because they are *financial* [well off] they may, from time to time, stray outside the boundaries of respectable activity without seriously damaging their respectability. A real man, whether he is married or not, is expected to engage in outside amorous adventures and to show that he has good verbal ability. At the same time, being able *to hold a good conversation* and being able *to run plenty of women*, if taken to an extreme, may damage respectability. The contradiction between marital fidelity (which is part of respectability) and womanizing (which is considered reputable) is partially resolved by the fact that *running women* is an expensive proposition which requires considerable financial security--a trait associated with respectability.

The Middle Lower Class

About 10 percent of villagers belong to the middle stratum of the lower class. Except for the absence of clerical and civil service activities, many middle-lower-class occupations are identical to upper-middle-class ones, albeit on a smaller scale. As a result, its members include peasant cultivators who sell much of what they produce, owners of small to mid-sized shops, and less successful skilled and semi-skilled tradesmen (masons, carpenters, painters, plumbers). Other common occupations include government manual labor (truck loader, medical orderly, postman, forest guard, etc.), other full-time wage-labor jobs (stevedore, telephone technician, bus driver, porter, etc.), and self-employed skilled work (tailor, shoemaker, seamstress, etc.). Incomes in 1970 ranged from $200 to $400 per annum for a farmer to $1,000 or more for full-time government employees and other wage-laborers.

On the whole, members of the sub-class have had less opportunity for education than members of the upper-lower-class. Many, for example, were born into very poor (i.e., lower-lower-class) families and achieved their position through years of effort and determination. Only a few have completed a full primary school education and many are functionally illiterate. Yet about 85 percent of families own their own homes and house lots. Nearly 70 percent also own a small piece or two of agricultural land. Although smaller and less expensively furnished than those of the upper lower class, most dwellings are supplied with electricity and have pipe-borne water in the yard. Only a handful of families have refrigerators (often bought from funds sent by overseas relatives) and only one or two have in-house sewage disposal.

A combination of occupations and dependence on remittances are marked among the middle lower class. Farmers, for example, are obliged to work at other activities besides gardening to maintain their families because of the small size or low productivity of their holdings. Even skilled laborers often need to supplement their trades with other ventures because of the irregularity of work opportunities. Nearly one-half of households are also dependent on cash from relatives outside the island. Many of these families are headed by married women whose husbands are employed overseas or elsewhere in the Caribbean.

Elite patterns of respectability are also emphasized by sub-class members. Its women are active church-goers and marriage is the norm among middle-aged persons of both sexes. The pattern of entry into marriage, however, differs among many members of the middle lower class. Although a number married in their early twenties, most did so several years later, often after living for some years in consensual unions. The decision to enter legal, Christian marriage-- the only respectable conjugal form in Vincentian society--often symbolizes a change in status, an indication that the concomitants of acute poverty and economic insecurity have been left behind. Elite and upper-lower-class villagers sometimes refer to members of this stratum as "poor but decent," indicating that economic indices alone do not define the manner in which Leeward Villagers rank each other.

Despite the emphasis on respectability among members of the stratum, behavioral dualism is still plainly visible. Males are not exempt from the general lower-class dictum that *a man is a man* and extra-conjugal mating, rum-drinking, and other expressions of masculine behavior are positively evaluated so long as they are not taken to an extreme.

The Lower Lower Class

Over 80 percent of villagers belong to the lower lower-class. Membership is by ascription and, apart from labor migration, there is little opportunity for life-style transformation. The village poor, as they will be called throughout the study, dominate the least skilled and lowest paying island and villages occupations: fishing, seine knitting, fish mongering and other *huckstering* [petty retailing], agricultural wage-labor, road gang work, subsistence and small-scale peasant agriculture, domestic service, seasonal agricultural labor migration, *scavenging* [garbage collecting], and street cleaning, and other low-status activities. In 1970, few of these occupations paid more than $1.50 a day; by 1986, this had increased to only $5.00 a day. Under-employment and seasonality also characterize many of these jobs, the net result being that annual earnings are rarely over $2,000. Low earnings and lengthy periods of inactivity makes it necessary for many members of the village poor to pursue two or more different economic activities during the year to guarantee a minimal livelihood. But even opportunities for casual employment are limited, and there is much unemployment, especially among teenagers and adult women.

Fewer than two-thirds of the village poor own their own homes and less than one-half own their own house-spots. Although a few homes are supplied with electricity, none contain indoor plumbing, refrigerators, or valued household amenities. Less than one-half of sub-class members own or have a shared interest in agricultural land although some 20 percent rent or sharecrop land owned by other people.

Housing and household amenities are the most tangible indicators of the material conditions of sub-class poverty. Most dwellings, whether owned or rented, are small, single-storied two- or three-room board structures supported on a stone or wood-pillar foundation. Although many are in good repair, others have split or rotting wall and floor boards, badly rusted roofs, and tilted foundations. Furnishings are usually sparse--a small wooden table, a couple of chairs, two or more locally-made bed frames and home-made mattresses, a small bench or two, and a china cabinet containing glassware, cups, and plastic and ceramic trinkets.

Unlike their better-off lower-class peers, the village poor rarely have more than a few days supply of food at hand. Goods are purchased nearly daily in village shops often on basis of long-established credit arrangements. Savings are low or absent and a house and piece of land are the only 'investments.'

Diet, dress, and education also distinguish the village poor from the sub-classes above it. Large amounts of sugar and starchy foods--rice, flour, ground provisions, and breadfruit--and small amounts of relish--meat, fish, and poultry--are consumed. Most women's clothing consists of ill-fitting garments made by semi-skilled village seamstresses from cheap cotton or synthetic material purchased in Kingstown. Men and boys usually wear T-shirts or cotton shirts and poor quality trousers bought in the capital. Those who own a good pair of leather shoes usually reserve them for attendance at church, weddings, fetes, and carnival and go bare-footed or wear inexpensive imported rubber sandals the rest of the time. Many of the village poor are only barely literate having completed only a few years of primary school.

The limited life-chances among the village poor find their most tragic expression in high rates of infant mortality. Adults are also afflicted with a variety of intestinal and other ailments, and although the village has a full-time trained nurse, the clinic is stocked with few medical supplies. More thorough medical treatment by private physicians in the capital requires a fee few members can afford. Even the medication prescribed by the district doctor is beyond the means of many villagers.

Although normative dualism is also pronounced among the village poor, acting out the behavior associated with elite and middle class mores is normally impossible. As a consequence, a distinction between ideal patterns of action--behavior associated with society-wide norms--and sub-class specific modes of conduct is prevalent. For example, although most members, especially women, hold marriage as the most desirable form of conjugal activity, few marry since they are unable to meet the material prerequisites associated with legal, Christian marriage. The 'solution' that has been adopted by the village poor to deal with this inability to enter a respectable conjugal union parallels that found among equally poor Trinidadian peasants:

> . . . the lower-class [Black Trinidadian peasant], without abandoning the general values of the society, develops an alternative set of values. Without abandoning the values of marriage and legitimate childbirth he stretches these values so that the non-legal union and illegitimate children are also desirable. . . . The result is that members of the lower-class, in many areas, have a wider range of values than others within that society. They share the general values of the society with members of other classes, but in addition they have stretched these values, or developed alternative values, which help them adjust to their deprived circumstances (Rodman 1971:195).

What Rodman calls "the lower-class value stretch" and the development of alternative values are expressed among the Leeward Village poor in a variety of areas--kinship group affiliation, domestic life, ways of making a living, and friendship patterns. Life is *hard* in this sub-class and its members exhibit many of the material conditions associated with the "culture of poverty" (Lewis 1966). These include unemployment and under-employment, low wages, unskilled occupations, a lack of savings, chronic shortages of cash, an absence of home food reserves, poor housing, low levels of education and literacy, and a constant struggle for survival.

Many kinship traits associated with the culture of poverty are present as well: marriage is the ideal though many never marry; the kinship system is bilateral although there is a greater knowledge of maternal kin; there is a high incidence of consensual unions and female-headed households; and physical violence in training children and punishing wives and common-law partners is prevalent. Yet the feelings of despair, apathy, fear, fatalism, unworthiness, etc., which are said to characterize "the attitudes, values and character structure of the individual" (Lewis 1966:21) in the culture of poverty do not apply to most poor villagers. This is not to say that there is no suffering here, that there is no display of frustration or self-pity. But these emotions are neither exclusive to the village poor nor dominant in their lives. Indeed, it is values and cognitive orientations emphasizing strength, resilience, reputation (among men), respectability (among women), wit, and pride that guide the behavior of most poor people.

If there is 'fear' among the village poor, it is manifested in a desire to avoid being labelled *undecent* [disreputable]. It is far better, for example, to possess none of the traits associated with respectability and reputation than to live or behave in such a manner that only pity or contempt are the reaction of fellow villagers. Thus a man who drinks heavily but does not get drunk and *play the fool* will gain the reputation as a person who can hold his liquor; the habitual drunkard gains nothing in reputation and loses what little respect he may have. Similarly, a woman with an illegitimate child may not be respectable but she has nonetheless proven that she is a *big woman* and not a *mule*. But if she continues to have children year after year from a series of men, particularly if these men refuse to support their children, she will be called a *whore*.

THE ORGANIZATION OF WORK

It has often been reported that many Afro-Caribbean rural people simultaneously or sequentially engage in several subsistence and/or cash occupations (see Comitas 1964; Dirks 1972:569; Frucht 1971; Greenfield 1966:82-83; Handler 1973:97-98; Herskovits and Herskovits 1964:53; Horowitz 1967a:22; Otterbein 1966:29; Philpott 1973:85, 87-89; Rodman 1971:37; M.G. Smith 1962b:63, 1965:198; R.T. Smith 1956:22, 25, 41-43). In an influential article, Comitas (1964:41) has labelled this phenomenon "occupational multiplicity" ". . . a condition wherein the model adult is systematically engaged in a number of gainful activities which form for him an integrated economic complex." Comitas also suggests that "occupational pluralists" in rural Jamaica are an economic type different from but related to peasants, farmers, and plantation workers which results from the fact that ". . . no one [occupational] alternative is sufficiently lucrative for individual full-time specialization. . . ."

The pattern of economic activity in Leeward Village, suggests that occupational multiplicity may be part of a larger syndrome of the vocational complexity in many rural, Afro-Caribbean communities. Although some of the components of this complexity in such communities have been pointed out in various studies, no attempt has been made to systematically describe and analyze the full range of features and processes which contribute to vocational intricateness in a particular community (Rubenstein 1984).

Occupational complexity in Leeward Village is partly the result of an attempt by poor villagers to ensure an adequate income in a situation of extreme economic deprivation. Vincentian social and economic organization--national economic stagnation, an inadequate social service apparatus, and class-based monopolization of scarce island resources--have placed severe limits on the well-being and advancement of the village poor. Although it has been impossible for them to fully counterbalance the effects of these constraints, they have, nevertheless, responded by generating and maintaining occupational forms and arrangements which help them cope with their poverty and marginality.

Occupational Preferences

Most villagers have been inculcated with middle- and upper-class vocational values and aspirations without having been given the means for realizing them. As a result, occupational preferences greatly exceed work prospects, especially among young people.

The data in Tables 5.1 and 5.2 are based on a questionnaire I administered to all students ranging in age from 11 to 15 attending the village primary school. The results in Table 5.1 are based on the question: "What job do you want to do when you finish school?" and the results in Table 5.2 are in response to the questions: "What do you think is the worst job for a man in Leeward Village?" and "What do you think is the worst job for a woman in Leeward Village?" The data in Table 5.1 show a clear preference for such high status island positions as medicine, nursing, teaching, and office and clerical work, as well as an interest, among boys, in such less prestigious but secure occupations as carpentry, auto mechanics, and police work. The worst occupations cited (Table 5.2) include street cleaning (*scavenging*), road repair work, farming, fishing, and laundering clothes. Although they were asked to name village vocations, many children listed activities which are considered to be disreputable (stealing, cursing, begging, rum drinking, going to jail, fighting

TABLE 5.1 OCCUPATIONAL ASPIRATIONS OF LEEWARD
VILLAGE SCHOOLCHILDREN ACCORDING TO SEX

Males			Females		
Occupation	No.	%	Occupation	No.	%
Carpenter	7	18.9	Nurse	34	45.3
Physician	6	16.2	Store clerk	17	22.7
Teacher	6	16.2	Teacher	14	18.7
Mechanic	3	8.1	Office clerk	4	5.3
Policeman	3	8.1	Bank clerk	2	2.7
Office clerk	3	8.1	Policewoman	1	1.3
Lawyer	2	5.4	Postmistress	1	1.3
Sailor	2	5.4	Stewardess	1	1.3
Magistrate	1	2.7	Seamstress	1	1.3
Mason	1	2.7			
Store clerk	1	2.7	Total	75	100.0
Tailor	1	2.7			
Engineer	1	2.7			
Total	37	100.0			

TABLE 5.2 UNDESIRABLE OCCUPATIONS IN LEEWARD VILLAGE

Males			Females		
Occupation	No.	%	Occupation	No.	%
Thief	22	23.7	Street cleaner	18	19.0
Street cleaner	21	22.6	Road laborer	18	19.0
Road laborer	16	17.2	Farmer	12	12.6
Farmer	7	7.5	Thief	11	11.6
Unemployment	7	7.5	Unemployment	8	8.4
Fisherman	7	7.5	Cursing	5	5.3
Fighting	3	3.2	Washerwoman	4	4.2
Making trouble	2	2.2	Fish vendor	3	3.2
Going to jail	2	2.2	Beggar	3	3.2
Cursing	2	2.2	Drinking rum	3	3.2
Murderer	1	1.1	Going to jail	2	2.1
Gambler	1	1.1	Working	2	2.1
Watchman	1	1.1	Domestic servant	2	2.1
Laborer	1	1.1	Stone gatherer	2	2.1
			Gossiping	1	1.1
Total	93	100.0	Prostitute	1	1.1
			Total	95	100.0

making trouble, etc.) as "worst occupations," highlighting the community preoccupation with respectability. Many also cited unemployment ("just sit down and do nothing"; "walk up and down the street") as an undesirable activity, thereby illustrating an acute awareness among young people of the economic troubles facing the community. More important, many of the "worst jobs" in Table 5.2-- road repair, farming, and fishing--are among the most typical village occupations. Alternately, the most commonly named occupations in Table 5.2 bear little relation to the activities really engaged in by adult villagers. There is, then, a contradiction between normative evaluation and statistical occurrence based on an opposition between the actual world of the middle and upper classes and the realities of the lower-class experience. Both M.G. Smith (1965:208) and Comitas (1964:45) have reported similar distinctions between occupational choice and employment opportunities in rural Jamaica.

> [T]he occupational aspirations of rural schoolboys and the prospects they face as adults could hardly differ more sharply. . . . Own-account farming or unskilled labor--the two least desired occupations--are almost the only alternatives before them (M.G. Smith 1965: 208).

> [G]enerally unrealistic vocational aspirations . . . keep the young in hope of high paying and prestigeful wage employment. Compounding the situation are ambivalent-to-negative attitudes towards the land itself and towards manual labor, both heritages from slavery (Comitas 1964:45).

These are "unrealistic vocational aspirations" only because, for most young people, they are unattainable; but they make good sense within the context of the overarching system of Vincentian behavioral evaluation. Medicine, nursing, the civil service, etc., are societal vocational ideas which have been internalized by these children via the formal school curriculum and informal home socialization. But although they are occupations which many parents view as ideals for their children, adult villagers, like their rural Jamaican counterparts, show less denigration of the enterprises which they themselves are obliged to carry out as a result of growing economic responsibilities. Parents are also more realistic about the possibility that their children will be able to achieve those vocations which are most prestigious and high paying. It is as if in the process of gaining economic responsibilities that there is a transformation of middle-class occupations from the realm of attainability to that of unattainability, accompanied by an elevation of certain lower-class jobs to a level of social acceptability. In other words, occupational values are 'stretched' to produce a normative dualism between societal occupational ideals and lower-class occupational realities.

The Sexual Division of Labor

The same holds true for the sexual division of labor. The data in Table 5.3 suggest a clear-cut though not absolutely rigid division of labor according to sex. Gender distinctions are most pronounced in skilled and semi-skilled trades and least in subsistence activities, marketing and selling, and professional and managerial positions. Since the itemization in Table 5.3 is based on cultural notions about the most normal and appropriate occupations for men and women, it obscures a flexibility in attitude about women doing men's work. The village ideal is for men to work outside the home and for women to carry out domestic functions (cooking, house-cleaning, child care, etc.). But if she is educated and has domestic help, it is acceptable for a wife to be employed in some prestigious outside activity such as teaching or nursing which matches her training. It is also appropriate for a poor woman to supplement her family's income through some respectable job such as shopkeeping or dressmaking which complements the work of her husband (who may be a farmer or tradesman). Even if she periodically helps her husband in an enterprise which produces the bulk of household income such as assisting for a few days during the planting season, she will be esteemed as a helpful wife. But there is a difference in the minds of villagers between work which either carries high status and thus confers respectability or which complements what the spouse is doing and activities which either carry low esteem (e.g., government road-repair labor), or are male-oriented (e.g., agricultural wage work), or prevent the completion of domestic duties. Though she may gain a reputation for being hard-working and energetic, such a women will suffer in terms of respectability. This is especially so if heavy manual labor--clearing land for planting, digging banks, pulling a seine net ashore--is involved. These are the lowest status and lowest paying occupations in the village, yet the ones in which sexual occupational replaceability is most highly developed. It is the force of economic circumstance which obliges many poor women, particularly unmarried mothers living in households in which there are no adult males, to take on these jobs.

TABLE 5.3 DIVISION OF LABOR BY SEX AND AGE

Activity	Men	Women	Boys under 15	Girls under 15
(a) Domestic Functions				
Sweeping the Yard	occ[a]	yes	yes	yes
Scrubbing floors	rare	yes	rare	yes
Cooking	occ	yes	occ	yes
Diapering children	occ	yes	no	yes
Bathing children	no	yes	no	yes
Supervising and punishing children	yes	yes	yes	yes
Combing children's hair	no	yes	no	yes
Shopping for food	rare	yes	yes	yes
Fetching water	occ	yes	yes	yes
Sweeping the house	rare	yes	yes	yes
Washing clothes	no	yes	no	yes
Ironing clothes	no	yes	no	yes
Gathering fruit, herbs, and spices in yard	occ	yes	yes	yes
Washing dishes	rare	yes	yes	yes
Building a fire for cooking	yes	yes	yes	yes
Looking after fowls and hogs in yard	yes	yes	yes	yes
Mending clothes and sewing	no	yes	no	yes
Gathering and cutting firewood	yes	yes	yes	yes
Making beds	no	yes	yes	yes
Baking	no	yes	no	rare
(b) Agriculture				
Digging banks	yes	rare	no	no
Cutting and burning bush	yes	rare	no	no
Planting	yes	yes	rare	occ
Weeding	occ	yes	no	no
Harvesting root crops	yes	yes	occ	rare
Picking high tree crops	occ	no	yes	no
Picking other fruits and vegetables	occ	yes	occ	rare

(Continued)

[a]occasionally

TABLE 5.3 (Cont.)

Activity	Men	Women	Boys under 15	Girls under 15
(c) *Animal Husbandry*				
Milking cows	yes	no	yes	no
Pasturing cows and donkeys	yes	rare	yes	no
Pasturing sheep and goats	yes	yes	yes	no
Butchering livestock	yes	no	no	no
(d) *Fishing*				
Trapping river fish and crayfish	occ	yes	yes	yes
Seine boat crew	yes	no	rare	no
Line fishing	yes	no	occ	no
Repairing fishing nets and equipment	yes	no	no	no
Pulling seine nets ashore	yes	occ	yes	rare
Knitting seine nets	yes	yes	no	no
Spear fishing	yes	no	yes	no
(e) *Hunting and Gathering*				
Hunting small wild game	yes	no	yes	no
Gathering wild plants and fruits	yes	yes	yes	yes
(f) *Skilled and Semi-skilled Trades*				
Mason	yes	no	app[b]	no
Concrete block maker	yes	no	no	no
Telephone technician	yes	no	no	no
Plumber	yes	no	no	no
Carpenter	yes	no	no	no
Tailor	yes	no	app	no
Painter	yes	no	no	no
Seamstress	no	yes	no	app
Tanner	yes	no	no	no
Shoemaker	yes	no	no	no
Watch repairer	yes	no	no	no
Picture framer	yes	no	no	no
			(Continued)	

[b]apprentice

TABLE 5.3 (Cont.)

Activity	Men	Women	Boys under 15	Girls under 15
(f) Skilled and Semi-skilled Trades				
Shipwright	yes	no	no	no
Tinsmith	yes	no	no	no
Cabinetmaker	yes	no	app	no
(g) Unskilled labor				
Truck loader	yes	no	no	no
Porter	yes	no	no	no
Garbage collector	yes	no	no	no
Stone breaker	yes	no	no	no
Agricultural laborer (for division of tasks see (b) above)	yes	yes	no	no
Repairing roads	yes	yes	no	no
Cutting cord wood	yes	no	no	no
Sawyer	yes	no	no	no
Construction laborer	yes	no	no	no
Stone gatherer	occ	yes	yes	yes
Laundress	no	yes	no	no
Janitor	no	yes	no	no
Street cleaner	yes	yes	no	no
Stevedore	yes	no	no	no
Road driver	yes	no	no	no
(h) Managerial, Professional, or High Status Activities				
Real estate speculator	yes	yes	no	no
Construction oversear	yes	no	no	no
Verger	yes	no	no	no
Priest/Minister/Preacher	yes	no	no	no
Librarian	no	yes	no	no
Church organist	yes	yes	no	no
Piano teacher	no	yes	no	no
Burial society officer	yes	yes	no	no
Estate overseer	yes	no	no	no
Gas station proprietor	yes	no	no	no

(Continued)

TABLE 5.3 (Cont.)

Activity	Men	Women	Boys under 15	Girls under 15
(h) *Managerial, Professional, or High Status Activities*				
Civil servant	yes	no	no	no
Customs officer	yes	no	no	no
Agricultural officer	yes	no	no	no
Draftsman	yes	no	no	no
Nun	no	yes	no	no
Handicraft teacher	no	yes	no	no
Postmistress	no	yes	no	no
Bank teller	occ	yes	no	no
Nurse	no	yes	no	no
Schoolteacher	yes	yes	occ	occ
Town Board Warden	yes	occ	no	no
Politician	yes	occ	no	no
Trade union official	yes	no	no	no
Office clerk	yes	yes	no	no
(i) *Other:*				
Bus driver	yes	no	no	no
Taxi driver	yes	no	no	no
Postman	yes	no	no	no
Policeman	yes	no	no	no
Agricultural station attendant	yes	no	no	no
Pesticide sprayer	yes	no	no	no
Bus conductor	yes	no	yes	no
Watchman	yes	no	no	no
Medical orderly	yes	no	no	no
Truck driver	yes	no	no	no
Forest ranger	yes	no	no	no
Domestic servant	no	yes	no	occ
Sales clerk	no	yes	no	no
Supermarket clerk	yes	yes	no	no
Shopkeeper				
(i) rum shop	yes	yes	no	no
(ii) provision shop	yes	yes	no	no
			(Continued)	

TABLE 5.3 (Cont.)

Activity	Men	Women	Boys under 15	Girls under 15
(i) *Other:*				
Shopkeeper				
(iii) other small shop	occ	yes	no	no
(iv) shop assistant	no	yes	occ	yes
Barber/hairdresser	yes	yes	no	no
Itinerant dry goods vendor	no	yes	no	no
Prostitute	no	yes	no	no
Midwife	no	yes	no	no
Laundress	no	yes	no	no
Chocolate maker	no	yes	no	occ
Coal maker	yes	yes	no	no
Copra maker	yes	yes	no	no
Selling agricultural produce	rare	yes	yes	yes
Selling fish	yes	yes	no	rare
Selling butchered livestock	yes	occ	rare	occ
Security guard	yes	no	no	no
Sales tax collector	yes	no	no	no
Time-keeper	yes	no	no	no

Unemployment and Underemployment

A consequence of the circumvention of the ideal pattern of the gender-based distribution of tasks among adult females and high vocational aspirations among young people of both sexes is much higher rates of unemployment and underemployment than among older villagers. Nearly 30 percent of the male labor force under 20 was totally inactive in 1970, as opposed to only 2 percent of the 20 and older cohort. The extent of female unemployment is masked by the domestic duties of those who are not employed outside the home. Still, the proportion of women primarily employed outside the home is much higher among those between 30 and 60 than among those between 15 and 30.

Occupational preferences alone do not account for higher rates of unemployment among younger people. Comitas's (1964:45) suggestion that young Jamaican males are sometimes unemployed because they do not normally maintain their own households and hence have few economic responsibilities and low financial needs applies to Leeward Village as well. Adolescent and teenage girls and young unmarried mothers who are living in their natal households also have fewer economic burdens than older women although, unlike young men, domestic chores take up most of their time if older household members are working outside the home. More importantly, a concomitant of high teenage unemployment may be that it reduces economic competition with older persons, individuals whose duties make them in greater need of the limited resources and opportunities they are permitted access to in both the village and the wider island society.

Underemployment, also severe among young villagers, is a problem which affects the poor at large. According to the 1970 population census, 22 percent of the village male working population and 32 percent of the female working population were employed for less than 7 out of the previous 12 months (Census Research Programme 1973:206).

OCCUPATIONAL COMPLEXITY

The restrictions imposed on the life-chances of the village poor have been instrumental in producing village occupational intricacy. This complexity is expressed by (1) the absolute number of different jobs engaged in by villagers, (2) a distinction between self-employment and wage work, (3) a dichotomy between village and extra-village economic pursuits, including temporary and seasonal labor migration, and (4) occupational multiplicity.

Table 5.4 lists a total of 76 different full- and part-time jobs found among lower-class village adults and Table 5.5 summarizes the primary occupations among the 137-member labor force in a random sample of 100, or nearly 25 percent, of the households in the village. Assuming that the same proportion of work force to non-work force members in Table 5.5 holds for the entire population, then the 76 occupations in Table 5.4 are distributed among less than 600 persons, for an average of one job for every eight working villagers. Certain occupations are predominant. Of the 41 activities in Table 5.5, farming is the most important, employing one out every five persons. Fishing, agricultural labor, shopkeeping, road work, domestic service, and teaching also are important vocations. The teaching category is made up mainly of uncertified teenage instructors from upper- and middle-lower-class homes. Farming, agricultural wage-labor, and fishing--primary food production activities--occupy over one-third of the work force while the whole area of food production and sale includes nearly one-half of the sample work force. Construction and repair jobs are major vocations as well employing nearly one in every five adults in the sample.

TABLE 5.4 LEEWARD VILLAGE LOWER-CLASS OCCUPATIONS

Males

agricultural station attendant	postman
barber	lay preacher
bus conductor	quarry laborer
bus driver	road gang driver
butcher	sales tax collector
cabinet maker	security guard
carpenter	seine fisherman
cattle raiser	sexton
concrete block maker	shipwright
construction laborer	shoemaker
construction overseer	spear fisherman
forest guard	stevedore
garbage collector	stone breaker
hunter	tailor
line fisherman	tanner
mason	telephone technician
medical orderly	timekeeper
painter	tinsmith
pesticide sprayer	truck driver
picture framer	truck loader
plumber	watchmaker
policeman	watchman
porter	wood-cutter

Females

chocolate maker	janitor
cook	laundress
dam fisherman	midwife
domestic servant	prostitute
hairdresser	sales clerk
handicrafter	seamstress
	(Continued)

144

TABLE 5.4 (Cont.)

Females

handicraft instructor   small-scale vendor
itinerant vendor

Both sexes

agricultural laborer   road gang laborer
agricultural produce vendor   seine hauler
baker   seine net knitter
burial society official   shopkeeper
charcoal maker   small-stock raiser
copra maker   stone gatherer
farmer   street cleaner
fish vendor   supermarket clerk
primary school teacher

TABLE 5.5   SAMPLE OF WORKING POPULATION CLASSIFIED BY
            PRIMARY OCCUPATION AND OCCUPATIONAL
            CATEGORY

Category	Occupation	No.	%
Production and sale of food	farmer	27	19.7
	fisherman	11	8.0
	fish vendor	2	1.5
	agricultural laborer	10	7.3
	shopkeeper	10	7.3
	grocery clerk	2	1.5
	animal herder	2	1.5
	estate overseer	1	0.7
	chocolate vendor	1	0.7
	Sub-total	66	48.2
Construction	mason	4	2.9
	carpenter	4	2.9
	painter	4	2.9
	road laborer	9	6.6
	construction laborer	1	0.7
	quarry laborer	1	0.7

(Continued)

TABLE 5.5 (Cont.)

Category	Occupation	No.	%
Construction	building contractor	1	0.7
	apprentice mason	1	0.7
	Sub-total	25	18.3
Domestic service	servant	8	5.8
	washerwoman	1	0.7
	Sub-total	9	6.6
Clothing manufacture	tailor	1	0.7
	apprentice tailor	3	2.2
	seamstress	1	0.7
	apprentice seamstress	2	1.5
	Sub-total	7	5.1
Education	primary school teacher	7	5.1
	handicrafts teacher	1	0.7
	Sub-total	8	5.8
Other skilled trades	handicrafter	2	1.5
	telephone technician	1	0.7
	forest guard	1	0.7
	Sub-total	4	2.9
Other semi-skilled and unskilled trades	bus driver	1	0.7
	stevedore	1	0.7
	garbage collector	1	0.7
	porter	1	0.7
	truck loader	1	0.7
	bus conductor	1	0.7
	gardener	1	0.7
Other semi-skilled and unskilled trades	shop clerk	1	0.7
	seine knitter	1	0.7
	Sub-total	10	7.3

(Continued)

146

TABLE 5.5 (Cont.)

Category	Occupation	No.	%
Clerical	office clerk	1	0.7
	time-keeper	1	0.7
	gas station manager	1	0.7
	Sub-total	3	2.2
Unemployed		5	3.7
	Total	137	100.0

Work and Time

There is a complex interrelation between self employment and wage labor, on the one hand, and full and part-time work, on the other. Table 5.6, which represents a rearrangement of the data in Table 5.4, lists 9 full-time own-account activities, 29 part-time self-employed enterprises, 22 full-time wage-labor tasks, and 16 part-time wage work activities engaged in by villagers. Of the 35 *different* self employment activities, 6, or 17 percent, are carried out solely on a full-time basis. Of the 36 *different* wage-labor jobs, 20, or 56 percent, are done exclusively through full-time effort. Several occupations are carried out both full- and part-time. The most important of these are selling agricultural produce, agricultural wage-labor, farming, line and seine fishing, dressmaking, and petty-commodity vending.

TABLE 5.6 LOWER-CLASS VOCATIONS

Own-account occupations: full-time activity
agricultural produce vendor   plumber
carpenter   seamstress
cattle raiser   shopkeeper
farmer   small-scale vendor
mason

Own-account occupations: part-time activity

agricultural produce vendor   preacher
barber   prostitute
cabinetmaker   seamstress
                                     (Continued)

TABLE 5.6 (Cont.)

Own-account occupations: *part-time activity*

chocolate maker	seine net knitter
charcoal maker	shipwright
copra maker	shoemaker
dam fisherman	small-scale vendor
farmer	small stock raiser
fish vendor	spear fisherman
hairdresser	stone breaker
handicrafter	stone gatherer
hunter	tanner
itinerant vendor	tinsmith
midwife	watchmaker
picture framer	

Wage-labor occupations: *full time activity*

agricultural laborer	policeman
agricultural station attendant	porter
bus conductor	postman
butcher	quarry laborer
concrete block maker	salesclerk
domestic servant	schoolteacher
forest ranger	supermarket clerk
garbage collector	telephone technician
handicraft instructor	time-keeper
medical orderly	truck loader
pesticide sprayer	watchman

Wage-labor occupations: *part-time activity*

agricultural laborer	road driver
burial society official	road laborer
construction laborer	sales tax collector
construction overseer	security guard
cook	sexton
janitor	stevedore
laundress	street cleaner
librarian	time-keeper

Extra-Village Employment

About 130 lower-class villagers, or some 20 percent of the adult working population, work outside the village for all or part of the year. The jobs done, their setting, their permanence, and the type of movement they require distinguish work found outside the community. Some 20 percent of the 130 villagers work in Kingstown, nearly 50 percent travel to Barbados, St. Kitts, and the United States as seasonal farm workers, and over 30 percent are employed in the St. Vincent Grenadines or in parts of St. Vincent other than Kingstown.

Full-time work involves nearly 30 percent of the extra-village labor force, 66 percent are employed outside the community on a seasonal or other temporary basis, and the remaining 4 percent work in other parts of the island part-time.

Sixty-six percent of those engaged in extra-village employment are temporary or seasonal migrants absent from the island for between three and six months, 30 percent are daily commuters, and the rest return to their homes only on weekends.

Most people employed outside Leeward Village but within St. Vincent are skilled and semi-skilled wage workers who commute daily to their jobs in Kingstown and other parts of St. Vincent. The most common occupations in Kingstown are journeyman or apprentice carpenter and mason and such unskilled and semi-skilled jobs as bakery apprentice, porter, stevedore, housepainter, and truck loader. The main activities outside the capital are truck and bus driving, truck loading, carpentry, and masonry.

Occupational Multiplicity

Comitas (1966:44) has suggested that "occupational pluralists" are an economic type different from but related to peasants, farmers, and plantation workers which results from the fact that "no one vocational alternative is sufficiently lucrative for individual full-time specialization." Although the proportion of men systematically engaged in several occupations is much lower than the 63-79 percent reported by Comitas for four Jamaican villages, occupational multiplicity in the village is still important. Indeed, in one way the Vincentian situation is more striking than the Jamaican one since occupational multiplicity in Leeward Village also involves women. Moreover, Comitas's (1964:49) own figures may be inflated since he deals only with households in which at least one member is a fisherman or fish vendor.

The working population in the sample of 100 households (Table 5.5) contains 84 men and 53 women. Of the 84 men, 25, or 30 percent, are simultaneously involved in two or more jobs. Of the 53 women, 13, or 25 percent, are engaged in more than one occupation. In all, out of the total of 137 men and women, 38, or 28 percent, have multiple own-account or wage-labor jobs.

As might be expected, the secondary jobs of these 38 villagers include many popular primary vocations. On the one hand, food production, especially farming, agricultural wage-labor, and fishing predominate as secondary occupations among those who are principally engaged in non-food producing activities; on the other, farming, fishing, agricultural and road labor when carried out as primary activities are commonly combined with unrelated or complementary occupations such as construction work.

Occupational multiplicity in Leeward Village also has a temporal dimension in which certain activities are carried out sequentially on a seasonal or life-cycle basis. For men, the annual pattern usually combines farming and periodic government wage work, the former often divided between own-account cultivation and agricultural labor. Work for the government typically means a total of only a few weeks employment on a road-repair gang divided into blocks of three or four days each. Among some men fishing and/or seasonal labor migration are added to these activities to produce a pattern involving migration to Barbados to cut cane from January to late March or early April, several weeks of inactivity, and two or three short periods of road repair interspersed with occasional fishing or agricultural wage-work and/or self-employed farming.

The life cycle dimension of occupational multiplicity refers to the involvement of many poor villagers in a half dozen or more different wage-labor and self-employed enterprises during their long working careers. Among men, combinations of fishing during youth and young adulthood, and independent farming, agricultural wage-labor, road repair, temporary or recurrent migration, and a host of unskilled manual labor activities during the later stages of the life cycle forms a common pattern. Among many women, domestic service, laundering clothes, part-time dressmaking, road repair labor, agricultural wage-work, peasant cultivation, and petty retailing have been important occupations during their working careers.

Case No. 1. Ivan Windsor, an impoverished villager in his mid-fifties, never attended school and began to work full-time from the age of 14. At various times he has worked as a fisherman, road laborer, unskilled construction worker, agricultural wage-laborer, and charcoal maker. He now divides his time between sharecropping and wood-cutting. Many villagers suspect that Windsor also engages in praedial larceny to help support is large family.

Case No. 2. Wilbur Harris, a lower-class farmer in his late-50s, began working in his mid-teens. In the village, he has been a wage-laborer, fisherman, sharecropper, estate wage-laborer, charcoal maker and seller, woodcut-ter, government road-repair worker, and small-game hunter. During the 1930s, Harris migrated to the Domini-can Republic to cut sugar cane. During the Second World War, he sailed to Aruba where he was employed as a common laborer in an oil refinery.

Case No. 3. Nellie Collins, a single mother in her mid-thirties, is now employed as a part-time domestic servant. This income is supplemented by the sale of home-made ice cream and a local curry dish at village dances, intermit-tent dressmaking, and the sale of estate and home-grown agricultural produce. In the past, she has done peasant farming, has run a small shop, and has laundered clothes. During the early 1960s she went to Trinidad for a year where she worked as a domestic servant in a middle-class household.

Case No. 4. Selma Walker is a poor villager in her early-forties. She has variously worked as a road laborer, seamstress, laundress, domestic servant, shopkeeper, and waitress. Unlike most lower-class village women, she has rarely done any sort of farming. Currently, dressmaking is her sole occupation.

Each of the features which make up occupational complexity in Leeward Village is an adaptive response to the limitations imposed by Vincentian socio-economic organization. In particular, occupation-al complexity counterbalances some of the effects of Vincentian economic stagnation and class stratification by granting poor villagers a degree of maneuverability in the economic arena. Of course, the unreliability of and low return from most of the occupations available to lower-class villagers have resulted in a preference for stable, well-paying wage labor. But the activities which provide remunerative, full-time employment are scarce and competition for them is great. Only a few villagers have been able to secure permanent, albeit not highly paying, positions as truck or bus drivers, stevedores, supermarket clerks, and the like. Although the resultant proliferation of low paying, short term occupations is itself a manifestation of Vincentian economic stagnation, the manner in which villagers take advantage of what little opportunity there is *to make a bread* is an indication of the adjustments they have had to make to their marginal socio-economic position. The constraints which force many women to ignore the culturally defined sexual division of labor, for example, should be viewed as a manifestation of the elasticity that must be present in the occupational sphere so that the limited opportunities that are offered can be utilized.

Many of the vocations pursued by villagers demand little training, cash outlay, or long-term commitment. Many of them also can be carried full- or part-time, on an independent or wage basis, and in combination with other enterprises. These features underlie the pattern of occupational multiplicity and have the effect of maximizing the possibility of individual and family security. For example, the greater number of own-account activities performed on a part-time than on a full-time basis (Table 5.5) is the result of being able to carry out independent jobs when wage work is unavailable. Thus line fishing, wood cutting, small-scale farming, stone gathering, and similar activities may be pursued when other labor outlets (e.g., road work, seasonal migration, and agricultural wage-labor) are scarce or absent. Similarly, agriculture may be undertaken alongside such activities as road and agricultural labor which do not normally occupy a full working day. Occupational multiplicity also minimizes economic risk by spreading an individual's labor over several different enterprises. Given the uncertainty of return from agriculture, for example, it is necessary to ensure that some cash will always be coming in by engaging in other short-term jobs (road repair work, seasonal migration, agricultural wage-labor, etc.) during the growing season. Finally, for many poor villagers, occupational multiplicity is simply a necessary survival mechanism since few extant occupations can satisfy even minimal subsistence.

CASH AND SUBSISTENCE OCCUPATIONS

Fishing, agricultural wage-labor, government road repair work, carpentry/masonry, shopkeeping, and domestic service are the primary activities of 56, or 42 percent, of the 132 members of the working population in Table 5.5. Peasant cultivation, the single most important primary and secondary occupation in the village, is treated separately in the next chapter.

Fishing

Fishing is the main occupation of some 8 percent of village men (Table 5.5). It is an important secondary activity as well. Several women are also employed part-time as fish vendors and net knitters while both males and females, including young boys and the occasional girl, regularly help pull seine nets ashore. The overall result is that the entire fishing process involves the full-time or occasional participation of nearly 15 percent of adult villagers, almost all of them members of the village poor.

Fishing is mainly an activity of young and early middle-aged men. Of the 11 fishermen in Table 5.5, seven are under 40. Fishing attracts younger people primarily because it demands no formal training and little if any financial outlay, and it may be carried out on a part-time or casual basis. Fishing is also a highly visible activity many of whose onshore tasks take place adjacent to the commercial hub of the village. Young teenage boys readily help pull boats and seine nets ashore. Those who show a particular interest in fishing are sometimes recruited on an *ad hoc* basis to fill out a seine boat crew whose regular members are absent. Seine fishing is also an exciting activity for a teenage boy. It is a collective hunting-like enterprise which demands short periodic bursts of intense physical effort. The cash rewards, meager in the long run, can be very profitable when the occasional large catch is made.

Fishing as a vocation commands little respect or prestige in the village, and although there are older men who have been fishermen all their lives, many teenagers and young adults treat it in a cavalier fashion. Yet it is in this lack of commitment to fishing--a quality which is a consequence of its unpredictability and un-reliability as a productive technique--that its significance as an occupational category lies. Fishing in Leeward Village is an inshore technique and the fishing grounds are the bay itself and several banks close to shore. It usually involves the passive and often frustrating exercise of waiting for an illusive quarry to enter a narrow ecological niche. Seine net fishing, for example, is confined to the shallowest portions of the bay, an area which rarely attracts large schools of fish. Though line fishing involves a much larger marine arena, it is generally considered to be an inefficient and time consuming technique (cf. Bottemanne 1959). As a result, earnings in most forms of fishing average a few dollars a day at most and often several weeks may pass without any fish being caught. Low and unpredictable material returns are met by fluidity in fishing crew membership as well as the constant entry into and exit from all kinds of fishing. Seine boat crews, for example, are mainly temporary 'groups' always gaining and losing members as more reliable economic alternatives are presented or withdrawn. Even those who may be considered full-time fishermen--perhaps half of all the men involved--take advantage of alternative economic opportunities when they become available. A seine boat captain, for example, will work as a road repair laborer from time to time during the year while many of his 'regular' crew will migrate seasonally to Barbados to cut cane. Still, the ease of entry into fishing means that those who might otherwise be unemployed can take advantage of it when they need to. Similarly, fishing is an activity which can be carried out part-time or integrated with other activities. Seines are thrown at or near daybreak or in early evening in accordance with the movements of the species that enter Leeward Bay. This enables crew members to combine fishing with other work such as self-employed trades and agriculture.

There are many fishing techniques employed, indicating an effort to maximize the use of the marine environment despite the presence of a limited technology. These techniques are: net fishing, line fishing, pot fishing, *tri-tri* fishing, spear fishing, and gathering. There are three types of net fishing: *seine fishing, net fishing*, and *seiner*. Line fishing also has several varieties: *banking, trawling* (also called *towing*), *glass box fishing, shore fishing*, and *rodding*.

Outfitting a seine is an expensive proposition. Although many of the materials used, including the two small rowboats and 23 foot seine boat, are constructed on the south coast of the island or in the Grenadines, the $1,200 or more total cost of net and boats is beyond the means of most seine boat captains. Of the five seines in the village, only two are owned by boat captains. Of the three others, one is owned by a prosperous non-fishing villager and two by overseas migrants.

There is much reciprocity and camaraderie among fishermen. Assistance in repairing nets, hauling boats out of the water, pulling a seine net ashore, and filling out a crew that is short a member or two is usually freely given. Fisherman are said *to live loving with one another* and disputes, particularly among seine captains, are normally quickly patched up. Cooperation among members of different crews is reinforced by the often close friendships among and between crews manifested by collective rum-drinking and general socializing. All these examples of reciprocity function to spread the risks and reduce the uncertainty of inshore fishing. Without them fishing would represent an even less attractive occupation than it does.

In theory, seine fishing is a commercial venture based on the marketing of fish according prices set by supply and demand in which some of the profit is reinvested to enlarge the size of the net. In practice, however, it tends to be a subsistence activity in which there is often little left for sale once the informal distribution of the small catch among the principles has taken place.

When the occasional large haul occurs, a more regularized sharing takes place. About 15 percent of the value of the week's yield is divided among the 10 or so persons who had regularly assisted in pulling the seine ashore during the preceding week. Many of these people are members of other crews. The remaining money is divided into three portions with the owner of the seine receiving two parts and the captain and crew equally dividing the remaining share. Twelve to fifteen percent of the owner's portion is then given to the captain.

Net fishing requires a much smaller crew and financial outlay than *seine fishing*. There are three fishing nets in the village, two of which belong to non-fisherman seine owners. The technique is used exclusively for catching small, beaked, seasonally-available fish called *balahoo* and involves three men, including the captain, using two small boats and a fine-mesh net 120 feet long and 16 feet wide.

Seiner is a trapping technique for catching tiny fish in a 'net' composed of extended sections of burlap sacks whose corners are held up by two people. It takes place at night with the fish attracted almost ashore by a lighted kerosene torch held by a third person. *Seiner* is a time consuming and not very productive way of catching fish and is carried out on an irregular basis by only a few poor villagers.

More popular are the various kinds of line fishing. Some types require a two-man crew while others can be carried out by a single person. *Banking*, a stationary fishing method on one of the 20 known banks outside Leeward Bay, involves the use of different kinds of lines, hooks, and bait. *Glass-box fishing* uses nearly the same equipment except for the *glass box*, a wooden cube with an opening at one end and a glass plate at the other. The box is partially submerged over the coral formations in and around the bay and the line manipulated in the direction of any fish that are spotted. *Trawling* (also called *towing*) is a mobile technique aimed at catching large species such as shark and barracuda using a course line and large multi-baited hook. The line is allowed to extend well behind the row boat while it is *pulled* through deep water by one or two rowers. *Shore fishing* takes place in late evening from the pier or beach front and involves the use of a line or a strung bamboo pole. *Rodding* resembles *shore fishing* and involves hooking small river species during the day or early evening using a rod and line.

Pot fishing is popular among several line fishermen. Fish pots constructed from chicken wire and thin strips of wood are baited with fruit and vegetable scraps and set on five inshore reefs and banks.

Tri-tri fishing is a technique pursued mainly by adult women and involves the trapping of tiny river fish in or near the mouth of the Leeward River using discarded burlap sacks weighed down by stones and covered with shrubbery. Since *tri-tri* are considered a delicacy in the island and fetch a high market price, most of them are sold rather than used for home consumption.

Spear fishing (also called *stick fishing*) is carried out on an occasional basis by a small number of teenage boys and young adults. Home made or store-bought spear guns are used, and fishing takes place over the corral formations along the side of Leeward Bay and neighboring inlets.

The gathering of crayfish and other crustaceans under river rocks and stones in the upper part of the valley is an activity which is mainly confined to young boys, girls, and women. Unless a large amount is collected, all the produce is used for home consumption.

Agricultural Wage-Labor

Agricultural labor is engaged in by the poorest villagers of both sexes in nearly equal proportion. The entire village agricultural labor force is made up of about 70 villagers, or about 12 percent of the adult working population. A little over half are employed on a more-or-less regular basis. The remainder are casually employed on both large and small holdings. At least half of the men and many of the women have other jobs as well. Wages in agricultural employment are the lowest in the island: in 1970, men and women were paid $0.90 and $0.70 for a half day's work, respectively.

156

Road Labor

Although road labor involving construction, repair, and cleaning work is considered to be the least desirable job in the village, it is a common primary and secondary occupation in the community. The rate of pay--$0.95 per day for men and $0.75 for per day for women in 1970--is only marginally better than agricultural wage-labor. The sporadic and short-term nature of the work--few villagers receive more than 30 days employment a year--mean that no men and only a few women engage in road labor to the exclusion of other activities. Unlike agricultural labor, road work is heavily dominate by women even though nearly all gang drivers are male. Road labor is a less physically strenuous activity than agricultural work and is easily integrated with domestic activities since notice of employment is issued well in advance in small blocks ranging from a few days to two weeks. Yet the fact that road labor, a highly irregular, low status job, is the *primary* vocation of so many women underscores the extent of underemployment in the community.

Road work includes cleaning drains, cutting down foliage that is obstructing traffic, street sweeping, gathering stones used in road repair, and patching pot holes. The last of these involves the repair of large depressions in the public roadways in the Leeward Village area by a gang of between 10 and 15 workers including a driver. The sequence of work includes filling the holes with crushed rock (the job of the women) after they have been swept clean (the job of the men) and covered with tar (the job of the driver and a male assistant). The stones are then pounded down (the task of the men) and covered with another layer of tar (the job of the driver and his helper). This a time-consuming and labor intensive effort whose results are short lived. Of this technique of road repair it has been said:

> Between 1957 and 1965, repairs and maintenance of roads averaged $300,000 a year and this expenditure was met from the local budget. It should be pointed out that road maintenance was partially used to solve the problem of unemployment, consequently persons were employed where equipment could have been used more economically and effectively. Government should try to find more effective avenues of employment for the unemployed (University of the West Indies Development Mission 1969:94).

Efficient or not, road work is an important supplementary source of

157

support for poor villagers. But road work also has a political dimension. The appointment of road drivers who received between $1.50 and $2.00 per day in 1970, or more than double the amount paid to ordinary workers, is based on support for the party in power and a change in government always brings a new set of drivers. Indeed, candidates for the new positions are pre-selected during political campaigns by influential middle-class villagers who submit their preferences to the elected district representative for consideration by the Public Works Department. Politically active villagers may also influence the choice of gang workers although most of this is in the hands of the driver who makes the selection by political affiliation, friendship, and kinship. Since friendship also follows party lines and since kin often have the same political leanings, the determining factor is support of the party in power. There are many more candidates than there are jobs and this engenders considerable resentment and promises of political retribution--a promise which is always fulfilled--on the part of opposition supporters.

Carpentry and Masonry

Masonry and carpentry are treated together as a single occupation because they are often carried out by the same person, because they are closely linked construction activities, and because they involve similar degrees of skill, training, remuneration, and status evaluation. Boys between 15 and 18 enter the trades by attaching themselves to a successful builder for a two or three year apprenticeship period. Although a few boys are employed in the village, most apprenticeship takes place in Kingstown or the Grenadines and involves weekly or monthly commuting. Wages are dependent on the location of the work. In 1970, apprentices in the village received $1.00 per day, those in Kingstown about $1.50 per day, and those in the Grenadines a standard rate of $2.00 per day.

There is often considerable movement from one contractor to another and of those who enter these trades few complete the necessary informal training to become independent builders. The monotony and tedium of the apprenticeship tasks, disputes with employers, the long absences from home when working in the Grenadines, the habitual lay-offs characteristic of all kinds of construction work, the anticipation of overseas migration, and the relative absence of economic responsibilities among young men contribute to a rapid turnover among apprentices. Those who persist,

158

however, are rewarded with a fairly reliable income. The most successful village carpenters and masons earned well over $250 a month in 1987 by combining short-term self-employed village construction work with longer term wage-labor in Kingstown and the Grenadines.

Shopkeeping

The presence in 1970 of a grocery store, 17 small food shops and *parlors*, 9 rum shops, and 3 bakeries in a community of 2,200 people indicates how important retailing is in Leeward Village. Together these 30 establishments employed some 45 villagers on a full- or part-time basis. Shopkeeping, is viewed as a desirable occupation, especially if it can be carried out on a large scale. Nearly all lower-class returned migrants give some thought to opening up a business of some kind and the most successful village shops are owned by such persons. But most shops are tiny and poorly stocked, and their owners nearly always have some other source of income to supplement their meager retailing earnings. Many shops also have a short life span. Low incomes, intense competition for a cash-poor clientele, defaults on the extension of credit, and political and personal disputes with customers result in the closing down of two or three shops every year. But the total number remains fairly constant--32 in 1971 and 36 in 1980--as new 'entrepreneurs' try their hand at retailing. Most shops also have a very limited inventory: a hundred pound bag or two of sugar and/or flour and/or rice, a couple of cases of *sweet drinks* [carbonated beverages], a few cartons of cigarettes, a small assortment of tinned goods, and several dozen bread rolls. These are occasionally supplemented by home-made confections, headache tablets, and ground provisions. The largest shops, all but one of which is located on the main road, are much better stocked and provide a good income for their middle- and upper-lower class owners. In addition to selling such staples as sugar, flour, and rice, they also carry *sweet drinks* of various types, a variety of imported canned goods, salted meat and fish, patent medicines and toiletries, and bread and cake. Retailing is largely a female enterprise and only seven of the shops devoted to the sale of food and/or rum--a bakery, two food shops, and four rum shops--are operated solely by men. Men also own and manage the non-food businesses, a handicraft shop, a shoemaker shop and a tailor shop. Almost all the smallest businesses are run either by married women whose husbands are involved in other activities or by single women who depend on shopkeeping for a large portion of their income.

Domestic Service

It is easy to underestimate the role of domestic service from the data in Table 5.5 which show that is an activity among less than 15 percent of the female working population. Supplementary case studies show that at least twice that many women have worked as servants at some time in their lives, many for several years. There are also many village girls and women currently employed as domestics in Kingstown who return home for only a day or two once a month and, therefore, were not included as part of the village population for census purposes. When employed in wealthy Leeward Village homes, the usual wage in 1986 was $50.00 per month plus meals. In some households where the domestic is an adolescent or teenage girl, board is also provided and a quasi-kinship relationship established if the girl is employed for several years. Although higher wages plus room and board are offered in private homes and hotels in Kingstown, like their teenaged male counterparts, many girls quit their jobs after a short time because of the confinement of urban employment, dissatisfaction with working conditions, or a desire to return to old friends and familiar surroundings.

HOUSEHOLD ECONOMIC ORGANIZATION

The economic organization of Leeward Village is largely a product of the occupational activities of its members. Work and wealth also affect household size and kinship composition, features which are discussed in Part III. Two aspects of domestic economy are treated here: household economic cooperation and patterns of food consumption. To highlight the main features of the domestic economy, it is assumed that those who occupy a common dwelling share the same food supply and that households contain one or more adults and two or more children of various ages. Although often this is not the case, it is best to avoid unnecessary complications at this point.

Economic Cooperation

A description of economic cooperation in Leeward Village requires treatment of the beliefs and practices about the division of domestic labor, the organization of outside economic activities, the sources of household support, and the control of property and earnings.

The Division of Domestic Labor. The division of domestic labor according age and sex is summarized in Table 5.3. As elsewhere in the Caribbean, domestic activities are the domain of women, girls, and, to a lesser extent, boys. Still, as the table makes clear, men are not excluded from the home scene as is implied in most Caribbean ethnographies (e.g., Philpott 1973:138-140; R.T. Smith 1956; Wilson 1973). The role of men in the home has been pushed to the side partly because domestic tasks have been lumped together in a unitary manner. For example, if all activities involving the care of children are treated as a single duty, then it is an area which obviously falls to women and girls. A finer analysis, however, reveals that men are not excluded from the domestic scene. When they are at home, they often take or share responsibility for supervising and punishing children. They also help prepare meals by fetching water from the roadside pipe, gathering fruits, herbs, and spices planted in the yard, pealing vegetables, and building the cooking fire. The feeding of chickens and other small animals kept in the yard is often done by men as well. On occasion, men also help with such 'female' jobs as sweeping the yard and diapering and bathing their children. In most households, there is also a degree of division of domestic work among the children based on sex and relative age. It is common, for example, for the eldest boy to be in charge of sweeping the yard and feeding the chickens while one of the girls has as her main job the sweeping out of the house. All children, however, are obliged to fetch water when it is needed.

Extra-Household Economic Activities. There is a symbiotic relationship between domestic and extra-domestic economic activities. For example, when all the adults are employed outside the home, household tasks fall to the remaining members regardless of age. It is common for a 12 year old girl to do almost all the cooking, cleaning, washing, and child care when older household members are away working. Conversely, when adult women are not employed outside the home, its younger members play a much smaller role in the day-to-day domestic economy.

The household and outside work life of spouses also complement each other. Whether living common-law or married a man is held responsible for providing the material means in cash or kind for feeding, clothing, and sheltering dependent household members while his spouse is charged with ensuring that domestic activities are successfully completed. She may do so by carrying them out herself or by making sure that someone else does them if she is otherwise occupied.

Outside the house and yard itself coordination of productive activities and complementarity of economic roles are far less common. When two or more adult household members are working, rarely are these activities the same. Task consolidation and occupational symbiosis are also uncommon. Only 18 of the sample of 100 village households are corporate productive units based on the extra-domestic cooperation of two or more of its members. When collective work does occur, it usually involves either casual agricultural help given by a woman to her spouse, or a division of labor in which the man farms and the woman sells any surplus produce.

Occupational multiplicity for individuals corresponds to occupational heterogeneity for households. Both arrangements ensure minimal economic viability by allowing the manipulation of different ventures, no single one of which can meet individual and household needs. The varied sources of household income summarized in Table 5.7 is another index of domestic economic variability. The table lists the primary source of support among the sample of 100 households. In 74 cases, support is derived mainly from the efforts of resident members; in 17, mostly from relatives outside St. Vincent; and in 9, mainly from contributions from outside the household but from within the island. Moreover, 87 of the 100 units have more than one source of support: 24 have two sources, 23 have three, 23 have four, and 17 have five.

Most support sources, whether external or internal, are not linked. Given the unreliability and low rewards obtained from most lower-class occupations, a collective effort, especially one based on common household membership, is an inappropriate economic strategy. This is partly because a group enterprise might reduce the ability of villagers to take advantage of periodic short-term economic options since the efforts of several persons would have to be quickly mobilized and coordinated. In a situation of constantly shifting economic prospects, an individual effort is more expedient than a joint one. Moreover, for most lower-class households the best economic strategy is for each adult member to pursue a different activity to reduce the risk that the failure of any one of them will critically affect household well-being.

TABLE 5.7 PRIMARY SOURCE OF ECONOMIC SUPPORT AMONG THE SAMPLE OF 100 CORESIDENTIAL UNITS

Source of Support	No. of units
Own-account activities of head	31
Wage-labor of head	24
Remittances from daughter(s) of head or head's spouse	6
Wage-labor of resident children of head or head's spouse	5
Own-account activities of resident spouse	4
Own-account activities of other members	4
Child support by non-resident fathers for children of head or head's spouse	4
Remittances from son(s) of head or head's spouse	4
Wage-labor of resident spouse	3
Own-account activities of resident children of head or head's spouse	3
Remittances from male consensual mate	3
Remittances from husband	2
Remittances from other relatives	2
Child support by non-resident fathers for children of head or head's spouse's children	1
Support from son in St. Vincent but outside Leeward Village	1
Support from daughter in St. Vincent but outside Leeward Village	1
Support from relatives in Leeward Village	1
Poor relief from government	1
Total	100

There is also little scope for household-based collective enterprise. Only the largest shops involve the joint industry of spouses while skilled and semi-skilled trades and wage-labor jobs do not lend themselves to household-based group effort. The activity which best supports the economic cooperation of household members is agriculture. Yet only one-half of village households have any access to land, and most cultivators find that they cannot even satisfy subsistence needs from their small holdings. In addition, the risks involved in farming--the failure or theft of crops, low market prices, and so on--make it unwise to jointly concentrate in it, particularly if there are more reliable jobs available. Agriculturalists are well aware of these risks and react to them by attempting to increase the number of work options open to them. Thus, a renter or sharecropper will leave his growing crops under the care of his spouse while he migrates to cut cane in Barbados and an owner-cultivator will work as a road laborer whenever employment becomes available, visiting his garden intermittently during the period of work.

Property and Earnings. One of the most important aspirations of villagers is the ownership of house. Possession of a dwelling and house-spot ends the payment of rent and the possibility of arbitrary eviction. House ownership also symbolizes social independence and a measure of financial security while the renting of a dwelling is viewed as a sign of material impoverishment. Villagers are not looked down upon simply because they do not own a house. Still, their unstable renter status is occasionally disparagingly referred to in arguments: "You feel you is somebody? You na ha un house!" But as has already been shown, nearly 30 percent of the sample of 100 coresidential units are living in homes which they do not own. A new board house measuring only 9 feet by 16 feet in 1970 required at least $1,500 for material and labor, a sum well beyond the means of most poor villagers. Acquiring a house spot is an even more expensive proposition. In 1971, a two-storied house on a lot measuring 32 feet by 64 feet sold for over $7,000. The house itself was valued at about $1,000.

Regardless of its mode of tenure, a house must be equipped with all sorts of necessities. Responsibility for acquiring beds, tables, chairs, cooking pots, dishes and glassware, and a china cabinet falls mainly on the head. Other working members are expected to help by purchasing things they themselves need or by making cash contributions to the head. Except for undivided family property and the few items which are jointly purchased by its members, household property is individually owned. Parents will even give their young children small animals (a chick, a piglet, or a lamb) to raise as their own and to dispose of as they wish. Similarly, except for those households in which the earnings of teenage members are expropriated by the head, the earnings and savings of members may be independently distributed so long as some contribution is made to the support of the home.

Compared to many peasant communities, the material wealth of the Leeward Village household is low. The total of household items, excluding clothing, owned by a family containing seven people, two adults and five children ranging between infancy and 14 years of age, is listed in Table 5.8. Rita Keane, 32, and Bobs Clarke, 34, have been living together for two years in the house that Rita inherited from her grandparents. It is a wooden structure, 16 feet by 17 feet, containing three rooms, a *drawing room* opening off from the front entrance and two bedrooms, one of which is used for storing tools and clothing. The house is valued at $1,000 and is in good repair. There is no kitchen in the 32 feet by 32 feet treeless yard and all cooking is done on a pile of stones at the side of the house. Water for drinking, washing, and cooking is drawn from a public stand-pipe on the main road some 40 feet from the end of the yard. Bobs is regularly employed as a truck loader and earns $7.00 for a six day, 48 hour week. Rita does not work regularly although she occasionally earns a dollar or two as seamstress.

As the table shows, Rita owns most of the household items, having inherited then from her grandparents or acquired then before she met Bobs. It is because of her ownership of the house and most of its possessions that Rita considers herself and is considered by villagers to be the head of the unit.

The value of the items in Table 5.8 is well under $1,000. By far the most expensive object is the sewing machine. But there are many households which exhibit much greater material poverty than this one while supporting a greater number of dependent members. In addition, unlike many lower-class villagers, Rita has a bank account containing over $200, money largely accumulated as gifts from former boyfriends. Bobs does not know about the account or the amount of money in it.

TABLE 5.8 HOUSEHOLD POSSESSIONS OF A POOR FAMILY

Item	Owner	Location
(a) *Furniture*		
2 small tables	Head	Drawing Room
2 side tables	Head	Drawing Room
2 chairs	Head	Drawing Room
China wagon	Head	Drawing Room
Wooden bed	Head	Drawing Room
Small bench	Head	Drawing Room
Shelf	Head	Drawing Room
Hat rack	Head	Drawing Room
Steel bed	Head	Drawing Room
		(Continued)

TABLE 5.8 (Cont.)

(b) *Cooking and Serving Items*

34 Drinking glasses	Head	Drawing Room
Metal tray	Head	Drawing Room
Glass pitcher	Head	Drawing Room
2 Glass dishes	Head	Drawing Room
5 China cups and saucers	Head	Drawing Room
1 Sugar Bowl	Head	Drawing Room
1 Dish Cover	Head	Drawing Room
4 Dinner plates	Head	Drawing Room
1 Bowl and cover	Head	Drawing Room
2 Plastic bowls	Head	Drawing Room
1 Glass bowl	Head	Drawing Room
3 Enamel cups	Head	Drawing Room
4 Tin Cups	Consensual mate	Drawing Room
1 Enamel plate	Consensual mate	Drawing Room
6 Tablespoons	Head	Drawing Room
3 Teaspoons	Head	Drawing Room
3 Forks	Head	Drawing Room
2 Dinner knives	Head	Drawing Room
1 Mixing spoon	Head	Drawing Room
1 Cutting knife	Head	Drawing Room
1 Enamel pot and cover	Head	Drawing Room
1 Iron pot	Head	Drawing Room
1 Coal pot	Head	Step landing
2 Can openers	Head	Drawing Room
1 Enamel tea kettle	Head	Drawing Room
1 Tea pot	Head	Drawing Room
1 Funnel	Head	Drawing Room
1 Enamel wash basin	Head	Drawing Room
2 Tin buckets	Head	Drawing Room and yard

(c) *Tools and Utensils*

1 Straw Broom	Consensual Mate	Drawing Room
1 Wooden handled brush	Head	Drawing Room
1 Shoe brush	Head	Spare room
2 Coconut brooms	Head	Yard
3 Small press irons	Head	Drawing room
1 large heating iron	Head	Drawing room
2 Cutlasses	Consensual Mate	Yard
1 Hammer	Head	Spare room (Continued)

TABLE 5.8 (Cont.)

(c) *Tools and Utensils*

1 Pair of pliers	Head	Spare room
1 Pen knife	Head	Bedroom
2 Dozen clothes pins	Head	Drawing Room
6 Diaper pins	Head	Drawing Room
2 Enamel basins	Head	Yard
1 Enamel chamber pot	Head	Bedroom
1 Plastic shopping bag	Head	Drawing Room
Sewing machine	Head	Drawing Room

(d) *Livestock*

4 Hens	Head	Yard
4 Chicks	Head	Yard
1 Cock	Head	Yard
1 Hen	Second eldest son	Yard
1 Hen	Youngest daughter	Yard
1 Chick	Youngest child	Yard

(e) *Decorative Items*

1 Mirror	Head	Drawing Room
4 Calendars	Head	Drawing Room, Spare room
8 Framed pictures	Head	Drawing Room
Newspapers papered to walls	Head	Spare Room

(e) *Decorative Items*

Assorted photographs and pictures on walls	Head	Drawing Room
1 Glass vase	Head	Drawing Room

(f) *Other*

2 Mattress covers (grass filled)	Head	Bedroom
1 Trunk	Head	Bedroom
2 Suitcases	Head	Bedroom
12 Pairs of curtains	Head	Drawing Room, Spare room, Bedroom
2 Spools of thread	Head	Drawing Room

(Continued)

TABLE 5.8   (Cont.)

(f)	*Other*		
	4 Needles	Head	Drawing Room
	1 Tape measure	Head	Drawing Room
	1 Change Purse	Head	Drawing Room

Food Consumption

Ensuring a steady supply of food is the most important concern of most lower-class households. Although signs of malnutrition in young children (distended bellies and skin sores) are obvious in only a minority of the poorest households, the diet among the village poor is high in carbohydrates and sugar and low in protein. This is because foods high in protein are more expensive than starchy vegetables and their derivatives. It is not uncommon for a poor family which has a few *fowls* in the yard to sell the eggs for 10 cents each to buy imported flour, sugar, and rice. Still, most families try to balance *food* [starchy material] with *relish* [meat and fish] although often the *relish* consists of nothing more than a tin of sardines or a few small fish. The data in Tables 5.9, 5.10, and 5.11 are based on the food consumed at home by three lower-class families. Not included is food eaten outside the household, namely purchases of cakes and sweets by children, bread, crackers and soft drinks by adults, and the food offered by kin, friends, and neighbors when their homes are visited. Most food, however, is consumed at home even when it is acquired from relatives and friends and most lower-class households eat three meals, *tea* [breakfast], *breakfast* [lunch], and supper. *Breakfast* is normally the heaviest meal while supper often has the same kinds of items taken at *tea*.

The household represented in Table 5.9 is the poorest of the three and this is reflected in its daily expenditure on food. The family in Table 5.10 is somewhat better off though some of the items consumed (the sweet potatoes, carrots, and tomato) were given to the household by friends and neighbors. Although the household depicted in Table 5.11 is the best off in terms of diet, the money value of the food consumed is somewhat illusory since some of what was eaten derived from the farming efforts of the head. As a result, the milk, eggs, lime, peas, and tomatoes, while given at prevailing market prices, were obtained at a lower real cost.

All three families are heavily dependent on imported foodstuffs: 55 percent of the expenditure of the household in Table 5.9, 56 percent of that spent by the family in Table 5.10, and 48 percent of the outlay of the unit in Table 5.11. Again, the lower proportionate expenditure on imports by the last family was a consequence of its partial support by the food grown by its head. Not all households are so fortunate and, as the next chapter will show, even those families having access to land do not always work it. A heavy reliance on imported food together with a serious underuse of village lands are central features of the economic impoverishment of the community and its members.

TABLE 5.9 DAY'S MENU FOR AN EIGHT PERSON HOUSEHOLD

Tea: 8:00 a.m.

Chocolate Tea:[a]

2 sticks unsweetened chocolate	.04[b]
1/2 lb. brown sugar[c]	.07
2 ounces powdered milk[c]	.08
1 pinch salt[c] (value less than .01)	.00
4 boiled sweet potatoes	.25
Sub-total:	.44

Breakfast: 12:00 Noon

Boilin/Cook-up:[d]

1 lb. rice[c]	.20
Dasheen tops (picked locally)	.00
1 tomato	.06
1/2 onion[c]	.02
1/3 cup cooking oil	.05
1/2 oz. cooking butter[c]	.06
1 tin sardines[c]	.30
Sub-total	.69

Supper: 6:00 p.m.

4 boiled sweet potatoes	.25
Mint tea:	
Mint (value less than .01)	.00
1/2 lb. brown sugar[c]	.07
1 pinch salt[c] (value less than .01)	.00
Sub-total	.32
Total	$1.45

[a]A hot cocoa drink [b]Based on 1971 prices [c]Imported items
[d]A stew

TABLE 5.10. DAY'S MENU FOR A SIX PERSON HOUSEHOLD

Tea: 8:00 a.m.

5 bread rolls[a]	.20[b]
Eggs:	
2 eggs	.20
1 oz. butter[c]	.05
Tea:	
3 oz. "Milo"[c]	.36
6 tsp. powdered milk[c]	.40
3/4 lb. brown sugar	.11
Sub-total	1.32

Breakfast: 12:00 noon

Boilin:

4 sweet potatoes	.25
2 dasheens	.25
1 lb. carrots	.16
1 lb. fish	.25
1 onion[c]	.05
1 tomato	.04
2 oz. cooking oil	.06
1/2 oz. cooking butter[c]	.06
Sub-total	$1.12

Supper: 7:00 p.m.

Limeade:

2 limes	.04
3/4 lb. brown sugar[c]	.11
Bakes:[d]	
1 lb. flour[c]	.16
1 tsp. sugar[c] (value less than .01)	.00
1/2 oz. yeast[c]	.05
1/2 oz. cooking butter[c]	.06
1 pinch salt (value less than .01)	.00
Sub-total	.42
Total	$2.86

[a]Made from imported flour [b]Based on 1971 prices goods
[c]Imported items [d]Fried bread

TABLE 5.11   DAY'S MENU FOR A FOUR PERSON HOUSEHOLD

Tea: 8:00 a.m.

Coffee:
4 tsp. coffee[a]	.15[c]
1/3 1b. brown sugar[a]	.05
2/3 bottle milk	.11
1 pinch salt[a]	.00
6 bread rolls[b]	.24
Eggs:	
2 eggs	.20
1/3 cup cooking oil	.05
Sub-total	.80

Breakfast: 12:30 p.m.; 2:00 p.m.

Limeade:
1 lime	.02
1/2 1b. brown sugar[a]	.07
Bakes :	
1/2 lb. flour[a]	.08
1 egg	.10
1 cup milk	.04
1/2 oz. cooking butter[a]	.06
1/2 oz. baking powder[a]	.02
1 pinch salt[a] (value less than .01)	.00
4 oz. cooking oil	.12
Sub-total	.51

Supper: 8:00 p.m.

Cook-Up:
1 lb. rice[a]	.20
2 lbs. peas	.72
1/2 lb. salted beef[a]	.45
3 tomatoes	.12
1 onion[a]	.04
3 stalks green onions	.03
4 oz. cooking oil	.12
1 oz. cooking butter[a]	.12
Sub-total	1.80

Total	$3.11

[a]Imported items   [b]Made from imported flour   [c]Based on 1971 prices

Chapter 6

Land Tenure and Use

Formed between the lateral spurs of hills branching off from the island's north-south mountain range, Leeward Valley contains nearly 1,500 acres of privately owned land divided into 289 separate holdings (Table 6.1). Agriculture has always been the single most important village economic activity and some 30 percent of the adult working population was employed in commercial and peasant farming during the early 1970s (Table 5.5). Small farming and agricultural wage-labor are also important secondary occupations since they involve 45 percent of the 213 people in Table 5.5 who are concurrently engaged in two or more economic ventures. Despite this leading role of agriculture, only 58 percent of the 289 holdings in the valley contained any cultivation in the early 1970s other than fruit trees. Moreover, most holdings which were worked were seriously underused. The net result was that less than 20 percent of valley land was farmed at any given time. This situation has improved somewhat in the last few years and many younger men are turning to farming for their livelihood. But Leeward Valley still contains much idle and under-cultivated arable property. Why this is so in a poor, land hungry community requires an analysis of the size and distribution of holdings, the way plots of land are held and transmitted, and the actual use to which land is put (Rubenstein 1975).

THE SIZE AND DISTRIBUTION OF HOLDINGS

Compared to earlier periods, the role of estate agriculture has decreased dramatically. In 1899, the Leeward Valley and immediately adjacent region's 1,300 acres were divided into only 12 holdings; in 1970, the 1,434 acres were divided into 289 pieces of land, a 24-fold increase during the 70 year interval. Still, the four largest farms in the valley--Leeward Valley Estate (280 acres), the two separate portions (80 and 73 acres) of the former Palm Park Estate, and Belaire Estate (100 acres)--made up nearly 40 percent of valley acreage although they formed only 1.4 percent of the total number of separate land holdings. As a result, most valley plots are small with a mean size of only five acres. Nearly 90 percent are below the average and one-third are between one and two acres (Table 6.1).

TABLE 6.1 DISTRIBUTION OF LAND HOLDINGS IN THE LEEWARD VALLEY AND IMMEDIATELY ADJACENT REGION, 1970

Size of holdings (acres)	Number of Holdings			Area of Holdings		
	No.	%	Cumulative %	No. of Acres	%	Cumulative %
0 - 1/2	16	100.0	5.5	2.7	0.2	0.2
1/2 - 1	51	17.6	23.2	30.7	2.1	2.3
1 - 2	93	32.2	55.4	125.9	8.8	11.1
2 - 3	53	18.3	73.7	115.9	8.1	19.2
3 - 5	40	13.8	87.5	154.5	10.8	30.0
5 - 10	17	5.9	93.4	111.0	7.7	37.7
10 - 50	15	5.2	98.6	350.6	24.5	62.2
50 +	4	1.4	100.0	542.3	37.8	100.0
Total	289	100.0		1,433.6	100.0	

THE TENURE AND TRANSMISSION OF HOLDINGS

Valley lands are held in the same way as village houses and house-spots. *Bought land* refers to property purchased by the present owner and accounts for 140, or 48 percent, of the 289 holdings.

Most of the 149 remaining plots are nearly equally divided between *inherited land*, property transmitted at death to a single heir, and *family land*, undivided holdings jointly bequeathed to two or more people. There is also a residue of 11 holdings which were either acquired as a gift during the former owner's lifetime or in which the claims are either unclear or in dispute.

Family ownership and joint purchases of valley land have produced a multiplicity of proprietary rights over holdings and there are 545 separate claims to the 289 pieces of land (Table 6.2). Since many villagers have rights over more than one piece of property, fewer than 400 people hold the 545 claims. Table 6.2 also shows that the total acreage of the 67 family holdings far exceeds the total of the 71 inherited plots. This is largely because Leeward Estate, a family holding, alone occupies nearly 20 percent of valley land.

TABLE 6.2 LAND HOLDINGS CLASSIFIED BY TENURE
         AND CLAIMS

Type of Tenure	Number of Holdings No.	%	Area of Holdings No. of Acres	%	Number of Claims No.	%	Claims by Village Residents No.	% of Total Claims
Bought	140	48.4	695.1	48.5	146	26.8	84	57.7
Inherited	71	24.6	215.4	15.0	71	13.0	48	67.6
Family	67	23.2	507.0	35.4	317	58.2	128	40.4
Other	11	3.8	16.2	1.1	11	2.0	6	54.6
Total	289	100.0	1,433.6	100.0	545	100.0	266	48.8

Although agriculture is the single most important village occupation, this does not mean that all villagers have access to farmland. The data in Table 6.3 summarize land holdings by members of the sample of 100 households and indicate that only one-third of units own any land of their own. Alternately, working land does not necessarily imply land ownership and one-sixth of households in the sample have some interest in agricultural land only as renters, sharecroppers, or rent-free users.

TABLE 6.3 LAND HOLDINGS AMONG THE SAMPLE
OF 100 CORESIDENTIAL UNITS

Type of Tenure	Number of Coresidential Units
Bought	18
Inherited	5
Family	10
Rented	12
Rent-Free	3
Sharecropped	2
No Interest in Land	50
Total	100

ATTITUDES TOWARDS LAND

Owning land and farming land in Leeward Village are not the same thing, and this fact explains much of its under-utilization. As elsewhere in the West Indies, land and its possession are valued in and of themselves. The possession of a piece of land has many connotations: pride in the ownership of something that is valued; prestige in being a propertied person in a community characterized by material poverty; continuity with the past when land has come down from the *old parents* [ancestors]; immortalization through the bequest of land to future generations; security against the loss of other income generating sources; and freedom from the regimentation and low status of estate wage labor.

Although it is the ambition of most villagers to own some land, that members of only one-third of village households do so shows how difficult it is to realize this goal. For the rest, acquisition of a piece of land is a long term objective, an aim which even accounts for the wage-labor migration of many villagers (cf. Otterbein 1966; Wilson 1973). Even persons in their early twenties, including overseas residents, are eager to buy a piece of property, if only for future house-building or to signal their relative economic prosperity. Although land may be mortgaged to finance some commercial venture or to fund removal abroad, it is rarely sold even in cases of great financial pressure. Only those who have left the island with no intention of returning will voluntarily dispose of their holdings. This does not preclude real-estate speculation and several villagers have profited from the purchase, subdivision, and sale of idle estate lands in the valley.

With so many referents--peasant cultivation, subsistence, wage-labor, economic security, real estate investment, sentimentality, prestige, freedom, pride, continuity, etc.--it is no wonder that villagers are so possessive of their properties and react strongly and swiftly to any infringement, actual or perceived, of their customary or legal rights. Praedial larceny, trespass, crop destruction, boundary disagreements, inheritance disputes, squatting, and other *land affairs* are a popular topic of village conversation and the most common cause of civil litigation. Legal squabbles even involve *family land*, that category of property meant to go from generation to generation without formal partition. As a legacy from the *old parents, generation to generation land* is supposed to symbolize familial continuity and solidarity. But as elsewhere in the West Indies (cf. Clarke 1966:65), impartible inheritance runs counter to both the codified legal system and the ambition of most villagers for unencumbered individual land ownership.

FOLK AND JURAL SYSTEMS OF TRANSMISSION

This contrast between a folk system of tenure and transmission of property and an overarching societal jural system has been reported throughout the English-speaking Caribbean (cf. Clarke 1971:200-242; M.G. Smith 1965:221-261; R.T. Smith 1971:243-266). In Leeward Village, as elsewhere in the region, the heirs of an intestate married man are his wife and legitimate children and of an unmarried man, his brothers and sisters. The customary system differs from the jural system in two ways: (1) it recognizes the right of certain categories of illegitimate or *bastard* issue and extra-legal spouses to inherit property and (2) it observes verbal declarations, the personal circumstances of potential heirs, and the sentimental relation that existed between the deceased and these heirs. The village's folk system of transmission finds its closest counterpart in the Carriacouan model described by M.G. Smith (1965:250):

> Where a male landholder dies intestate leaving children of different birth status, the legitimate heirs have a right to inherit, while the illegitimate only have a claim of conditional character. Where there are no legitimate children of an intestate male, his illegitimate issue inherit

without hindrance. . . . The illegitimate children of intestate women inherit equally with the legitimate. During their lifetime, the widows of intestate landholders exercise complete control over their husbands' land, but may not alienate it.

The customary system in Leeward Village differs in two ways from the Carriacouan one. First, a man's illegitimate children produced before his marriage to their mother inherit equally with the legitimate or *lawful* issue of the union. Second, where there are no *lawfuls*, a man's *bastard* children inherit "without hindrance" only if the following conditions are met: (1) the property is not *family land* and (2) the deceased was himself illegitimate, or, if legitimate, his *lawful* siblings choose not to exercise their legal claim. Conversely, if the land is of the *generation to generation* type, the joint male owner was *a lawful*, he married and produced legitimate offspring, and his *outside children*, as they are called, were produced in a long defunct or short-lived union, then these illegitimate children have no folk or legal claim to a portion of the inheritance. In either of these two polar situations, disposition of property, supported by community sentiment, is straightforward. At times, however, disagreements and contention may break out, as, for example, when an almost forgotten brother suddenly arrives from overseas to press his legal claim to his brother's land, 'disinheriting' the dead man's consensual mate of many years. In these cases, village sympathy usually rests with the common-law wife and the man's illegitimate children.

Land Disputes

Villagers are well aware that according to formal Vincentian jurisprudence illegitimate children and consensual mates are not entitled to inherit except by testamentary disposition but, as the following cases illustrate, they also believe that blood ties and years of cohabitation should not be ignored.

Case 1. Godfrey Wilson died intestate leaving behind a house, house-spot, and a two-acre piece of *bought land*. Wilson, who had lived alone during much of his adult life, had most of his meals provided by an unmarried sister, Adelle, who also lived alone. A long-lived non-cohabitational union between Wilson and Lena Jones had produced two children, both of whom Wilson had always supported and with whom he had *lived loving* [been on amiable terms] right up to his death. But Wilson was legitimate as were his three full sisters and a half-sister, the product of his father's first marriage. After his death, Wilson's half-sister's husband, a man with considerable experience in *land affairs*, took charge of the disposition of the dead man's property. Two acres of agricultural land were given jointly to the three full sisters; the house was put up for rent and the proceeds earmarked for Adelle, the poorest sister and the one who had provided her brother's meals; two cows and a calf were taken by the administrator on his wife's behalf; the clothing and other personal effects were given to the half sister's son; and the household furniture was transferred to another sister. Nothing was given to Wilson's children. Although no one expected Lena Jones to be granted part of the inheritance because their union had terminated many years before, villagers believed that the children who had enjoyed Wilson's faithful support and affection should have been included in the distribution. Although he did not involve his wife in the transmission of the most valuable part of the inheritance, the two acres of land, the administrator, an East Indian in an Afro-Caribbean village, was termed a "robbery *Coolie* bitch" for leaving Wilson's children out.

"Robbery" may take more dramatic forms than a contradiction between societal jural and local folk norms. It often involves what villagers call *t'ief land*, property which is seen as fraudulently acquired by the standards of both systems. *T'ief land* is obtained in one of two ways: a resident agent or caretaker placed in charge of the land by a migrant owner claims that the land has been abandoned or that the former proprietor has died without any legal heirs; or one or more family heirs obtains a title deed which excludes the other customary owners. As two of the following cases indicate, those who have been dispossessed are often prevented from gaining legal redress because of the large expense involved in what are normally protracted and unpredictable juridical battles.

Case 2. Martha Hadaway purchased nearly three acres of Crown land during the early years of this century. She bequeathed the land in a will to her three daughters, one of whom, Linda, acquired title to the property after the death of the other sisters. Linda then transferred the land in a deed of gift to one of her sons. A son of another excluded beneficiary consulted a lawyer but did not have the funds to pursue the matter.

Case 3. Tracey Bowen died intestate leaving behind two acres of land which belonged, according to legal and customary usage, to his two *lawful* daughters, Nancy and Laura. Nancy, however, took possession of the whole piece, worked it for many years, and willed it to her daughter Verene. Laura, Bowen's other daughter, died, leaving six children, one of whom frequently complained about his mother's and siblings' dispossession. In 1970, Verene, in an apparent attempt to legitimize control over the land in a manner which would partially recognize the claims of her collateral kin, secured its legal administration into two equal portions with one of Laura's daughters.

Case 4. Lawrence Adams had still not paid off his two-acre piece of land when he died in the 1940s. His brother, Christopher, took over the land, completed the payments, and acquired a title deed. Upon migrating to the United States in the late 1940s, he placed a friend, Janet Deare, in charge of the land. A few years later Janet transferred responsibility for the land to Paul Phillips, an enterprising farmer, who began to cultivate it, a traditional right of anyone who is *response for* [in charge of] a piece of land. In 1969, Phillips filed the following statutory declaration:

"I Paul Phillips . . . do solemnly and sincerely declare as follows:
(1) Christopher Adams was seized of a parcel of land situated in Leeward Village. . . .
(2) The said Christopher Adams resided in the United States of America for many years.
(3) Better a letter dated 8th January 1952, I was put in possession of this parcel of land by the said Christopher Adams.
(4) Christopher Adams died in America in the month of March 1955 and was survived by his wife who also died in the same year.
(5) That from the same year 1955, I have been in

uninterrupted possession and have paid all the taxes for the said parcel of land.

(6) That I am unaware of anyone other than myself who has made any claim to the said parcel of land or any part thereof or any interest therein."

Phillips was wrong on two grounds. First, he was put in charge of the land by Janet Deare, not Christopher Adams. Second, although Adams had no children of his own, he had a *lawful* sister whose son, William, had tried to exercise his claim by repeatedly 'trespassing' on the land, thereby indicating that Phillips was not in un-molested occupation of it. After making some preliminary inquires about his legal rights, William was forced to drop the matter because of a lack of funds.

Deviations from the Folk Model

Acquiring *t'ief land* is not the only way the folk norms of the disposition of land and other property are ignored or circumvented. Indeed, 'exceptions' to both traditional and jural norms of transmission seem to be the rule in Leeward Village. If there is a structural principle at work informing the process of actual transmission, a good label for it is "personalism," a concept developed by Rodman (1971:159) to describe the quality of family relations among lower-class Black peasants in Trinidad. Personalism in kinship behavior refers to ". . . the extent to which the content of a kinship relationship grows out of interaction (instead of being prescribed by the formal tie)" (Rodman 1971:159). The role of personalism in Leeward Village inheritance patterns is most evident in the case of testamentary disposition where the choice of heirs is a product of the quality of the relationship between property owner and various potential beneficiaries. In some cases, a legal heir may be excluded because of a dispute with the testator; in other cases, a distant relative or even non-kin may be granted some or all the legacy because of the quality of the relationship with the donor; in still others, kin of equivalent genealogical distance may receive unequal allotments based on their differing social circumstances and per-ceived material needs. The following cases illustrate each of these possibilities.

Case 5. Albert Simmons disinherited his only child, the legitimate issue of his first marriage, because he and the son had not spoken for years because of a long-standing dispute. Naming the son the beneficiary of "a penny and a glass of water" (to protect himself from the charge that he had accidently disowned him), Simmons willed all the property, including a valuable piece of agricultural land, to his childless second wife.

Case 6. When Paul Phillips, the owner of the *t'ief land* in Case 4, died he left behind three pieces of land and a house. His will bequeathed none of this property to his three *outside* children, presumably because he had never been on good terms with them. Instead, he left one piece of land--the *t'ief land*--to the servant who had cared for him during his last days. Most of the remaining property was assigned, in trust, to the two offspring of an *outside* child to be given to them at jural adulthood. Nothing was left to the other grandchildren since he was also not on speaking terms with them. In fact, he had never met the two grandchildren who were to inherit the bulk of his property, but at least he had never quarreled with them.

Case 7. In his will, John Millington parcelled up his two and one half acre plot of land among his seven legitimate children. Alex, the eldest, received the largest share, three-quarters of an acre, because he was a married man with a family. Two other sons, both unmarried, received one-half acre each. The four daughters were jointly allotted three-quarters of an acre because being women Millington believed that they would be less likely to farm the land than their brothers.

Less than 10 percent of land and other property is disposed of in wills. Choice, however, continues to hold even in intestacy and its operation may be seen, in part, through the proposed transmission of land by its owners. In a non-random sample of 44 village landholders, the following consignment intentions were given: 18 persons had not yet decided or were otherwise uncertain about the disposal of their property; 12 proposed to leave it to their children; 10 planned an unequal allocation amongst children and other kin; and 4 intended conveyance by the extent of economic help given by their children and other persons.

Those who planned equal filial transmission had most or all their children still living with them. Among males, all these issue were legitimate; among females, both *lawful* and *bastard* children were included. Like their counterparts elsewhere in the West Indies, villagers look forward to help from their offspring in old age. Though they recognize that this personalized filial obligation is not always met--some children are just *bad-minded*; others are too poor to help; and still others have family obligations of their own which demand most of their resources--Leeward Villagers believe that if it is fulfilled, then it should be rewarded through the bestowal of property. Among the ten landowners who planned unequal distribution, three proposed leaving their land to their wives alone (in fact, two of the three are childless); one plans to allot it jointly to his wife, two of his many children from various extra-marital unions, and to a foster son; one intends to transfer it to one of his sons on the basis of a request from his dead brother from whom he acquired the land and who was the godfather of the prospective heir; one aims to allocate it only to some of her grandchildren but has not decided which ones; one will leave it to his first son and eldest child; one will bequeath it to her two daughters, her only children still at home; and one will hand it down to two of his sons.

More instructive of the economic basis of many of these transfers and the way they are rooted in personalism are the intentions of the four landholders who cite material aid as their main consideration. One plans to leave her estate to "the nearest one who takes care of me"; another "according to treatment" received from his children; a third to "who will *mind* [support] me"; and a fourth to one of her sons in England because "he is the one who has me *standing up* [alive and well]. The others don't *notice* [show any concern for] me."

The intended transmission among most of these 44 villagers may not be carried out in the manner in which they would like since, if they follow past community practice, they are unlikely to formalize their choice through testamentary disposition. Yet it is just an improbable that most actual conveyances will conform precisely to the folk model of intestate inheritance. Again, one or more of the customary heirs (and occasional non-heir) may "walk in and take all." More likely, the heirs themselves may informally partition the property in terms of their own relative needs and interests. As a consequence, *family land* often loses many of its claimants, sometimes even being transformed into *inherited land* in the process. There are a variety of reasons why some of the legitimate heirs do not exert their rights in the land: they are engaged in a more remunerative economic activity and have no interest in farming; they have migrated from the island and do not intend to return; they view the piece of land as a reward to those co-heirs who took care of the landowner during old age; they see the plot as too small or unproductive to bother with; they want to avoid the inheritance disputes that sometimes occur when there has been two or more generations of transmission; they have other more valuable holdings; and they do not want to interfere with the long time cultivation of the land by one or more of their peers.

The Productive Utility of Family Land

Such deviations from the customary transfer of *family land* suggest the need to reevaluate the traditional view about the productive utility of jointly held property. Several observers have described family land in negative terms: on the one hand, it is said to be either abandoned or under-utilized ". . . because working it would arouse family antagonism" (Brierley 1974:90); on the other, it is argued that multiple ownership retards its agricultural development even in cases where it is cultivated (Clarke 1966:66; Finkel 1971:299; Lowenthal 1961:5). Clarke (1971:221), for example, has argued that in Jamaica:

> . . . the possibility of members of the family living in other parts of the island, returning to exercise their claim, either to cultivate the land, or erect their home on it, or to reap the produce of the trees, acts as a deterrent on economic use.

In St. Lucia the norms of *family land* use appear to be taken even further.

> [T]he *rights* to [*family*] land are equally shared, and the legacy of the land becomes the communal property of the entire family. Thus, for example, if one of the heirs clears a field and plants a crop on it there is nothing to prevent all the other members of the family (including brothers, sisters, nephews, and nieces) from harvesting the crop when it is mature. This arrangement of communal land rights within the family serves as a strong deterrent to agricultural development since the more ambitious and enterprising farmers feel that it is not worthwhile

planting crops under these conditions (Finkel 1971: 299).

Given these sorts of considerations, *family land* is said to have little beyond sentimental significance.

> From the aspect of land use it [*family land* in Jamaica] is inevitably wasteful and incompetent. A good deal of family land is under-used, occupied by the old people, who are physically unable to develop it. Other multiple owned holdings are completely unproductive save for the food trees planted by the ancestors . . . . Misuse of land in the form of exhaustion or neglect, under-use because of lack of capital, or multiple ownership restricting development, are all practical results which have to be weighed against the strong sentiment and high values attached to the system (Clarke 1971:240-241).

Such views do not generally apply to Leeward Village family holdings. The 67 family plots in the valley have a total of 317 joint owners but only 128, or 40 percent, of them are village residents (Table 6.2). Most owner absenteeism is a product of extra-island wage-labor migration and results in an average of only two claimants per parcel of land. Although there is some reluctance to farm *family land* when there are many claimants present or when rights to the property are in dispute, for family members who are otherwise landless the migration of heirs is beneficial. Not only does it make more land available to those left behind who wish to cultivate (cf. M.G. Smith 1965:240-241), it also reduces the scope for family disputes regarding access to and use of communal property. Even when all family heirs are absent--a regular occurrence in Leeward Village--the property is never abandoned. Caretaking arrangements are always made and this enables otherwise landless villagers, kin and non-kin alike, to work a plot of land without the expense and constraints of leasehold and sharecrop transactions. Part or all of 14, or 21 percent, of the 67 family holdings are also farmed by renters and sharecroppers. The net result of caretaking, renting, and sharecropping is that a slightly larger proportion of family holdings than bought or inherited plots--61 percent as opposed to 57 percent --are cultivated, a difference which is magnified when account is taken of the generally smaller size and relatively lower subsistence and commercial value of *family land*. Conversely, for many of those who migrated *family land* was used as collateral security for borrowing the funds to finance overseas removal. Even in cases of non-cultivation, the productive potential of *family land* is not forgotten and its possession may be considered a form of security against adversity. In this regard, Clarke's (1971:208) finding for Jamaica applies equally to Leeward Village.

> [T]emporary non-exercise of a claim on family land does not, in the traditional system, preclude a subsequent exercise of that right. For example, a brother may return to the family land, occupied by his other brothers and sisters, after years of residence elsewhere and it would still be recognized by his family that he had the right "if he had the need," to erect his house on the land and share in the crops of any of the fruit trees planted by his forbears on the property.

In Leeward Village, as in rural Jamaica (Clarke 1971:238), produce from several family holdings, especially tree crops, is also distributed to heirs not engaged in the plot's cultivation, including relatives living in other parts of the island.

THE UTILIZATION OF FARMLAND

Ground provisions--yams, sweet potatoes, tannias, dasheens, and eddoes--form the basis of the diet of most villagers and are planted on most cultivated holdings. A variety of other fruits and vegetables such as corn, peas, beans, tomatoes, cabbage, bananas, plantain, cacao, onions, peppers, peanuts, and cucumbers are also grown on many plots. All pieces of land except the smallest contain one or more breadfruit, mango, or coconut trees. Except for the largest farms, most of the starchy tubers and much of the tree crops are used for subsistence. Surplus *provisions*, fruits, and many of the other vegetables are sold in the village or in the Kingstown market by the women and girls of the household.

Although there are seasonal variations in rainfall on the island --the 'rainy' season lasts from May through November and the 'dry' season from December through April--a mountainous topography means that there is some precipitation throughout the year resulting in a long planting season for some crops and a variable one for others. Tubers are planted from January to May; bananas from December to April or May; corn, a three-month *catch crop*, from June to December; and peas in March and April.

Many cultivators use the *MacDonald's Farmers' Almanac*, an annual astrological handbook published in the United States which accords with the local belief that planting should coincide with the lunar cycle. It is generally believed that planting should not take place at or near full moon since the *strength* of the moon at that point will *force* the body of the plant resulting in low yields.

Agriculture is based on a partial division of labor according to sex. Men are normally responsible for *cleaning* the land, i.e., cutting down and burning the natural vegetation that has accumulated since the last planting, and women are in charge of weeding the growing plants. The sowing of seeds, the planting of cuttings and tuber sections, and the harvesting of crops, however, are performed by both sexes.

As elsewhere in the island, valley cultivation is unmechanized. The main tools are imported iron hoes and *cutlasses* [machetes]. Indeed, cultivation on some of the valley's estates has 'devolved' from full-fledged agriculture to simpler horticultural-like techniques. Up to the end of the 1950s ox-drawn plows and the occasional tractor were used on Leeward Valley Estate. A decrease in markets for crops suitable for mechanization (cotton, sugar-cane, and arrowroot), the introduction of banana cultivation, a crop that is difficult to mechanize, and decreases in estate cultivation led to a gradual disappearance of draft animals and tractors.

Estate lands are not the only holdings that are under-utilized. Many peasant holdings have not been worked in years and less than 20 percent of all valley acreage was cultivated in the early 1970s. This under-use of arable land is a perennial economic problem throughout the West Indies and occurs even in those countries where agriculture is the mainstay of the economy (see Augelli 1962:438; Finkel 1971:298; O'Loughlin 1968:100-104; Philpott 1973). Although there are a few reports which document some of the factors producing this situation (e.g., Brierley 1974; Edwards 1961; Finkel 1964), little has been done to systematically describe and interrelate the various features which have yielded a particular land use pattern in a given West Indian territory. I shall try to do so here since many of the factors which influence valley cultivation are relevant to an understanding of the overall organization of village economic life.

There are four sets of factors which account for the undercultivation of valley lands: demographic factors, ecological factors, economic factors, and ideological factors (see Rubenstein 1975).

Demographic Factors

Several interrelated demographic features play a role in determining the scope and intensity of valley cultivation. The first three of these are directly related to labor migration out of the valley, a process which is the topic of the next chapter.

Leeward Village has followed the general pattern of Vincentian migration and between 1957 and 1965 many landowners and agricultural laborers left the island for Great Britain. The migration of proprietors is evident in the already mentioned fact that of the total of 545 claims to valley acreage, only 266, or less than one-half, are represented by claimants currently residing in the village (Table 6.2).

Many of the migrant claimants were among the most ambitious cultivators in the valley. In fact, successful farming often provided the funds to finance overseas migration. Although migrants almost always leave their land in the care of a relative, friend, or some other agent to work as they wish, the degree of cultivation by these non-owners, many of whom are the aged parents of migrants or persons untrained in farming, is habitually much less intense that previously carried out by the owner.

Some of the hardest-working agricultural laborers, sharecroppers, and renters have also migrated and the entire agricultural labor-force consists of approximately 70 men and women. To intensively operate a holding over 10 acres requires the employment of agricultural workers. The migration of former field laborers has produced a shortage of workers on these holdings, and the bulk of them are either idle or grossly under-cultivated. The overseas removal of sharecroppers and renters has adversely affected cultivation even on the smallest of holdings. Both forms of working land are habitually associated with efforts to supplement other forms of income by working the property of those who cannot or will not do so themselves.

Migration from the village has nearly always involved far more men than women, producing a sex ratio of 588 men per 1,000 women in the 20 to 60 age range. The effect on farming is that there are not enough men to complement the work done by the women. A habitual complaint voiced by women who would like to farm their land is that they cannot secure male laborers to dig banks for them.

Much of the *bought land* in the valley is owned by elderly or late middle-aged men. Many plots are also held by agriculturally inexperienced women who inherited the land at the death of their husbands. The result is that much acreage is concentrated in the hands of elderly people and non-farming widows. The shortage of laborers, renters, and sharecroppers merely aggravates this situation.

Ecological Factors

The techno-environmental factors affecting the extent of cultivation in the valley include the location of plots, topographic and soil conditions, holding size, cultivation techniques, and the physical changes that have resulted from over 200 years of intensive cultivation.

Most of the valley plots owned by villagers are located either at or near the head of the valley or along its upper sides. Nearly 30 percent of all village holdings are also situated in regions adjacent to or some distance from the main valley region. The distant location of and travel time required to reach these plots, compounded by a steep and rugged topography, makes their cultivation difficult for farmers of middle age and older. The paid workers needed to help farm some of the larger peasant holdings are also reluctant to go so far, especially when there is employment closer to home. Remote holdings producing cash crops are also plagued by the problem of transporting produce to market. Most farmers, for example, who began growing bananas during the early 1960s gave up within a few years because of the expense of shipping their produce to Kingstown and the damage caused to the fruit when it was moved over such long and rugged distances. The individual stems had to be *headed* [carried on the heads of laborers] by paid workers from remote fields to secondary roads servicing the valley and the poor quality of these byways produced considerable bruising to and hence rejection of the fruit by the marketing authorities.

Many of the holdings that were obtained after the 1902 volcanic eruption--and this includes nearly all peasant plots--are located in the least fertile and most steeply sloped parts of the valley. Large portions of several plots are almost uncultivable since much of their area includes ravines, gutters, and other inclines. Soil erosion, partly attributable to the steep gradient of holdings, is a problem which affects many plots. Poor drainage, thin soils, and a rocky surface contributes to an absence of cultivation in some areas as well.

Nearly 90 percent of plots are under five acres and over one-half are under two acres (Table 6.1). The smaller the holding, the less economical is its cultivation. Most forms of mechanization, fertilization, crop rotation, or fallowing are impractical on such small parcels of land. Cash crops are also ruled out since almost all that is grown is consumed by the household. Small holdings also preclude anything more than part-time cultivation. This makes the cultivation of distant and agriculturally marginal plots even more uneconomical and has led some landowners to abandon cultivation completely especially when wage-labor activities become available.

Despite a legacy of proto-peasant cultivation during slavery, many landowning villagers have no agricultural experience. This is especially true of those who inherited their land but also includes many villagers who purchased their land for reasons other than its cultivability. In short, many owners do not work their land either because they do not have the requisite skills or because they are not interested in farming.

Economic Factors

The extent and intensity of agricultural activity in the valley is strongly influence by production costs, market conditions, profit levels, work patterns, and the alternative uses to which both land and labor may be put.

There is a widespread reluctance to work as an agricultural laborer and villagers will engage in it only if they have no choice. Agricultural labor, as has already been pointed out, is the lowest paying economic pursuit in the island. It yields a level of remuneration which hardly meets minimal household needs. Even if they were eager to work as full-time laborers, most workers cannot find steady employment since only a handful of the largest landowners make use of agricultural laborers on a more-or-less regular basis. There is also considerable friction between employers and laborers. The latter complain of low wages, poor working conditions, and the excessive demands of their employers. The former, in turn, express concern about the unavailability or tardiness of laborers and low worker productivity. The inability to secure an adequate and reliable labor force because of wage and work disputes prompted Leeward Valley Estate to switch from agriculture to arboriculture by planting the entire estate in coconuts in 1969.

Economic ties among workers themselves have adversely affected cultivation. *Swap labor*, or labor exchange, has always been popular among smallholders. It usually involves men assisting each other in digging banks on a reciprocal basis but may also include the exchange of bank digging and crop weeding between men and women. The exchange of labor helps foster cultivation in two ways. First, since collective effort is involved, the monotony and solitude of farm work is reduced. Second, since labor exchange is based on a balance being struck between work given and work received, the debts incurred must be canceled out during the same planting season. Independent cultivation becomes partially transformed into a group effort, governed by the need to repay the help of others and, more important, to ensure that there is enough work to occupy the labor team on the land of individual members.

Labor exchange has decreased in the valley over the years and a minority of cultivators now participate in it. Its decline is attributable to the migration of many farmers, animosity among those who formerly exchanged labor as a result of political disagreements, and reduced cultivation among older individuals. Still, those who continue to *swap labor* are among the most active cultivators in the valley.

The unreliability of market conditions and the disappearance of some traditional markets have forced many farmers to sharply curtail production or restrict their efforts to satisfying the smaller and less profitable domestic market. The production of such cash crops as cotton, arrowroot starch, bananas, copra, and cassava starch are dependent on unpredictable external markets and price levels. Since most Vincentian exports shipped outside the Caribbean constitute a minute fraction of world production or, as in the case of arrowroot, are competing against natural and synthetic substitutes, prices and hence profits are beyond the control of islanders. For example, until the 1960s cotton and arrowroot were the chief cash crops in the valley. The disappearance of the markets for these crops forced many farmers to leave much of their land idle or switch to less lucrative substitutes.

Personal economic failures because of climatic forces (too much rain, drought, hurricanes), soil depletion, and poor farming techniques have also prompted some farmers to abandon or reduce cultivation. The absence of farm insurance and government indifference has meant that many cultivators are either unable or unwilling to try again. For example, crop failure owing to heavy winds was a major reason for sharply reduced valley banana production throughout the 1960s. Conversely, many smallholders are willing to plant or extend their cultivation but lack the funds for plants, seeds, cuttings, fertilizer, and occasional paid help.

For most crops, farming requires a planting-weeding-reaping cycle of between three to nine months before produce is available for sale. Although different items mature at various times during this period, many of these are for home consumption and the cultivator who lacks a large cash reserve must rely on credit-purchase at local or Kingstown shops. Accounts at shops are kept viable by periodic reductions in the accumulated deficit. Since peasant farming provides cash so irregularly, it is necessary to pursue other income generating activities which yield a more regular source of cash. This means that less time and effort are available for cultivation.

Some villagers are unwilling to plant or are selective in what they cultivate because of a well-founded fear of praedial larceny. Crops which bring high returns are especially attractive to thieves and this encourages the planting of less remunerative substitutes for which market demand may be weaker.

Many holdings are not worked simply because agriculture is not the only use to which land may be put. Most of the recent acquisitions under one acre have been made by overseas migrants and are meant as house sites rather than farm plots. Some 180 acres, or 12 percent of valley lands, are also used to pasture livestock, particularly cattle. Stock-rearing demands less labor than cultivation and is pursued by older men who were active farmers in the past but who are now content with the smaller returns from their animals. Some of these men, together with several wealthy villagers, have purchased potentially productive land for real estate speculation. Such land is normally taken out of cultivation or is only half-heartedly farmed as the owner waits for the opportunity to profit from its resale.

Finally, although working the land is the single most important economic activity in the village, most community members are not engaged in it. As was shown in Chapter 5, a host of other occupations are present in the village, many of which demand far less skill and effort and produce higher income levels than farming.

Ideological Factors

Hourihan (1973:29) has correctly pointed out that there is in St. Vincent ". . . a widespread aversion towards agricultural labor by Vincentian youth" and that, generally, white-collar work is preferred to any type of manual labor. In the questionnaire administered to Leeward Village schoolchildren, not a single one cited agriculture as a desirable activity (Table 5.1); conversely, agriculture was named one of the worst occupations in the village by these schoolchildren when they were asked to name undesirable jobs (Table 5.2).

Although *working a hoe* is viewed in negative terms, farming as such not denigrated. Instead, it is the actual field labor itself which is seen as demeaning and agricultural workers are occasionally pejoratively called *field niggers* by other villagers. In short, given the low esteem in which manual agricultural labor is held, most people try to avoid it if they can and accept nearly any alternative that is available.

The low status villagers themselves attach to agricultural labor is matched by the lack of encouragement given to farmers by the government. Department of Agriculture field workers rarely visit the community to lend advice despite the presence of the Agricultural Field Station on the outskirts of the village. Cultivation also receives low priority in national budgets and development planning and it is nearly impossible for a smallholder to secure a government farm loan.

Many of the factors that are contributing to the under-utilization of valley land are interconnected. Uncontrollable market forces, low agricultural wages, and ecological and climatic calamities provide a body of constraints against which the demographic limitations and agrarian beliefs and values are either formed or acted upon. For example, all cultivators are faced with poor or unstable markets, labor shortages, and failures because of environmental forces. The result is either marginal profits or outright losses, a situation which encourages the reduction or abandonment of cultivation and the search for economic alternatives. Similarly, low earnings are partly responsible for the general aversion towards agricultural wage-labor and provide an incentive to look for work elsewhere. If the alternative to working the land is migration, the resultant sex imbalance in the working population together with the general shortage of labor pose a serious problem for those who might otherwise be willing to plant.

Chapter 7
Labor Migration

Labor migration has long been the most important strategy used by poor villagers to promote their economic well-being and raise their social standing (cf. Richardson 1983:xi, 6, 171-182). More than any other process or institution it has supported enhanced life styles through the accumulation of greater wealth than is possible within the island or the development of remunerative and prestigious skills through education. Migration from the village probably began immediately after Emancipation in 1838 as part of the widespread exodus of former Vincentian slaves to other islands in search of higher wages. Removal from the community has continued up to the present with villagers taking advantage of migration opportunities whenever they occur. Concomitant with the economic and status implications of exodus from the village are a host of features which are summarized in Philpott's terms "migration-oriented society" and "migrant ideology" (1968, 1971, 1973) and Richardson's "migration ethos" and "migration culture" (1983:xi, 23-24). These include the demographic, social, cognitive, and sentimental implications of migration for both the sending society and for the migrant in the host country. Each of these features is revealed in an examination of migration from the community.

HISTORY AND DEMOGRAPHY OF MIGRATION

The only data on the extent of migration during the 19th century comes from census reports. In 1871, the valley population was 753; in 1881 it was 740; and in 1891 it was 734 (St. Vincent 1871, 1881, 1891). These decreases are probably attributable to participation of residents in the removal of Vincentian agricultural laborers to Trinidad, Guyana, and Central America.

A large body of descriptive material based on surveys and interviews I conducted between 1969 and 1972 reveals the pattern of migration during this century. The data in Table 7.1 summarize past migration among villagers over the age of 15. The rate of migration is much higher among males in all age cohorts except the youngest one and complements the skewed sex ratio of 100 women per 44 men over the age of 20 in the community. The data also show an overall high rate of male migration: of the 213 men over 30, 126, or 59.2 percent, have a history of past migration. Although the table suggests that there is either a progressive increase in the rate of male migration according to age or that there was a higher rate of male removal in the past, other data collected indicate that most of the men left the village before they were 30 and that most of the migration occurred after 1950. An additional explanation of the pattern of removal that does seem credible is that previous migration streams were based on temporary removal while those since the late 1950s to England, the United States, and Canada have involved the long-term or even permanent migration of villagers. Indeed, hundreds of native-born villagers are still living elsewhere, a fact accounting for much of the youthfulness of the village population.

TABLE 7.1 MIGRATION HISTORY OF VILLAGERS OVER THE AGE OF FIFTEEN

Age	No.	Males Migrants %	Migrants as a % of Total Male Population	No.	Females Migrants %	Migrants as a % of Total Female Population
15 - 19	117	2	1.3	1.7	105	2	2.0	1.9
20 - 29	74	24	15.8	32.4	135	23	23.0	17.0
30 - 39	48	23	15.1	47.9	85	23	23.0	27.1
40 - 49	52	23	15.1	44.2	83	16	16.0	19.3
50 - 59	46	31	20.4	67.4	76	16	16.0	21.1
60+	67	49	32.2	73.1	137	20	20.0	14.6
Total	404	152	100.0	37.6	621	100	100.0	16.1

The data in Table 7.2 summarize the destinations of the migrants in Table 7.1 and indicate that certain countries and regions--Trinidad, Aruba, Curaçao, Barbados, San Domingo [Dominican Republic], the Grenadines, the United States, and England--received the bulk of migrants. The table also shows that migration destinations are gender based. Removal to Cuba, San Domingo, and Barbados, for example, involved greater numbers of males since the main employment was the cutting of sugar cane, an activity which has never involved the recruitment of females.

TABLE 7.2 MIGRATION OF VILLAGERS ACCORDING TO SEX AND LOCATION

Location	Males		Females	
	No.	%	No.	%
Trinidad	30	19.7	47	47.0
Aruba	25	16.4	11	11.0
Barbados	24	15.8	5	5.0
Cuba	14	9.2	0	0.0
San Domingo	12	7.9	0	0.0
Grenadines	11	7.2	11	11.0
Curaçao	10	6.6	6	6.0
Panama	3	2.0	1	1.0
Guyana	1	0.7	1	1.0
St. Lucia	0	0.0	3	3.0
Grenada	0	0.0	3	3.0
Elsewhere in the Caribbean	4	2.6	0	0.0
U.S.A.	10	6.6	2	2.0
England	7	4.6	10	10.0
Elsewhere	1	0.7	0	0.0
Total	152	100.0	100	100.0

The returned migrants from the United States in Table 7.2 represent only a fraction of recent migration to that country. Most of those listed are farm workers who were hired to cut cane and/or pick fruit along the eastern seaboard. Since the 1960s, nearly equal numbers of men and women have also left for the United States with the intention of settling there for many years and these people are not represented in Table 7.2. Similarly, the greater number of women than men classified as having returned from England obscures the fact that the amount of migration there has been much higher among men than among women. Indeed, most returnees are the wives of men still living in England.

The pattern of removal to the locales in Table 7.2 has paralleled the island-wide temporal sequence. Migration to Trinidad began in the 1920s, reached a peak during the Second World War when work in the oil refineries and U.S. military bases became available, declined after the War, and continues to attract many villagers. Migration to Aruba and Curaçao, where Leeward Village men were employed as oil refinery workers, began during the 1920s, continued up through the 1930s and 1940s, when women entered the migrant stream as well, and was reduced to a trickle during the early 1950s. Removal to Barbados is a recent phenomenon which began in the 1960s with the migration of men as sugar-cane cutters and women as temporary or long-term domestic servants. Cuban migration was confined to a short period during the 1920s when Leeward Village men were employed there as cane cutters. Removal to the Dominican Republic also involved seasonal cane cutting during the 1920s and 1930s. Migration to the Grenadines began in the 1960s. It has consisted of agricultural laborers of both sexes going there for a few months at a time as farm workers, as well as skilled, apprentice, and semi-skilled construction workers migrating there for a month or two before returning home. Removal to the United States has been of different types and has occurred in different stages: migration to New York City during the early 1920s in which permanent removal was the usual outcome; recent migration to large urban centers, particularly New York City and Washington, D.C., in which the intent of most migrants is permanent or long-term residence; and the already mentioned seasonal migration of agricultural laborers which began in the early 1960s. Migration to England consisted of a movement which began during the mid-1950s and continued up through the mid-1960s. Most of these migrants are still in England.

Based on island emigration statistics and expected community natural increase figures, it is estimated that 534 people migrated from the community between 1960 and 1970 alone, producing an annual net migration loss of 2.4 percent per year. This is a much higher rate than in the country as a whole and suggests that Leeward Village is more affected by migration than most other regions in St. Vincent. The annual loss during the decade meant that nearly all the natural increase was counterbalanced by migration:

without removal from the community Leeward Village would have had a 1970 population of 2,779, or 19.2 percent larger than it really had.

The current residence of villagers who married between 1945 and 1970 gives additional evidence of the high rate of community migration. Table 7.3 summarizes the current residence of the 168 men and 174 women who married during this period and are still alive. The data indicate that 48.3 percent of the men and 35.6 percent of the women are living outside St. Vincent, the majority in England.

TABLE 7.3 CURRENT RESIDENCE OF VILLAGERS
WHO MARRIED BETWEEN 1945 AND 1969

Location	*Males*		*Females*	
	No.	%	No.	%
Leeward Village	65	38.7	95	54.6
St. Vincent	22	13.1	17	19.8
Trinidad	9	5.4	7	4.0
Elsewhere in West Indies	12	7.1	7	4.0
England	51	30.4	35	20.1
U.S./Canada	7	4.2	13	7.5
Other	2	1.2	0	0.0
Total	168	100.0	174	100.0

MIGRATION-ORIENTATION AND IDEOLOGY

Philpott (1968:475) has defined a migration-oriented society as ". . . any society in which a significant proportion of the population is involved in seasonal, temporary or permanent out-migration." Although he fails to describe what he means by "a significant proportion," he terms Montserrat, a Caribbean island-society in which there was a mean annual migration rate of 2.9 percent between 1946 and 1960, a migration-oriented society (Philpott 1968:466, 1973:21). In quantitative terms, then, Leeward Village, with a migration rate of 2.4 percent between 1960 and 1970, is a migration oriented community. But a migration-oriented community or society is characterized by much more than the sheer removal of large numbers of people. An important features of such a society or community is that emigration becomes *institutionalized*, an outcome which is usually the result of its having been a significant phenomenon for a long period of time. In becoming institutionalized, a host of beliefs and values about migration are formed. Some of these are summarized in Philpott's term "migrant ideology," ". . . the cognitive model which the migrant holds as to the nature and goals of his migration" (1968:474). In Montserrat this cognitive model includes ideas about the length of the migration (that it is a temporary phenomenon), the reason for migrating (to earn money), and the nature of the commitment to members of the sending society (the obligation to send remittances to close kin).

The factors governing Leeward Village migration, especially over the past 25 years, are broadly similar to those which produced the mass movement from Montserrat to England described by Philpott (1973:29-36, 108-112). Societal economic stagnation, poor life chances, and limited opportunities for advancement have propelled people out of the village. These incentives for migration have, of course, long been present in the community and are acted upon whenever there are opportunities to go to regions which show promise of producing the requisites of a better way of life back home.

The features which characterize migration-orientation and ideology in Leeward Village include a widespread desire to leave the island, a 'definition' of migration as a temporary phase, an obligation *to have in mind* those left at home, manifested in the requirement to send remittances to and/or sponsor the migration of close relatives and good friends, and a continued involvement with the household from which migration took place (cf. Philpott 1973; Richardson 1983).

Among young villagers in particular migration is viewed as far more than an economic process. It is a rite of passage--a stage in the process towards jural adulthood--whose delay or unattainability often causes bitterness. In reply to my question of why he wanted to go to England to join his mother, one man in his early twenties replied that he wanted "to become a man." The questionnaire on occupational choice given to the village schoolchildren contained the question "Would you like to leave St. Vincent after you finish school?" If they answered 'yes,' they were instructed to also answer the question "Where would you like to go?" Of the 108 responses to the first question, 107 expressed a desire to migrate. The favorite destinations were the United States (43 percent), England (33 percent), and Canada (17 percent), a reflection of the presence of close relatives in these countries as well as an acute awareness of contemporary migration trends and outlets.

Motives for migrating among villagers range from those that are strictly economic (e.g., a desire for increased prosperity) to those that are either social (e.g., a wish to reunite with relatives) or personal (e.g., a desire to gain the prestige associated with migration)(cf. Richardson 1983:18-19, 25, 46, 90). The most important motivation, however, is the material one and it is expressed in both "push" and "pull" terms. Among the reasons offered by the schoolchildren when asked why they would like to migrate and why people generally leave the island were: "St. Vincent is a poor island"; "America pays more to work"; "I think I can earn my living there [in the United States]"; "Some people leave St. Vincent to earn more money"; "[People leave] to go and work for their children"; "I would get a better job [abroad]"; "There is plenty of work there [in Canada]"; "[I want to leave] to better my position"; "St. Vincent has no work for me to do"; "There are more industries there [in the United States]"; "It have plenty of money and work there [in the United States]"; "[I want to leave] to make a better living"; "[People leave] to send money to their parents and they will not go hungry."

Like their counterparts elsewhere in the Caribbean (see Brookes 1969; Crane 1971:71, 210, 213; Hill 1977:230; Lowenthal 1972:218; Philpott 1973:69, 178, 187-188; Richardson 1983:25, 156, 172-174), most villagers view removal from the community as a temporary phenomenon, an idea which undoubtedly originated as a result of the migration outlets available to them before the opening up of England. For example, although many men spent up to 20 years in Aruba, Curaçao, or Trinidad during the 1930s, 1940s, and 1950s, the loss of jobs at the oil refineries and military bases and host government repatriation schemes forced many of them to go back home. Similarly, migration to Cuba, the Dominican Republic, Panama, Barbados, and other Caribbean and Central American destinations has been based on temporary contracts involving seasonal agricultural labor or work on particular construction projects.

The mass migration to England dramatically changed the length of the migration period and is only gradually being met, starting with younger people, by a transformation of the migrant ideology. Unlike most previous migration outlets which were based on short-term agrarian or construction industry employment booms, migration to Britain (and more recently to the United States and Canada) was a product of widespread labor shortages in various industrial, transportation, and service areas. Although most of these migrants may never resettle in St. Vincent, many express a desire to someday return home (cf. Philpott 1973:187-188; Richardson 1983:156). The principal behavioral manifestations of this return orientation are: (1) an affiliation with fellow islanders in the host society and a general preference for marriage to other Vincentians; (2) a continuing involvement in the affairs of the domestic unit from which migration took place; (3) the remitting of money to close family members in the village; (4) the sponsorship of near kin and good friends who also wish to migrate; and (5) the acquisition of dwellings, agricultural land, and other property back on the island (Rubenstein 1979).

Overseas Social Relations

Leeward Village migrants seldom break their home ties (cf. Lowenthal 1972:227). Most overseas friendships tend to be formed with either fellow villagers or with other Vincentians (cf. Philpott 1973:178-179, 189-190). Discussions with migrants who have worked in neighboring islands and relatives of emigrants in England suggest intensive interaction among village peers in the receiving society, including cohabitation during the initial period of migration and residential proximity throughout the overseas sojourn (cf. Philpott 1973:178-179). Those living in one London district call the area "Richmond Road" because that is the name of Leeward Village neighborhood many of them came from (cf. Philpott 1973:168). To be sure, much of this may be explained as a continuation of pre-existing village and island friendship ties, the presence of a common body of shared interests and experiences, and a distrust of strangers, including other West Indians. But affiliation with other villagers and fellow islanders is also a consequence of continuing social and sentimental involvement with the sending community and an intention to return home someday (cf. Philpott 1973:178-179). Alternately, migrants who have decided to remain permanently in the host society often begin to reduce or end interaction with their fellows (cf. Philpott 1973:178-179). The exact whereabouts of scores of migrants, nearly all of them male, is unknown for this reason. Sometimes marriage to a migrant from another island or to a non-West Indian gradually results in a decision not to return to St. Vincent, accompanied by absorption into a non-island-based social network. In other cases, as the following example indicates, it is disputes with relatives back home which precipitate a complete break in migrant-network ties.

Since Lester Anthony had no savings of his own, his removal to England in 1956 was entirely financed by his mother, Mary Anthony, who mortgaged a piece of *family land* to raise the $150 boat fare. Before his departure Lester promised his mother that he would build her a new house with the money he would earn in England. Upon his arrival in England, Lester moved in with a cousin with whom had been raised. Lester soon found employment and was able to remit the entire passage money to Mary within a few months. Since he intended to return home someday, Lester asked his mother to open a joint bank account in St. Vincent to which he made regular deposits in addition to the monthly remittances he faithfully sent for his mother's support.

Sometime in 1958 Lester wrote to Mary demanding that she send him his bank book because a friend who had just come over to England had informed him that she was squandering his savings on his two younger sisters. Angered by this accusation, Mary wrote a vitriolic reply and transferred the joint account, which by then contained some $400, into her own name. All correspondence between mother and son ceased. Lester soon moved into a flat of his own and gradually began to reduce his interaction with all family members in England including several from his natal household. In 1959 he married a Jamaican and moved north to Manchester, further altering his social field. In 1971, his mother helped finance the building of a new house using the funds in the former joint account. His attendance at the funeral of a close family member in London in 1982 was the first time he had been seen by any of his relatives and former friends for many years.

The return orientation is also expressed in the high rate of island endogamy among migrant who marry abroad (cf. Philpott 1973:170). Many villagers in Britain have even formalized pre-existing unions by sending for their extra-residential or common-law partners in the village. Some men who were having trouble finding the right partner in England have gone as far as sponsoring women selected for them by close kin back home. These tendencies are generally encouraged by the families of migrants who believe that as long as the spouse is a Vincentian, the migrant will continue to be commited to them.

202

Home Domestic Involvement

Long periods of absence from the village have barely altered the home orientation of many migrants. Husbands continue to support their village wives and children despite 20 or more years of separation; friends receive their annual Christmas *raise* [cash gift]; and an overseas wedding or funeral brings the ringing of village church bells. Any news from home--deaths, local scandals, national political machinations--quickly spreads within migrant networks; and next year brings the promise of a long dreamed of trip home. Many fulfill this promise and between 1969 and 1971 alone nearly 150 villagers living in the West Indies, North America, and England visited the community for periods ranging from several weeks to several months.

Ties to the village even involve preoccupation with the day-to-day affairs of the sending household. This is especially the case among those who headed their domestic groups and is manifested in an attempt to continue to *rule* those left behind. In one case a migrant in England instructed his wife to build an addition to the second story of their house so that their daughter who, he calculated, would soon *come young lady* [begin to menstruate] would not be able to keep sleeping on the first floor unsupervised by her mother. Other less dramatic instructions are also given by migrants.

Brooklyn, NY

Dear Mary,

You is the oldist one in the home and you make Danny [Mary's sister's boy friend] coming there and pass order. You had to be a damn shame. If Doris [Mary's sister] want her man let her go in the Street and meet him but please tell him I say do not come in my grandmother house. If Doris is so low to make all like Danny blow in her face is up to her. I try my best but nothing in it. So let him take care of her and stop him from coming there. If he dont stop go to the [Police] Station.

Emaline
[Mary's mother]

New York, NY

Dear Doris

I am glad to here that Jimmy [a family friend] is working the [family] land. You must all not trouble anything for him. Tell him I say I would send him some money to plant some potatoes give you all, and when it want to *clean* [weed] I will send him money to clean it. I here the three boys [Doris' brothers] is giving you trouble. Dont cut them but beat them. Keep them clean and give them food.

Emaline
[Doris' mother]

[Barbados]

Hi Doris,
You must keep everything at home clean and donot beat those children too much. I know the work is hard but try and donot make those children walk dirty. Make Leeward Village people see we is somebody.

Your true sister Mary.

New York, N.Y.

Hello Doris,
Now your uncle Selvin is going to send for you soon, but in the meantime, I would like you to wash Paul and Mento [Doris' brothers] clothes for me, and I will send something extra for you for washing them; and I want you to behave yourself, try and not get yourself mix-up with any boys to make any children, for your uncle will be mad with you, and he will not send for you anymore.

I am your true mother
Emaline.

Remittance Obligations

It has often been pointed out that the remittance of money and other gifts to members of the sending community is an important West Indian migrant obligation (e.g., Frucht 1968:202; Hill 1977:230; Philpott 1973:140-143; Richardson 1983:26, 47, 49; M.G. Smith 1962b: 58). Although it is likely that this responsibility has been unconsciously internalized as part of the socialization process in migration-oriented societies (see Philpott 1973:141), self-interest, based on the return expectation, probably plays a role as well (see Dirks 1972:572; Richardson 1983:26). Philpott's (1973:176) explanation of the meeting of remittance obligations among Montserratian migrants in London applies equally to their Leeward Village counterparts:

> Virtually all migrants believe that they will someday return to Montserrat if only for a holiday or for retirement. Migrants anticipate the general community approval of a man (or woman) who 'never sent an empty letter all the time he was out.' More important they fear the specific displeasure of their family members should they return without having met their obligations. This is expressed in statements such as 'I'd be ashamed to face my people, if I hadn't done my best.' Also, there is the notion of insurance, of holding their place with their families in Montserrat, because of the possibility of sickness, declining employment or restrictive legislation compelling them to go home and even seek the help of their families there.

Leeward Village migrants are expected to send money to their mother (or other female who reared them), to any children they may have left behind, to other close kin, particularly those with whom they were raised, and to close friends (cf. Philpott 1973:142). Not all migrants meet their responsibilities to those at home and some carry them out in an irregular or apparently reluctant fashion, especially if they have been away for several years. Although informal sanctions may be employed to deal with this (see Philpott 1973:175-178), there is nothing to compel the migrant to send money back to the village. The amount and frequency of remittances are also not specified except by the ability of the donor; low or irregular remittances are tolerated if it is felt that the emigrant is sending 'anything he has.' Villagers are also aware that migrants are bound to develop important obligations in the host society. If they marry and begin raising children, for example, it is recognized that this will affect their ability to meet in the same manner their responsibilities back home. It is also recognized that some children are just *better-minded* than others--they were simply born that way--and will, therefore, more faithfully execute their kinship duties. Still, a village migrant who has not fulfilled his obligations knows that he will be condemned for being *bad-minded* or *ungrateful* not only by family members but by the community at large should he ever return. In fact, generosity in sending money home usually goes unacknowledged for fear that this may provoke the jealousy of those who are not so lucky (or even bring unwelcomed requests for financial help). Conversely, information about remittances which are felt to be inadequate are quickly and widely circulated by the neglected party to attract public sympathy and perhaps even financial aid.

The role of remittance obligations may be seen in the following extracts from letter written by migrants.

Brooklyn, NY

Dear Mary,

Well I am glad that you received the money that I did send for Xmas because you all told the whole of Leeward Village how I was a bad mother. Now you send and tell me about the passport. I did not pay that much for my own and this money I sent to you if you want to sit down and eat it out is up to you. I sent enough to take out your picture, your passport, and so on, and you sit down on your ass and would not turn around and try to get out of Leeward Village. Plenty want the chance and cannot get it. I am sending $4.00 [U.S.] in this letter to pay the light bill. You will find two dollars in this letter. Give to change it. Give Doris [Mary's sister] three [Eastern Caribbean dollars] to pay her [typing] lesson and give Mac [Mary's brother] 25 cts, Bruds [another brother] 12 cts, Danny [another brother] 12 cts, Mento [another brother] 12 cts, Paul [another brother] 12 cts, Ellen [Mary's daughter] 12 cts.

Emaline [Mary's mother]

[London, England]

Hello Noreen,

I did not manage to send you all any cards for the Christmas but I still like to wish you all a Merry Christmas and a Happy New Year and I hope that you all may enjoy yourself and have a good time throughout the holiday. Well I send you this £1.10. I hope that it may be of great use to you and tell Mildred [Noreen's mother] that I will send her something for the New Year. I just couldn't make it for Christmas.

Carl [a cousin raised in
the same household with her]

[London, England]

Hello Noreen,

How are you, my dear. This is my very first letter to you since I am in England. The truth is my first few years in England were pretty Brown [difficult] with me. I couldn't write to no one because I never like to write an empty letter [one containing no money]. I enclose £1.10s.

Your dear friend Myrtle.

In the sample of 100 village households, 26 counted on off-island remittances for at least 25 percent of their support while only 36 households received no external funding. Although only 4 of the 100 households were totally dependent on off-island residents for support, 64, or nearly two-thirds, received some cash from overseas. Moreover, nearly every village household currently receiving no remittances has a history of external cash contributions from present or former members.

A Case Study of Sponsorship

The relation between off-island residents and those back in the village involves more than just material support and a sentimental attachment to home. Continuing involvement with village kin is also manifested in the obligation to help household members and close friends who also wish to migrate. Excluding dependent offspring and spouses, aid in removal to England from the mid-1950s to the early 1960s consisted of loaning some or all the nearly $150 passage money needed for the one-way boat trip, meeting the migrant upon disembarkation, and providing lodging until the new arrival had secured employment and housing. Figure 7.1 schematically summarizes the sponsorship 'chain' created when Clifford Tobin decided to go to England in 1956. While its size makes it far from typical--some migrants mobilized all their passage money themselves while others where part of a chain with less than a dozen 'links'--it has the advantage of encompassing in a single case the more important features governing financing and sponsoring arrangements, as well as the continuing interaction between migrants and their families back home.

Clifford Tobin (1 in Figure 7.1), a poor tailor in his early twenties, was among the first Leeward Village migrants to go to England. Since Clifford had little money of his own, others helped finance his passage. His mother, Florence, with whom he was still living, sold her cow, and his cousin (MMDS), Edward Taylor (2), who had been reared by Florence, lent him $100. Clifford was *received* in England in 1956 by his friend, Jacob Skinner, one of the first villagers to migrate to England. Clifford lived with Jacob for a month or two and then moved into a room of his own. During his first few years overseas Clifford sent his mother a monthly remittance of about $15. Occasionally, he also remitted funds to one of his sisters (FD) raised in a different household but with whom he was 'on good terms.' From time to time, he also sent a few dollars to two of his matrilateral parallel cousins (MMDD), girls who had been raised with him in the same home. After his marriage in the early 1960s to a woman from a large community north of Leeward Village whom he had met in England, the regularity of these remittances decreased. With three children to support he stopped sending money to all but his mother and even reduced the frequency of remittances to her to once every two or three months. Like many of his counterparts, Clifford has been back to the island twice on extended holidays. Since the death of his mother in 1984, he has started to make plans to rebuild the old family house and intends to return home for good in the next couple of years.

Clifford's mother did not press him to return the *cattle money* which had helped pay for his passage and this enabled him to help finance the migration of his cousin, Edward Taylor (2), in addition to repaying the $100 loan. Edward, who had some savings of his own, added these to the money received from Clifford, and sailed for England in 1957. He was received by Clifford and lived with him for several months.

For the next two years, Edward regularly remitted $25 to his aunt, Florence. He also sent about the same amount two or three times a year to his aunt (MMD), Mary Adams, who, together with Florence, had raised him. After his marriage in 1957 to a fellow Vincentian, the amount and frequency of his remittances gradually began to decrease to the point where Florence could only expect to receive a few dollars at Christmas.

When Edward left for England he had already produced four children in two extra-residential unions.

208

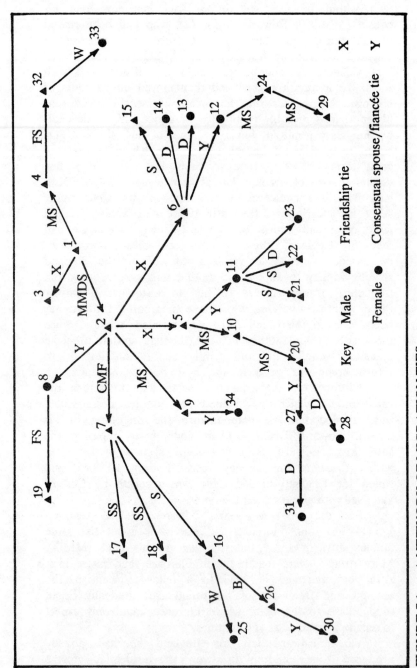

FIGURE 7.1   A NETWORK OF MIGRATION TIES

Unlike most male migrants, he continued to send money to his children for the next dozen years partly because he had originally intended to send for and marry one of their mothers. He eventually changed his mind--she was *dotish* [dim-witted] and apparently promiscuous (each time she gave birth his aunt, Mary, was obliged to examine the neonate to make sure it was his)--and in 1959 wrote to Mary asking her to find him a wife in St. Vincent. Mary decided against a Leeward Village woman, stating that they were too *tamarind* ["sour" like the fruit, i.e., of bad disposition], and instead selected a partner, Jane Shallow (8), from a nearby community. Edward and Jane exchanged letters and pictures for several months and were married soon after she arrived in England late in 1959.

In 1959, Clifford Tobin (1) helped finance the passage of his Leeward Village friend, James Samuel (3). Clifford's mother, Florence, was not pleased with her son's action stating that James's family, who she argued were better off than her own, should have helped him instead.

In 1961, Clifford, with some funding from Florence, sponsored his brother (MS), Kenneth Tobin (4), with whom he had been reared. After arriving in England, Kenneth continued to correspond with his pregnant girl friend back in the village and supported their child after it was born. But he abruptly stopped writing to her after being informed by several village migrants who followed him that the child was not his. The next year, Kenneth decided to marry a girl from St. Vincent whom he had met in England. Learning of his plans, his mother, Florence, wrote to him stating that she felt that he was marrying too soon and that she had not sent him abroad "to look for a wife." Kenneth went ahead anyway and surprised his mother who feared that his marriage would lead to a reduction in remittances by continuing to send her some $10 a month for the next several years. He also kept up the practice of sending money every Christmas to his aunt (MMD), Mary Adams, and to one of the aunt's daughters, as well as an occasional *raise* to one of his brothers (FS), Gary Simmons (32), who was reared in a different household and who he later helped sponsor. In recent years, however, the frequency of remittances to his mother has decreased to once every three to four months.

Nothing has been sent to other persons for many years.

Edward Taylor (2) helped finance the migration to England of five people: two friends (5 and 6), a fiancée (8), a former girl friend's father (7), and a brother (9).

In 1957, Edward loaned half of the money to pay for the trip to England of his friend, Benjamin Duncan (5). Benjamin raised the rest of the passage money by borrowing funds from his mother, by selling his pig and goat, and by using the few dollars he had managed to save.

Edward also loaned $75 to another friend, Elton Prince (6), who went over in 1957. Elton accumulated the balance needed by selling the shares he had in two cattle and by using savings from his farming efforts. Elton lived with Edward for a short time before moving out on his own.

In 1958, Edward helped finance the migration of his girl friend's father, John Lyscott (7), since he was still corresponding with the girl and supporting their child. When he had migrated, Edward had left his two cattle under the joint care of John and his aunt, Florence. He instructed John to sell the cattle, give Florence the share she was entitled to, and use the remainder to help pay for his boat ticket. John supplemented this with funds accumulated from farming.

In 1960, Edward sent for his brother (MS), Horace Taylor (9), who had been away working in Trinidad for the previous two years. Because Horace had been steadily employed in Trinidad, Edward's family in the village was not concerned that he had not followed the tradition of sponsoring kin before non-kin. However, since Horace had not been able to save much money while living in Trinidad, Edward was obliged to lend him most of the passage money.

Kenneth Tobin (4) who had been sponsored by his brother, Clifford Tobin (1), assisted only one person, his brother (FS), Gary Simmons, when he migrated to England in 1969. Though the amount loaned to him is not known, the aid Kenneth gave to his half-brother is a rare instance of agnatic siblings who have never lived together assisting each other in migrating.

Benjamin Duncan (5) who had been assisted by his friend, Edward Taylor (2), was instrumental in the migration of two people, his brother (MS), Frank Duncan (10), and his common-law wife, Alice Lyscott (11). Benjamin sent for Frank only a few months after his own arrival and was obliged to contribute the entire passage money since Frank had neither savings nor mortgagable property. Frank lived with Benjamin for several months before moving out on his own. In 1958, Benjamin sponsored his common-law wife, Alice (11), and they married soon after her arrival. At various times during the 1960s, he and Alice sent for their three children (21, 22, and 23).

Elton Prince (6) who had also been aided by his friend, Edward Taylor, had been living with his common-law wife, Ruby Joseph (12), when he left for England. He regularly sent money to Ruby, sponsored her in 1959, and married her shortly after she reached England. Elton currently remits funds only to the aunt who raised him (he has no siblings and both of his parents are dead). After Ruby joined him they continued to send money to Ruby's parents who were taking care of their three children. During the 1960s, they sent for the three children (13, 14, and 15), the last one joining them in 1969. Ruby still sends money to her mother on a regular basis.

John Lyscott (7) who had been sponsored by his daughter's former boy friend, Edward Taylor (2), faithfully remitted funds to his wife and children from the time he migrated in 1958 until his return to the village in 1971. In 1960, John contributed most of the passage money for his son, Orwin's (16), overseas removal, and he was the main source of sponsorship funds for Orwin's two sons (17 and 18) who joined their father in 1969. Unlike most migrants, Orwin never repaid the money loaned to him by his father.

Jane Shallow (8), whom Edward Taylor had sponsored and married in 1959, has always met her remittance obligations. Long after her arrival in England she continued to send money regularly to many persons in her home community including her parents, her father's mother, her father's sister, and some of her cousins and close friends. She also often sent clothing to her son from a previous union who was being raised by his paternal grandparents. In 1968, Jane helped sponsor a half-brother (FS)(19) with whom she had been reared.

Horace Taylor (9), who had been sponsored by his brother (MS), Edward Taylor (2), in 1960 continued to send funds to the aunt, Florence Tobin, who had helped raise him after his mother's death. Although he only remitted funds two or three times a year each *raise* amounted to some $50. He also sent at least $15 twice a year to another aunt, Mary Adams, who had a hand in rearing him as well. At the time of his migration Horace had been involved for several years in an extra-domestic union with Emily Lynch (34) in which three children had been produced. He sent for and married her in 1961. Emily remained in England until 1963 when she abruptly returned to the village. Two explanations are given for her return. The one states that Horace sent her home after he discovered that she was having an affair with another West Indian; the other suggests that her mother was complaining about the difficulties she was having taking care of Emily's three children. Horace continued to support Emily until she became pregnant as a result of a union with a villager. For several more years he send money to his eldest daughter for the support of her and her two siblings.

Frank Duncan (10) who had been sponsored by his brother (MS), Benjamin Duncan (5), has sent no money back to his mother for the past several years although he regularly remitted funds during his first few years in England. Since Benjamin did not require that Frank quickly pay back the passage money, the latter was able to send for their brother (MS), Claude Duncan (20), in 1958.

Ruby Joseph (12) who had been sponsored by her common-law partner, Elton Prince (6), helped send for her brother (MS), Phillip Jeffers (24), with whom she had been reared, in 1960. Phillip, who still occasionally remits funds to his mother, sent for his brother (MS), Bertram Jeffers (29), in 1964. The latter regularly sends money to his parents back home.

Orwin Lyscott (16) who had been sponsored by his father, John Lyscott (7), sent for his brother (B), Adolphous Lyscott (26), in 1961, a year after his own migration. Although Orwin was still living with his parents when he migrated he had fathered two children (17 and

18) in an extra-domestic union with Agatha Hannaway (25). Orwin married Agatha shortly before leaving for England and sent for her a few months later. The two children were left in the care of Agatha's mother and were supported by their parents until they were sponsored in 1969 with the money borrowed from (and never paid back to) John Lyscott. Neither Orwin nor Agatha now send money to anyone in the village.

Adolphus Lyscott (26), Orwin's brother, sent for and married his girl friend, Clara John (30), a year or two after his arrival in England. Adolphus occasionally remits funds only to his mother while Clara sends money to her mother and sister every month.

Claude Duncan (20) who had been sponsored by his brother, Benjamin (10), was living with Dorothy Ophelia (27) when he went to England. Dorothy joined and married him a few months later, leaving her two children, a daughter (28) from Claude and a daughter (31) from a previous union, under the care of Claude's mother. In 1962, they sent for the two girls. Claude still remits money to his mother every month while Dorothy sends a small *raise* to her parents only on holidays.

Gary Simmons (32) who had been assisted by his half-brother, Kenneth Tobin (4), had been living with Caroline Primus (33) in a village near Kingstown when he decided to migrate. He married Caroline a few days before his departure and she joined him a few months later leaving their children behind with her mother. Caroline was forced to return home two years later because her mother was having trouble *ruling* [controlling] the children and because her eldest daughter had become pregnant.

As a result of the initial migration of Clifford Tobin in 1956, 33 people were assisted in going to England over a 14-year period. To be sure, had Clifford not migrated many of these people would have found some other way to mobilize their passage funds since these are usually gathered from several sources. Still, the role of kinship and friendship in initiating and perpetuating migration streams and fostering remittance patterns cannot be underestimated. A small range of categories of persons was involved in the Tobin network: nine brothers (all but one of whom were reared together); nine children, six fiancées, three friends, two wives, two grandchildren, one cousin, and one 'potential' father-in-law (CMF). As a result, the main principles involved in sponsorship are male sibling-ship based on coresidence, parenthood, marriage, betrothal, and close friendship. In Tobin's network there is a dichotomy, except among children, between same and opposite-sex links: siblings who sponsor each other are always males while cross-gender links only operate between spouses or those who are betrothed, the sponsor always being a man. Although this is not the case for all migration networks in the village, Tobin's chain highlights the tendency for men to sponsor their brothers, wives, and girl friends and for women to sponsor their children. The network also shows that although many migrants continue to remit funds to their families for many years, there is a gradual reduction in the frequency of remittances over time, especially among married men. In fact, it is expected that women, particularly mothers and daughters, will 'more have in mind' their kin than will men and the two roles of mother and daughter reinforce each other when a women leaves her children under the care of her own mother.

MIGRATION AND THE LOCAL ECONOMY

Most of what is remitted by migrants is spent on day-to-day household subsistence support. Remittances are also used to build, renovate, or enlarge a house, to upgrade household facilities, especially to provide electrification and indoor plumbing, to acquire household furnishings, to buy shoes, clothing, and other personal items, to participate at weddings and other village ceremonial events, and to discharge accumulated debts. They are employed as well to buy house-lots and agricultural land, to establish small businesses such as rum shops and bus service to the capital, to pay for sending children to secondary school, and to finance the overseas removal of additional family members.

There is no doubt that direct economic aid from overseas relatives has raised the income level, material quality of life, and social position of those who are in receipt of regular remittances (cf. Frucht 1968:206-207; Lowenthal 1972:221-222; Lowenthal and Comitas 1962:206; Philpott 1973; Richardson 1983). Nutrition, health care, and even sanitation among many families may have been improved along with access to previously unattainable and prestigious consumer goods. The building of new homes has given employment to village artisans, the acquisition of agricultural land has transferred revenue to several cash starved landholders, and the attainment of a secondary school education has improved the vocational prospects of many village children. The use of remittances to finance the migration of others has also multiplied the opportunities for individual and family life-chance improvement (cf. Frucht 1968:201; Philpott 1973:129-135). But this does not mean that remittances and the entire migratory process of which they are a part have been a panacea for the community's economic ills.

As has already been shown, the migration of land owners, sharecroppers, and estate laborers has been instrumental in the under-utilization of valley lands. Remittances from these and other villagers have also enabled some people to avoid ill-paid or low status forms of employment such as estate wage-labor and subsistence cultivation. This, in turn, has adversely affected local agricultural production while raising dependence on expensive imported food substitutes (cf. Philpott 1973; Richardson 1983:27).

Overseas investment in house plots and farmland has also reduced valley agricultural production. Such holdings normally remain uncultivated or are worked well below their capacity by the resident dependents (often aged parents) or agents (often non-farmers) of migrant owners (cf. Richardson 1983:159, 165). Land fragmentation also results from off-island purchases and renders uneconomical the commercial cultivation of the one- or two-acre plots that are normally acquired by migrants. Competition for available acreage, especially plots destined for housebuilding, has likewise inflated land prices well beyond the reach of landless peasants eager to work land of their own.

The investment of remittances in such standard enterprises as bars and grocery shops has had little developmental effect as well. Small in scale and capital investment, employing only family members, and serving as a distribution outlet for expensive imported food and drink, such ventures can hardly be said to add to village economic productivity.

It would be shortsighted, if not immoral, to place any blame for the effects of migration and remittances on individual migrants or their families. To be sure, the principal reason for migrating is a desire for self-improvement and the long term goal is to come back to the village a prosperous person (cf. Philpott 1973:108). But more than just showing that material wealth is a major criterion for social placement and personal evaluation in the island, this goal suggests that the basis for prosperity has to be sought elsewhere, a further sign of the depressed condition of the local economy. Stated otherwise, if the village offered the kind of productive outlets that could be tapped through the investment of remittances or other overseas savings, these would have been utilized to begin with:

hard-won rural economic surpluses or remittances from working-class overseas occupations would scarcely have been used to finance migration to other places except for the paucity of local investment opportunities in the first place (Lipton 1980:12).

PART III

KINSHIP AND
SOCIAL ORGANIZATION

Chapter 8
Kindred Organization

INTRODUCTION

From the late 1940s to the early 1970s Afro-Caribbean peasant family life was the subject of considerable anthropological and sociological research. A host of book-length ethnographies, collections of articles, synthetic and theoretical studies, and scholarly debates were published during the period (e.g., Blake 1961; Clarke 1966; Davenport 1968; Goode 1966; Gonzalez 1969; Greenfield 1966; Henriques 1953; Mintz and Davenport 1961; Otterbein 1966; Rodman 1966, 1971; Schlesinger 1968a, 1968b; M.G. Smith 1962a, 1962b, 1966; R.T. Smith 1956, 1960, 1964; Solien 1960). Of special interest to Caribbeanists were the causes, structural features, distribution, and normative status of the non-marital conjugal unions, high rates of illegitimacy, and female-headed households that were found in most rural communities. Several competing models attributed these and related features of family life to either the persistence or reinterpretation of West African kinship organization (e.g., Herskovits and Herskovits 1947), the disruptive effects of slavery (e.g., Henriques 1953; M.G. Smith 1962a), cultural pluralism (M.G. Smith 1965), the culture of poverty (e.g., Rodman 1971), class stratification (e.g., R.T. Smith 1956), wage-labor migration (e.g., Gonzalez 1969; Otterbein 1965), or community organization (e.g., Clarke 1966).

Having dealt with Black peasant kinship organization for some 25 years, anthropologists turned their attention to other issues during the 1970s, to studies of verbal performance (e.g., Abrahams 1983), friendship (e.g., Wilson 1971), overseas migration (e.g., Foner 1978; Philpott 1973), recreation (e.g., Manning 1973), drug use (Rubin and Comitas 1976), and urban life (e.g., Brana-Shute 1979; Lieber

1981; Laguerre 1982). The few studies published during the past 10 years hardly match those produced during the heyday of Caribbean family research. Marian Slater's "The Caribbean Family: Legitimacy in Martinique" (1977) is the product of five months of field research carried out in 1956. The comprehensive and more contemporary national study by Roberts and Sinclair (1978), though it contains a wealth of statistical and qualitative data on union formation and sequencing in Jamaica, is based entirely on structured interviews, involves the responses only of women, and lacks a community-level social and ecological context. The last book length account of kinship in the region, Max Paul's "Black Families in Modern Bermuda" (1983), is a brief and only slightly revised version of a doctoral thesis based almost solely on formal interviews conducted among mainly middle-class families. Although Caribbean family studies has by no means been abandoned as a field of inquiry, it seems that it has been concluded that most of the problems that were of concern in the past have been adequately dealt with. A study of Leeward Village kinship formations, conjugal arrangements, and domestic group life suggests that this conclusion is premature. In particular, an analysis of the village kinship system indicates that some of the most fundamental concepts underlying Caribbean family research--the household, parental roles, mating--have been uncritically defined and improperly operationalized, that synchronic patterns of family organization have been transformed into temporal sequences using methodologically unsound procedures, that theoretical disputation has often been based on inadequate empirical description, and that not enough attention has been paid to folk systems of description and explanation. It goes without saying that if it lacks a sound empirical foundation, ignores folk classifications and other emic inputs, utilizes poorly formulated concepts, and employs questionable methodological procedures, the entire edifice of West Indian family studies rests on an inherently unstable foundation. A call for a review of traditional issues is not mine alone. In recent years such pioneers of Caribbean family studies as Raymond T. Smith, Hyman Rodman, and Nancie Gonzalez have rethought or radically altered their original positions on the developmental cycle of the domestic group (R.T. Smith 1973), the serial distribution of conjugal forms (Voydanoff and Rodman 1978), and the consanguineal household (Gonzalez 1984) through analyzing new data collected since their original research.

This need to question 'first principles' and long held verities from the findings on Leeward Village may seem somewhat surprising given that the general features of the village kinship system resemble those found in other Afro-Caribbean rural communities. The kindred, an ego-centric category of kin, is the maximal consanguineal unit, two conjugal forms besides legal, Christian marriage are present, there is a double standard of sexual behavior between the sexes, and there exist a plethora of complex and variable household groupings and domestic arrangements including those which do not contain a mating pair as their principals (cf. Clarke 1966; Davenport 1968; Gonzalez 1969; Greenfield 1966; Henriques 1953; Horowitz 1967a; Philpott 1973; Rodman 1971; Slater 1977; M.G. Smith 1962a; R.T. Smith 1956).

The three related domains of kindred, household, and conjugality have dominated the attention of students of Caribbean kinship. Since the pattern of Leeward Village mating influences the organization and composition of the household and since the kindred is the category from which most domestic group personnel are recruited but among whom sexual congress and marriage are prohibited, it is best to begin a discussion of the village kinship system with the kindred.

Leeward Village kindreds are large and vaguely defined categories of blood relatives similar in structure to the kin networks reported elsewhere in the region (see Davenport 1968:249-253; Gonzalez 1969:86-87; Lowenthal 1972:105-106; Otterbein 1966:128-129; Philpott 1973:114-116; Powell 1982; Rodman 1971:135-137; R.T. Smith 1964:33-35). An examination of its importance in the lives of villagers requires the treatment of its structure and functions, the system of kinship terminology, and the content of kinship relationships.

KINDRED STRUCTURE AND FUNCTIONS

Although the existence of the kindred has been reported by many Caribbeanists, kinship and family studies in the region have long focused primarily on the household and conjugal domains. For example, M.G. Smith (1962a:3, 9) bases his well known comparative analysis of household composition in a sample of Caribbean societies on the following assumption:

I shall try to extract principles which govern family relations among the populations under study from data on mating and household composition. I call these regulatory principles family structure. From the given facts of domestic grouping and mating practice I shall try to derive the principles of family structure in each sample. . . . We may explain the form and development of household groups by the principles of family structure, and since we must derive these principles by the analysis of domestic groups, we can use the data on household composition to verify or illustrate them . . . .

Otterbein (1966:x) takes Smith's suggestion a step further in his study of family organization in the Bahamas when he argues that ". . . household composition was found to be the primary determinant of interpersonal relations [kinship, affinity, and fictive kinship]." In an early review of the Caribbean kinship literature, R.T. Smith (1964:34) also argues that ". . . kindred ties arise out of domestic relations, mating, and local community ties" (R.T. Smith 1964:34).

These unidirectional views ignore the dynamic quality of Caribbean conjugal, domestic, and kindred organization, and relegate extra-household kin ties to a minor position within the entire system of kinship and affinity. Although the kindred has not always been viewed in this way in Afro-Caribbean anthropology (cf. Davenport 1968:249), most studies have either neglected it outright or have pushed it to the background through the overwhelming attention paid to the household. For example, R.T. Smith (1964:33) notes that:

. . . it is quite true that the concentration of attention upon the household as a functioning unit of child-care and economic organisation has tended to divert attention from the network of relationships linking households to each other. It is important that these relationships be studied with as much exactitute as possible . . . .

Yet he goes on to add that:

[B]ut it would be ridiculous to regard the household in a purely negative way, or to forget that 'family' functions require frequent social interaction and not merely a token recognition of consanguineal or deactivated conjugal relationships (1964:33).

In fact, it has been the kindred rather than the household that has been generally viewed in a "purely negative way." It is partly for this reason that Powell (1982) is only able to cite scattered and often indirect evidence of kinship networks in three studies (Clarke

1966;   R.T. Smith 1956; Rodman 1971) in her recent review of the kindred literature.

Methodological considerations account for some of this neglect of the kindred in Caribbean family studies.

> The most tangible aspect of the family is the household, and being physically discrete, it can be dissected, analyzed, and compared with considerable precision (Davenport 1968:249).

> Field studies of West Indian family organization are forced to rely heavily on household composition data in view of the lack of reliable explicit rules about family relations (M.G. Smith 1962a:197).

In other words, concentration on the household and the concomitant neglect of the kindred may be simply the product of field-work exigencies rather than the role that these social forms really play in the lives of West Indians.

The kindred has not always been treated in an epiphenomenal way in Afro-American anthropology. Detailed attention has been paid to it, for example, among Blacks in the United States (see Aschenbrenner 1975; Shimkin, Shimkin, and Frate 1978; Stack 1970, 1974) and South America (see Whitten 1965). The importance attributed to Black kindreds--or extended families as they are sometimes called--by these writers suggests that the deterministic role of the Afro-Caribbean household should be questioned (cf. Wilson 1973:140).

The Leeward Village kindred is a bilateral, egocentric collection of all known or reputed consanguineal relatives of an individual regardless of genealogical distance. Since the definition of kindred boundaries and the recollection of particular members varies from person to person many full siblings do not even share the same collection of relatives and there are nearly as many of kindreds in the village as there are villagers. The entire kindred is usually called by the term *family* (cf. Davenport 1968:249; Philpott 1973: 114-115). Individual kindreds are often very large and it is not uncommon to find some containing well over 200 identifiable members. The distinction made elsewhere in the region between *near family* and *far family* (see Davenport 1968:250; Philpott 1973:114-115) is also made in Leeward Village although with far less precision. For some villagers *near family* includes all cognates to the first cousin range, i.e., parents, grandparents, parents' siblings, parents' siblings' children, siblings, siblings' children, children, and grandchildren. For others *near family* extends to the range of second cousins, i.e., lineally to great-grandparents and great-grandchildren and collaterally to the children of siblings' children and the children of the children of parents' siblings' children. For still others *near family* includes all cognates to whom an exact genealogical link can be traced. The definition of *far family* is accordingly just as variable although many villagers would agree that its boundaries are delimited by relatives to whom no precise consanguine tie can be shown. Occasionally, affines are also included in *near* or *far family* using some intervening tie to establish the link as when ego refers to alter as his *family* because ego's child is alter's sister's child. The lack of agreement on its boundaries and the occasional inclusion of in-laws are examples of the fact that in Leeward Village as in other regions ". . . an individual's recognition of kindred is situationally selective" (J. Freeman 1961:208). In an influential treatment of the kindred Freeman (1961:210) has emphasized the cross-cultural imprecision in the recognition of kindred membership limits:

> The ethnographic evidence suggests that a sharp line of demarcation is never drawn, but rather . . . there is 'a shading off as degrees of relationship become more distant' . . . the outer limits in recognition varying . . . from one society to another, and within a society, even from individual to individual.

The data in Table 8.1 which summarize some of the demographic features of the *near families* (defined for comparative purposes as extending only to the first cousin range) of 15 villagers, three men and 12 women, ranging in age between 18 and 83 support Freeman's assertion. The 15 villagers were able to name a total of 1,146 *near family* of whom 862, or 75.2 percent, were still alive. Of the 1,146 total, social interaction of some sort was or had at some time been maintained with 512, or 44.7 percent, of them. Of the 862 living kin, 483, or 56.0 percent of whom were living in the island, relations were still maintained with 314, or 36.4 percent, of them. Of the 314 with whom there was some affiliation, only 66, or 21.0 percent, were current household members. While it is, of course, impossible to make any kind of statistically significant generalizations from such a small number of the hundreds of kindreds in the village, within this limited sample the following features were present: (1) *near families* of around 60 living members are common (with a range of 32 to 128); (2) the number of kindred members living in St. Vincent averages around 30 (with a range of 17 to 54); (3) relations are currently being maintained with some 20 members (with a range of 3 to 59); (4) and it is typical for about five members of the *near family* to be household residents (with a range of 0 to 13).

TABLE 8.1 KINDRED SIZE AND AFFILIATION

Respondent		Kindred Members					
Sex	Age	Total Named	No. of Living Members	No. of Members St. V.	No. of House Members	Total Affil- iation	Current Affil- iation
Female	35	80	69	37	3	42	25
Female	83	81	42	21	0	33	15
Female	73	87	40	20	0	35	10
Female	63	128	79	51	12	89	59
Female	67	60	47	19	2	21	11
Female	38	87	51	27	13	30	14
Female	67	56	37	17	0	13	3
Male	28	49	43	33	1	16	7
Female	18	60	57	29	4	27	21
Female	47	110	88	54	3	57	42
Male	22	32	30	20	10	15	14
Male	53	81	69	49	5	43	33
Female	48	102	93	48	5	47	34
Female	35	94	82	35	3	29	19
Female	31	39	35	23	5	15	7
Total		1,146	862	483	66	512	314

Despite the volitional basis of kindred affiliation a perusal of household composition shows that particular patterns of interaction are commonplace. From the perspective of ego, the most common relationships are with mother, father, mother's siblings, mother's parents, mother's sisters' children, siblings, sisters' children, children, and daughters' children. The matrilateral emphasis in kindred affiliation--an aspect of the 'matrifocal' complex in lower-class Afro-Caribbean kinship (see Gonzalez 1969; R.T. Smith 1956)--is partly a product of extra-domestic mating in the community since the children of these unions are normally raised in their mothers' households. From the vantage point of household heads, other patterns of membership are also common. In male-headed units, typical consanguineal members are children, daughters' children, and spouse's or mate's daughters' children. In women-headed households, the most common relatives of the head are children, daughters' children, sisters, and sisters' children. For both male- and female-headed residences, the most frequent consanguineal relations are between parents and children, mother's parents and daughters' children, mother's mother's mother and daughters' daughters' children, mother's siblings and sisters' children, and mother's sisters' children and mother's sisters' children.

But a mere perusal of the most typical household configurations presents only a limited picture of the range of association among kindred members. In his analysis of Black Trinidadian family organization Rodman (1971) identified four principles of family interaction, each of which is partially applicable to Leeward Village kindred organization. "Individualism" refers to ". . . the extent to which the individual remains unbound by strong ties of kinship" and is manifested by a general weakness of kinship ties, a tendency to place personal interests above those of family, and the absence of communal ownership of household or other property (Rodman 1971:159-163). "Personalism" which has already been discussed for the allocation of land in Chapter 6 means that the content of a kinship relationship develops out of nature of the interaction between kin instead of by formal prescription. The result is a meagerness of formal expectations associated with particular kinship relationships so that individuals have considerable leeway in acting out a given relationship as they see fit (Rodman 1971:163-166). "Replaceability" is ". . . the extent to which it is possible to replace one person by another in a given kinship role" (Rodman 1971:159). Lastly, "permissiveness" refers to ". . . the extent to which there exist a variety of permitted patterns of behavior in a given situation" and is marked by a degree of randomness in the use of kinship terms and the practice of shifting children between residences and maternal surrogates. "Permissiveness" is the most general of the four principles.

> The existence of individualism, personalism, and replaceability can all be considered as aspects of the permissiveness of the kinship system, for it involves "permission" for the kinship bonds to be as fluid and elastic as these characteristics make them. The interdependence of these characteristics is thus evident. Since the formal kinship bonds are weak (individualism) there is room for kinsmen to negotiate the terms of their relationship (personalism),

and to terminate the relationship and enter a similar one with another person (replaceability) (Rodman 1971: 172).

Although "individualism" is far less evident in Leeward Village than it appears to be in rural Trinidad, Rodman's four structural principles, mediated by other less general principles which Rodman does not consider, help account for the form and content of kindred relationships. These additional features are age, gender, birth and union status, coresidence, genealogical distance, and interpersonal conflict.

Age

A newborn infant, of course, has no choice in the initiation or termination of relationships with kindred members living in other households. The degree of interaction with these non-resident kin tends to be limited and generalized until, from about the age of five, children start to wander from home on their own or in the company of age peers. The choice of kin to visit is based on the strength of the relationship with them and children seek out those who are most *loving* [have shown them the most affection or have been the most generous to them]. Choice of kin affiliation based on affectivity may even result in a temporary or permanent shift in residence. Although the pattern of what has variously been called "child-dispersal" (Blake 1961:83-86), "child-shifting" (Rodman 1971:101-102), "child-keeping" (Stack 1974:62-89), and "child-lending" (Sanford 1974) is usually initiated by members of the sending or receiving household, the personal preference of the child is often the determining factor. Actual or perceived bad treatment at home or incompatibility with a new member head the list of factors prompting children to move in with other relatives.

> *Case No. 1.* Paula Prescott grew up in her maternal grandparents' home where she was left when her mother migrated to England. Although her father had never acknowledged her as his offspring, Paula's paternal grandmother, Agatha Lewis, accepted the child as *family* and the latter frequently visited her home where she was always well received. At the age of 12 Paula ran away from her grandparents' home and joined Agatha Lewis's household. Agatha was very fond of the child and had no objection to her joining her household. Although Paula's

maternal grandparents were opposed to the move, they did not force the girl to return home because she had left on her own accord. Instead, they informed Paula's mother who was living in England and this prompted the latter to send for her daughter shortly thereafter.

Case No. 2. Alvin Thompson ran away from his mother's home to join his maternal grandmother's household at the age of nine because he did not like his mother's new common-law partner. His grandmother welcomed him into her home where he had been a frequent visitor since birth. His mother who had reared him up to that point did nothing to prevent the move.

As children pass through adolescence into young adulthood the pattern of interaction with kindred members becomes more complex as gender, coresidence, personal preference, conflict, and other factors begin to play larger roles. The most intensive interaction with kindred members coincides with the maximum size of the network and occurs between the ages of 30 and 50.

Gender

Several scholars have remarked on the marginal domestic and kinship role of lower-class Black West Indian men and the con-comitant dominance of these spheres by women (e.g., Clarke 1966; Gonzalez 1969; Rodman 1971; R.T. Smith 1956; Wilson 1973). The unimportance of kinship for men and its significance for women is, of course, a matter of degree and emphasis rather than mutual exclusiveness and there are many cases in which village women have little to do with extra-household kin and in which men are intimately involved with their families. In general though the related domains of household and kindred are more important to women than to men. Moreover, although involvement in domestic affairs tends to be greater among elite than among poor men, their filiation with non-household kin is normally limited (cf. Wilson 1973:122-147). In comparison to women, men are also generally able to identify fewer kindred members, know less about those whom they can name, and interact with a smaller portion of those they are familiar with.

Yet there is nothing in the ideology of kinship which states that men and women ought to be differentially committed to their kindreds. Indeed, it is said that *"family* ought to *live loving,"* that they ought to greet each other warmly whenever they meet, and that they should help each other in any way they can (cf. Philpott 1973:114). Villagers are well aware that these requirements are often not met, particularly by men. Some men are said to *selfish* [reclusive] or *likrish* [stingy] and therefore have little to do with their kin or treat them no differently than others. Alternatively, from an early age males form relationships with non-kin and by the time they reach adolescence or young adulthood receive most of their emotional and social gratification and expend much of their material resources in extra-kinship relationships.

Birth Status and Conjugal Form

There is considerable variation in the recognition of and interaction with members of the paternal half of the kindred depending on birth status--whether a person is a *lawful* [legitimate] or a *bastard* [illegitimate]--and conjugal form--whether a person is the issue of a coresidential or extra-residential union. A *bastard* is not normally as acquainted with his father's as with his mother's kin, especially if the union between the parents is no longer extant. There are, of course, exceptions to this depending on residence of the kin, *their* birth status, and the intensity of the relation between ego's parents and their consanguines. For example, a *lawful* person may have a markedly lop-sided matrilateral bias in his kindred if his father is a *stranger* [non-native-born villager] who married into the community and rarely visits his home area while a *bastard* who is the product of a defunct extra-domestic union may have a more-or-less symmetrical kin network if he was informally adopted by his paternal grandmother. Still, with most men being not as close to their kin as most women, there is normally some matrilateral skewing even in the kindreds of legitimate villagers.

Coresidence

Davenport's (1968:249) generalization about lower-class Jamaican households holds true for Leeward Village as well: "The fundamental feature of the household is its organization according to the principles of kinship." Kindred membership forms a major criterion for household residence since it is the kinship collectivity from which the latter finds most of its members. Within the framework of the typical kinship categories and relationships already outlined coresidence of kindred members is often governed by considerable choice. A woman, for example, will migrate and leave her children under the care of her mother or sister, remitting cash to ensure the support of the household. The child may then be shifted to its father's home if the grandmother becomes ill or the sister decides to migrate as well. This fluidity in household membership suggests that the kindred as a whole or at least some defined portion of it may be as much a 'unit' of coresidence as the household itself, a hypothesis considered in more detail in Chapter 10.

The relation between kindred and household is not one of independent versus dependent variables. Kindred ties themselves are also affected by household composition as when the intensity of interaction among household personnel reduces the social, emotional, and material resources that might otherwise be available to non-resident kin. In short, the relationship between kindred and house-hold membership is much more dynamic and variable than some writers have suggested (e.g., R.T. Smith 1964:34; Otterbein 1966:34).

Genealogical Distance

Other things being equal, the degree of interaction and the depth of sentiment among kindred members decreases with collateral distance (cf. Philpott 1973:114-115). The closest relations are between parents and children, sisters, maternal grandparents and grandchildren, and mothers' sisters and sisters' children. But this is a tendency not a hard and fast rule and other factors, especially personalism and permissiveness, often serve to counterbalance it. Even within the nuclear family gender tends to differentiate parent-offspring interaction and while the mother-child bond is the strongest and most affective kinship tie in the village (cf. Clarke 1966:158-159; Davenport 1968:251; Wilson 1973:135), the stronger tie is between mother and daughter.

Conflict

The personalism, optative quality, and lack of jural or moral sanctions in most kindred relations means that disputes between its members are often difficult to resolve and may lead to long term or even permanent estrangement. Although disputes between close kin usually remain outside the official domains of police-station and courthouse, because the kindred is a vaguely defined, unbounded, acephalous ego-centric network not a hierarchical, closed corporate group means that there are only informal and limited mechanisms for settling disputes among members. For example, if a mother expels her daughter from the home after learning that she has become pregnant or a husband beats his wife because he has seen her idling on the streetcorner kindred members may try to intervene but they can do little to force the parties to seek an accommodating solution to their problems. Equally important, such cases often involve appeals to friends and neighbors whose efforts may be just as fruitful as those of close kin.

Personal Choice and Preference

Age, gender, birth status, union type, coresidence, genealogical distance, and personal disputes are some of the factors which temper kindred recognition and interaction. Yet as was shown in their discussion, choice and preference often override these other factors. Men often choose to have less to do with their relatives than women and long dormant ties may be reawakened. A fundamental feature of the Leeward Village kindred, one which it shares with kindreds generally, is that:

> . . . it present an individual with a wide range of optative relationships--relationships which, in the absence of any binding descent principle, it is possible for him to accentuate as he pleases or as it suits his special interests (Freeman 1961:210-211).

A consequence of the personalism and permissiveness that define kindred behavior in Leeward Village is that kinship ties are dyadic rather than group-based. This is even reflected in the manner in which kindreds are referred to. Normally, the term *family* is employed for a specific blood relationship as in the often heard expressions "He is my *family* [related to me by a consanguineal tie] and "You and me is *family*, ain't it?" In the few cases in which *family* is employed to refer to all a person's relatives the connotation is often derogatory ("Them Smith *family* [all persons who share Smith blood regardless of present surname] too wicked").

Leeward Village kindreds are the maximum set of consanguines with whom ego can initiate kinship relationships of varying content. Although the intensity of interaction decreases with genealogical distance, the idiom of blood ties may be used to reinforce existing relationships or to reactivate those which have either been defunct for some time or have never been utilized. Conversely, the presence of choice makes it possible to end existing relationships or to refuse to engage in 'new' ones. Although this gives ego considerable flexibility in this area of social life, this malleability is a two-edged sword for it means that others may act contrary to one's interests in exercising their own preference.

If a given relationship proves valuable to an individual, the remoteness of the collateral tie is ignored. On the other hand, consanguineal links are often 'forgotten' or pushed to the background because certain family members are *beneath notice*, because there is a long-standing grievance between the parties, or because interaction with them is felt to be socially inappropriate or materially disadvantageous. In such cases ego may even be reluctant to acknowledge that a kinship connection even exists; if pressed, he may reveal at most that he and alter are "supposed to be some kind of *family*" with the exact tie left unspecified.

> *Case No. 1.* Nella Collins is on close terms with her second cousin (FMFSS), Thomas Wilson, even though she is the illegitimate child of a man whose maternal grandfather produced Thomas's father in an extra-domestic mating union. Moreover, she only sees Thomas who lives in a suburban community on the south coast of the island when she visits him in his government office in Kingstown or when he visits his mother in Leeward Village. Their relationship, reinforced by occasional gifts of agricultural produce by Nella and periodic cash gifts by Thomas, has been strengthened in recent years because Thomas is a high-ranking civil servant with national political aspirations. He often assists Nella with bureaucratic paper work and is counting on her support in recruiting other family members if he decides to run for office. Although Nella has a warm regard for Thomas, she only grudgingly acknowledges her blood tie to Irma Williams, an aunt (MFD) living on the outskirts of the village, who is a member of a family whose behavior and level of living are ridiculed by villagers.

> *Case No. 2.* Janice Jeffers is on *good terms* with her cousin (FZS), Orwin Woods, although her father, through whom she traces her relationship to Woods, was not married to her mother, hardly supported his daughter, and

permanently migrated to Cuba in the 1920s when she was still an infant. Woods, a middle-class villager and a leading member of a national political party, can guarantee that Janice will receive occasional work on a road gang when his party is in power. Meanwhile Janice has as little as possible to do with her uncle (MB), Albert Findlay, even though they grew up in the same household and now reside on the same *family* plot of land. Albert is considered one of the most *dotish* [foolish] of villagers, a reputation earned by dressing in rags, occasionally walking naked through the streets, and begging passers-by for money. Indeed, Janice herself often curses her uncle or abuses him in other ways.

The optative, dyadic, and self-interested bases of kindred organization make it difficult to delineate its typical functions. The 'folk model' merely states that *family ought to live loving* and that this should be expressed by help in time of need: the lending of money when a person is *broken*; the giving of food when a person is hungry; and moral or emotional support in crisis situations. Yet these obligations often go unfulfilled and when they do occur they are usually between relatives who are united by extra-kinship ties as well. In fact, these same obligations are said to characterize close friendship. In addition, an entire kindred or even large portion of it never acts collectively apart from its embeddedness in a unit recruited using non-kin principles as well. Weddings, funerals, and wakes are all attended by friends, neighbors, patrons, employers, and clients as well as by kindred members.

Given the variability and vagueness of kindred boundaries, it is difficult to attribute to Leeward Village kindreds even the regulation of sexual activity and marriage (cf. Philpott 1973:115). Sexual intercourse with all members of the kindred is not considered incestuous although a few women refuse to have relations with any man to whom a genealogical tie can be traced. On the other hand, first cousin marriage has occasionally taken place even though most people consider such unions *nasty* [perverse] because "the blood is too close."

But this is not to say that the kindred is unimportant in Leeward Village. On the contrary, it is the very vagueness of its stated functions, the lack of clarity of its boundaries, the absence of sanctions compelling compliance to its 'obligations,' and the presence of replaceability, personalism, and permissiveness in affiliation with its members which is the essence of its significance.

Operating as they do within a socio-economic milieu characterized by restrictions on their social mobility and economic well-being, the best interests of most poor villagers would be ill served by rigidly bounded, corporate kinship groups with clearly defined rights, duties, and obligations. Instead, an elastic, open-ended kindred system permitting adjustment to changing circumstances is the most appropriate adaptive mechanism given the marginal social and economic situation which defines the lives of most villagers. For example, the openness of the kindred allows the tapping of alternative kinship ties depending on current circumstances. A woman may appeal to her mother's sister to care for her child while she is working in Kingstown; she may also conveniently 'forget' that she is distantly related to a man she is willing to have an affair with (or suddenly 'remember' a remote tie to a man whose persistent entreaties for sex she wants to divert); a child may move to his grandmother's house if he is not getting enough to eat at home because of the addition of new siblings to the household; and a man may appeal to a distant kinsman for a cash loan or a job. Of course, the variable and optative quality of the kindred permits others to refuse to fulfill their kinship 'obligations.' Still, this is the price which must be paid to maintain the overall flexibility of the kinship system.

KINSHIP TERMINOLOGY

Kinship terminology in Leeward Village resembles the pattern of nomenclature found elsewhere in the Caribbean (cf. Henriques 1953:137-138; Otterbein 1966:117-127; Philpott 1973:115; Rodman 1971:145-155; R.T. Smith 1956:160-162). Kin are often called and addressed by non-kin terms; kinship terms of address frequently bear little or no resemblance to an actual biological link or the 'normal' term used to describe the same genealogical tie; non-relatives are sometimes addressed or even referred to using kinship terms; some kinship roles have a host of terms to describe them while others have very few; and an exact genealogical reckoning is often used to describe a relationship in place of an existing kin label. In short, Leeward Village kinship terminology, like the rest of the kinship system, is marked by openness and variability. Compounding the complexity of the folk system of nomenclature is an alternative mode of terminology. Rooted in the island's European heritage, it follows standard English kin naming practice and is based on what villagers believe to be the appropriate terms of address and reference for various categories of kin. Together with the folk alternatives to them, these terms are summarized in Table 8.2 which contains the consanguineal kinship terminology and Table 8.3 which lists the terms used for affines. Many of the mainstream terms--brother, sister, cousin, father, mother, uncle, aunt, grandfather, grandmother, son, daughter, grandson, sister-in-law, brother-in-law, mother-in-law, father-in-law, auntie-in-law, uncle-in-law, son-in-law, and daughter-in-law--although recognized and occasionally used by villagers when a precise designation is sought are nonetheless viewed as somewhat formal and so are not common in everyday discourse. Some of these formal terms are also recognized as being inaccurate from the perspective of the elite system of kinship terminology. It is felt, for example, that, strictly speaking, the terms *father/mother-in-law* should be used to refer only to spouses' parents while *son/daughter-in-law* should be employed solely for children's spouses. In particular, it is known that a parent's spouse is a step-parent and a spouse's child, a step-child, and although these are considered the more proper terms their usage hardly occurs. Similarly, the terms niece and nephew are known to all villagers and are thought to be the more accurate and prestigious terms to use, but they are rarely employed. Instead, either a precise description of the biological tie is used (e.g., "She a me *sissie gal*" ["She is my sister's daughter"]) or, as is more common, reference is made to the terms for parents' siblings: "I have to call her *tantie*" or "He have to call me *uncle*" (cf. Philpott 1973:115).

Village kinship terminology is also complicated by the frequent use of first names and agnomina as terms of address and reference (cf. R.T. Smith 1956:160-162). The three categories of nicknames in the village are *fun names*, *play* or *fond names*, and *home names*. A *fun name* is a pejorative reference term used to emphasize some physical deformity or moral flaw. One villager is referred to as *Tip-Toe-Cockie* because a withered leg causes him to walk on the toes of one foot, while another is called and referred to as *Pitiful* because of her poverty and quarrelsome behavior. *Play names* or *fond names* carry no such derogatory connotation although many of them either have meaning, highlight personal or physical characteristics, or are a contraction or mispronunciation of existing names. All villagers, including family members, call and refer to one elderly woman as *Nendeare*, a merging of *nennie* [godmother] and Deare, her surname. Many *play names* which connote some phenotypical feature have skin color as their referent (e.g., *Black-Man, Red-Man, Whitey, White-Man, Black-Girl, Brownie, Red-Boy, Reds, Blanco, Congo Queen*). *Play names* and those *fun names* which carry only a mild pejorative are commonly used as substitutes for both first names and kinship reference terms.

TABLE 8.2 CONSANGUINEAL KINSHIP TERMINOLOGY

Term of Reference	Term of Address	Biological Relationship
Ego's generation:		
Brother;buddie;bruds; first name	Brother;buddie;bruds; first name	F,FS,MS
Sister;sissie;sis;tita; first name	Sis;tita;first name	Z,FD,MD
Cousin;cuz;first cousin; first name; description of relationship ["We are two brother's children."]	Cousin;cuz;first name;cousin + first name	FBS,FBD, FZS,FZD, MBS,MBD, MZS,MZD
First ascending generation:		
Pop;father;dad;puppa; daddy;poppy;pappa;dadda	Pop;daddy;poppy;pappa; dadda	F
Mother;mom;mamma; mommie;mumma;old queen; first name	Mother;mom;mamma; mommie;first name	M
Uncle;uncle + first name; description of relationship ("He is my father's buddie.")	Uncle;uncle + first name	FB,MB
Tantie;aunt;auntie;first name; tantie + first name; description of relationship	Tantie;auntie;first name; tantie + first name	FZ,MZ
Second ascending generation:		
Grandpa;grandfather; granddaddy;grandpuppa	Grandpa;grandfather; grandpuppa; granddad; graddaddy	FF,MF
Grandma;grandmother; mammie;old queen	Grandma;grandmother; mammie;momma	FM,MM

(Continued)

TABLE 8.2 (Cont.)

Term of Reference	Term of Address	Biological Relationship
First descending generation:		
Son;boy;pickney;child; first name	Boy; child; first name	S
Daughter;girl;gal; pickney;child; first name	girl;gal;child; first name	D
First name;description of relationship ["He is my sister's child."]	First name	BS,ZS
First name;description relationship	First name	BD,ZD
Second descending generation:		
Grandson;grandboy;grand-child;grandpickney; grand;first name	First name	SS,DS
Granddaughter;grandgal; grand;grandpickney; first name.	First name	SD,DD

TABLE 8.3 AFFINAL KINSHIP TERMINOLOGY

Term of Reference	Term of Address	Affinal Relationship
Ego's generation:		
Wife; first name	First name	W
Girl friend; friend; keeper; concubine; first name	First name	Consensual spouse
Husband; first name	First name	H
Boy friend; friend; fellow I'm keeping with; first name	First name	Consensual spouse
Sister-in-law; first name; description of relationship ("She's my wife's sister.")	Sister; sis; first name	WZ, HZ

(Continued)

238

TABLE 8.3 (Cont.)

Term of Reference	Term of Address	Affinal Relationship
Brother-in-law; first name; description of relationship	Brother; bruds; first name	WB, HB
First ascending generation: Mother-in-law; description of relationship ("She is my father's wife.")	Surname	FW, WM, HM
Father-in-law; description of relationship	Surname	MH, WF, HF
Auntie-in-law; description of relationship ("She is my my father's brother's wife.")	Surname; first name	FBW, MBW
Uncle-in-law; description of relationship	Surname; first name	FZH, MZH
First descending generation: Son-in-law; description of relationship ("He is my daughter's husband."); first name	First name	DH, WS, HS
Daughter-in-law; description of relationship; first name	First name	SW, WD, HD

Agnomina which are nearly exclusive to the domestic domain or used only by a close set of kin are known as *home names*. One woman whose first name was Elaine began to be called *Tantain* by her sister's first child who was trying to pronounce Tantie Elaine. The name stuck and her own children began to call her *Tantain* when they began to speak. Other nieces and nephews and a sister born after the name had taken hold followed suit but her parents and older siblings who had previously addressed and referred to her by her 'real' name continued to do so.

The use of *home names* and widespread *fond names* arises through what Rodman (1971:150-153) calls the "principle of imitation." A child, for example, will call his mother by her nickname because others in the same household are doing so. The limited number of *titles* [surnames] in the community and the wide ramification of kin ties also encourages the use of agnomina. This is because the actual name or the kinship term of reference would prove confusing if there is more than one person with that name or if the speaker has more than one known relative within the particular kinship category (cf. Manning 1974).

But not all people have nicknames and their use is sometimes viewed by both elite villagers and high status islanders as a symbol of the lower-class way of life (cf. Manning 1974). When respectable villagers are assigned nicknames, these often symbolize their elevated social position. Some of these clearly indicate status differentials (e.g., *Cap*, a foreshortening of captain is the term of address and reference for a well-off and politically active villager) or are duplications or approximations of kinship terms used in the first ascending generation (e.g., *Mother* Miller, *Momo*, *Mamain*, *Dado*)(cf. R.T. Smith 1956:161).

Leeward Village kinship terminology is also complicated by the frequent use of kin terms to address and even refer to non-relatives. Villagers often call each other by such terms as *family*, *uncle*, *tantie*, and *daddy*. The latter three terms are usually employed by young people to address non-kin elders (cf. R.T. Smith 1956:161), sometimes people they have met for the first time. Occasionally, the term *daddy* is even used in addressing a younger person of high status or wealth, especially if he is also white.

The use of kin terms for non-relatives and first names and agnomina for kin diverges from the rules governing mainstream Vincentian terminology. Gender differences are always observed, but distinctions between lineals and collaterals and between members of adjacent generations or age categories are often ignored. The "principle of imitation" accounts for some of this divergence but this usually affects only *fond names*, *home names*, and certain categories of kin. The *fond names* of some villagers are known and used by everyone in the community regardless of relative age or the link between the parties. Most *fond names* or first names, however, are more restricted or used by only certain kin. Many village men have *fond names*, for example, but these are almost never used as terms of address by their children and there was only one instance in which children called their father by his first name. The use of nicknames to address other males in the first ascending generation is also rare and an uncle may be addressed by a *fond name* only if it is one used by all villagers and by his first name only if it is preceded by the term uncle. Conversely, members of the first and second descending generations are always addressed by their first name or by a *play name*.

This contrasts sharply with the practice of naming female

maternal kin. A mother may be addressed by her first name, by a *play* or *home name*, by the term *tantie* or by the 'normal' terms associated with the role of genetrix (see Table 8.2). A mother's sister may be called by her first name, by a *fond* or *home name*, by the term tantie, or by one or more of the usages usually thought to be associated with the role of biological mother. A mother's mother may be addressed by a *fond* or *home name* or by the ideal terms associated with motherhood. Although imitation is involved in the establishment of these variant terms, it does not account for their presence as acceptable alternatives to mainstream norms of nomenclature. As the examination of kinship relationships will show, the extant system of naming is a product of parental roles and associated features of household organization. Leeward Village households are fluid and elastic units which quickly respond to changes in social and economic incentives and constraints such as labor migration opportunities, the dissolution of conjugal unions, or the addition of members through closely spaced births. Wage-labor migration in which mothers are obliged to leave the village in search of work to support themselves and their children as well as fosterage in which offspring are sent to live with close kin to alleviate their mother's economic burden often mean that a mother's mother or mother's sister takes on the maternal role. It is as a concomitant of the replacement of personnel that these relatives are accorded the kin terms which are most appropriate to their actual behavior. In a like manner a young unmarried woman normally continues to live at home after she has begun childbearing and often comes to be addressed by the term *tantie* or by her first or nickname if her own mother or older sister is either the most dominant household member or the person most responsible for the child's day-to-day care (cf. Rodman 1971:145-155; R.T. Smith 1956:143-146, 162). It would be both confusing and inaccurate for a child growing up in this situation to address both women by the same term and the child is permitted to select the term which best fits the content of the roles being performed on its behalf. Sometimes a kind of compromise is reached with the child calling the genetrix, *mommie*, and the mater, *momma*.

Relative status, perceptions of personal advantage, and situational factors affect the choice of kin terms outside the domain of child rearing. High status kin are usually addressed by the respectable alternative of a given kinship term rather than by the common term (e.g., cousin instead of *cuz*) and remote kin ties are often translated into close ones with the aid of such terms as uncle and *tantie*. Permissiveness in the use of kin terms is also extended to non-kin when they are called *family, uncle, tantie*, and *daddy* either to draw on the sentiment and idiom of kinship or, when terms used to address members of the first ascending generation are employed, to symbolize status and material differences (cf. Rodman 1971:148; Wilson 1973:142-147). Thus several members of the village elite are addressed by such terms as *uncle*, *daddy*, and *mother*, often followed by their surname or an abbreviation of it, to appeal to the respect associated with the age and generation differences such terms connote as well as to bring these persons into the orbit of kinship with its expectations of financial and other assistance.

KINSHIP RELATIONSHIPS

The variability and complexity in the system of kinship terminology is a manifestation of the form and content of village kinship relationships. The belief that *family* should *live loving* is manifested in the expectation that parents should *mind* [support] their children when they are young, that this should be reciprocated with respect, obedience, and domestic assistance, and that these children should help their parents in old age. Siblings should also *live loving* and help each other in times of need. No fixed rights or duties are associated with other kin, just the general expectation that they should help one another in crisis situations. Apart from these general sentiments little is usually said about the content of kinship links (cf. Philpott 1973:114; R.T. Smith 1956:159).

Fathers and Children

When a child results from a conjugal union, whether based on a nuclear family household or not, the genitor is expected to *mind* his offspring, thereby acquiring the rights and responsibilities associated with the role of social father (Rubenstein 1980). These include the obligation to provide the child with a surname and a class of socially recognized kin, the right to expect obedience and respect from the child and to punish the child for wrongdoing, responsibility for some of the child's actions, and the right (but not necessarily the obligation) to make the child an heir. *Minding* a child, in turn, presupposes *owning* [accepting paternity in] the child. Whether a child is *owned* by the genitor--or even *owned* by any man--is often a complicated matter. Some children are not *owned* at all; others are *minded* by men who do not *own* them. Occasionally a child is *owned* by two men, and in a few cases acknowledged paternity changes over time. Privately some men admit that they have sired children who are *owned* by other men. All of this means that it is necessary to distinguish between pater (social father), genitor (the socially acknowledged biological father), and the genetic father (the actual biological father)(Barnes 1961).

Although some women succeed in forcing reluctant genitors to accept the ownership of their child through a maintenance suit, admission of paternity normally rests with the man. If he has no cause to doubt her fidelity or the siring of their other children, which is normally the case among married couples, a man will not question his woman's pregnancy. Conversely, a man may deny that a child is his, sometimes claiming that he has never engaged in sexual intercourse with the woman or has paid her for her services. This occurs if the woman who tries to *give* [assign paternity of] the child to him is known to be promiscuous, if the child bears no physical resemblance to him, if their union was very brief or furtive, or if he is unable or unwilling to *mind* the child. If a man does decide to own the child this normally indicates a willingness to *mind* it as well. But not all men who *own* their children later *mind* them, and a child may be *minded* by someone who does not *own* it. In cases where the father does not *own* his child, or *owns* it but does not *mind* it, the burden falls on either the mother who is then said to *mind* her own child or on the mother's mother or some other relative who *minds* it for her. A further complication may arise when a father does not *own* his child but his own mother accepts the child as her son's based on its physical resemblance to family members. In such event the son's mother is said to *own* the child although this does not oblige her to support it.

A child may also be disowned by a genitor based on a claim of mistaken paternity. Such a disclaimer may occur if the growing child begins to resemble the father less and less, if it is discovered that the woman was having an affair with another man at the time of conception, or if it is found that she has also *given* the child to someone else. In all these cases the discovery is usually based on *commess* conveyed to the man by kin or friends. For example, when Kevin Charles heard that his daughter from an extra-domestic union was not his, he changed his mind about arranging for mother and daughter to join him in England, where he had migrated during the woman's pregnancy. The following is an excerpt from a letter which he wrote to a close family member explaining his decision.

> Well Noreen I saying this but I know that you would all
> not like to hear such but I am sorry about this child

affairs. Well I have heard that the child is not mine and how its black and I don't decide to mind no other man's child. What so ever they get when I was at home let them make that do. I am entirely finish. I even had the birth paper [to be used for sponsorship purposes] but I am going to send it back to them without a line. My child is not suppose to be so black as I heard from those fellows that came up late. Its up here I hear everything.

Illegitimate children who are both *minded* and *owned* by their fathers usually take their surnames, although this does not guarantee that they will be incorporated into their circle of kin. As *unlawfuls* they have no legal claim to their fathers' property or to the property in which these men hold shares. If a man decides both to *own* and *mind* his child, the amount and regularity of support is also dependent on whether the child is a *lawful* or a *bastard*. If the child is legitimate, support will nearly always continue until he or she reaches early or mid-teens even if husband and wife separate. The ongoing union between the partners does, however, directly affect the support that *unlawfuls* receive, suggesting that *minding* is contingent on sexual access to the mother (cf. Sanford 1975:170). The random sample of 100 households contained 293 children under the age of 15, 143 of whom were produced in unions which are no longer extant. Of these 143 children, 75, or 52.5 percent, received no maintenance from their fathers while 10 of the 68 supported children were maintained through court orders against their five fathers. Consequently, only 58, or 41 percent, of the 143 children received unconstrained upkeep from their non-resident fathers. Most of the supported children were under 10. Few village illegitimate children over this age receive support if they are the product of defunct unions.

The degree and quality of interaction between father and child also depends on whether the child is legitimate and whether both are living in the same home. Children produced in extra-domestic unions usually see their fathers only when the latter visit their mothers' homes. Since inter-household conjugal affairs rarely last for more than a few years if they are not converted into common-law or marital unions, affiliation between fathers and their non-resident children is not usually intense (cf. Philpott 1973: 115). Children have even less to do with their fathers after the union ends, particularly if this is accompanied by the reduction or cessation of economic support.

Although interaction between father and child is stronger when the former is a household member, the connection is not a particularly warm one and this is reflected partly in the rare use of *fond names* by children. Much of this remoteness is a consequence of the male role in household affairs and the kinds of interests fathers and children share. Although it is true that many men help with household duties the domestic scene is largely dominated by women, and men generally spend much of their time and find much of their social and emotional gratification outside of it. Little scope for father-child collective activity exists since most male economic tasks are carried out on an adult peer group or individual basis. Only if the father owns a large commercial establishment do his children regularly help him. The largest shopkeepers, for example, all have their children and other young household dependents working with them and the tie between these men and their children seems much closer than is typical in the village.

The father-child link under shared residence also varies with the child's birth status. If the offspring is illegitimate, the relationship is even more remote and impersonal than if the child is a *lawful*, a tendency which reflects the instability of unions between unmarried pairs. Alternately, legitimate issue are a man's *lawful* offspring, his heirs; they legally carry his surname and will normally inherit his property.

The tie between a genitor and his resident children forms a model for the father-substitute, a role usually played by a step-father or grandfather. Involvement between step-father and step-child is even less intense than between biological father and child, especially in the many cases where the step-father is neither married to the child's mother nor the head of the household. Well aware that their step-children will always side with their mothers in domestic quarrels, many men in this position consider themselves (and are often considered by others) to be *passengers* [passers-by or hangers-on] in the home. This is sometimes combined with resentment over having to *mind* someone else's children. When the surrogate father is a grandfather, however, the paternal relation is often warm, sometimes more so than between actual genitor and offspring. This is because the tie uniting grandfather and grandchild is indissoluble, because such men are middle-aged or older and spend far more time at home than their younger peers, and because the burden of supporting their *grands* is often not great since most of their mothers are migrants who remit funds for the support of the children and other household members.

Mothers and Children

A woman whose child no man will *own* or *mind* will say she is both mother and father to the child. This means that when a genetrix also assumes the role of pater all parental rights and duties belong to her; it supports the view that the mother-child tie is the most important of all consanguineal links among lower-class Black West Indians (Clarke 1966:142; Rodman 1971:80-89; R.T. Smith 1956; Wilson 1973:135). Villagers say that it is the duty of a mother to *care* [rear] her child, and, if the father is not supporting it, to *mind* it as well. However, as elsewhere in the region (see Clarke 1966:99, 177-181; Gonzalez 1969:52-53; Sanford 1974, 1975), maternal rights and duties in Leeward Village may be temporarily transferred to or shared with others. Some mothers neither *care* nor *mind* their children; some *care* them without *minding* them; others *mind* them but do not *care* them. In the sample of 100 households, 68, or 23.2 percent, of the 293 children under 15 were living in units which did not contain their biological mothers. The five mothers of 13 of these children were dead. Of the remaining 55 children--18.8 percent of the total of 293--39, or 70.9 percent, were being *minded* in full or in part by their 24 non-resident mothers. Of the 39 mothers living apart from these 55 children, *minding* was provided by one of six mothers living in Leeward Village, four of nine living elsewhere in St. Vincent, nine of twelve in other parts of the Caribbean, and ten of twelve in England, Canada, and the United States. The inverse correlation between *minding* and distance from the village is a product of the greater financial resources of those mothers living outside the village, especially those living and working overseas where wages are very high by island standards. Conversely, nearly all the 15 mothers living in St. Vincent had surrendered one or more of their children to help reduce the financial burden that *minding* entails.

But most mothers *care* their own children and those who are unable to do so usually continue to *mind* them. A genetrix *cares* but does not *mind* her children if *minding* is being carried out by the children's father(s) or has been delegated to some other household member. If a child is not being *minded* by its father and if the mother has no means to support it herself, *minding* commonly falls to the mother's mother. If the genetrix remains a household member, various parental rights and duties connected with nurture, grooming, nursing, discipline, and training are shared among the genetrix, grandmother, and other capable household members. The right to assign temporary or permanent custody over the child to some other person is retained by the genetrix even if she does not *mind* the child and only plays a small part in the rearing process.

A maternal grandmother is also the most likely candidate for *caring* a child if its mother is not a household resident. Most cases of *minding* by mother-substitutes are short term arrangements in which the genetrix asks the fosterer to *keep* [temporarily *mind*] the child for her. For example, a mother may transfer the responsibility for *caring* her child to her mother if she is working in Kingstown as a domestic servant yet still maintain rights over the child by continuing to *mind* it. In the same way, a married couple may temporarily leave their children with the wife's parents when they migrate often sending for them only years after they have settled. Even when *keeping* arrangements are temporary, day-to-day nurture and training rests with the fosterer who also acquires the right to demand help with household chores.

When *keeping* continues for a long period of time--several years or more--and support from the biological mother is low or infrequent, the fosterer begins to assume greater rights over the child and may even become the child's mater. This often happens when destitute mothers give their children to distant kin or even non-kin for *minding* and *caring* in the hope that the children will be more adequately looked after. In many of these cases the transfer is initiated by childless couples or elderly women with no resident children or grandchildren to help with domestic duties, grocery shopping, and running errands.

Unlike the father-child relationship, considerable warmth and affection mark interaction between mothers (or mother-substitutes) and children. Tenderness and attentiveness may be short-lived, however, if children are produced in rapid succession. If there are additional females in the home, a grandmother, elder daughter, or mother's sister, much of the actual *caring* for the other children may be transferred to them while the mother concentrates on the newborn child.

Both boys and girls are encouraged by example and gentle prodding to begin to help with domestic duties from an early age. It is common for a young girl of three or four to wash her own panties, carry water in a small pan from the road-side pipe to the house, help look after younger siblings, and assist in sweeping out the house and yard. Young boys are also expected to carry water, sweep the yard, and *make messages* [run errands]. But the main burden of help with housework falls on girls and by the age of 10 or 12 they are expected to be making a major contribution to the domestic scene by helping with house cleaning, clothes washing and ironing, cooking, and child rearing.

Although boys are still required to fetch water, sweep the yard, and run errands well into their teens, most of their time is spent away from the house in the company of friends. Most village boys leave school at about the age of 14 and begin to look for work. A mother will rarely rebuke her son for not finding a job since she is well aware that local employment prospects are poor. The boy will be encouraged to enter a trade such as carpentry, masonry, or tailoring and household members may even arrange this for him by seeking out an apprenticeship with a village tradesman. When the boy begins to work he is expected to turn over some or all his earnings to his mother. This arrangement does not usually last for more than a year or two after which most mothers must content themselves with whatever their sons are willing to dole out to them. A desire for even greater independence, an opportunity to migrate to the capital or overseas, or entry into a common-law union removes most men from their natal households by their mid- to late twenties. Unless they migrate overseas or intend to soon return home, contributions to their mother's support either ceases or consists of no more than a token dollar or two a month after they move out.

The early life cycle of females is normally quite different. Daughters are given little free time and their unsupervised activities away from home are limited (cf. Wilson 1973:128). A mother's concern about her daughter's movements increases when the latter *comes young lady* [begins to menstruate] at which time she is admonished to "keep from boys" (cf. Clarke 1966:97; Greenfield 1966:108-109). This warning is usually ineffective and most poor girls become pregnant while they are still living at home. A first pregnancy is usually a traumatic one. The girl will almost certainly receive a beating and may even be evicted from the household for a period of between a few hours to several weeks (cf. Clarke 1966:98-99; Philpott 1973:117-118; R.T. Smith 1956:145; Wilson 1973:128). A mother will nearly always call her daughter a *whore* during the scolding that follows the discovery of her pregnancy. But morality as such is not the crucial issue. Rather, from the mother's perspective the girl has jeopardized her chances of eventually marrying or otherwise achieving respectability; she has also challenged her authority through her disobedience and attempt to *play big woman* [pretend she is a full adult](cf. Philpott 1973:118; R.T. Smith 1956:144-145; Wilson 1973:128-129); and she has added to the economic burden of the household since unions leading to early first pregnancies are usually short-lived, involve low or infrequent child-support payments, and almost never culminate in marriage.

Most mothers soon become reconciled to their daughter's

248

condition and later pregnancies bring less comment, especially if they involve the same father. The mother-daughter relationship usually remains close even if the daughter eventually leaves the household, an occurrence which is far less frequent than among sons. Several mothers and daughters continue to cook some or all their meals together even when they are living in separate households and a mother will readily look after her daughter's children (and vice versa) if the latter is otherwise occupied.

Migrant daughters are expected to send regular remittances to their mothers even if they have left no children behind to be cared for. This expectation is much stronger than for sons, and daughters who do not meet it are considered *ungrateful*.

Siblings

Sibling relationships range from close and intimate to hostile and competitive according to gender, relative age, and coresidence. Generally, the bond between same-sexed siblings is warmer than between those of opposite sex because of greater shared interests and household responsibilities. Sisters are normally closer than brothers because of their more intimate joint involvement in the related domains of household and kindred. There are many cases, for example, of two or even three sisters living harmoniously in a family dwelling throughout their lives.

Age also affects the sibling relationship. There is often a maternal-like, asymmetrical tie between an older sister and a younger brother even if their mother is also a member of the household. Alternately, overt hostility or mutual avoidance often characterize interaction between older and younger sister or between a brother and sister of about the same age in households where material poverty and many children mean competition for both food and adult attention.

The tie between the offspring of the same mother who are living in different households is usually only quantitatively different from that of brothers and sisters reared under the same roof because of the constant visiting back and forth that usually occurs in this situation. On the other hand, half-siblings who share the same father are nearly always raised in different households and often have little to do with each other. Indeed, given the physical mobility of many men, the children of the same father may never have met one another or, for that matter, may not even known of each other's existence.

Chapter 9

Sex, Mating, and Marriage

Villagers are well aware that parenting can be a complex phenomenon composed of several discrete patterns of behavior and functions divided among people who may not be living in the same household. The form, content, normative status, and distribution of the conjugal alternatives available to villagers account for much of this complexity.

As in many other Afro-Caribbean peasant communities, there are three mating forms in the village: *extra-residential mating*, also known in the literature as the "visiting union" (Roberts and Sinclair 1978), a conjugal form in which the partners live in separate households; *consensual cohabitation*, sometimes called "common-law marriage" (R.T. Smith 1956) or "concubinage" (Clarke 1966; Henriques 1953), a union which involves the joint residence of couples who are not legally married to each other; and legal, Christian marriage.

Although each of these unions has features which distinguish it from the others, the fundamental distinction is between the two non-legal types--"non-legal" since they involve neither the official approval nor disapproval of the juridical system--and formal marriage. As elsewhere in the Caribbean, neither the state nor the norms governing lower-class conjugality oblige couples either to marry or to form durable coresidential unions if children result from their mating (cf. Davenport 1968:258). On the other hand, formal marriage, as opposed to non-legal mating, is considered to be a permanent, legally-binding and religiously-sanctioned union among the lower-class. Divorce in rare, even among couples who have separated for many years. In a poor community like Leeward Village, legal marriage also carries with it a rather formidable set of material prerequisites: a church wedding and lavish reception;

250

economic support of the wife and children of the union; ownership of a fully equipped and furnished house; and economic viability in the form of a reliable source of income. There is little possibility of fulfilling these expectations among lower-class village men given the limited economic opportunities and resources available to them.

THE PATTERN OF CONJUGAL BEHAVIOR

It has often been argued that the mating alternatives present in many Black West Indian peasant communities are sequentially distributed according to age. Where, as in Leeward Village, three mating alternative are present, it is said that most young adults are in visiting unions, a majority or plurality of middle-aged persons are cohabiting consensually, and most older persons are married or widowed (see Davenport 1968; Lowenthal 1972:110-111; Horowitz 1967a, 1967b; M.G. Smith 1966:xxi-xxiii). Although this distribution of conjugal forms refers to correlations between current age and union type, it has usually been inferred that the mating types follow one another in a sequential pattern according to advancing age. For example, in analyzing synchronic household census data collected in a highland peasant village in Martinique, Horowitz (1967b:478) discovered that most adolescents and young adults between 15 and 24 were mating extra-residentially, a plurality of adults between 25 and 39 were cohabiting consensually, and most people over 40 were married. Horowitz (1967b:478) transformed this static pattern into a diachronic sequence in the following manner:

> Consensual cohabitation frequently follows a period of extra-residential mating, and is often deferred until a woman is pregnant or has borne children. Consensual cohabitation almost always precedes marriage, and marriage is usually delayed until some or all children have been born. Thus, older adolescents and young adults tend to mate extra-residentially; middle-aged adults are more likely to cohabit consensually, although a substantial number are married; and marriage is elected by older persons.

Many other studies also have insisted that marriage is 'delayed' until middle age or older among peasant and other poor West Indians (see Blake 1961:138-143; Davenport 1968:256-265; Ebanks, George, and Nobbe 1974:231; Greenfield 1966:118; Lowenthal 1972:105; Nag

1971:107; M.G. Smith 1966:ii; R.T. Smith 1956:138, 147, 178-181). The actual temporal sequence of conjugal behavior in Leeward Village suggests that these findings are rooted in the methodological error of uncritically translating a pattern of synchronic distribution of mating forms into a pattern along a time axis (Rubenstein 1977b).

The data in Table 9.1 summarize the distribution of mating and parental status found in 1970 among the 402 Leeward Village males over the age of 15. Prevailing mating behavior and parental status derived from a total village census resulted in the differentiation between eight conjugal forms. Although this kind of categorization has become standard in the literature (see M.G. Smith 1962b:31-32; R.T. Smith 1956:115-119), the concern here is with extant behavior rather than with whether an individual has been married or has lived with a common-law partner some time in the past. Only the category "childless single" refers to overall marital/parental status rather than mating as such: men are childless and single if they have never had children and have never participated in a union involving cohabitation. On the other hand, men are classified as consensually cohabiting or married only if their unions are still on-going while the four categories based on widowhood or separation imply that neither cohabitation with another partner nor the birth of offspring in a visiting union followed the dissolution of the previous union. A widower, for example, who is now producing offspring in a visiting union was classified as a "single father" while a man who had separated from his legal spouse and was living common-law at the time of the census was placed in "consensually cohabiting" category.

The data in Table 9.1 suggest that mating forms exhibit a gradual shift from age cohort to age cohort. In particular they imply a 'movement' towards marriage with advancing age.

The data in Table 9.2 summarize the distribution of mating and parental condition among the 621 Leeward Village women over 15. The synchronic pattern of mating forms among women is not as neatly patterned as among men. Much of this is a product of the higher rate of male wage-labor migration (see Chapter 7) which has produced an 'excess' of "single mothers" in the community. Still, consensual cohabitation shows a pattern of decreasing in importance with advancing age.

Material collected from official courthouse records on the 184 marriages which took place in St. Vincent between 1945 and 1969 in which at least one member of the pair was permanently residing in the village at the time of the marriage casts doubt on the validity of the temporal patterns implied in these two tables and suggests

TABLE 9.1 ADULT MALES CLASSIFIED BY AGE AND MARITAL/PARENTAL STATUS

Union Type	15-19 No.	15-19 %	20-29 No.	20-29 %	30-39 No.	30-39 %	40-49 No.	40-49 %	50-59 No.	50-59 %	60-69 No.	60-69 %	70 + No.	70 + %
Childless single	116	99.1	37	50.0	6	12.8	6	11.5	4	8.7	0	0.0	0	0.0
Single father	0	0.0	16	21.6	5	10.6	1	1.9	4	8.7	2	4.5	0	0.0
Consensually cohabitating	1	0.9	15	20.3	23	48.9	16	30.8	4	8.7	4	9.1	4	18.2
Married	0	0.0	6	8.1	12	25.5	24	46.2	30	65.2	22	50.0	15	68.2
Separated from consensual spouse	0	0.0	0	0.0	1	2.1	3	5.8	2	4.3	10	22.7	0	0.0
Separated from legal spouse	0	0.0	0	0.0	0	0.0	2	3.8	0	0.0	2	4.5	0	0.0
Widowed by consensual spouse	0	0.0	0	0.0	0	0.0	0	0.0	0	0.0	1	2.3	0	0.0
Widowed by legal spouse	0	0.0	0	0.0	0	0.0	0	0.0	2	4.3	3	6.8	3	13.6
Total	117	100.0	74	100.0	47	100.0	52	100.0	46	100.0	44	100.0	22	100.0

TABLE 9.2 ADULT FEMALES CLASSIFIED BY AGE AND MARITAL/PARENTAL STATUS

Union Type	15-19 No.	15-19 %	20-29 No.	20-29 %	30-39 No.	30-39 %	40-49 No.	40-49 %	50-59 No.	50-59 %	60-69 No.	60-69 %	70+ No.	70+ %
Childless single	84	80.0	21	15.6	3	3.5	5	6.0	5	6.6	4	5.7	5	7.5
Single mother	15	14.3	51	37.8	22	25.9	23	27.7	16	21.1	18	25.7	15	22.4
Consensually cohabiting	5	4.8	38	28.1	26	30.6	17	20.5	8	10.5	4	5.7	1	1.5
Married	0	0.0	18	13.3	27	31.8	24	28.9	32	42.1	15	21.4	9	13.4
Separated from consensual spouse	0	0.0	4	3.0	6	7.1	9	10.8	6	7.9	8	11.4	14	20.9
Separated from legal spouse	0	0.0	2	1.5	0	0.0	2	2.4	1	1.3	3	4.3	1	1.5
Widowed by consensual spouse	0	0.0	0	0.0	1	1.2	1	1.2	5	6.6	5	7.1	4	6.0
Widowed by legal spouse	1	1.0	1	0.7	0	0.0	2	2.4	3	3.9	13	18.6	18	26.9
Total	105	100.0	135	100.0	85	100.0	83	100.0	76	100.0	70	100.0	67	100.0

that the relationship between mating types and age is more complex than the three-fold lineal progression from visiting through common-law mating to marriage. Marriage in the community is entered via one of three routes: of the 182 marriages for which there is data, 13, or 7.1 percent, did not involve any previous mating between the pair; 88, or 48.4 percent, were entered directly from a visiting union; and 81, or 44.5 percent, were preceded by consensual cohabitation. In short, marriage more often follows extra-residential mating than it does consensual cohabitation despite the contrary inference suggested by the data in Tables 9.1 and 9.2. In addition, 116, or 63.0 percent, of the 184 married women did not have any children from previous mates when they married while 30, or 16.3 percent, had only one child from an earlier union with another man. Only 15, or 8.8 percent, of the 170 married women for whom there is data had a prior history of consensual cohabitation with former mates. Of these women, only five had more than one such common-law union.

Conversely, most non-legal unions, whether extra-residential or based on cohabitation, do not evolve into marriage and the form that one union takes is not a good predictor of the form of a later union. Many villagers participate only in visiting unions, others move from common-law 'back to' extra-residential relationships, and still others whose marriages have *mashed up* or who have been widowed resume mating in either visiting or free coresidential unions.

Equally instructive of the temporal pattern of union formation is data on the actual age at which marriage takes place. The material in Table 9.3 is a compilation of data on the 109 men and 125 women classified as "married" in Tables 9.1 and 9.2. Of the 109 married men, 16.5 percent are below the age of 40 and 83.5 percent are above the age of 40; of the 125 married women, 36.1 are below the age of 40 and 63.9 are above the age of 40. This distribution makes it tempting to argue that most villagers who marry do so after the age of 40.

Table 9.4 presents the age at which the persons in Table 9.3 really married and, therefore, represents the sequential distribution which can only be inferred from the data in Table 9.3. The information in the two tables are nearly the mirror image of each other. Where Table 9.3 suggests that 83.5 percent of married men elected matrimony after the age of 40, Table 9.4 shows that 69.7 percent of them were already married by the time they were 40. The data on the married women shows the same contradiction between the synchronic inference and the actual sequence of entry into marriage.

TABLE 9.3 MARRIED ADULTS CLASSIFIED BY PRESENT AGE

		15-19	20-29	30-39	40-49	50-59	60-69	70+	Total
Males	No.	0	6	12	24	30	22	15	109
	%	0.0	5.5	11.0	22.0	27.5	20.2	13.8	100.0
Females	No.	0	18	27	24	32	15	9	125
	%	0.0	14.4	21.7	19.2	25.6	12.0	7.2	100.0

TABLE 9.4 MARRIED ADULTS CLASSIFIED BY AGE AT MARRIAGE

		15-19	20-29	30-39	40-49	50-59	60-69	70+	Total
Males	No.	0	42	34	20	10	3	0	109
	%	0.0	38.5	31.2	18.4	9.2	2.7	0.0	100.0
Females	No.	19	52	27	24	3	0	0	125
	%	15.2	41.6	21.6	19.2	2.4	0.0	0.0	100.0

If the sequential pattern of mating in Leeward Village shows less regularity than is reputed to exist in other Caribbean communities like it, this does not mean that the village conjugal system is 'disorganized' or follows a random pattern. When elite and middle-class villagers marry--and most of them do--they do so between their late teens and mid-twenties and such unions are almost never preceded by consensual cohabitation or the birth of children. When marriage among other villagers takes place it does so at a much lower rate and it occurs several years later--but still much before the age of 40--and it is almost always followed by several years of *friending* or *living*. This class-based pattern of conjugality is a consequence of a combination of the differential opportunities for fulfilling the expectations associated with marriage and the social availability of common-law unions only among poorer villagers. However, when conditions change, a re-evaluation of the appropriateness of existing conjugal forms often follows. Such was the case when migration opportunities to England began to open up.

The mass migration to England from the village dramatically affected the extent and age of marriage among the village poor. Of the 184 marriages that took place between 1945 and 1969, 48, or 26.1 percent, took place during the four year peak period, 1959-1962, of removal to England. Most of these unions involved poor villagers under the age of 40 whose male partner migrated within a few months of the marriage. In every case the expectation of removal from the island was the main incentive for marriage to a *friend* or *keeper*. Several concomitants of migration, especially the kind of long-term sojourn that going to England promised, prompted the decision to marry. Removal to Britain contained the expectation of material security, if not prosperity, and meant that the social and economic concomitants of marriage could for the first time be met. This was associated with the feeling that consensual cohabitation in England was either morally unacceptable or legally prohibited and discouraged men from sending for their *keepers* and continuing to live with them as before. Migration to the "mother country" was also believed to represent an elevation in status and respectability and marriage was seen as a necessary ingredient in this transformation. Information from early migrants that Britain's tax structure severely penalized unmarried men prompted several villagers to legitimize already existing unions. These kinds of considerations also encouraged many of the men who migrated to England during this period to sponsor and marry their partners within a year after their arrival.

If the Leeward Village data has any generality, early marriage and a more complex pattern of conjugal sequencing may also be the norm in other Afro-Caribbean peasant or peasant-like communities, a feature which has been obscured through the uncritical interpretation of static census data. Additional reasons for this complexity in Leeward Village besides overseas migration may be discovered by examining the form, content, and meaning of the conjugal forms available to community members.

SEXUALITY AND SEXUAL ACTIVITY

Sexual activity in Leeward Village takes only one socially approved form, with *bulling* [male homosexuality] and *zammie* [lesbianism] considered *nasty*. As elsewhere in the Caribbean, village children learn almost nothing about sex from adult household members (cf. Blake 1961; Clarke 1966:98; Greenfield 1966:108-109) since such talk between minors and elders in the home context is thought to be *common* [vulgar] or disrespectful. Girls are strongly admonished, however, not to *talk to* [have anything to do with] boys when the begin to *see their flowers* [start menstruating] (cf. Clarke 1966:97; Greenfield 1966:109). Several women recounted how they were even told that babies were brought by ships or airplanes. Boys are not warned about *talking to* (a euphemism for a sexual relationship) girls. Unlike the latter, they do not bring *trouble* (i.e., an unwanted pregnancy) to the home.

Despite the taboo on the discussion of sex between parent and child, *nature* [the sex drive] is considered a fundamental human urge and there is much talk about *sex affairs* [sexual matters] in the village. Both males and females are felt to possess *nature* although it is acknowledged that some persons are *hotter-skinned* [possess more *nature*] than others. Being *hot-skinned* or *rammish* [having the quality of a ram-goat] is viewed as a manly virtue and a male who shows little interest in sex is considered abnormal. Precociousness in boys is felt to be a sign that virility will characterize their adult behavior and such infants will admiringly be called *mannish* [trying to act like a man](cf. Clarke 1966:91; Wilson 1973:151).

Unless he is fully committed to mainstream norms of respectable Christian behavior, a man, whether married or not, is expected to be interested in having sexual relations with a variety of different partners (cf. Clarke 1966:91; Philpott 1973:119; Rodman 1971:59-61, 115-116; Wilson 1973:150-152). Success as a lover results in the enviable reputation of being a *saga boy* [rake]. Elite and

middle-class married men--persons who are concerned with respectability as well as reputation--face a contradiction between marital
fidelity (which is part of the syndrome of respectability) and
controlling [having exclusive sexual access to] several women (which
is part of reputation). The contradiction is resolved in several ways.
The ability to *run women* requires a sound financial base--an
attribute of respectability--from which to provide one's lovers with
the gifts, especially money, expected in most affairs (cf. R.T. Smith
1956:137-138; Wilson 1973:152). The notion that sexuality is innate
also means that its expression is largely uncontrollable. A man who
is engaging in extra-marital unions is, therefore, unable to do
otherwise because of his *nature*. The kinds of partners a married
man is involved with help salvage his respectability as well. If they
are *nasty* [unclean] and *undecent* [disreputable], his esteem will
suffer. But if they are *nice* [attractive and well groomed] and do not
run off at the mouth, a discrete affair should not affect respectability. The manner in which the intrigue affects the relationship
between the spouses is also critical. If it brings *boderation* [trouble]
to the home or, worse still, leads to a public altercation between
the two women, the man's overall social standing may be damaged.

An important feature of sexual reputation is the fathering of
children (cf. Clarke 1966:91; Wilson 1973:150-151). Indeed, to be a
full man is to have children and middle-aged childless males are
pitied in private and occasionally scorned in public with the
expression: "You na even have a *seed* [child]." Men sometimes
privately boast about children they have sired but are mistakenly
owned by others.

"What is fame for the man is shame for the women" is the way
villagers express the contrary set of behavioral expectations about
female sexual activity (cf. Rodman 1971:60). Ideally, they ought to
act respectably by not mating outside of marriage (cf. Horowitz
1967a:51-52). A woman who does not behave in this way may termed
a *whore* even if she does not accept gifts from her lovers. The
terminology used to describe the mating of women highlights the
double standard in sexual activity. A girl who has been deflowered is
said to have been *spoiled* and if she becomes pregnant is said to
have had a *fall* or to have *spoiled her chances* (for marriage). The
following extracts from a sermon entitled "Sex and the Single Girl"
delivered by the village's Seventh Day Adventist minister during a
well attended three-month long crusade are indicative of the general
concern about sexual behavior shared by all village religious leaders
and their respectable community supporters.

"That long white wedding veil and gown that you wear is still a symbol of purity. I see some people walk up the aisle and, oh, some of them should go in black. . . .

"Young ladies, let me warn you, all young men want is fun and frolic and if you allow yourself to be a football to be kicked from player to player, then you've got some very good footballers around. . . .

"Its a very sad picture to see a mother sitting there with ten sometimes twelve children in the home and not a father around and no one whom she can surely point to as the father either because she doesn't know which is the father. . . .

"The bible says that fornicator or that adulterer is not going to get into the Kingdom. . . .

"Young ladies let us come to you now, for there are many such tonight who are so foolish to give over themselves freely to men like this and when the men come with nice, flattering, lovely words you fall victim of their pleads and they give you one child, two, three. Afterwards they'll go off and marry somebody else and you are left there to suffer all the rest of your life. . . .

"Some of you may have been living in concubinage, living in illicit, illegal sexual relationships, for years and years upon years. And you say, 'Well, why should I go through the expense of marriage.' It doesn't take expense, my friends. All it takes is a willingness and all that you put into it, and it could be done for you freely. But that's not the problem tonight. Your problem is not just I don't have the money or I don't have a house. Your problem is the problem of conversion--that you don't have Jesus--and because you don't have Him you don't see the necessity or you don't see the urgency of coming out of the life of sin. That's your problem."

Despite such moral and religious admonitions, encouragement from respectable villagers, warnings from parents not to *speak* to boys, and the acceptance of marriage as the ideal social and spiritual arena for the expression of sexuality and the production of children nearly all Leeward Village females begin their conjugal careers outside of marriage. The ineffectiveness of mainstream norms in channeling the sexual behavior of lower-class Afro-West Indians has often been reported in the literature together with a variety of sometimes competing explanations and theoretical positions. Some involve the role of material poverty (the inability to afford a church wedding; the absence of a reliable income source; general economic insecurity; lack of funds to buy a house) (Blake 1961:137-142; Clarke 1966:74, 77-78; Davenport 1968:256, 260; Greenfield 1966:100-101; Horowitz 1967a:54, 1967b; Rodman 1959, 1961, 1971:67); some refer to the unwillingness of men to accept the economic and legal respon- sibilities of a binding marital union (Blake 1961; Davenport 1968: 260; Rodman 1961, 1971:67-69; R.T. Smith 1956:138) or to support the children from previous unions (Clarke 1966:75); others involve the absence or ineffectiveness of kin or community sanctions on sexual behavior (Blake 1961; Clarke 1966:82; Davenport 1968:257-258; Rodman 1971:104; R.T. Smith 1956: 147); still others concern the social and moral acceptance of non-marital mating (Clarke 1966; Davenport 1968:256; Henriques 1953:87-89; Rodman 1959, 1961, 1971; M.G. Smith 1966; R.T. Smith 1956:181-182, 224); and at least two refer to ignorance about the sex act among young females (Blake 1961; Greenfield 1966:109). Each of these positions has some relevance to the Leeward Village situation. Economic considerations play an important role in community conjugal behavior. The extra- legal marital forms are especially attractive to village males and R.T. Smith's (1956:138) generalization about their relation to legal marriage in rural Guyana applies equally to Leeward Village.

> Young men are far less eager to marry or set up house [than young women], for it means that they have to provide a house, as well as support for a wife and family. . . . If young men are reluctant to marry, they are certainly not reluctant to have affairs with young women, and they form attachments which often result in pregnan- cy. In this eventuality it does not by any means follow that the man will be expected to marry the girl. He will certainly be expected to support the child if he is able, and he may continue his attachment to the girl, and other children may be born. Once he has accepted responsibility for the child he has some sort of tie with its mother and the relationship may endure until they can set up house together, probably in a common-law relationship. On the other hand, the pregnancy itself may precipitate an estrangement, particularly if the man denies paternity and the girl has to apply to the court for an affiliation order.

Non-legal unions are begun and ended with relative ease in Leeward Village and the material obligations they entail--economic aid to the partner during the life of the union and the *minding* of the issue that result from it--are only obligatory as long as the relationship is viable. For reasons described below, the only real recourse available, suing the father for the maintenance of illegitimate issue, rarely takes place.

Economic considerations also are instrumental in perpetuating non-legal mating, especially the visiting union, among poor women. The terminology used to describe village sexual activity vividly illustrates that a Leeward Village woman's sexuality is one of her most important economic assets.

To work one's front, e.g., "She can really *work* she *front*." Front refers to the female genitalia and the analogy is to working a piece of agricultural land for material gain.

Money, e.g., "You had better put some clothes on that little girl, I can see she *money*." *Money* refers to the vagina and its intrinsic economic utility.

To make fares, e.g., "She does *make fares* all about." *Making fares* refers to prostitution--the direct commercial exchange of sex for money--the analogy being to a bus conductor collecting fares from the passengers.

To hand up, e.g., "He does *hand up* plenty." *Handing up* means giving cash gifts to the partner in an extra-residential union.

To have a sweet hand, e.g., "His hand *sweet*." This refers to the quality of a man who "does *hand up* plenty."

Whore, e.g., "She too *whore*." The term is employed to describe the behavior of women who engage in several affairs either concurrently or in rapid serial succession regardless of whether they also *make fares*. The assumption is that all sexual activity has an actual or potential monetary component.

To fool/trick someone, e.g., "She/he done *fool* he/she." Although the phrase has non-sexual referents as well, when describing sexual activity it implies either that a man has had intercourse with a woman without fulfilling his promise to give her something, or that a man has given a woman a child and is not supporting it, or the a woman has taken money from a man without providing the agreed sexual access.

To keep a woman, e.g., "He does *keep* she." *Keeping* refers to the relationship between extra-residential or common-law partners in which the man *keeps* the woman by supporting her.

To make/strike bargain, e.g., "They done *make bargain* to meet tonight." Although used in other contexts as well, when referring to mating the expression implies that a couple has reached agreement to have sexual intercourse for monetary payment.

To be sure, marriage also carries economic expectations but these are less clearly visible than in non-legal unions because of an overlay of moral, jural, and status implications. Lacking this veneer, monetary considerations are laid bare in the non-legal union. A man is expected to be *response for* [economically responsible for] or at least give periodic gifts in cash or kind to his partner in exchange for sexual access and many women deliberately seek out men whom they feel are *financial* [well-off]. Many unions dissolve when support ceases and, in fact, some men deliberately stop *handing up* or do not *hand up* at all, despite promises to the contrary, when their sole intent is a short-term casual union. At the same time, a man is not expected to give his girl friend money every time they have inter-course for this is reserved for women who *make fares*.

Some women will boast about generous partners who "*hand up* their hand well" and a few women are quite explicit about the relation between money and sex.

"You think you can go with them men and not look for nothing."

"Before he can do that [gain sexual access] he had to *hand up*."

In reply to the question of why they *got in with* particular partners different women answered:

"He said he like me and used to *hand up* and thing."

"He used to *hand up* dollars and thing."

"He used to treat me a kinda nice by *handing up* his hand."

The material basis of sexual behavior normally begins with motherhood. Before they begin to have children of their own village girls enter unions for other reasons: like males they possess *nature* and find it difficult to resist the persistent efforts of attractive suitors; information about coitus and its reproductive consequences are sometimes vaguely understood; and they are 'unprotected' by any kin except their mothers or mother-substitutes.

Children learn the rudiments of sexual behavior either by eavesdropping on the conversations of adults, through information imparted by older friends, or through youthful experimentation with another child. Initiation into sexual activity is variable. A few girls are sexually active by the age of 10, sometimes with men many years their senior, and a few boys begin to experiment, usually with girls several years older than them, from about the age of eight. Most villagers, however, do not begin full sexual activity until their mid teens. Yet the fundamentals of sex and reproduction are imperfectly understood by many teenagers, particularly girls, and not a few blame their first pregnancy, sometimes claiming it resulted from their initial act of coitus, on their ignorance of reproductive behavior. Greenfield's (1966:109) findings in Barbados also apply to many Leeward Village girls:

Repeated admonitions about "staying away from boys," young female informants complained, never include a discussion of "what to stay away from." Many girls interviewed claimed "that they did not know that what they did could cause a child." They were angry at their mothers for not preparing them for motherhood, but admitted that they would behave the same way with their own daughters.

Despite the almost total absence of parental sex instruction, a mother will try to ensure that her daughter obeys her admonition to *keep from* boys. If she suspects that her daughter is *speaking to* [having an affair with] someone, a sound beating is almost certain to occur. Yet there are two features of the village mating system which render maternal warnings and physical punishment inoperative. First, males are given complete sexual freedom. Villagers are either unaware of the contradiction created by the double standard of mating--trying to control their daughters while permitting their sons "to go all about" means that other people's sons have potential access to these girls--or rationalize it by placing all the blame for an extra-marital pregnancy on the girl. Second, kin, friends, and neighbors do not normally intervene in the affairs of young girls, feeling that other villagers will accuse them of being *macoes* [busy-bodies] (though this does not preclude considerable gossip about the girl's behavior) and often the mother is the last to find out about her daughter's liaison. Among village men there is the added fear of being charged with sexual jealousy. Even fathers and brothers do not try to control the mating of their daughters and sisters for this reason. It is said that some men are eager to "eat the *zaboca* [avocado pear] and eat the seed too [copulate with both a mother and her daughter]" and a few women are even reluctant to engage in a cohabitational union if they have a teenaged daughter at home for fear that their partner will find their new *daughter-in-law* too much of a temptation. Indeed, when a teenaged member of a household becomes pregnant and paternity is not readily known, a father or step-father is occasionally held responsible by the community until the identity of the actual genitor is established.

> *Case 1.* Clive Jessop had been living with Beryl Gordon for five years when the latter learned that her 16-year-old daughter, Tharma, the product of a previous union was pregnant. Tharma refused to name the genitor and the rumor quickly spread that Clive was responsible for the young girl's condition. Beryl was extremely distressed and half believing the rumor, assembled Clive, Tharma, and a small group of friends and neighbors who were to act as witnesses. When all had gathered in the house, Clive turned to Tharma and asked her whether he had ever said anything to her "out of place." She replied that he had not, broke down and began to cry, and confessed that a neighbor's son, a boy of about her own age, was the father of the unborn child.

> *Case 2.* Nella Collins had been living with her father, John, for about two years when she became pregnant as a result of a clandestine affair with a married man in Kingstown. Nella's care in concealing the union soon prompted the rumor that John Collins had *breed* his own daughter. One of Nella's brothers happened to overhear

this charge in a conversation between two neighbors and reported it back to her. Nella then successfully *actioned* the neighbor for slandering her.

Case 3. When Jack Thomas was informed by one of his relatives that his 13-year-old daughter was *friending* [involved sexually] with a man in his early twenties he appeared disturbed but said he would do nothing about it: he would neither rebuke his wife for permitting it to happen; nor would he punish the daughter; nor would he try to prevent the relationship from continuing by confronting the young man. He was not getting along with his wife and he said that any action on his part would only lead her and others to accuse him of "wanting to be there with she [the daughter]."

Considerable controversy has been generated in the literature about the normative status of lower-class Afro-Caribbean mating vis-à-vis societally sanctioned conjugal practices. It has been argued, for example, that it is such factors as those discussed so far--poverty, ignorance about sex, the double standard of mating, and the lack of parental control over sexual activity--that alone account for lower-class conjugal behavior. Those who hold this position (e.g., Blake 1961; Goode 1966) also subscribe to the view that legal marriage is the only socially acceptable union among lower-class Black West Indians. Other researchers have countered with the radically different position that lower-class Caribbean conjugality is governed by a set of norms and cultural principles which diverge from those of the middle and upper classes. For example, Henriques (1953:87) long ago reported that among poor Black Jamaicans "There is no moral sanction against concubinage" and that ". . . the black people have an entirely different conception of sexual morality from the coloured and white sections." Both of these opposing views may be questioned on conceptual grounds. The first suggests that since marriage is the *ideal*, then no other union is *morally tolerated*. The second implies that since non-legal unions are *socially acceptable*, then they are also the *most preferred* forms of mating. Each interpretation, then, ignores the distinction between ideals, norms, mores, and preferences. In addressing the interpretation of marriage as the only allowable mating form among lower-class West Indians Rodman (1971:119) argues that:

Marriage may very well be the ideal pattern, or the

preferred pattern; but to say that the non-legal union is deviant because marriage is preferred is clearly fallacious. It is also possible for the non-legal union to be normative, although less desirable than marriage.

Conversely, non-legal mating may be normative without necessarily being either the *only* morally acceptable conjugal form or the ideal mating arrangement.

Marriage in Leeward Village is the ideal conjugal type among most adults and it is the ambition of nearly all women to marry (cf. Henriques 1953:86). Still, non-legal mating forms are socially acceptable although they carry little prestige for women and lack respectability for both sexes. Few lower-class villagers hold the view that sexual congress should only occur within marriage although most believe that marriage is the most acceptable arena for sexual expression. Males, whether married or not, are given complete sexual freedom and while mating for young teenaged girls is felt to be inappropriate, adult women are normally permitted to engage in premarital unions without community censure if they do not *makes fares* or change partners in rapid succession. It is also felt that mating for both sexes ought to begin at about the age of 16 and that marriage should take place at about the age of 20 or 21 (cf. Blake 1961). Many villagers also believe that consensual cohabitation is an appropriate forum for testing personal compatibility before proceeding to marriage, quoting the widespread West Indian proverbs "come see me and come live with me are two different things" and "better a good *living* than a bad marriage" to support this position (cf. Clarke 1966:82-83; Rodman 1971:64). Equally important, although marriage is viewed by most villagers as a more desirable form of union than consensual cohabitation, morality or respectability are not the critical issues in the evaluation of the two unions (cf. Henriques 1953:87-88; Slater 1977:162-166). Rather, marriage is seen as a more *stationary* [stable] and serious union since it is defined as being life-long and contains the obligation to support a wife and children. All this points to a duality between mainstream and lower-class-specific mating norms and the need to examine the form and content of the three village mating alternatives.

EXTRA-RESIDENTIAL MATING

Depending on the prominent features of the union, extra-residential mating is variously termed *liming*, *talking*, *pass-by*, *friending*, and *keeping*, and the partners are called and refer to each other as *friend*, *girl friend/boy friend*, and *keeper*. *Friending* is the most common village mating form. For nearly all villagers, it is the first union entered, and a great many elderly women have never been in any other kind. The relationship is popular among nearly all men, including those who are currently married. Many women who have never participated in a coresidential union have produced all their children with one or more married *keepers* (see Table 9.2).

Extra-residential mating is probably as popular in other Caribbean communities. But it has received far less attention than the other two conjugal forms and this is partly because of the narrow way it has been defined in the literature. For example, in an influential study of Caribbean conjugality, M.G. Smith (1962b:168) has restricted 'mating':

> . . . to those unions which involve conception, cohabitation, or community consensus and familial action. Where paternity is disputed, I cannot speak of mating. Where the community and kin of a couple who live apart and regard them as mates, the relation possesses duration and tolerance, if not approval, of the partners' families, as well as public recognition. We cannot speak of clandestine or casual relations as mating, since such relations lack public recognition or family sanction.

More recently, Roberts and Sinclair (1978:60) have argued that:

> . . . a clear distinction must be made between sexual association and the existence of a union. For while the latter of necessity implies steady sexual relationships between the couple, it is possible for a woman to engage in occasional sexual contacts without being involved in a union. A union cannot rest on sexual relationships alone.

But clandestine unions in Leeward Village--and I suspect in other communities as well--are such an important part of community conjugal behavior that their neglect would obscure many of the mating system's basic components (cf. Freilich 1961, 1968). Some of the terms used to describe visiting unions are usually reserved for surreptitious relations. The term *liming*, when used to refer to an on-going extra-residential affair, implies that the union has not yet become well established, that it may never become regularized, and that its existence is not widely known or acknowledged. Similarly, the term *talking* ("He and she are *talking*") and *pass-by* ("He just *pass-by* and make a child") also refer to unrecognized or short-term unions. Among young teenaged girls, fear of parental punishment constrains them to keep their mating secret (or at least restrict knowledge of it to a small circle of close friends who sometimes serve as go-betweens in arranging secret rendezvous between the partners). There is also an effort to keep unions which are based on the direct exchange of sex for money from becoming public. A man gains little prestige from such relations and may even lose the esteem of his peers for *running whores*. Since he is likely to also be in a more stable union, his regular partner may fuss about his philandering, especially if she feels that the money he is spending on his *keeper* should go to her instead. Similarly, the woman in the 'irregular' union may also be in a durable union, sometimes even legal marriage, and only *make fares* to supplement her income. A few married women whose husbands are overseas also engage in carefully concealed unions so as not to place their marriages in jeopardy.

As important as they are, economic considerations are not the only ingredient in extra-residential unions. Leeward Village women are said to have a "weakness for sex" which derives from their *nature*. This "weakness" manifests itself in their susceptibility to persistent suitors. Many women readily admit that they *got in with* a particular man because of his *good talks* [sweet and convincing words] and aggressive manner ("He always behind me to be there with him."). Males take pride at being adept at *sweet-talking* or *chatting* females. Their patience and determination are rarely strained even when they are verbally abused or totally ignored, both of which commonly occur during the early stages of *chatting*, a process which often goes on for months. *Sweet talk* consists of expressions of affection, boasts about one's personal qualities, declarations of sincerity, and, especially if the woman already has children, promises of financial help (cf. Wilson 1971:151-152). Verbal declarations are often supported by hand-delivered or mailed love letters containing expressions of undying love and devotion, promises of fidelity, sometimes combined with direct or veiled references to marriage, and a request for a reply. David Hadaway, a villager in his mid-twenties, was attracted to Mildred Roberts, a girl in her late teens, whom he had met on a visit to a nearby village. Though he was living with a woman in Leeward Village at the time, he wrote to Mildred as follows:

Hello Mildred. This is to let you know that I am in love with you. You member the last time we spoke at the [stand]pipe me and your cosin, and I told her that I love you, and you did not tell me yes or no. But Sunday your cosin told me every thing was fine with me loving you. So I write you that you will write back and express your love in writing because you are *shame-face* [to tell me face-to-face]. Please love me. I will not love another girl as long as I have you. A thing I want to put to you is, I will like to come home by your mother and say that I love you. So write back quikley and say if I must do that. Look Mildred all my mind is on you. I love you, I love you too the end of time.

This is your future husband
Mr Romance
David Hadaway

Many such love letters are written in vain and most young, unattached women are *sweet-talked* by several prospective suitors during a single year without *taking on* any of them. David Hadaway was more fortunate than many of his peers for although Mildred was already *talking to* someone in her village she decided to write back. Like her Leeward Village counterparts, she expressed concern about David's sincerity and long-term intentions.

Hello David

I got the letter what you wrote me and I must say those few lines set me on top of the world. About your love to me I cant not stop that because it is love. Know body can't stop love. But I must tell you the truth. I am in love with a boy already. I truly love him with all my heart and it is very hard to leave a boy who I love so long. Alice [her cousin] did not tell you that. Boy you see these days is good luck and also bad luck. When Alice tell me all what you said about loveing me I tell she I know that before you ever tell her so, because I use to see how you is watching me. David I can't really believe what you said you love me and also you will like to come home to my mother for me. You see I am just 18 years old and is I alone is home with my mom and dad. All my brothers and sisters is away so I have to stay with my mother a little more. We will talk about that a little later on. My love to you is just the same as your love to me but I hope you is not fooling me. So until I herc from you again.

I am,
Always your love
Mildred Roberts.

As the following note from a 16-year-old girl to a man in his mid-twenties indicates some women go further than this by making verbal or written requests for money to test their partner's sincerity before deciding to fully commit themselves to a new union.

Leeward Village P.O.

Hello My Beloved boy Friend Donald
How are you? I am asking you this favour. Plese I want to go down in Clearbay [a neighboring village] Friday and come back Monday Morning. I want a Suit case and shoe so I am askin you Plese if you will give me them. Harold i will do any thing for you because i love you and I want you to love me. As long as a reel fish has a tail my love for you will never fail. O.K.

I am your
girl Friend Jane Sandiford

More experienced women are less likely to use *sweet talk* in making these requests. The following note was written by a married woman in her late thirties whose husband was away in England to a prospective lover in the village.

Leeward Village

Hei Hillary
This is Eunice. Why the hell you treating me so. You always promiceing me something and not giving me. Any way my dear I was looking for you last night and cant find you. Any way please some money for me. I dont even have so much as a red cent in my hand this morning to make our tea. After you see I send to you this morning you can emagine. I will treat you nicely dont be afraid.

I am Eunice

The stability of extra-residential unions parallels this variability in affectivity and commerciality. Some visiting unions last for several years and there are a few which have been extant for over 20 years. The majority, however, are short-lived affairs lasting no more than a year or two. Since they are based on individualism, extra-residential unions may be terminated when either party wishes to do so. And since they are non-legal and do not involve the kind of material, social, and domestic obligations associated with coresidence, they appeal to lower-class males: they permit sexual gratification and the gaining of prestige (if several partners are involved simultaneously or consecutively) without the need to enter a legal or consensual union in which the economic and other obligations may be difficult or impossible to meet.

The absence of well defined rights and responsibilities uniting extra-residential partners is a main reason many such unions end after a short period of time. The woman is expected to be sexually faithful to her partner, who, in turn, is required to reciprocate with gifts of money or other material items. Beyond this, little is specified about the way the relationship should unfold and various kinds of behaviors are permitted. Some women regularly wash and cook for their non-resident boy friends, while others never do so. Some unions are very intimate, while others are confined to sexual release. Some unions involve constant visiting between households, while others are based on furtive nocturnal encounters at some deserted locale or in the home of a third party. Some unions demand regular cash outlays to ensure their viability; others are marked by the near absence of gift-giving. There is a measure of male sexual-exclusiveness in some relationships; others are an attempt to simultaneously *control* several women. Some show promise of being transformed into marriage, while others are fleeting affairs soon to be terminated.

Permissiveness also characterizes the relation between the man and his partner's parents in those cases in which a formal (and sometimes written) request has been made to begin or regularize a visiting union. The granting of permission to visit the home is made according to the suitor's appearance, family background, reputation and economic well-being, and on the expectation that legal marriage may eventually take place. Economic considerations are always at the forefront. In one case, a mother accepted her daughter's boy friend because he offered to 'lend' her some money to buy goods for her small peddling business; in another, a father was reluctant to interfere in the relation between his adolescent daughter and a grown man because the latter was always giving him gifts; and in still another, both parents browbeat their daughter into marrying a man she was not fond of because he was a prosperous returned migrant. Alternately, if the suitor is poor, unemployed, or working for low wages, parental approval is often withheld.

CONSENSUAL COHABITATION

Living, keeping, and *living common law* are the folk terms used to describe consensual unions based on cohabitation. That *keeping* is employed for both visiting and coresidential relationships suggests that villagers see a close resemblance between the two forms of union. Common-law partners are referred to and refer to each other as *keepers* or *friends* again implying that the two non-legal unions share much in common. The mere presence of the two non-legal mating alternatives in Leeward Village is also an important adaptive feature of village mating. Both extra-residential mating and consensual cohabitation allow sexual and procreative functions to be carried out without the necessity of entering a permanent, legal union.

Still, *friending* and *living* differ in several respects. As a mating form which they know is practiced among middle-class persons, the visiting union is not normally condemned on grounds of morality or respectability. The common-law union, a conjugal type hardly ever found among the middle class and elite, not only conflicts with basic religious teachings but also deliberately violates the societal norm of legal, Christian marriage as the only acceptable union for sexual coresidence. Conversely, consensual cohabitation is an unequivocal sign of the rejection of societal patterns of respectable mating, a signal that mainstream norms are ineffective in channeling behavior among lower-class villagers.

Consensual cohabitation is also confined to adults and only a few couples under 20 are *living common law*. This is partly because the union is reserved mainly for women with children; since most women do not begin to produce issue until the age of 18, early coresidence is discouraged. *Living* also demands a degree of economic responsibility in the form of the support of a *keeper* and provision for or maintenance of a dwelling, even if it is only a rented house, that most young men are unable or unwilling to undertake. Conversely, the consensual union provides a more reliable base for the *supportance* of a woman and her children than does the visiting union. This is because the division of labor among common-law partners involves the provision of money and/or food by the man and the carrying out of domestic functions by the woman. Indeed, from the perspective of day-to-day domestic life, there is often little to differentiate consensual from legal unions (cf. R.T. Smith 1956:178-179). Consensual unions are also more durable than extra-residential unions. Many last for five years or more, and there are couples in the village who have been *living* for over 20 years. For these reasons many lower-class villagers feel that despite the damage to the woman's respectability *living* is preferable to *friending* when there are several children to support. On the other hand, many younger women with only a child or two are unwilling to accept the additional behavioral constraints and domestic responsibilities of *keeping*. They are also discouraged from entering these unions by their mothers who fear that this may spoil their chances of eventually marrying.

Because they provide a more dependable basis for the support of women and their children than extra-residential mating yet free men from the economic and legal obligations of marriage consensual unions are a popular mating form in Leeward Village with 39.3 percent of men and 25.6 percent of women between 30 and 50, respectively, *living common law* (Tables 9.1 and 9.2).

Still, consensual cohabitation is not the same as marriage and the two unions should not be confused. Just as the obligations of economic support and domestic responsibility distinguish *living* from *friending*, so do they mark the difference between *living* and marriage. The social and economic expectations surrounding marriage--elaborate and expensive ceremonial, a house and furnishings, a life-long, morally- and legally-sanctioned commitment, and a reliable income base--are also absent in the consensual union. *Keeping* is viewed as a voluntary arrangement which may be terminated at any time by either partner. Once the relationship ends, the obligation to support the woman also ends. The fundamental impermanence of *living* also means that many middle-aged villagers have participated in three or four of them, sometimes going back to a former partner after a later union has proven unsatisfactory. For many men, it is easy to replace consensual mates with each other. Several cases were observed in which men *dispatched* with one *keeper* and moved in with another on the same day or *ran* one partner and replaced her with another within a day or two.

The instability of consensual unions is also manifested in the manner in which the rights, duties, and obligations of the partners are defined. Even during the life of the union the requirement of being *response* for the *keeper* and the children of the union is seen as less binding in the consensual union than in marriage. A woman

is expected to *do for* her *keeper* but is not obliged to provide his
meals or wash his clothes because they "are only living together and
not married." Similarly, a man is expected to be *response* for his
concubine but cannot be compelled to support her because she is not
his legal spouse. Permissiveness in the consensual union, especially
regarding economic support, acts as a rationale either when the
union's expectations are not being actualized but the partners do not
want to *mash up*, or when there is a desire to end a union which is
not satisfying to one or both partners. An unemployed man, for
example, may be excused for not supporting his *keeper* because he is
not obliged to do so; a *keeper* who has *butt* [cuckolded] her partner
may be absolved by both the mate and the community since she is
not required to provide him with exclusive sexual access, especially
if his support to the household is insufficient for its maintenance. In
both cases, however, the decision to tolerate the breach in expected
conduct is left to the partners themselves.

MARRIAGE

Legal, Christian marriage is the ideal mating form in Leeward
Village because it conforms to both lower-class and mainstream
notions of respectable conjugal behavior, because it is the only
mating form acceptable to all the island's religious denominations,
because it is the dominant conjugal form among the society's middle
and upper class, and because it is thought to represent an actual or
potential transformation in life-chances. When asked whether it is
better to marry or to live together, villagers unreservedly choose
marriage, often quoting the Bible--"It is better to marry than to
burn" (First Corinthians 7:9)--as support. Marriage involves several
behavioral expectations which, together with conformity to religious
morality, confer respectability on married people. A married man
should give up his philandering and "cleave to his wife." He should
not be seen *knocking about* [loafing] on the roadside, *liming*
[carousing] on street corners, or frequenting rum shops. A married
woman "should keep herself to herself" and not be seen engaging in
idle roadside *commess*. She should spend most of her time taking
care of the home and appear neat and well groomed in public. Above
all, she should not *butt* her husband. If she observes these expectations she will earn the term of address, *mistress*, a label symbolizing
the deference and respect that ought to be shown to married women
(cf. Philpott 1973:123). Such respect does not come automatically and
if the *worthless behavior* (e.g., cursing and quarreling in the street

by the woman and habitual drunkenness by the man) that characterized the couple's pre-nuptial behavior continues, respectability is
denied them and they are treated and thought of in much the same
way as they were before they married.

Marriage is also the ideal mating form in Leeward Village
because of the rights, duties, and obligations associated with it.
Unlike consensual cohabitation, marriage is viewed as a permanent,
legal union in which the responsibilities of the partners are clearly
defined and obligatory. This holds especially for its economic referents and helps explain why marriage is desired by most women and
avoided by many men (cf. R.T. Smith 1956:138).

> "The husband has *response* of *minding* the wife, giving her
> whatever she has need of. The wife has *response* for the
> husband in keeping him clean and getting him something
> regular to eat."

> "You are responsible for a wife when married but when
> *common-law* anything could happen."

> "You never went to church so you can always leave the
> woman [under consensual cohabitation] but if married she
> can always take you to court to maintain her."

> "When married you can always say you have a husband to
> take your *response*; when *common-law* the boy could come
> and go and pretend to love you and come only for sex."

Given these requirements and the presence of two socially
acceptable alternatives to it, it is not surprising that marriage is the
least common conjugal form in Leeward Village. In 1970, 38.3
percent of men and 24.2 percent of women over the age of 20 were
in an ongoing marital union (see Tables 9.1 and 9.2). Although this
at first suggests that marriage occurs more frequently than *living*--
during the same time 23.2 percent of men and 18.2 percent of
women in the same age cohort were in common-law unions--overall
the consensual union is more popular. Many villagers have been
involved in two or more relationships based on *living* while only a
handful have been married twice. In addition, many of the currently
married couples entered marriage via consensual cohabitation.

Other social and economic expectations associated with it also
act to discourage some people from marrying. The woman ought to
be childless, in her early twenties, and living with her parents. Her

suitor, who should have the means to adequately support a wife before contemplating marriage, should either formally visit the girl's home to express his interest in marrying her or, better still, write a letter to her mother containing a proposal of marriage. If he is accepted, a date for the wedding should be set. The ceremony ought to be held in a church, preferably outside the village to heighten the formality of the events and ensure a large, conspicuous motorcade back to the village to celebrate an elaborate and expensive *keep-up* [reception] in a banquet hall rented for the occasion. The costs of the wedding should be borne by the couple and their parents according to their means. After the marriage the couple should settle down to life-long monogamous neolocal residence in a dwelling which the husband owns and has furnished (cf. Clarke 1966:76-79; Greenfield 1966:100-101; Horowitz 1967a:51-52; Otterbein 1966:33-56; Philpott 1973:122-123; R.T. Smith 1956:168-177).

The decision to marry is a male prerogative and is based on such considerations as romantic love (if the couple is young and has not been cohabiting consensually), the personal qualities of the mate (thrift, industriousness, sexual fidelity), economic circumstances (the opportunity to migrate, the securing of enough money to build a house), and religious conversion. This is not to say that the woman or her parents, if she is still living at home, play no role in the decision to marry. Many suitors are found wanting because they are too poor, come from disreputable families, are notorious philanderers, and so on. But, the decision to marry at all as opposed to remaining single is made by men and most women would like to marry if they had the chance, a generalization supported by the village expression that for women "when it comes to marriage, before none, any." When asked why they had not married women almost invariably replied "I can't marry myself" while men said they could not afford to get married or that they had yet to meet the right partner.

Still, many villagers do marry though their unions hardly follow the formal expectations associated with the matrimonial state. Some, for example, involve poor people in their fifties who have a simple *license wedding* [court-house ceremony without a reception] after having lived together for many years. In practice, then, marriage may be entered into in a variety of ways. Some unions are preceded by extra-residential mating, others by consensual cohabitation; in some cases, the bride is childless, in others, she has one or more children from her fiancé or from a previous mate or series of mates; many marriages involve a well-attended church ceremony and an elaborate reception but some are preceded by only a *license wedding* attended by bride, groom, and two witnesses; in some cases, provision is made for separate residence in a dwelling owned by the groom, in others, the couple merely moves into the bride's household for a period which may range from a few months to several years. More specifically, of the 184 marriages involving villagers which took place between 1945 and 1969 the ideal pattern of entry into marriage was followed in 11, or six percent of them.

The feature most commonly associated with the ideal is a church wedding and between 1945-1969 there were only three *license weddings*. But the presence of a church wedding is no assurance that an elaborate reception will also take place. In 52, or 29.4 percent, of the 177 marriages for which there is data, there was no reception at all; in 30, or 16.9 percent, the reception consisted of an informal gathering of a few friends and close kin who partook of some wine and cake. The size of the reception is usually linked to the kind of union that immediately preceded the marriage. Although there are many exceptions, the tendency is greater for couples who have been *living common law* for several years to have a much small *fête* [reception] than for those who have never lived together. The association between reception size and previous union status is partly social and partly economic. Couples who have been living together before their marriage cannot expect much help from their parents since financial aid of this type is normally associated with continuous residence in the natal household until marriage. Such couples also tend to have fewer economic responsibilities, hence a greater opportunity to have saved enough money for an expensive *fête*. Conversely, couples who entered marriage via *living* find it difficult to finance a large *fête* since they have usually had the burden of supporting a household containing children produced during or prior to their cohabitation. Such couples are usually poor to begin with since common-law unions are unacceptable among prosperous villagers. Elaborate receptions are also less common among coresidential couples because it is sometimes felt that while they ought to regularize their unions in the sight of God by having a church wedding, an elaborate reception is more appropriate for younger couples who have never lived together. Indeed, if they have a large reception they may be accused of squandering their money or trying to *show themselves* [show off] although they also risk being mocked for having a *t'ief wedding* if there is no reception at all.

But the youthful marriage of childless couples, although it typically involves a large *fête*, normally rules out the possibility of simultaneous house ownership and neolocal post-marital residence. Most young, childless women marry men either their own age or a few years older than themselves. This almost invariably rules out possession of a dwelling since young men, even if they are regularly employed, will have had insufficient opportunity to accumulate enough capital to buy or build their own home. Conversely, men who already own a property--persons at or near middle age--usually marry women who have already produced issue for them or others and are only a few years their junior. Although the formation of new and independent households occurred in 127, or 69.4 percent, of the 183 marriages for which there is data, the dwelling was owned by the husband in only 62, or 33.9 percent, of cases. Of the residence types associated with patterns other than the ideal, matrilocality was the most common with 43, or 23.5 percent, of couples moving in with the wife's parent(s) after the ceremony. The most usual modes of house tenure among neolocally residing couples were removal to a dwelling rented by the husband (29, or 22.8 percent, of the 127 cases of neolocal post-marital residence) and residence in a house owned by the wife (24, or 18.9 percent, of cases). In only 18, or 18.5 percent, of the 178 marriages for which there is data, was there any provision of housing, including the purchase, building, repair, or rental of a dwelling in preparation for the marriage.

The expectation of life-long faithful monogamy is also rarely achieved. Of the 183 marriages for which there is data, 23, or 12.6 percent, ended in informal separation. Divorce, as a means for terminating an unsuccessful union, is ruled out in most cases because of the expense involved, the hope of some wives for reconciliation, the expectation by both partners that they will not remarry, and the ease with which later non-legal unions can be entered. Adultery and the cessation of economic support are the two main causes of marital breakdown. Fourteen of the 19 cases of union dissolution for which there is data were motivated by adultery. In three cases it was the husband's *wildness* [philandering] that caused his wife to leave him; in four cases the couple *mashed up* after the husband discovered that his wife had *butt* him while they were residing in the same household; and in seven cases the wife *butt* the husband while the latter was working off the island. In four of these seven cases the husband learned of his wife's philandering only after she became pregnant. In the five remaining cases of marital breakdown, the union ended after the migrant husband stopped supporting his wife.

There are few married men other than those who entered matrimony at an advanced age or who are strongly committed to Christian moral precepts who have not at some time had an outside affair. The three cases of the husband's philandering leading to separation merely highlight the fact that male adultery rarely precipitates a *mashing up*. Many wives openly complain to friends and neighbors about their husbands' liaisons and the bitterest quarrels between spouses as well as the severest cases of wife-beating are a consequence of male philandering. Some wives openly confront their husbands' *keepers* and a few have even physically attacked them. But most wives are obliged to resign themselves to their husbands' behavior, speaking out only when they feel that the money given to the *keeper* is adversely affecting the economic well-being of the household. The following letter illustrates the nature of this concern.

At Home.

Dear Dafford,

    Well, this is Avril explaining her mind to you once and forever more. Now, Dafford, I haven't enough strength into me to talk, because what you was to gave me to make it you put into another woman of yours, so that they can walk and bounce on me so I write because it's no use talking when you don't mean to change. Dafford it is eight years since we all knows each other and it now happens that you say you got married. It is just a year since this had been done and you are not behaving like a married man. This thing is looking funny to see that you are married to me and you're still going around with another woman.

    Now I am quite satisfy to go and work for my child because God see that he needs a help. You have Denise [his girl friend's daughter] and her mother over us.

From
Avril

Although less common and blatant than male adultery the extra-marital affairs of wives is greater than one might expect given the strong community sentiment against it. Of the 212 village women who were or had at some time been in a marital union 44, or 20.1 percent, had had an extra-marital affair. Sexual frustration among the wives of migrants prompts some of these women to enter an outside union. Economic considerations encourage other women to form short-term liaisons to supplement the meager earnings of their husbands from the gifts of money received from their lovers. The double standard of mating is also a contributing factor since it

280

produces the contradiction that all wives (except one's own) are eligible sex partners (cf. Freilich 1961, 1968). Most men, whether they are themselves married or not, would not hesitate to "beg for a piece of the thing" from a married woman if they felt that they could "get through." Indeed, intercourse with a married woman would only add to their esteem among their peers. Differential mating norms also mean that wives take great care to conceal their affairs from their husbands and few cases of female adultery result in marital breakdown. To be sure, there will be much gossip about their philandering, especially among close kin and affines, but little effort will be made to inform their husbands or otherwise break up the adulterous union.

Chapter 10

The Household

Like their counterparts elsewhere in the Afro-Caribbean, Leeward Villagers consider a family composed of a legally married couple and their children as the ideal arena for sexual expression, procreation, child rearing, cohabitation, domestic group life, and economic cooperation (cf. Blake 1961:110-113; Horowitz 1967a:51-52; Philpott 1973:120-123; R.T. Smith 1964:35-36; 1970). This household arrangement is highly evaluated since it originates from adherence to both societal and lower-class-specific norms of respectable mating and because it implies the economic viability and independence of the family group through the efforts of the husband-father. Yet with less than one third of village households composed in this way, conformity to the ideal is the exception rather than the rule. Several factors produce deviations from the nuclear family household ideal. Visiting unions create units lacking a coresident mating pair; common-law marriage results in households which depart from the conjugal ideal; labor migration affects household composition through a shortage of marriageable males, lengthy absences of married men from their families, and the removal of parents of both sexes; natural and socio-economic forces such as death, union dissolution, and migration generate households composed of solitary individuals of both sexes and varying ages; and child-shifting and informal adoption complicate even those units which have a nuclear family core.

The presence of exceptions to the elementary family residential ideal and the resultant 'messiness' in the configuration of household groups have long been recognized in Caribbean family studies and have stimulated the production of various competing and often confusing classifications of the different 'types' of domestic arrangement found in lower-class communities (e.g., Clarke 1966:117-135; Greenfield 1966:190; Henriques 1953:105-114;Horowitz 1967a:43-45; Otterbein 1966:190; Philpott 1973:147-152; M.G. Smith 1962a). A basic but often unquestioned assumption underlies most of these typologies: the household is the fundamental unit of Caribbean social organization (Ashcraft 1968:64; Otterbein 1966:x; Philpott 1973:113; R.T. Smith 1960:67).

In Chapter 8 concentration on the household in Caribbean family studies was said to be a product of the exigencies of fieldwork. Overemphasis on the household may also be challenged on conceptual and empirical ground. This is not to say that the household is unimportant in the day-to-day life of villagers or that R.T. Smith's (1964:33) already quoted contention that ". . . it would be ridiculous to regard the household in a purely negative way" should be dismissed. Rather, it means that Wilson's (1973:135-140) contrary position, developed from his study of household composition and morphology in Providencia, a tiny island in the Western Caribbean, that "Until preoccupation with the household and family is reduced to a proper perspective, the mainstreams and wellsprings of Caribbean social life will never be understood" also needs to be considered.

> [T]he importance of the household does not lie in its structure. In terms of social relations based on kinship, its makes no differences whether the structure is conjugal or affinal, whether the family is matrifocal or nuclear. The domestic realm is the culturally defined province of the female no matter whether there is a spouse present or not, no matter whether he is a legal or common-law spouse. The societal relationships of women are built upon kinship ties, and all men are peripheral within the kinship sphere (Wilson 1973:135-140).

Wilson is no doubt overstating his case and most Caribbeanists would find his position that the household is relatively *unimportant* unconvincing. Nevertheless, several researchers have pointed out that too much concentration on the household has detracted from an analysis of inter-household relationships (Greenfield 1961:73; Philpott 1973:113; R.T. Smith 1964:33; M.G. Smith 1962b:7-9; Solien 1960:101). Still, except for Solien's (1960) early work in Belize this awareness has not been translated into a re-evaluation of the structure and function of the Caribbean household. The organization of households in Leeward Village suggests that such a rethinking is in order.

HOUSEHOLD COMPOSITION

Many different residential configurations are present in the community including two-generation male-headed nuclear families, three-generation female-headed units consisting only of consanguineal kin, married couples living by themselves or with one or more grandchildren, and adults living alone. A perusal of the 'shapes' that households take, of course, cannot show how these units came into being: a family consisting of a mother and children may either a product of a husband's migration or the result of one or more visiting unions. Nor can descriptions of household configuration give any indication of its internal workings (cf. Wilson 1973:135-140). Still, a description of the demographic and morphological characteristics of households can be a useful first step in determining the generation, maintenance, transformation, and functioning of domestic groups.

As the next section shows, there is a need in Leeward Village to distinguish between coresidence, or living together in the same house, and domestic group life. Though the two notions generally overlap the concern at this point is with joint residence as opposed to cooking and eating together and in this respect the total village population of 2,245 persons is distributed among 433 residential units for a mean size of 5.2 persons per residence. There are relatively few units with 10 or more members (see Table 10.1)--39 out of the 433--but these contain a total of 447 people, or 20 percent of the village population. Table 10.1 also shows that 60 percent of residences are headed by women and that 60 percent of villagers are living in female-headed units. The difference in the size of male- vs. female-headed units, however, is not significant.

Villagers hold that a man in the role of husband/father ought to head his household and *rule* its members if he owns the dwelling and is responsible for the support of its members (cf. M.G. Smith 1962a:17). As head he is ultimately responsible for everything that goes on in the home and acts as final arbiter in household decision-making. He decides who may visit or live there; he directs the disposition of household property; and he takes charge of crises affecting the unit such as death, unlawful trespass, and litigation (cf. M.G. Smith 1962a:18). The head also represents the unit in relations between households or with formal agencies. But he normally leaves the carrying out of day-to-day household activities to the other members and only interferes when these are not being discharged to his satisfaction.

TABLE 10.1 CORESIDENTIAL UNITS CLASSIFIED BY SEX OF HEAD AND NUMBER OF PERSONS

Number of Persons	Male Head		Female Head	
	Number of Units	Total Persons	Number of Units	Total Persons
1	26	26	35	35
2	19	38	32	64
3	18	54	25	75
4	15	60	25	100
5	14	70	35	175
6	14	84	25	150
7	18	126	29	203
8	22	176	16	128
9	10	90	16	144
10	5	50	10	100
11	6	66	5	55
12	1	12	4	48
13	2	26	1	13
14	1	14	2	28
15	1	15	0	0
20	0	0	1	20
Total	172	907	261	1,338

When one or more of the prerequisites associated with headship is absent, the identification of the head becomes problematic. A wife may *rule* the home by virtue of her ownership of the house and her husband may *rule* her because he is a *big man* [adult male] and the main breadwinner. The prospect of divided responsibility has led M.G. Smith (1962a:15-17) to distinguish between "headship" and "dominance," the former referring to the quality of "that person whom the community as well as the household members regard as the head of the domestic group" and who "tends to assert headship whenever necessary."

Headship is formal leadership and entails formal responsibility. Dominance is actual influence but does not entail corresponding responsibility as a matter of course. . . . For example, a childless couple who live in a homestead rented or owned by the woman, and who are economically dependent on her may nonetheless have the man as the head. The converse also occurs; we occasionally find a childless couple under a female head although the man is the mainstay of the domestic unit. In both these cases the person formally recognized as the household head is not its dominant member. . . . Unless bedridden or otherwise incapacitated, widows retain formal headship despite dependence on their resident children, since the alternative is incompatible with the kinship roles of mother and child. Likewise, unless incapacitated or insecurely mated, men retain formal headship, however dependent they are on their mates, since the alternative is incompatible with the principle of male precedence which regulates relations between the sexes at this level of West Indian society (M.G. Smith 1962a:17).

In Leeward Village there were some 50 coresidential units out of the 433 in which dominance and headship overlapped, conflicted, were disputed, or in which formal leadership was shared by two or more people. Most involved either the control of the dwelling by a married or common-law woman or the disability through disease, senility, or feebleness of the person who would normally be head. In each case, assignment of headship was made by the majority opinion of unit members supplemented by the views of neighbors and other persons familiar with the internal operation of the unit.

The data in Table 10.2 summarize the kinship composition of the village's residential units according to the sex of the head. A few of the categories need some elaboration. Nearly all the half-siblings (categories 14 and 16) are mother's children rather than father's children. The foster children (17 and 18) refer to informally adopted non-kin. "Other materterine kin" (22) are "persons whose mothers or maternal grandmothers were sisters or the children of sisters" (M.G. Smith 1962a:41) while "quasi-kin" (26) include the affines and mates of kin not covered by the other categories (e.g., granddaughter's common-law partner) as well as the kin of deceased or non-resident affines or former mates not covered by the other categories (e.g., the children of a former consensual mate). "Non-kin" (27) include live-in servants, temporary wards, and close friends of the head or other members.

Close kin, spouses, and consensual partners form the bulk of coresidential group personnel. Children, grandchildren, and spouses and common-law partners alone account for 82.7 percent of household members. Most of the remaining personnel include great grandchildren, siblings and half-siblings, sibling's children, and spouse's or consensual partner's children and grandchildren.

TABLE 10.2 HOUSEHOLD MEMBERS CLASSIFIED BY
RELATIONSHIP TO HOUSEHOLD HEAD AND SEX OF HEAD

		Male Head		Female Head		Total	
Category of Kin		No.	%	No.	%	No.	%
1.	Spouse	89	12.1	8	0.7	97	5.4
2.	Consensual mate	33	4.5	21	1.9	54	3.0
3.	Son	178	24.4	251	23.3	429	23.7
4.	Daughter	199	27.1	296	27.5	495	27.3
5.	Son's child	15	2.0	46	4.3	61	3.4
6.	Daughter's child	77	10.5	285	26.5	362	20.0
7.	Spouse's child	13	1.8	0	0.0	13	0.7
8.	Consensual mate's child	28	3.8	0	0.0	28	1.6
9.	Son's grandchild	0	0.0	10	0.9	10	0.6
10.	Daughter's grandchild	3	0.4	30	2.8	33	1.8
11.	Spouse's grandchild	15	2.0	0	0.0	15	0.8
12.	Consensual mate's grandchildren	11	1.5	0	0.0	11	0.6
13.	Sibling	5	0.7	12	1.1	17	0.9
14.	Half-sibling	2	0.3	19	1.8	21	1.2
15.	Sibling's child	10	1.4	14	1.3	24	1.3
16.	Half-sibling's child	3	0.4	8	0.7	11	0.6
17.	Foster child	9	1.2	3	0.3	12	0.7
18.	Foster child's child	0	0.0	2	0.2	2	0.1
19.	Parent	2	0.3	7	0.7	9	0.5
20.	Child's spouse	2	0.3	2	0.2	4	0.2
21.	Child's consensual mate	0	0.0	6	0.6	6	0.3
22.	Other materterine kin	5	0.7	21	1.9	26	1.4
23.	Other kin	0	0.0	14	1.3	14	0.8
24.	Spouse's other kin	20	2.7	2	0.2	22	1.2
25.	Consensual mate's other kin	6	0.8	0	0.0	6	0.3
26.	Quasi-kin	2	0.3	8	0.7	10	0.6
27.	Non-kin	8	1.1	12	1.1	20	1.1
Total		735	100.0	1,077	100.0	1,812	100.0

There are significant differences in the distribution of these kin between male- and female-headed homes. Of the 735 members of male-headed units, 16.6 percent are the spouses or consensual partners of the head while of the 1,077 members of female-headed units, only 2.7 percent fall into this category. Second, grandchildren compose 30.8 percent of female-headed units but only 12.5 percent of male-headed ones. Third, collaterals (categories 13, 14, 15, 16, 22, and 23) are not as well represented in male-headed units, forming 3.4 percent of the membership, as in female-headed ones where they compose 8.2 percent of the membership. Fourth, the children and other kin of spouses and consensual partners make a significant contribution to male headed residences, forming 12.7 percent of the membership, but almost none to female-headed ones where they compose only 0.2 percent of the membership. These differences in kinship composition are the result of variability in the formation and internal organization of male- and female-headed units.

Table 10.3 reduces the sample of 100 homes to 36 types to account for the distribution in Table 10.2. Units are distinguished by the sex of the head, the presence of the head's spouse or mate, the jural status of the head's conjugal union if one is present, and the relation between the head and the other members. To be sure, such a detailed classification makes comparison cumbersome. But it permits a finer-grained analysis of residential composition and organization than the simpler schemes presented in most other studies.

Some of the distinctions pointed out in Table 10.2 are also evident in Table 10.3, and together the two tables present a detailed synchronic picture of village residential group composition. Men usually *rule* homes in which their mates or spouses are members either because they are in charge of the dwelling, because they are the main breadwinners, or because, being men, they are able to exert their will backed by the potential use of community sanctioned force. Of the 49 non-single person female-headed units in Table 10.3, only five (numbers 7, 24, 33, 34, and 36) contain a married or common-law couple as their principal members. In all five cases the woman owned the dwelling and most of its furnishings. Alternately, of the 41 residences that do not contain a married or common-law couple as their principals, only four (2, 3, 8) are male-headed and one of these (2) is composed of two unrelated men. Only one of these four residences involved true 'patrifocality' in which a father was forced to do all the *minding* and most of the *caring* for his four illegitimate children after his common-law mate who had migrated to the United States stopped corresponding with him. One of the two remaining units consisted of a father and son temporarily living alone while the wife-mother was in Barbados seeking medical treatment while the other consisted of an elderly disabled widower, one of his daughters, and the daughter's three children.

Women nearly always *rule* homes in which there are no men in the role of spouse or mate. Some of these have developed from nuclear family units through the death, desertion, or long-term migration of a spouse or common-law partner. Others are the product of visiting unions in which a woman and her children continue to live in the family home after her parents have died and the adult males have left. Still others come into being when a woman leaves her natal household to provide a separate dwelling for herself and her children.

TABLE 10.3 TYPE OF CORESIDENTIAL UNIT CLASSIFIED BY SEX OF HEAD

	Type	Male Head	Female Head	Total
1.	Single person	3	6	9
2.	Unrelated pair	1	0	1
3.	Head + children	2	19	21
4.	Married couple	3	0	3
5.	Consensual couple	1	0	1
6.	Married couple + children	12	0	12
7.	Consensual couple + children	3	1	4
8.	Head, children + grandchildren	1	8	9
9.	Head + grandchildren	0	3	3
10.	Head, child, grandchildren + great grandchild	0	1	1
11.	Head, grandchild + great grandchildren	0	1	1
12.	Head + great grandchild	0	1	1
13.	Married couple, children + grandchildren	3	0	3
14.	Married couple + grandchild	1	0	1
15.	Head, children + collaterals	0	4	4
16.	Head, children, grandchildren + collaterals	0	2	2
17.	Head + collaterals	0	3	3
18.	Head, children, grandchildren + unrelated persons	0	2	2
			(Continued)	

TABLE 10.3 (Cont.)

	Type	Male Head	Female Head	Total
19.	Married couple, children + head's child	1	0	1
20.	Married couple, child + spouse's child	1	0	1
21.	Married couple, children, grandchild, spouse's child + grandchildren	1	0	1
22.	Married couple, children + head's mother	1	0	1
23.	Married couple, children + spouse's collateral	1	0	1
24.	Married couple, head's children + grandchild	0	1	1
25.	Married couple, spouse's children + grandchildren	1	0	1
26.	Married couple + spouse's great grandchildren	1	0	1
27.	Married couple + spouse's collaterals	2	0	2
28.	Married couple, spouse's collaterals + unrelated child	1	0	1
29.	Married couple + unrelated child	1	0	1
30.	Consensual couple, children, mate's children + grandchildren	1	0	1
31.	Consensual couple, children, mate's children + mother	1	0	1
32.	Consensual couple, mate's children + grandchildren	1	0	1
33.	Consensual couple + head's children	0	1	1
34.	Consensual couple, head's children children + grandchild	0	1	1
35.	Consensual couple + mate's collateral	1	0	1
36.	Consensual couple + head's collateral	0	1	1
Total		45	55	100

The data in both Table 10.2 and 10.3 show that grandchildren comprise a much smaller portion of the personnel of male- than female-headed units. Extra-residential mating and migration of the mothers of these children account for the presence of most of the grandchildren in both types of homes. Their stronger representation in female-headed units is partly a consequence of the readier acceptance of illegitimate issue in these families. In residences headed by married men higher class affiliation or aspiration often results in the eviction of a daughter who keeps producing *bastard* issue.

Collaterals also form a greater portion of personnel in female- than male-headed units. Since most men who aspire to domestic group leadership leave their natal households in their early twenties, they almost never acquire headship in households in which their collaterals (siblings and siblings' offspring) are already members. Men gain household headship by either (1) forming a single-person household, (2) acquiring a dwelling in which to place a wife or *keeper* and children, or (3) joining an established family which often includes the collaterals of a spouse or common-law partner and gradually assuming headship over it. Conversely, the higher representation of collaterals in women-headed units is largely a consequence of the child care provided when its single mothers migrate in search of work to support themselves and their offspring.

It is also evident from the data in both Table 10.2 and 10.3 that children and other kin of spouses and consensual partners are well represented in male-headed residences but make almost no contribution to female-headed ones. Men almost always enter and leave coresidential unions as individuals while women are usually accompanied by one or more of their children when they do so. Even when they surrender headship to a husband or common-law partner this rarely affects the continuing residence of their children and other kin.

In summary, the difference in the composition of male- and female-headed coresidential groups is the result of the following tendencies: (1) married or consensually cohabiting men *rule* their households; (2) mature single mothers head their households or otherwise live in units led by women; (3) there is a greater tolerance of illegitimacy in female-headed units; (4) women rear their own children and/or other dependents regardless of the type of union they are in; (5) women stay behind in the parental home after their brothers leave; and (6) men enter consensual or marital units as individuals rather than as members of a kinship group.

Although there are significant differences between the composition of male- and female-headed units, there is one basic similarity which unites them. Both the absolute range of the different kin in Table 10.2 and the resultant configurations formed from the sample of these in Table 10.3 are indicative of the accommodative capacity of Leeward Village households. To be sure, a few basic categories of kin and affines--children, grandchildren, siblings, siblings' children, great grandchildren, and spouses and mates--form the bulk of household personnel. Still, both the presence of other kin and non-kin as well as the elaborate way in which the most important categories of kin are arranged to form residential units suggest that plasticity and permissiveness characterize the make-up of village households.

The variability in both the range of persons making up village households and the manner in which these persons are combined to form particular residential units is only part of the complexity of village household organization. The structure of the domestic group and the manner in which its functions are carried out indicate that most village households are unbounded, fluid, non-corporate 'units' which are extremely sensitive to the operation of socio-economic forces that lie outside them, and that the form they take and functions they perform at any particular time are adaptive responses to these forces (cf. Brown 1977).

HOUSEHOLD ORGANIZATION

The lower-class Afro-Caribbean household is usually defined as "a group of people occupying a single dwelling and sharing a common food supply" (R.T. Smith 1960:67; cf. Ashcraft 1968:480; M.G. Smith 1962a:11). It has long been recognized that the "group of people" in question need not comprise a family, particularly a nuclear family. But although more and more researchers have been following Solien's (1960) suggestion that it is necessary to distinguish both analytically and empirically between the related concepts of household and family (e.g., Ashcraft 1966; Brown 1977; Philpott 1973:113-114; Rodman 1971:100-108), the separation of the two concepts has largely meant that the importance attached to the family in earlier studies (e.g., Henriques 1953) has been shifted to the household in later ones (e.g., Otterbein 1966:ix; M.G. Smith 1962a; R.T. Smith 1960, 1964:31-34). This change in focus has been accompanied by two implicit assumptions about Caribbean social organization, the second being a corollary of the first: some sort of minimal, corporate or quasi-corporate kinship *group* exists as the basic unit of rural Caribbean social life; if this minimal unit is not the family, then it must be the household. The organization of Leeward Village domestic groups suggests that these assumptions are the product of an uncritical definition of the household.

Once the distinction between the family ". . . defined as a group of people bound together by that complex set of relationships known as kinship ties, between at least two of whom there exists a conjugal relationship" and the household, a unit which ". . . implies common residence, economic cooperation, and socialization of children" (Solien 1960:106) is made it becomes evident that households are not invariably composed of families and that families do not always reside together as households. Although this distinction has proven to be an important one in Caribbean kinship studies, the complexity of domestic group organization in the region (see Brown 1977; Ashcraft 1966) suggests that additional conceptual clarifications are necessary. Bender's (1967) refinement of the household concept is particularly useful in this regard. Bender argues that just as the family and household are logically and often empirically discrete, the term household itself contains two logically distinct aspects-- coresidence and domestic functions--which are often also empirically autonomous. Coresidence, defined as living and sleeping together in a common dwelling, and domestic functions which mainly encompass ". . . the provision and preparation of food and the care of children" (Bender 1967:499) are conceptually discrete attributes of the household that may vary independently under certain conditions or in certain societies.

The nature of Leeward Village domestic organization suggests the need for still another logical distinction (Rubenstein 1983a). Although it follows the clarifications made by Solien (1960) and Bender (1967), this additional refinement also takes note of kin group attributes traditionally associated with the family, especially the nuclear family. As long as the concepts of family and household remained united in Caribbean family studies, the link between such family functions as sexual expression and regulation, reproduction, socialization and economic co-operation (see Murdock 1965:1-22) with a particular residential grouping presented no ambiguity. With their analytical and empirical partition the relation between the functions formerly attributed to the family and the structural unit needed to carry them out becomes problematic. The relation between family structure and family function has received considerable treatment in the literature (see Bender 1967; Levy and Fallers 1959; Goody 1972; Spiro 1953; Yanagisako 1979). Consideration of the vexing question of whether the family is best defined structurally or functionally may be avoided if all relevant variables, structural as well as attributional and including those associated with both the family and the household, are examined within the same framework. Figure 10.1 schematically does so by distinguishing between (1) economic production, (2) coresidence, (3) sexual expression/regulation, (4) commensality, (5) reproduction, and (6) socialization. Probably the best label to attach to the unit in which all these variables coalesce is the *domestic group* (Goody 1972:4-5; cf. Ashcraft 1966:268; Brown 1977:258) whereas the unit in which all the functions, save extra-household economic co-operation are congruent should be termed the *household*.

As Table 10.4 indicates, there are 15 possible combinations of the six attributes of domestic group organization. The division of the domestic group into these spheres is necessitated by the complexity of family life in Leeward Village, an intricacy which has often been alluded to but never thoroughly examined in the Caribbean literature. In fact, by dividing commensality into distinct food preparation and food consumption spheres, by including domestic functions not listed in the figure (e.g., housekeeping and dwelling maintenance), and by splitting these into the areas listed in Table 5.3 an even finer (and more unwieldy) analysis would have been possible. For the sake of brevity and clarity and to reduce the repetition that would result because of the overlap of some of these attributes, only a few of the 15 combinations are discussed.

TABLE 10.4 CROSS-TABULATION OF DOMESTIC
GROUP ATTRIBUTES

	Coresidence	Sexual Regulation	Commensality	Reproduction	Socialization
Economic Production	1	2	3	4	5
Coresidence	--	6	7	8	9
Sexual Regulation	--	--	10	11	12
Commensality	--	--	--	13	14
Reproduction	--	--	--	--	15

294

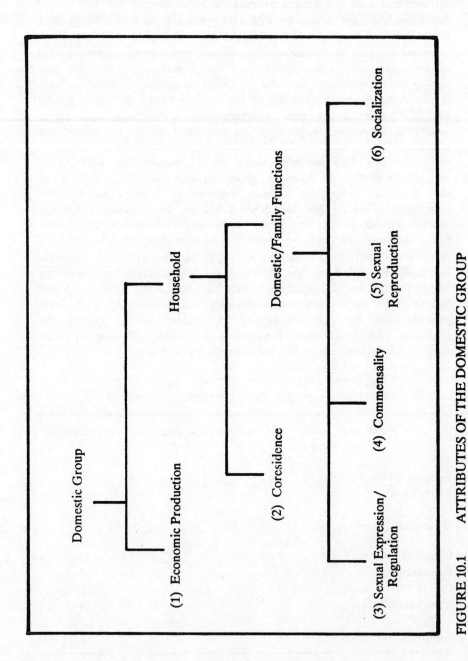

FIGURE 10.1   ATTRIBUTES OF THE DOMESTIC GROUP

Economic Cooperation

It is felt that where circumstances permit, the household should form a unit of joint economic co-operation and hence, constitute a domestic group. As has already been shown in Chapter 5, coordination of extra-household economic activities and complementarity of work roles is rare and only 18 of the sample of 100 village coresidential units are also domestic groups based on collective farming or shopkeeping involving at least two of its members.

Extra-household productive activities are not the only ones marked by a low rate of economic coordination. Economic individualism characterizes the ownership of property and the distribution of earnings. Except for undivided family property and the relatively small number of household items which are jointly purchased by those who share the same residence, houses and their contents are individually owned and may be disposed of as the owner sees fit. Only the property of immature household members and the earnings of teenagers who are working for the first time, come under the control of the household head. In short, even disregarding extra-domestic joint economic activity, the Leeward Village household is not a unit of corporate productive activity (cf. Greenfield 1966:126).

Coresidence and Commensality

Sharing a dwelling, from both an analytic and folk perspective, refers to joint occupation of an undivided structure with a common entrance. According to villagers "where you sleep is where you live." In addition to proximity in sleeping arrangements, coresidence means access to most or all parts of the house and use of its furnishings and amenities. Commensality, on the other hand, refers to the customary joint consumption of food by a group of people one or more of whom is responsible for its preparation. In local idiom, it is the collectivity who "eat from the same pot."

Of the 433 coresidential units in the village, 343, or 79.2 percent, are also joint commensal units defined by the common preparation and consumption of food. Of the 430 collective units of consumption in the village, 343, or 79.8 percent, are also groups of people who share an undivided dwelling. In other words, 20 percent of both coresidential units and units of joint food preparation and consumption are not true households. The sample of 100 coresidential units provides a more detailed picture of the relation between eating together and sleeping together. Eighty-six of these are also commensal groups; six coresidential groups contain two commensal units each; one is made up of three units of consumption; and seven coresidential units are part of commensal units which contain other coresidential groups. The data in Figure 10.2 schematically depict the relation between coresidence and joint consumption found among nine villagers, two middle-aged sisters (1 and 2) and the children and grandchildren of one of them. The two sisters shared the elder sister's (1) three-room cinder block house along with the grandson (9) and last child (5) of the younger sister. Together these four people made up a separate unit of coresidence (A1). The elder sister prepared all her own meals and formed an independent one-person commensal unit (B1). The younger sister, along with her two last children (4 and 5) and two of her grandchildren (6 and 9), also constituted a discrete unit of consumption (B2). The younger sister's son (4), together with his nephew (6) and elder sister (3) and her two children (7 and 8), comprised a distinct coresidential unit (A2) in a house belonging to his mother. The elder daughter (3) and children formed a separate unit of commensality (B3) in that house.

Most cases in which coresidence and commensality overlap are not this complex. The majority, including the example just cited, also involve considerable food sharing and occasional shifts of residence among commensal and housing units. Yet cases in which a coresidential unit is composed of two or more units of consumption and ones in which those who "eat from the same pot" do not live together occur with enough frequency that it would be imprecise to describe village domestic organization using the traditional monolithic usage of the household concept.

The two varieties of overlap between coresidence and joint consumption have similar causes. The presence of two commensal groups in the same dwelling is normally a product of the inability of the junior of these to form an independent household because of the expense of renting or building a house and providing it with the required furnishings (cf. Brown 1977:264-265; Greenfield 1966:114-118, 127; 1971). In most cases, the autonomous commensal groups originally comprised a single food sharing unit which fissioned when one of its members, usually the daughter of the head, decided to assume partial economic independence by undertaking separate cooking arrangements. Often such a hiving off from the household represents a developmental stage in the formation of a fully autonomous household which comes into being when the members are able to secure their own dwelling.

297

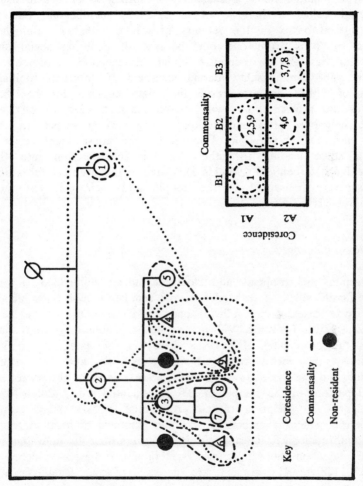

FIGURE 10.2   OVERLAP BETWEEN CORESIDENCE AND COMMENSALITY

The extension of consumption over two or more dwellings also represents an attempt to cope with extant economic circumstances and is an elaboration of the normal pattern of food sharing in the community (cf. Brown 1977; Gonzalez 1969:70). Persons who were formerly members of a common household are sometimes obliged to move to a separate house because of the formation of a consensual or marital union or because of increases in membership due to closely spaced births or the re-entry of former members. But they continue to "cook from one pot" because of enduring social and sentimental ties and to minimize budgetary expenses. More often, however, joint commensality among members of different dwellings consists of either an extra-residential mate cooking for her boy friend or the provision of meals for an indigent, aged or disabled relative, neighbor, or friend residing in a nearby house. In the former case, the preparation of meals for the non-resident mate is often a stage leading to either his full incorporation into the household (cf. Greenfield 1966:114-115) and/or the eventual formation of a separate household of the couple and their children when financial resources permit.

Sexual Regulation and Reproduction

Despite the conjugal and domestic norms embedded in the nuclear family village folk model, sexual regulation and reproduction are, in most cases, either fully or partially autonomous. To be sure, reproduction in Leeward Village, as in all human communities, involves the channeling of the sex drive via the categories of kin defined by the incest taboo. Nevertheless, the *units* of sexual regulation and the production of children are often not the same. Of the 530 persons in the sample of 100 coresidential units, 224, or 42.3 percent are the offspring of extra-residential mating. Since sexual regulation is generally associated with the presence of legal marriage in the anthropological literature it is also important to note that of the 306 people in the sample produced in unions based on common residence, 128, or 41.8 percent, are the issue of consensual cohabitation. In addition, out of the total village population of 2,245, 71.8 percent were born outside of legal marriage.

Reproduction and Coresidence

Sexual reproduction, of course, requires the presence of a unit of coresidence minimally composed of mother and child. But coresidence does not require that reproduction (or even mating) take place and there are many village homes (see Table 10.3) that do not or have never contained children. Conversely, many residences contain children who were born elsewhere and entered the unit during infancy or early childhood.

Extra-residential mating and the instability of many common-law unions often mean that neither the reproductive nor the child-rearing unit is coterminous with the unit of sexual regulation and activity. In the sample of 100 coresidential units, 82 contain children under 15. Of these 82 units, only 18 include both parents of all resident children under 15. In addition, 23.2 percent of the children under 15 in the sample are living apart from their mothers. Similarly, nearly one-half of these 293 children are the product of unions which are no longer extant.

The low correlation between sexual regulation, reproduction, and socialization is a product of the system of village conjugality and the practice of child-shifting, temporary fosterage, and wage-labor migration. As has been shown, each of these features of village social organization has been generated as adjustments to island-wide and local-level social and economic conditions.

HOUSEHOLD CHANGE

Much has been written about the developmental cycle of the lower-class Afro-Caribbean household (e.g., Davenport 1968; Greenfield 1966, 1971; Horowitz 1967b; Otterbein 1963, 1970; Philpott 1973:147-153; M.G. Smith 1962a; R.T. Smith 1956). Most writers agree that there are a variety of different life-cycle paths that households may follow and that these are a product of the organization of mating, the allocation of parental roles, post-marital residence rules and preferences, the inheritance of property, and migration. In Leeward Village the morphology and development of the coresidential forms in Table 10.3 are a product of (1) the community's three mating alternatives, (2) the allocation of the mothering role to persons other than the genetrix, (3) a residence rule which constrains the long-term cohabitation of two pairs of married or common-law adults, (4) a high rate of labor migration which results in the fosterage of children and a high community ratio of adult females to adult males, and (5) the de facto inheritance of family property by the women who remain behind in the parental home after their brothers leave.

The residence arrangements in Table 10.3 and the processes that have generated them are not equally available to all villagers. Those in which the principals are consensually cohabiting pairs or single mothers are dominated by members of the village poor. Residential stability also varies among the different village strata. Although changes in household personnel occur among all village classes, poorer families experience the most entry and exit of members because of in- and out-migration, the formation of new households or commensal units, child-shifting, the formation and dissolution of common-law unions, and births and deaths. The greater kinship complexity and size of most poor households together with the need for its members to quickly adjust to changing external conditions such as labor migration opportunities are also manifested in dramatic alterations in household membership over very short periods of time. Except for a brief article by Otterbein (1970), short-term modifications in household form have been ignored in Caribbean family studies in favor of analyses of the 'typical' long-term transformations most households go through over their life cycle. As important as such analyses are for an understanding of the general pattern of community household development, preoccupation with them has impeded an appreciation for the equally important micro-changes that mark the structure and operation of the domestic domain.

Eighty-one of the sample of 100 coresidential units in Leeward Village had a different membership in June 1972 than they did in February 1970. The degree of change and the personnel involved are indicative of both the openness of the lower-class household and the role that kindred membership plays in the recruitment of household members. Of the 81 affected units, eight showed changes resulting from birth and death alone: seven added members through births to existing residents and one showed an addition through birth and a loss through death. Of the remaining 73 units, 14 disappeared entirely. Of these 14, four merged with existing village households, four left for other parts of the island, two migrated abroad, and three combined merging with existing households for some of its members with movement out of the village or island for others. Excluding births and deaths, the remaining 59 units experienced 132 changes in personnel involving in-movement, out-movement, or a combination of the two. Twenty-four units showed one change in membership, 14 showed two changes, six showed three changes, six showed four changes, two showed five changes, three showed six changes, and one showed seven changes.

TABLE 10.5 CORESIDENTIAL IN-MOVEMENT AND OUT-MOVEMENT, 1970-1972

		Under 15 Years of Age				*Over 15 Years of Age*					
		Move In		*Move Out*		*Move In*		*Move Out*		*Total*	
Relation to Head		No.	%	No.	%	No.	%	No.	%	No.	%
Head	No.	0	0.0	0	0.0	1	3.1	4	8.3	5	3.8
	%	0.0		0.0		20.0		80.0		100.0	
Spouse	No.	0	0.0	0	0.0	1	3.1	3	6.3	4	3.0
	%	0.0		0.0		25.0		75.0		100.0	
Consensual Mate	No.	0	0.0	0	0.0	4	12.5	1	2.1	5	3.8
	%	0.0		0.0		80.0		20.0		100.0	
Child	No.	0	0.0	12	54.6	11	34.4	26	54.2	49	37.1
	%	0.0		24.5		22.5		53.1		100.0	
Other lineal	No.	25	83.3	7	31.8	3	9.4	5	10.4	40	30.3
	%	62.5		17.5		7.5		12.5		100.0	
Collateral	No.	4	13.3	3	13.6	5	15.6	6	12.5	18	13.6
	%	22.2		16.7		27.8		33.3		100.0	
Affine	No.	1	3.3	0	0.0	3	9.4	2	4.2	6	4.6
	%	16.7		0.0		50.0		33.3		100.0	
Non-kin	No.	0	0.0	0	0.0	4	12.5	1	2.1	5	3.8
	%	0.0		0.0		80.0		2.0		100.0	
Total	No.	30	100.0	22	100.0	32	100.0	48	100.0	132	100.0
	%	22.7		16.7		24.4		36.4		100.0	

302

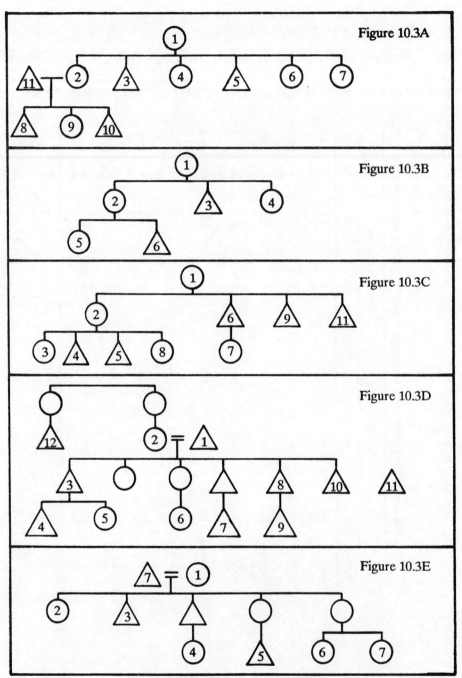

FIGURE 10.3   COMPOSITION OF FIVE HOUSEHOLDS IN 1970

The data in Table 10.5 summarize these 132 alterations in the 59 coresidential groups in terms of kinship relation, age, and direction of movement. The changes were closely divided between in-movements (46.9 percent of the 132 cases) and out-movements (53.1 percent). Most of those who moved in either direction were over 15 years of age (60.6 percent). The bulk of in-movement involved lineals, mainly daughter's children under 15, and children, collaterals, and mates or spouses over 15. Most of those who left were children and other lineals, particularly daughter's children, under 15 and children, collaterals, and lineals, especially daughter's children, over 15. Most of the collateral kin who moved in either direction were sisters and sister's children.

In-movements were nearly equally divided between persons coming to join the unit for the first time and those returning home after having lived elsewhere. Most new members were grandchildren under 15 who were joining their grandparent(s) because of the migration of their mothers. The bulk of members coming back home were migrant children over 15 and minor children who had been living in other village households or other island communities for a short period of time.

Nearly all out-movements involved permanent or long-term household members. Those under 15 were children or grandchildren moving to another house in the village, to another village, or, in the case of some of the grandchildren, to join their parents overseas. Out-movements of those over 15 were also dominated by children and grandchildren who were moving to another village household or migrating to another island or overseas.

Several specific cases of household change among poor villagers, some involving a longer period of time than the nearly two and one-half year interval discussed so far, illustrate the manner in which the processes that have been described operate in practice. The cases also highlight many of the features of village kinship that have been described in the last three chapters.

> *Case No. 1.* In 1970, Jean Brown (1 in Figure 10.3A), a 38-year-old women, was living in a small, three-room board house with her six children (2 through 7) and three grandchildren (8 through 10). Her eldest daughter, Sara (2), aged 22, and her three children formed a separate commensal unit. All of Jean's children, except Sara, were the product of a coresidential union with George Baker who had been killed in 1965.
>
> Shortly after George's death, Edmond Lewis (11),

304

Sara's boy friend and the father of all her children, moved into the house and it was this event that sparked the generation of Sara's independent domestic unit. Less than a year later, Sara gave birth to their second child (9). The house was already overcrowded and the couple and their two children moved into a rented dwelling in the same neighborhood. Sara had a third child two years later and they remained in the house until January 1970 when Edmond contracted to go to Barbados for three months to cut sugar cane. Jean's house was then in the process of being enlarged and Sara decided to move back in with her mother while Edmond was away but continued *to do* for herself and her children.

Edmond returned at the end of the cane season but remained for only a few weeks before going back to Barbados to look for work on his own. During his brief visit home Sara became pregnant and gave birth to a son in early 1971. Shortly after the birth, Jean's second eldest daughter (4), a girl of 11, left to work as a *little domestic* in the home of a distant affine and member of the village upper lower class.

At about the same time, Albert Walkin, who had been *keeping* with Jean since the death of his common-law partner the year before moved into the renovated house and became part of her domestic group.

Case No. 2. Emily Cyrus (1 in Figure 10.3B), aged 58, was living in a three-room wattle-and-daub house in 1970 with her three children (2 through 4) and two grandchildren (5 and 6), the latter being the issue of her eldest resident daughter, Jane (2). The two youngest children (3 and 4) were the offspring of a 20-year-long union with Sanford Douglas, a salaried government worker. Emily and Sanford had lived together for three of four years in Emily's house during the late 1950s but had 'reverted' to *friending* after considerable "disturbance in the home" as a result Sanford's relationship with two other women. But Emily still cooked, washed, and ironed for him and he, in turn, continued to support their two children.

The father of Jane's two children also supported them until Jane *got in with* another man in 1970. The affair though short-lived, resulted in the birth of a child later that year. A few months after the birth, Jane, then

29 years old, moved to Kingstown to study nursing, leaving her three children under her mother's care. She soon met a middle-aged man whom she married after the birth of their child in late 1971. The couple and child moved to a rented house in the village a few months later and were joined by the three children Jane's mother had been looking after. Jane and the four children spent much of their time at Emily's house where the two women cooked all their meals together.

Case No. 3. In early 1970, Wilma Lowe (1 in Figure 10.3C), aged 59, was living in an old, dilapidated wattle-and-daub house with her daughter Violet (2), 21, and Violet's three young children (3 through 5). Wilma formed a single-person domestic unit while Violet *did* for herself and her three children.

Later that year, one of Wilma's sons, Tracy (6), a man in his early thirties, sent one of his daughters, Merle (7), aged 10, the product of an on-going common-law union, to live with Wilma to help her grandmother with domestic chores.

Early the next year, Tracy and Wilma jointly purchased and repaired an old board house as a replacement for the wattle-and-daub structure which had become almost uninhabitable. After the repairs were completed, Tracy, Wilma, Merle, Violet, and the latter's three children moved into the house. Tracy continued to visit and support his common-law mate, a woman with whom he had lived for eight years.

Later that year, Violet gave birth to a fourth child (8). Like the other three, they were produced in visiting unions.

During the same year, another of Wilma's sons, Norville (9), aged 27, *dispatched* from his common-law spouse after she had *butt* him and returned to his mother's household.

Early in 1972, the four-year-old son (10) of another of Wilma's sons (11), Thomas, came to live with her after the child's mother migrated to Canada. Thomas, who had been living with the woman in Kingstown, continued to work in the capital but began to spend weekends in the village after her departure.

In May 1972, Violet (2) and her four children joined

Manley Daniel, the father of her last child, in a board house he had recently built.

Case No. 4. Alex Joseph (1 in Figure 10.3D), aged 60, and his wife, Carmina (2), aged 50, have been married for over 30 years. Of their nine children, only a 21-year-old son, Wilbert (3), was still living with them in January, 1970. The other members of their household were a migrant daughter's son (4) and daughter (5), another migrant daughter's daughter (6), and a migrant son's son (7). In 1971, the daughter's children (4 and 5) flew to England to join their parents who had left them in the care of their grandparents when they went abroad during the mid-1960s.

Later that year, one of Alex and Carmina's sons, Sherwin (8), aged 26, who had been working illegally in Barbados since 1968 was deported to St. Vincent and rejoined his parents' household. With him came his three-year-old son (9), the result of a recently *mashed up* common-law union in Barbados.

Later that same year, another of their sons, George (10), aged 20, also returned to the household after having worked in Barbados since 1969.

In March of 1972, a friend of George's (11) from a distant coastal village took up residence in the household after finding employment in the community as a mason.

In May of the same year, Carmina's (2) cousin (12), a man in his early forties, joined the household after having *dispatched* from his consensual mate.

Case No. 5. In February of 1970, Prunella Lee (1 in Figure 10.3E), a 52- year-old married housewife, was living in a small, cinder-block house with her two youngest children (2 and 3), aged 11 and 12, and three of her grandchildren (4 through 6), the offspring of migrants. Clarence (5), a boy of 10 was a temporary though frequent visitor to the home and in a few days he was back with Prunella's mother who had raised him from infancy after 'taking' him from his natural mother whom she felt was not capable of properly looking after the child.

Prunella's husband, Harold (7), who had been working as a construction laborer in the Grenadines for the past several months, returned home during the middle of the year.

Patsy (4), Prunella's son's 12-year-old daughter, who had joined the household late in 1969 after having lived with her maternal grandparents for several years, left to meet her mother in England in 1971.

Later that year Prunella herself went to the United States to join one of her sons. She took Cathy (6), aged six, with her at the request of the girl's mother who was also living in the United States. Prunella returned to the village six months later accompanied by another of Cathy's mother's children, an 18-month-old girl (7).

But Prunella's main intention in visiting the United States was to establish legal residence there via her son's citizenship status so that she could in turn sponsor her husband, Harold, who was not the father of the migrant son. Harold left for the United States in early 1972.

Case No. 6. This case involves the domestic and coresidential groups depicted in Figure 10.2 and the changes which have affected them since 1970.

Matty's son (4), Raymond, left home in 1971 at the age of 22 after a series of disputes with his mother. He moved in first with one half-sister then with another before settling with some friends for nearly a year. He migrated to the United States in 1972, has since settled his differences with his mother, and regularly sends her remittances. Gladys (3) continued to live in her mother's old board house long after the latter built a new concrete structure in 1972. Her younger daughter (8), Nella, joined the household of her father and his childless wife in a neighboring village in the mid-1970s. By the time the old board house was destroyed by Hurricane Allen in 1980, Gladys's older daughter (7) had given birth to a son in an extra-residential union. After the hurricane they rented a house.

Dudley (6) who had shared the old house with his aunt, uncle, and the aunt's two children moved into his grandmother's new house after it was built. He remained there until joining his mother in Trinidad in 1979.

Matty's last child, Brenda (5) married in 1974 and settled in a rented house with her husband. The marriage proved unsuccessful although one child was born during the first year and Brenda rejoined her mother's household

308

in 1976. She remained there until migrating to Barbados in 1978 to live with an older sister who had gone there many years before. She sent for her daughter, Penny, the next year. Penny remained with her until 1982 when she was taken to the United States by her grandmother, Matty, who was going to visit a daughter, Barbara, the mother of Grantley (9), who had migrated there several years before after having worked in Barbados as a domestic servant during the 1960s. Penny remained in the United States when Matty returned home several months later. Matty then assisted Brenda with her plane fare when she went to the United States the next year.

Grantley (9), Barbara's only child, had been left with Matty when his mother first migrated to Barbados. He joined her in New York in 1981. Matty has been living alone since that time. Her elder sister, Flo Tracy (1) continued to live by herself in the house next door until her death in 1984 at the age of 81.

The quantitative and case study material presented in this chapter have shown that village households are neither bounded nor static, nor do they go through any simple, predictable cycle. This evidence also underscores M.G. Smith's (1962a:8) important but often overlooked observation about the nature of West Indian family structure.

Apart from such socioeconomic conditions as migration, the inter-household movements of adults tends to exhibit the influence of conjugal and consanguine ties, and these are also important in governing the residential distribution of children. The simple fact that mating relations may take alternative forms, and that all of these alternatives influence the constitution of linked household groups, will show that familial and domestic relations are by no means coterminous, and that the latter cannot be reduced to the former. It follows that the appropriate unit for the analysis of family relations is the total population of a household sample rather than the constituent households themselves.

But this finding together with R.T. Smith's observation (1964:33) that ". . . concentration on the household as a functioning unit of . . . organization has tended to divert attention from the networks of relationships linking households to each other" does not apply solely to the complex way in which domestic structures and functions intersect or to the tendency for households to shift personnel back and forth. It also applies to other areas of social organization, to ties between friends, neighbors, and other non-kin (cf. Brana-Shute 1979:2).

Chapter 11

Friendship

The most obvious criterion for village membership is birth into an established family in the community and residents born elsewhere in St. Vincent are called *strangers* or referred to as "not from here" even if they have lived in Leeward Village for most of their lives. Differentiation by birth-place helps temper both the fact that the village is far from closed or corporate and the negative sentiments often heard about the village and its members. It also reflects the fact that although almost all villagers maintain social ties with outsiders, most interaction, kinship and otherwise, takes place among members of the local group. As important as the non-kinship component of such interaction is it has never received much attention in the literature. Indeed, the scholarly work on lower-class Afro-Caribbean social organization often reads as if it is informed by the following syllogism: kinship and domestic organization are the main arenas of social life; males are marginal to both arenas; therefore, males are marginal to Caribbean social life (cf. Brana-Shute 1976, 1979; Wilson 1969:71). For example, from the premise that ". . . the household . . . is one of the most important functional units of the social system . . ." R.T. Smith (1956:51, 221) concludes his influential study of family life in rural Guyana with a hypothesis that simultaneously marginalizes males within the household and relegates them to an ascriptively-based low position within the Guyanese color-class system:

> We maintain that the matri-focal system of domestic relations and household groupings, in the villages we have studied, can be regarded as the obverse of the marginal nature of the husband-father role. We further argue that

there is a correlation between the nature of the husband-father role and the role of men in the economic system and in the system of social stratification in the total Guianese society. Men, in their role of husband-father, are placed in a position where neither their social status nor their access to, and command of economic resources are of major importance in the functioning of the household *at certain stages of its development* (1956:221).

Similarly, in his study of poor Black families in Trinidad, Rodman (1971:177-178) argues that:

Husbands and fathers are often marginal members of the nuclear family . . . . The man's role as worker-earner lies at the center of an explanation of lower-class family relations in Trinidad. The man is expected to work and to earn for his family; his status within the family hinges on how adequately he provides. Unfortunately, the lower-class man is involved in much unemployment, underemployment, poorly paid employment, and unskilled employment. Because of these handicaps in his occupational role he is frequently unable to fulfill his provider role. This situation is so all-pervasive that it has ramifications for the entire system of family and kinship organization.

The man's worker-earner role is crucial because it links the work and family worlds, in which the man plays two of the most important roles in his life. The consequences for the man are particularly far-reaching when damage is done to him in this crucial joint role. He loses status, esteem, and income power, and this influences his position in the community and the family. He is held in low esteem by the members of his own family when he is unable to fulfill their expectation of him as a provider.

The quarrel which such views is that they ignore the role played in the lives of West Indian men by worlds and status systems other than those deriving from work, national systems of stratification, family life, and domestic organization (Brana-Shute 1976, 1979; M.G. Smith 1966:x-xv; Wilson 1969, 1973). As Lieber (1976:324) argues in his analysis of street life among poor Black men in Port-of-Spain, Trinidad:

> [A]ny understanding of the form and roots of commitment
> to street life fails if it sees this commitment as essential-
> ly "reflecting" dissatisfactions with home and family
> concerns. Such a point of view is tacitly embedded in
> much sociological thinking, reflecting as it does the
> indefensible notion that homes and families must be *the*
> pivotal domains of nonoccupational social life, and that a
> departure from attachment to these domains reflects their
> operational inadequacies, rather than the discovery of
> appeal elsewhere (cf. Brana-Shute 1976:54; Wilson 1969:71).

Substituting rural for urban and village for city, Lieber's (1976:324)
portrayal of street life in Port-of-Spain, Trinidad well fits the
Leeward Village situation.

> Aloofness from residentially based sodalities partly
> arises from the well recognized hesitance on the part of
> many poor, urban Black men to attach themselves to
> household links and activities as centers of significant
> social affiliation. Instead, men tend to commit much of
> their time and involvement to events and locales which
> are public and visible, and which evolve from the dynamic
> flow of the city's very active street life. In the streets of
> the city men locate a variety of points which become for
> them regular congregating spots--bases of operation. These
> points or nodes, and the webs of street life engagements
> they punctuate, then become pivots of appeal for young
> men ready to make choices about how to spend their time.

What Lieber's and other recent studies are making clear is that
the social arena in which poor West Indian men achieve status
recognition, social esteem, and personal fulfillment is the friendship
network (see Abrahams 1983; Austin 1983; Brana-Shute 1979; Dirks
1972; Wilson 1969, 1973). As in most other societies, friendship in
Leeward Village is mainly a non-kinship inter-household phenomenon,
a fact that goes a long way to explaining why it has been neglected
in a literature which has been preoccupied with the household or
with inter-household interaction based on kinship ties (Wilson 1969,
1971). The social landscape occupied by friendship ties, especially
among men, include public or semi-public domains--streetcorner,
bayside, pier, bridge, and rum shop. Apart from the semi-exclusive
back rooms of some rum shops, these are all public domains. Except
for fish selling and seine net mending along the bayside, leisure

activities--another domain traditionally neglected in Caribbean ethnology--dominate these locales. Drinking, story telling, and domino playing in the shops, and idle conversation, playful banter, and just *looking on* at the other locales are the main activities engaged in. Since behavior in these arenas looks as if it is unbounded and "loosely structured," it is harder to study than its counterpart in more formal and spatially-organized groupings such as the household--the domain taken to be dominated by women and children--and this has been a main factor accounting for its being overlooked (cf. Brana-Shute 1976:53-54).

Research since the early 1970s has resulted in a revised picture of behavior in public places and the forms of social interaction in which this behavior is embedded. Dirks (1972:171) well summarizes current thinking on the significance of networks in Afro-American research.

> The Afro-American community has been variously portrayed as weak, fragmentary, ineffectual, loosely organized, disoriented, disintegrated, amorphous, indistinct, and underdeveloped (Mintz 1966:932; 1968:317; T. Smith 1954:55; Wagley 1960:8; 1961:198). I find these descriptions neither accurate nor useful. They are clearly the result of a bias towards a 'group-based model of society' (Whitten & Szwed 1970:45) which fails to assign any value to alternative forms of social organisation. In the study of Afro-Caribbean communities, where informal interpersonal alliances appear to play an important part in the competition for resources, this model is not by itself adequate (Mintz 1968:317). An additional perspective is required. This perspective is provided by network theory.

What the Leeward Village material shows is that what still needs to be recognized is that friendship is not limited to men either in regard to existential satisfaction or social recognition; West Indian women and children also form intense and satisfying relationships with peers and patrons, neighbors and acquaintances, and these need to be studied as well.

FORMS OF FRIENDSHIP

Friendship always contains varying combinations of several features--affection, intimacy, volition, a supra- or extra-kinship recruitment basis, instrumentality--and, therefore, should not be distinguished solely by a single referent (Paine 1970:155). Still, it is useful to differentiate between three forms of friendship in Leeward Village: "close friendship" (Cohen 1961:353), an intense but informal and voluntary union marked by considerable "emotional and social propinquity"; "casual friendship" (Cohen 1961:353), or what Paine (1970:145) has labeled "acquaintanceship," a minimally affective relationship which "does not contain within it any duties, liabilities, privileges, or rights specific to the relationship itself"; and "expedient friendship" (Cohen 1961:353), ". . . an alignment of two persons . . . in which some gain, material, social, or some combination of them accrues to both parties as a direct result of their affiliation with each other" (cf. Wolf 1966).

Close Friendship

Close village friendship is an informal, voluntary relationship between members of the same sex. Close male friends often call or refer to each other by the term *pardna* [partner] or by the kinship term *buddie* [brother] while women who are close friends refer to each other using the kinship term *sissie* [sister]. Close friends are said to *live loving* or to *live just like family*. Some men say that "me *buddie* better to me than me own brother," at once an admission that kinship and friendship are distinct domains and that the latter may compensate for some of the deficiencies of the former. Close friends are also called *best friends* while a friend who is not quite as close as a *buddie* or *sissie* will be called a *social friend* or *good friend*.

Many friendships, especially among men, have been extant since early childhood. Congruent life styles, common vocational backgrounds, and residence in the same neighborhood form the basis for these long-lived relations. Shared political party support strengthens such partnerships (and vice versa) as does employment in the same trade. Fishermen, for example, find most of their close friends among their fishing peers and even members of different seine boat crews freely help each other in seine hauling, net knitting, and the filling out of a crew which lacks a member. Reciprocity is extended to the social arena as well where it finds its most important expression in collective drinking in one of the three village rum shops located along the beach front.

Close friendship with its broad and deep affective base also provides its partners with psychological support and emotional release, approval for belief and action, and a sense of personal worth and dignity. But moral support requires behavioral reinforcement. This means taking the side of the friend when he or she is being *advantaged* [taken advantage of] by others: good friends should back each other up in arguments and even lie for each other in court. The material base for close friendship is also important although it is often manifested in the *expectation* of economic reciprocity rather than in the routine exchange of goods and services. Close friends should give each other *anything* [whatever they are capable of giving]: they should lend each other money and give each other food. They should also help each other with economic tasks such as selling market produce, house building and repair, and child minding. Among women, these expectations are most often met by the exchange of food. If a woman has just finished cooking and a good friend drops by she will matter-of-factly be offered a plate of food without being asked. Among men, close friendship is a forum for distributing raw agricultural produce, collective drinking, sharing information about jobs or the availability of sexual partners, and migration sponsorship. Equally important, it is the main forum for male sociability in the community and many men spend much more time in the company of their male peers than they do with their household members.

Despite these positive referents, the obligations surrounding friendship are generally described from a negative point of view, from the perspective of the manner in which friends ought not to treat each other. A friend should not be *licrish* [parsimonious] or *selfish* [inhospitable]; he or she should not *macoe* [spy on] you, spread *commess* [gossip] about you, or *tief* [steal] from you. Close friendship especially implies mutual trust based on the sharing and keeping of confidences, a moral requirement that often goes unmet. Villagers are well aware of the network quality of friendship and other social ties and although they believe that it is desirable to have one or more good friends, they are aware that even best friends cannot always be trusted with secrets. Indeed, most friendships among women seem to be terminated when confidential information is revealed to others.

Casual Friendship

"Casual friendship" or "acquaintanceship" in Leeward Village is a relation between persons who are said to *move well* or *go good*. Although many casual friends are also neighbors the nature of the relationship means that they are neither privy to each others secrets nor expected to support each other against common enemies or help each other economically. No specific set of rights and privileges characterizes the relationship between acquaintances and its affective content is minimal. Expedient friends may be social equals or members of different socio-economic strata. In the former case, many acquaintances who are also neighbors will sometimes exchange food and help each other with child-minding, minor house repair, and *making messages* [shopping] and this may over time transform their relation into close friendship.

Since they are not on intimate terms and usually do not visit each others homes, men and women may be casual friends without fearing that they will be suspected of having an affair. For the same reason, casual friendship often links villagers of different social standing and economic position where it functions as a vehicle for the transmission of *commess* and the performance of minor economic services such as trivial help with domestic chores and *making messages*. Such transactions sometimes become regularized with the lower status partner receiving small amounts of food and cash from the higher status one. Some asymmetrical acquaintanceships develop such a strong instrumental base that they are transformed into informal patron-client ties, or what Pitt-Rivers (1954:140) has aptly called "lop-sided friendship."

Expedient Friendship

"Expedient friendship" (Cohen 1961) or what Wolf (1966) has termed "instrumental friendship" also has a minimal emotional or expressive content. But just as close friendship normally satisfies more than the mutual psychological needs of the participants, expedient friendship also contains a ". . . charge of affect . . . as a device for keeping the relationship a relation of open trust or open credit" (Wolf 1966:13). Similarly, just as acquaintanceship may be "balanced" or "lop-sided" in terms of the social and economic standing of those involved, instrumental friendship may link both social equals or those who stand in a hierarchical relation to one another. Moreover, as Wolf (1966:16) has argued:

When instrumental friendship reaches a maximum point of imbalance so that one partner is clearly superior to the other in his capacity to grant goods and services, we approach the critical point where friendships give way to the patron-client tie (Wolf 1966:16).

Whether patronage, strictly speaking, should be considered a form of friendship or not is less important than the need to keep up the appearance of affect if the relationship is to continue to be a "friendly" one rather than a simple business arrangement.

The importance of emotion, even if it is only feigned, is also evident in what is probably the most common form of expedient friendship in Leeward Village, casual extra-residential mating. The terminology used to describe the various patterns of behavior associated with such unions (see Chapter 9), together with the supporting case-study material indicate that informal sexual relations, particularly clandestine ones, have material gain and physiological release as their main components. To be sure, not all expedient relations between men and women involve the minimally affective exchange of sex for money. Hauling a seine net ashore, working on a road repair gang, exchanging agricultural labor, attending a funeral, wedding or wake, belonging to a migration chain, or membership in a political-party faction all involve ". . . coalitions of persons, recruited according to structurally diverse principles by one or more existing members, between some of whom there is a degree of patterned interaction and organization" (Boissevain 1968:550). The various principles and modes of recruitment of a migration network were described in Chapter 7 while the structure and function of the kindred as an ego-centric network was explored in Chapter 8. These may be supplemented by descriptions of a *swap labor* network among farmers, food distribution ties linking cultivators to family and friends, dyadic friendship ties among women, asymmetrical friendship relations, and a house moving action-set.

SWAP LABOR TIES

An "action-set" is a limited and circumscribed network of people temporarily mobilized by a central ego to carry out a particular task (Mayer 1966; cf. Boissevain 1968; Whitten and Wolfe 1973). Although it has boundaries, a defined membership, a leader, and an overarching collective purpose it is a "quasi-group" rather than a true group since:

> . . . the basis for membership is specific to each linkage, and there are no rights and obligations relating all those involved; . . . Moreover, the action-set could not exist without the ego around whom it is formed (Mayer 1966: 109).

Although fewer cultivators now participate in it than in the past, *swap labor*, or the balanced reciprocal exchange of farm work, is still a common mode of agricultural exploitation on small valley holdings. As suggested in Chapter 6, it involves men assisting each other on a rotating basis in *cuttlassing bush* [clearing a piece of land of unwanted natural vegetation] and digging banks in preparation for planting, and the exchange of bank-digging for weeding between men and women. *Swap labor* is a social as well as an economic event in which the sponsor of the day's work supplies a large mid-day *cook up* [a stew consisting of root crops and fish or meat] and an occasional bottle of rum.

Figure 11.1 depicts the network of *swap labor* ties radiating out from seven men (1 through 7). The network may not be complete since the additional ties branching off from the individuals with whom the seven men exchanged labor were not traced. Despite this shortcoming, the pattern in Figure 11.1 is that of a "partial" socio-centric network containing 17 men and two women in which there is a high degree of "connectedness" in some of its "zones" (Barnes 1972). The self reported basis of the exchange, the tasks traded, and the number of days involved are shown in Table 11.1. Most of the men stated that friendship formed the foundation of the exchange. In only a few cases were kinship and neighborhoodship also important. Although a couple of the men were also close friends, the minimum sentiment required for *swap labor* is that the parties *go well* [get along with each other]. Other considerations not mentioned by the participants also seem to influence the exchange of agricultural work. Most of the men have holdings near to each other, and a few have adjacent plots of land. Most of the men are renters rather than landowners and those who trade labor tend to rent their holdings from the same owner. Most of the plots are between one and three acres in size and contain similar croppings of starchy tubers. All are poor farmers, and most of the men are married and of middle age or older.

Labor exchange has decreased in the valley over the past 20 years and a minority of cultivators now participate in it. Many of those who habitually traded labor in the past have migrated, often using their savings from agricultural work to help finance their passage overseas. There has also been a gradual reduction in cultivation among many older farmers who were actively involved in *swap labor* in their younger days. Many of the crops which were particularly suited to joint labor such arrowroot and cotton farming are no longer grown. Animosity as a result of political differences has also alienated several men and women who previously exchanged labor. It is important to note, however, that those who continue to trade labor are among the most active cultivators in the valley.

320

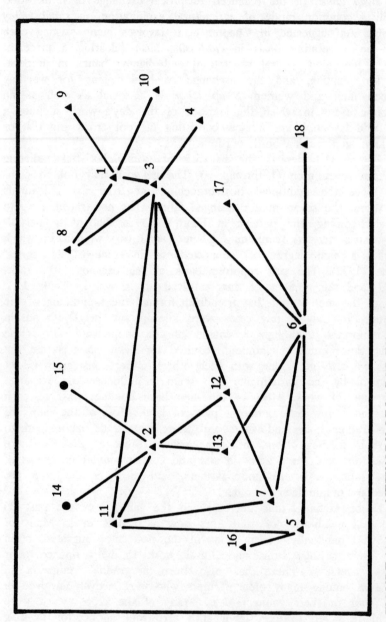

FIGURE 11.1   NETWORK OF LABOR EXCHANGE TIES

TABLE 11.1 LABOR EXCHANGE TIES

Ego	Alter	Relationship	Duration	Task
1[a]	8	adjoining plots	NK[b]	NK
	9	brothers	NK	NK
	3	common religious leadership	2 days	NK
	10	NK	2 days	NK
2	11	friends; neighbors	1 day	cutlassing bush
	12	friends	3 days	cutlassing bush; digging banks
	3	friends; same church	2 days	digging banks
	13	friends; adjoining plots	2 days	digging banks
	14	kinship	1 day	weeding in exchange for cutlassing
	15	NK	1 day	weeding in exchange for cutlassing
3	11	friends	1 day	digging banks
	12	friends; adjoining plots	1 day	digging banks
	8	friends; adjoining plots	1 day	digging banks
	6	friends	1 day	digging banks
4	3	friends	2 days	cutlassing bush; digging banks
5	16	friends; adjoining plots	1 day	cutlassing bush; digging banks
	6	friend	1 day	cutlassing bush; digging banks
	11	friend	1 day	cutlassing bush; digging banks
6	13	adjoining plots	NK	NK
	17	adjoining plots	NK	NK
	18	adjoining plots	NK	NK
7	11	friends	2 days	digging banks
	12	friends	2 days	digging banks
	6	friends; in-laws; adjoining plots	2 days	digging banks

[a]See Figure 11.1
[b]Not known

FOOD SHARING

Even if fewer farmers now engage in *swap labor* many cultivators still distribute some of the fruits of their gardening to a circle of family and friends. Data is available on the sharing of agricultural produce by 45 village farmers. Twenty-three of these cultivators gave some produce to non-household members. Of the remaining 22, only one was explicitly adverse to sharing food with others stating that "De neighbors dem too bad." Most of the rest who gave some reason for not sharing food with others stated that they either had very small yields--hardly enough for themselves and their families at home--or that they had not yet reaped anything during the current planting season. Of the 23 farmers who distributed some of their produce to others, 12 gave produce to neighbors, 8 to friends, 6 to their daughter(s), 4 to their sister(s), 1 to a mother, 2 to their workers, 1 to an employer, 1 to a minister, 1 to those who exchanged labor with him, 2 to "anyone who wants" [i.e., to no one in particular], and 10 to a variety of distant kin and close and distant affines or former affines. One informant described the balanced reciprocity that underlies many of these exchanges as follows: "When I have, I give; when they have, they give." Others stated that they allocated produce because the recipient, a friend, neighbor, or relative, was poor. Most of the children, sisters, and other relatives who received gifts of food did not cultivate land of their own. Except for close family members, good friends and neighbors, and the most destitute of villagers who could not survive except by the generosity of those around them, the gift of food--a yam, a pound of tomatoes, a heap of peas, a few limes--is a symbolic gesture, a sign of the affection underlying the relation, rather than an important dietary contribution. Still, enough farming and non-farming villagers receive such gifts that their cumulative material effect is significant.

LOP-SIDED FRIENDSHIP

As in other kinds of instrumental friendship, some charge of affect, familiarity, and trust underlies the link between patron and client. This is necessary if the relation is not to take on the form of a simple employer-employee tie. Patronage is sometimes reflected in the terminology used by the two partners in addressing one another. The higher ranking person will generally call the lower ranking one by a last name, first name, or agnomina while the latter will reciprocate with a kinship term such as *uncle*, *tantie*, or *daddy* which is normally employed to address older persons. Most superordinate-subordinate friendships in Leeward Village are dyadic, although those involving ties between politically influential villagers and their clients take the form of action-sets during political campaigns and are based on the direct or delayed exchange of party support for economic aid. Whenever there is a change in government, for example, all road drivers and other minor local government positions and almost all road worker jobs are transferred to supporters of the victorious party. High ranking villagers closely connected to the local candidate or other central party members collect names of active rank-and-file party champions during the campaign, and these are forwarded to Public Works Department officials responsible for the recruitment of district overseers and local road drivers. Such types of exchange highlight the essential feature of patron-client ties.

> *Patron-client* contracts tie people . . . of significantly different socio-economic status (or order of power), who exchange different kinds of goods and services. Patron-client contracts are phased vertically, and they can be thought of as asymmetrical since each partner is quite different from the other in position and obligations (Foster 1963:1281).

Not only do the "different kinds of goods and services exchanged" between patrons and clients distinguish asymmetrical from symmetrical expedient friendship the form of exchange also varies between the two kinds of relationship. Symmetrical expedient ties are characterized by balanced reciprocity, for example the exchange of equivalent amounts of manual labor during the current growing season, and patron-client ties are marked by generalized reciprocity.

> The two partners to the patron-client contract . . . no longer exchange equivalent goods and services. The offerings of the patron are more immediately tangible. He provides economic aid and protection against both the legal and illegal extractions of authority. The client, in turn, pays back in more intangible assets. These are . . . demonstrations of esteem . . . information on the machinations of others . . . [and] promise of political support (Wolf 1966:16-17).

Since they link members of different class segments, lop-sided friendship in Leeward Village has an integrative effect on community social life because it counterbalances the economic differentiation and social distancing produced by class distinctions. But interaction between patrons and clients is rather variable although the relationship is classified by villagers as belonging to the general domain of friendship. Some hierarchical friendships are marked by easy familiarity, others by considerable formality and expressions of deference; in some relationships patrons and clients freely exchange gossip and confidences with each other while in others the flow of *commess* is predominantly from client to patron; some male patrons drink with their clients while others do not. Still, most examples of patronage share at least two recurrent characteristics. Domestic interaction is almost always confined to the home of the higher status friend or, among men, to public places such as rum shops. As well, considerations of hygiene and palatability constrain most patrons from accepting cooked food from their clients. This is condoned by the latter who accept that their food is "too poor" for *high class* people. Even when the client eats at the home of the patron, the two do not normally eat together at the same table. Conversely, uncooked food in the form of garden produce normally flows from client to patron.

The case of Earl Weyland, a poor married villager in his early fifties gives some idea of the operation of the various features of lop-sided friendship. Weyland who combines farming and woodcutting activities to support his large family, is on good terms with Orwin Walkin, a prosperous middle-class farmer five years his junior. Weyland visits Walkin's shop every Saturday evening to drink with some of his acquaintances and to chat with Walkin and his wife. The relationship between the two men may be termed friendship rather than patronage even though it is asymmetrical. While they exchange different kinds of goods and services, they act informally in each other presence and tend to play down the obvious differences in their relative status. On the other hand, the relationship between Weyland and Walkin's wife is highly formal and circumspect, following true patronage in its form and content. Weyland always addresses her as *Mistress* Walkin, gladly runs errands on her behalf, and extols her virtues to others.

Mr. Walkin has granted Weyland a piece of land to work for free. In turn, Weyland annually distributes some $30 worth of provisions to Mrs. Walkin, a contribution both parties view as voluntary rather than part of a normal sharecropping arrangement. When he visits the Walkins in their home, he is often given food to eat and he sometimes receives a meal or a loan of a dollar to two when he visits Mrs. Walkin in the shop during the week. Still, when his services as a woodcutter are needed he receives payment on a commercial basis in keeping with the complicated and time-consuming effort even a small job involves.

Like some other poor men, Weyland has several other friends with whom he maintains asymmetrical expedient friendship, calling on them when he is *broken* and bringing them gifts of agricultural produce when he has a surplus.

The most common form of patron-client tie in Leeward Village is godparenthood. Most villagers try to ensure that at least one of the sponsors of their children's baptism is an influential villager and as a result many high ranking persons have a dozen or more godchildren. The formal expectations of godparenthood include participation in the baptism and confirmation of the child, social and material help in its upbringing, and punishment of its wrongdoing. As in most other village social relationships, these expectations often go unmet, especially by high ranking villagers, and what remains is only the prestige of having wealthy and respectable people whom one can call *faddy* [godfather] and *nennie* [godmother]. The often heard expression, "I don't have a *godfather*," to explain the difficulty in getting a government or other job in Kingstown simultaneously expresses the importance of dyadic ties in securing employment and the fact that actual godparents are often remiss in their duties. Still, the possession of a high status godparent is seen as desirable by all villagers. Even if they are *licrish* [stingy] such individuals can occasionally be relied upon for a small cash handout, advice on legal or bureaucratic matters, and help in completing a passport application.

DYADIC FRIENDSHIP TIES AMONG WOMEN

Friendship among West Indian women has been neglected even in those studies which decry the general lack of attention paid to friendship in the West Indian literature (e.g., Brana-Shute 1979; Lieber 1981; Wilson 1973), reinforcing the view that these women are inexorably tied to the hearth and home. Greenfield's (1966:106) summary of the domestic duties of married women in Barbados represents the standard view in the literature.

Most of her time is spent in the home while that of the man is spent outside of it. . . . In the performance of her

> duties [cooking, clothes washing, housekeeping, child rearing, and domestic management] a wife is expected to keep to herself. The more limited her contacts are with people outside her house and yard, the better her husband likes it. . . . They have very few friends and visit other women only on rare occasions. Their only contact with other people is at the standpipe, the shop, and at religious meetings or other affairs such as weddings and funerals.

Yet even if it is true that ". . . females dominate the household and domestic life in Caribbean societies" (Wilson 1973:127), this does not mean that the home and family are the only arenas in which they achieve a sense of social worth and emotional fulfillment. There is scant evidence in the literature to support this suggestion although R.T. Smith's (1956:77) description of the daily routine of Guyanese women implies that Greenfield (1966:106) is either overstating his point or that there is considerable intra-Caribbean variability in the freedom of movement granted to West Indian women.

> The afternoon is the time for a little leisure and for visiting friends or relatives. Daughters visit their mothers, and, as everywhere, women gossip and discuss their neighbours' shortcomings (R.T. Smith 1956:77).

Leeward Village women also spend their free time socializing with friends, neighbors, and kin. Although gossip--and gossip about gossip--forms the basis of much of this interaction, friendship ties among woman serve as more than just conduits for the exchange of *commess*. Emotional support, material aid, domestic assistance, and help with extra-household tasks mark many village friendships. To be sure, the movements of women, especially if they are married, are more restricted than those of men, and they will be rebuked by their husbands and gossiped about by others if they are perceived as spending too much time idling in public. But this does not preclude their having friends and acquaintances, including women who are far less respectable than themselves. The latter may be casual and instrumental friends--neighbors, clients, and others--who run errands on their behalf, help them with domestic work, and carry gossip to them. Nor need interaction between friends be confined to the home of one or the other. Waiting for the mail van to arrive at the Post Office, for service in a shop, for a bus leaving for town, or for fishing boats to return to shore, provides ample opportunity for socializing with other women.

As the following cases illustrate, close friendship normally unites women of comparable socio-economic standing. Many women spend much time with their friends, and, given their domestic responsibilities, residence in the same neighborhood is an important consideration. Similarity in age is less significant than common interests and beliefs and shared political sympathies. The exchange of goods, though found in most unions, usually symbolizes the nature of the tie rather than being itself instrumentally significant. Friendship ties among women are normally dyadic rather than clique-based, a trait characteristic of male friendship ties. They also appear to be shorter-lived than ties among their male counterparts and many woman-to-woman friendship relations have only existed for two or three years.

Case No. 1. Eugena Skerritt, a 64-year-old middle-lower-class married woman restricts most of her friendships to women living in the same part of the village. Of her four close friends, two are also married and share her class position. One of these friends, a next door neighbor, is nearly 20 years her junior, another is in her mid-sixties, and two are in their seventies. These women have been her friends for many years and she periodically visits all them in their homes. Only one of these women hardly ever returns these visits. Mrs. Skerritt still cultivates a small piece of *mountain* land and occasionally exchanges garden produce with the three friends who also plant gardens.

Case No. 2. Deddie McDonald, a poor 48-year-old woman has lived alone since her separation from a common-law partner with whom she cohabited for many years. Occasionally employed as a road-gang laborer, she receives most of her support from her two daughters, one living in England and one living in a neighboring village. She and Martha Anderson, a 56-year-old farmer and agricultural laborer, who has also been separated for several years from a common-law partner and is also assisted by overseas children, have been best friends for only two years. Strong support for the PPP party forms much of the basis for their close association and nearly every evening since the party came back into power in 1972 they visit the local party headquarters, a rum shop owned

328

by a leading member of the national party executive, to discuss local political issues. The shopkeeper is also Martha's patron. She has been employed by him as a laborer, exchanges agricultural produce with him, looks after his land when he is off the island, and advises him on local political support and the machinations of village Labour Party members.

Case No. 3. Sheilla Wilson, a poor 39-year-old woman with four children, has been living for three years with a man who is irregularly employed as a road laborer. Like many village women whose movements are restricted by the burdens of child care, most of Sheilla's friends are located in the immediate neighborhood. One of her best friends, Irene Blake, a neighbor four houses away, is also her half-brother's wife, and she visits her several times a week. Irene, aged 32, whose husband is permanently employed as a government handyman, is much better off than Sheilla and often gives her food to eat when she visits her home. Irene, who hardly ventures from home, does not return Sheilla's visits.

Sheilla and Mildred Donaldson, a poor woman in her late-forties who has been separated from her husband for many years, is also a neighbor and close friend. Sheilla visits Mildred in her yard every afternoon although Mildred, who rarely leaves her home, almost never reciprocates these calls. The two women occasionally share cooked food with each other and though neither plants a garden, they sometimes even exchange produce obtained from other people. Sheilla is also on good terms with Mildred's married daughter who visits her mother's home several times a week and with Mildred's 40-year-old married sister who lives next door to Mildred. On any given afternoon, the four women can usually be found *cooling out* [lounging] under the broad breadfruit tree in Mildred's yard. Not coincidentally, the four women and their respective household members all support the same political party.

Case No. 4. Rena Kirby, a 30-year-old woman who has been living-common-law for two years with a truck loader, is a member of the village poor. Unlike nearly all villagers she has no close family in St. Vincent, and this may account for her often repeated statement that "friends sometimes better to you than family." Still, she admits that she keeps the discussion of intimacies to a minimum when dealing even with good friends: "I talk anything about which I don't care about." Rena considers four women as close friends, Irene Woods, Jena Jackson, Denise Kirk, and Norma Anderson. The resultant friendship network is loosely knit and none of these women are more than acquaintances to one another.

Irene who is a few years older than Rena lives in Kingstown and Rena has known her for only three years. Rena visits Irene about three times a year and the latter has visited her in Leeward Village on two occasions. Irene who is better off than Rena sometimes gives her a dollar or two and has bought her some underclothing. When Inez was hospitalized in early 1971 Rena brought her some coconut water.

Rena is much closer to the other three women all of whom live in the same part of the village. Rena has known Denise, who is only 17-years-old, since birth and they have been good friends for two years. As is common in the village, their friendship began after Denise had a dispute with one of Rena's enemies, a neighbor living two doors away. Rena and Denise, who live within shouting distance of each other, meet and chat in the road nearly every day and regularly visit each other's homes. Denise is supported by her mother in the United States and is therefore rather better off than Rena. As a result, she often gives Rena fruit and vegetable produce she has purchased and offers her cooked food when she visits her home. She has also lent Rena money on a couple of occasions. Rena sometimes reciprocates with cooked food and occasionally gives Denise's niece a penny or two.

Rena and Norma Anderson, a middle-class widow the same age as Rena, have been friends since their school days. Although Rena calls her a close friend, their relationship more resembles acquaintanceship. Norma owns a small shop close to her home and Rena visits her there daily, often making small purchases during the visit. But Norma has never returned these visits and their relationship is confined to *old talking* [chatting] and the exchange of *commess*.

Jena Jackson, a poor 48-year-old woman who is also

cohabiting consensually has been Rena's closest friend for
the past four years. Rena visits Jena about three times a
week and the latter reciprocates about half as often. As
well, they usually *old talk* at least once every day either
in Jena's yard or in the adjacent roadway. Although their
union is based mainly on the exchange of *commess*, the
sharing of certain personal intimacies, and support for the
same political party, some material exchange also occurs.
Jena, who has many friends among the fishermen,
occasionally gives Rena some fish she has obtained from
them. When the one friend drops in on the other and food
is being served, she is sure to receive some.

A HOUSE MOVING ACTION SET

Carl Chambers a poor, middle-aged villager purchased an old
board house from the owners of Leeward Valley Estate where he was
employed as a part-time overseer. Although Chambers was living
rent-free in the overseer's quarters with his adult daughter and her
three children, he decided to move the house from the estate to his
small piece of agricultural land some 400 yards away. By local
standards this was not far to transport a house using manual labor
alone and many larger dwellings have often been physically removed
from one end of the village to the other, a distance of nearly a
mile. Since house moving is a large-scale, labor-intensive exercise
involving the dismantling of the dwelling, its transport in small
sections to the new site, and its reconstruction, a well coordinated
effort is needed. Accordingly, Chambers sought the direct and
indirect help of a total of 23 people including household members,
distant kin, friends, estate workers, fellow political party supporters,
and clients (Figure 11.2). Sixteen of the 24 links between Chambers
and his 23-member action-set were direct while eight were "second
order contacts" (Barnes 1972:8-9) using two intermediaries, a
daughter (1 in Figure 11.2) and an estate employee, as connections
to the other members of the work team. The daughter recruited six
helpers using ties of kinship, co-parenthood, close friendship,
acquaintanceship, and party support while the estate worker, who
did not herself join the crew, asked her son to help with the job.
Only one "zone" (Barnes 1972:11), or delimited portion of the
network, namely the sector connecting 1, 20, and 21, contained
lateral links without reference to the central ego and hence
exhibited beyond minimal "density" (Barnes 1972:13). At the same

time, several of the links were based on "multiplex relations" (Barnes 1972:12) since they combined at least two distinct types of ties. Client/party, kin/party, acquaintance/party, mate /employee, and employee/neighbor ties were combined in six of the 24 links. Most of the ties were egalitarian, binding together villagers of similar rank and wealth. Only five part-time estate employees (7, 11, 12, 13, and 14), persons recruited by Chambers to work on the plantation, and the two men (15 and 16) classified as "clients" because he had granted them free cattle-grazing rights on his land, stood in a slightly asymmetrical relation to him.

Members of the action set neither constituted the whole of Chamber's social field nor were they selected on an ad-hoc basis. Eight of the 16 men were skilled or apprentice carpenters, an important consideration given the care and experience needed to properly dismantle and reassemble an already built structure. Four of the seven women were employed to cook the large mid-day meal that is an expected as part of what is always a laborious full-day effort. All the participants, including the carpenters and cooks, also took part in the actual carrying of disassembled house sections to the new site.

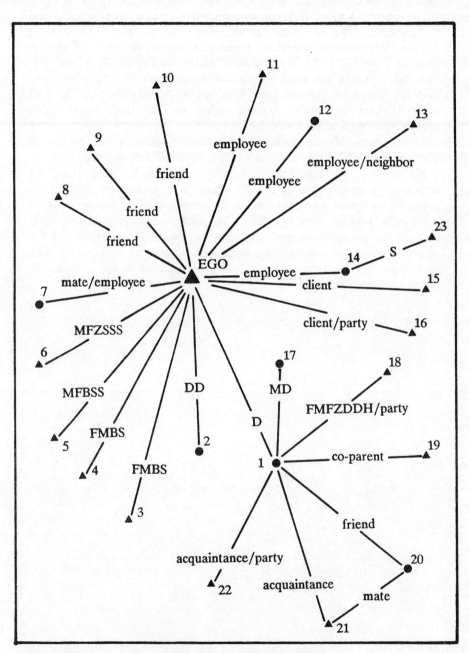

FIGURE 11.2   A HOUSE MOVING ACTION-SET

Chapter 12

Black Adaptive Strategies

This study began with the premise that although Afro-American poverty has been the subject of much scholarly attention, a great deal still remains unknown and several substantive areas, including the varied and complex ways in which poor people cope with economic adversity, have received far too little attention. Most studies, for example, have tended to either look at various features of poverty in a single institutional setting such as the family or have concentrated on a single process such as the formation of social networks in several different arenas. Even in concentrating on a single setting or process too many investigators have tried to explain the causes and consequences of Black West Indian poverty from an inadequate empirical base. The result has been that much of the theoretical disputation has been inconclusive simply because the various positions have lacked enough documentation. Indeed, there almost appears to be an intellectual aversion to holistic ethnography, at least as far as the study of poverty is concerned, a reaction, no doubt, to the shortcomings of the early ethnohistorical studies of Melville J. Herskovits (1937, 1958, 1966; Herskovits and Herskovits 1947) which saw much of Black West Indian society and culture as a survival from the African heritage (see Whitten and Szwed 1970).

The current view is that though the outlines of many African traits can be identified in contemporary West Indian culture, most of the aboriginal lifeway was destroyed or irreversibly transformed by the conditions of slave society. According to Mintz (1974:11-12):

> With few exceptions . . . enslaved Africans were sys-
> tematically prevented from bringing with them the person-
> nel who maintained their homeland institutions: the

complex social structures of their ancestral societies, with their kings, courts, guilds, cult-groups, markets and armies, were not, and could not be, transferred. Cultures are linked as continuing patterns of and for behavior in such social groupings. Since the groupings themselves could not be maintained or readily reconstituted, the capacity of isolated representatives of African societies to perpetuate or recreate the cultural contents of the past was seriously impaired. In addition, the slaves were usually unable to regroup themselves in the New World settings in terms of their origins; the resulting cultural heterogeneity of most slave groups limited that which could be shared culturally. It was not, after all, some single "African culture" that was available for transfer [see also M.G. Smith 1955:11-26, 1957].

The consequence of this interpretation of the role of the African heritage is that most scholars, whether they use the term or not, would probably agree that lower-class Black West Indians are a neoteric--a newly emergent--people (Gonzalez 1969:10-11). Although much has been written about the Black neoteric way of life some of the most fundamental questions about the origin, operation, and normative status of forms of behavior and belief people like those in Leeward Village do not share with other members of their societies remain unresolved. Which of them are really "retentions" or "reinterpretations" from the African past and which actually emerged during the era of island slavery (see Abrahams and Szwed 1975; Frazier 1957, 1960, 1966; Herskovits 1937, 1958, 1966; Herskovits and Herskovits 1947; Whitten and Szwed 1970)? Do the distinctive traits point to a culturally different tradition among the poor rural folk or are they merely situational, *ad hoc* responses to poverty conditions (see Liebow 1967; M.G. Smith 1965; Valentine 1972)? Are they class-based lifestyle variations or inadequate and partial imitations of middle- and upper-class Vincentian ways of behaving (see Blake 1961; Frazier 1966; Goode 1966; Henriques 1953; Moynihan 1965; Valentine 1972)? Of course, complex questions like these can only be addressed from a full and sound data base.

I have tried to speak to the indeterminacy of these issues in West Indian ethnology by describing the multiple ways and various arenas in which Leeward Villagers deal with their poverty. Using a cultural ecological research strategy, the study focused on three areas of adaptation to material deprivation. These were the economic sphere where the problem of gaining an adequate livelihood is the main concern for most people; the domain of family and household where kin and affines are enlisted for survival; and the realm of non-familial social life where friends, neighbors, and patrons are tapped or appealed to for social and economic help.

Together with the findings from other studies, the material on coping with poverty in each of these spheres is sufficient to address some of the problems of theory-building in Afro-Caribbean anthropology. To be sure, a single study does not a theory make and the conclusions drawn are meant for further comparative treatment and verification.

A variety of particular adaptive strategies and coping mechanisms were identified in the three arenas of economics, kinship, and friendship. The most important of these included: the formation of a proto-peasantry and a viable pattern of conjugal and domestic group life during the slavery era (Chapter 2); the emergence of a full-fledged peasantry and participation in wage-labor migration soon after Emancipation (Chapter 2); intense involvement in party-politics (Chapter 3); the generation and growth of a peasant-like village based on a complex but flexible form of community organization (Chapter 4); the development of an elaborate system of local social differentiation based in part on a distinction between reputation and respectability (Chapter 4); the utilization of vocational strategies ranging from occupational multiplicity to extra-village employment to migration overseas (Chapter 5); the presence of a permissive system of land use and transformation (Chapter 6); the emergence of a "migration culture" which includes the continuing commitment to those who have been left back home (Chapter 7); the manipulation of kindred ties in accordance with individual needs and interests (Chapter 8); the presence of an elastic kinship terminology system (Chapter 8); variability and fluidity in conjugal arrangements (Chapter 9); an elaborate system of household composition and organization in which flux and malleability are defining features (Chapter 10); and the utilization of personal friendship ties of various sorts for meeting social and economic needs.

Most of these strategies for coping with livelihood constraints are manifestations of three general principles of local social organization: the formation of dyadic ties and social networks; permissiveness in regard to belief and behavior; and cultural dualism. Probably the most controversial of these principles is the dualistic one, and for this reason I examine the hypothesis that most poor villagers are bicultural by comparing a dualistic model of village of belief and behavior to the more traditional conceptual frameworks used in Caribbean and Afro-American anthropology.

DYADIC TIES AND SOCIAL NETWORKS

The traditional preoccupation in anthropology with the study of bounded, corporate groups has resulted in either the neglect or misinterpretation of many features of Afro-Caribbean social organization (Brana-Shute 1979; Dirks 1972; Lieber 1981; Whitten and Szwed 1970:43-49). Employment of an ethnohistorical research agenda involving a search for African kinship groups (e.g., Herskovits 1937, 1958, 1966; Herskovits and Herskovits 1947), the uncritical application of a Euro-American model of social stratification and family life (e.g., Henriques 1953; Blake 1961), and the late development of a body of concepts for dealing with 'loosely structured' social forms accounts for most of this neglect. Only since the 1960s, for example, have concepts and models been available from network analysis and exchange and action theory to handle the non-group qualities of dyadic ties and social networks (Barnes 1972; Boissevain 1968; Mayer 1966; Foster 1961, 1963; Whitten and Wolfe 1973; Wolf 1966). This is not to say that networks and their constituent dyadic ties have gone unnoticed in Caribbean anthropology. In an important summary of the common socio-cultural features of the region, Mintz (1971:40) suggests that:

> Probably the main basis of social interaction among rural lower-class people--who make up the bulk of the population in Caribbean societies--is to be found in their ability to establish short- or long-term dyadic social relationships with those around them, either along lines of common interest, or to satisfy particular individual needs. In other words, rather than forming themselves into "groups" around some institution or in terms of kinship rights and obligations, these folk create radial sets of two-person linkages, and at the center of each such series is a single individual. . . . [T]he distinctive quality of Caribbean rural social structure may be its heavy emphasis on individual dyadic ties, as opposed to membership in social groups having some corporate or institutional or kin basis.

Mintz offers godparenthood and links between agricultural produce-vendors and their clients as examples of dyadic social relations. Other Caribbeanists have also pointed to the presence, directly or indirectly, of dyads and networks in such varied areas as friendship (Brana-Shute 1976, 1979; Lieber 1981; Dirks 1972; Wilson 1973), patron-client ties (Dirks 1972), conjugal behavior (Rodman 1971), kindred organization (Gonzalez 1969:85-87; Philpott 1973:114-116; Rodman 1971), household composition (Goldberg 1984; Rodman 1971), and labor migration (Philpott 1968, 1973). But few researchers have noted the functions that such social formations perform in the region although Mintz (1971:41) suggests that their genesis lies in ". . . a heavy individualistic emphasis in social relations" and that such "individualization" represents ". . . an adaptive response to the intense westernization, lengthy colonial trajectory, heterogeneous population origins, and the rather special economic history of the Caribbean area."

Other investigators have elaborated on how Caribbean individualization represents an "adaptive response" to extant societal conditions. In a small community in the British Virgin Islands, Dirks (1972:569) found that:

> . . . networks are formed on the basis of personal alliance
> as an adaptive response to resources of a shifting,
> impermanent nature, while groups develop a supra-
> individualistic quality in response to more stable and
> permanent resource bases.

For example, Dirks found that friendship and other non-group relations were formed as flexible social forms for exploiting geographically scattered, unstable, and impermanent regional employment and other economic opportunities. The same can be said for the dyads and networks formed among the young Black men in Port-of-Spain, Trinidad, studied by Lieber (1981). Although he fails to draw out its implications, success in the illegal marijuana trade clearly is contingent on the presence of flexible shifting interpersonal coalitions.

Caribbean women are not exempt from the process of network building. Although he gives little documentation to support it, Richardson's (1983:51) contention about the significance of flexible interpersonal coalitions in the "migration culture" of St. Kitts and Nevis parallels those in other studies.

> A typical female, in order to maximize her cash-receiving
> position in the light of economic uncertainty, has
> depended on herself, on a male mate--sometimes more
> than one--and eventually on children working abroad.
> Individual needs have been fulfilled more often than not
> by establishing male-female "family" alliances. These
> flexible alliances, supported by children and other

relatives, have seen family members geographically dispersed beyond St. Kitts and Nevis. This dispersal further enhances a cash receipt position for individuals and might be considered an adaptation to the economic circumstances surrounding the common people of the two islands. "Family" on St. Kitts and Nevis is an elusive ever-changing structure and a social adaptation to change and uncertainty.

"Network theory" has also been used to explain Black adaptation outside the Caribbean. In a famous study of Black streetcorner men in Washington, D.C., Liebow (1967) has detailed the emotional, sentimental, and economic implications of shifting networks of friends among poor and often unemployed ghetto males. More recently, Shimkin, Shimkin, and Frate (1978) and Stack (1970, 1974) have documented the economic and child-rearing functions of kindred networks among poor Black American women while Whitten and Szwed (1970:45), generalizing for all the Americas, have argued that:

> . . . in many New World Negro rural communities, where by one means or another individuals are kept effectively outside of the sources of economic change, *definable, bounded groups are maladaptive, and survival for them is thereby limited*. Constant subjection to varying inputs from externally generated cash seems to favor the development of *networks* of individuals, making up strings of *quasi-groups*.

The presence and significance of dyadic ties and ego-centric networks in Leeward Village lend support to Whitten and Szwed's proposition. Starting with the formation of flexible conjugal and domestic group arrangements during the slavery era, the presence of non-groups has always marked village social organization. Indeed, the community itself as a social unit features many network characteristics--openness in membership and migration, a heterogeneous membership, the absence of corporateness, and a form of social interaction based on a combination of conjugal, kindred, friendship, and neighborhood ties. These same features seem to form a coherent pattern which characterizes many other Afro-American rural communities. But, as Dirks (1972:565) correctly suggests, this has not prevented the organization of such communities from being interpreted in a negative light.

The Afro-American community has been variously por-
trayed as weak, fragmentary, ineffectual, loosely organized, disoriented, disintegrated, amorphous, indistinct,
and underdeveloped (Mintz 1966:932; 1968:317; T. Smith
1954:55; Wagley 1960:8; 1961:198). I find these descriptions
neither accurate nor useful. They are clearly the result of
a bias towards a 'group-based model of society' (Whitten
& Szwed 1970:45) which fails to assign any value to
alternative forms of social organization. In the study of
Afro-American communities, where informal interpersonal
alliances appear to play an important part in the competition for resources, this model is not itself adequate
(Mintz 1968:317).

Dirks calls for "network theory" to balance this perspective. This is
what was done in describing Leeward Village community organization
as the cumulative product of the activities of its members--of the
manner in which its residents have actively shaped the local social
and economic world around them. An open community, for example,
is partly a manifestation of extra-village employment, wage labor
migration, a high rate of exogamy, the extension of friendship
beyond its boundaries, the easy way in which village membership is
gained, and the other features of individualizaion already discussed
in Chapter 4. But it is equally important to recognize that community "weakness" from the perspective of a "group-based model of
society" is the counterpart of social integration from the point of
view of informal social ties based on friendship, neighborhoodship,
and other "loosely structured" social ties. Social solidarity and a
sense of separateness from other communities is achieved via
residential propinquity, streetcorner gatherings, gossip networks,
kindred affiliation, shared political support and other intra-community ties that occur outside organized, bounded social groupings.
    The paucity of closed, corporate groups at the community level
is also a reflection of the importance of dyads and networks in the
economic arena. The recruitment of seine boat and road gang crews,
apprenticeship to trades, labor exchange ties among peasant cultivators, help with house moving, and other collective enterprises
are all based on the network principle. The organization of labor,
the ownership of household property, and the disposition of employment earnings are also individualized as is the decision to transfer
land from one generation to another and to sponsor the migration of
and remit funds to particular kith and kin.
    Economic individualism towards kin is both cause and conse-

quence of the presence of dyads and networks in the related domains of kindred affiliation, conjugal behavior, and domestic organization. The kindred, an ego-centric category of kin, is the largest collection of relatives recognized by community members; kinship terminology is situationally selected and the relations it supports are subject to individual negotiation; parental role behavior results from the quality of dyadic interaction rather than membership in a pre-existing domestic group; sexual relations are worked out by the two individuals concerned with little reference to other kin; and the household is a fluid and elastic collection of relatives, not a permanent, bounded kinship group.

The presence of non-groups is probably most evident in non-kinship arenas. Collective labor tasks--dragging a fishing net ashore, moving a house, working on a government road repair gang, participation in *swap labor*--involvement in politics and membership in a streetcorner *liming* clique, all involve ad-hoc often temporary coalitions of persons recruited to meet the needs of the individuals involved. Even close friendships, especially among younger people, are often temporary unions, highly charged for a short period of time and then suddenly terminated by accusations of rumor mongering or gradually deactivated as new relations begin to develop.

PERMISSIVENESS

Dyads and networks are formed and maintained by individualism--by the degree to which individual villagers remain unconstrained by strong social bonds, kinship and non-kinship alike. In turn, individualism itself is a manifestation of the behavioral and normative permissiveness which marks much of what villagers think, do, and say. To be sure, villagers are not unconstrained by existing social ties; nor can the bulk of their behavior be reduced to a simplistic cost-benefit tally. Still, the evidence suggests that, in many situations, there are a number of moral and behavioral alternatives from which to choose, the selection taking place on the basis of personal inclination and perception of advantage; that kin and other social ties seem to be rather ineffective in channeling behavior, at least in comparison to what appears to be the case in other peasant or peasant-like communities; that the form and content of relations tend to be worked out by the actions of individuals rather than by pre-existing definitions of appropriate behavior; and that substitutes are readily found for particular relatives, sexual partners, and friends (cf. Rodman 1971).

341

Recognition of the presence of permissiveness and its corol-
laries--individualism, personalism, and replaceability--reveals the
process by which poor villagers have attempted to work out a viable
solution to the difficulties that have been imposed upon them by a
hostile social environment and unfavorable economic conditions. It
does so by directing attention to the human creative component in
ecological analysis--to the role played by decision-making, choice,
trial-and-error, and innovation in the adaptive process (Bennett
1969:11-19). Awareness of the importance of choice and strategy in
the generation of social forms and values has grown since their
incisive treatment first by Raymond Firth (1951) and later by
Fredrik Barth (1966a, 1966b). Acknowledging an intellectual debt to
Barth, Boissevain (1968:545) describes the formation of social groups
in the following manner:

> Social forms do not drop ready made from heaven. Nor
> are they merely taken over blindly from preceding
> generations, or simply borrowed from neighbouring
> societies. They are generated or adapted by individuals or
> aggregates of individuals acting in accordance with their
> own interests within the limits imposed by existing social
> forms and values which, in their turn, were generated or
> adapted in the same way in the past.

While the use of decision-making models of Afro-Caribbean
adaptation has not been extensive, their potential application has not
gone unnoticed.

> [W]e must conceptualize Afro-American cultures not simply
> as historically derived bodies of materials, as patterns of
> and for behavior, but also as materials actively employed
> by organized human groupings in particular social con-
> texts. Without the dimension of human action, of choices
> made and pursued--of maneuver--culture could be regarded
> as a lifeless collection of habits, superstitions, and
> artifacts. Instead we see that culture is *used*: and that
> any analysis of its use immediately brings into view the
> arrangements of persons in social groups, for whom
> cultural forms confirm, reinforce, maintain, change, or
> deny particular arrangements of status, power, and
> identity (Mintz 1974:18).

The potential utility of a decision-making approach to Leeward

Village adaptive processes is even reflected in statements of villagers themselves on the 'rules' governing various areas of activity. Much of what Leeward Village people do, or say they do, is governed by what Rodman (1971:137) has termed an "orientation to circumstances" to describe behavior and its evaluation in the poor Afro-Trinidadian village he studied.

> The *accordin'* attitude is one reflection of the orientation to circumstances. It provides an excellent illustration of the fluidity of lower-class life. To question after question asking for the correct or expected behavior the villager would reply, "Well, accordin' . . . " and then suggest several alternative lines of behavior that might be taken, depending on circumstances. With this outlook, it is frequently possible for the villager to fit his behavior to the circumstances and to benefit from a flexible *accordin'* culture rather than suffer from a fixed Procrustrean one (Rodman 1971:173).

There is, of course, no reason for the conscious explanations of informants to mirror the external observer's interpretation of the same behavior or situation. Indeed, it is difficult to differentiate 'analytic' from 'folk' interpretations in such instances and easy to unthinkingly transform the one into the other (Harris 1968:575-582). Nevertheless, it remains important to note that the actions of individual actors, their interpretation of these actions, and the resultant social patterns all point to the utility of a generative choice model of adaptive behavior.

As a recurrent and patterned manifestation of choice-making behavior, permissiveness is evident in most areas of village social and economic life. Permissiveness allows existing conjugal relationships to be terminated or new one to be formed; it enables people to address non-kin by kin terms or to ignore a connection to a close blood relative; it lets poor women circumvent the norms governing the sexual division of labor; it sanctions the decision to sponsor the migration of some children but not others or to leave property only to certain potential heirs; it allows men to deny the fathering of a child that is obviously their own or for some women to *give* the same child first to one man and then to another; it fosters multiple household membership, shifting friendship and political alliances, and the sequential or concurrent manipulation of respectability and reputation seeking behavior.

It would be ridiculous, of course, to suggest that a society or community could be characterized by complete permissiveness--that there are no structural constraints or set of jural or moral norms and rights governing social roles and associated behavior. Permissiveness in kindred affiliation, for example, was shown to be tempered by age, gender, birth status and union type, coresidence, genealogical distance, and interpersonal conflict. It would be equally naive to imply that the behavioral maneuverability and normative flexibility fostered by a permissive social system comes with no strings attached. Just as ego is free to begin or end a given kin, conjugal, or other social relation or to appeal to one or another set of normative 'rules' governing interaction, so alter has the choice to accept or reject ego's moral or behavioral claim on him. Permissiveness is a two-edged sword which must be wielded with both skill and delicacy, if its benefits are to be enjoyed. Some players because they are shrewder, more articulate, or harder working than others are better at manipulating their social environment, and it is these individuals--*saga boys*, self-made local entrepreneurs, successful labor migrants--who form a model for the others.

Although it has received detailed treatment only in the study of kinship behavior among rural, lower-class Afro-Trinidadians (Rodman 1971), permissiveness is relevant to other Caribbean populations where the same social and economic features are present: an unreliable economic base, community openness, variability in kinship organization, etc. One of manifestations of permissiveness, however, is less obvious, probably because its various implications are still unclear. Permissiveness operates outside the exclusive domain of class- and community-specific behavior and belief to include within the repertoire of normative and behavioral alternatives available to its members many of the social forms and accompanying beliefs, values, and attitudes characteristic of middle- and upper-class people. This additional source of social and ideological variability has been termed "biculturation."

BICULTURATION

Biculturation and terms related to it--"the lower-class value stretch" (Rodman 1971:190-200); "contraculture" (Bryce-Laporte 1970); "duality of cultural patterning" (Reisman 1970); "normative dualism" (M.G. Smith 1966:xxx); "plural acculturation" (Crowley 1957)--point to the double cultural orientation among many New World Blacks. The bicultural model is the most recent of several conceptual frameworks which have been employed to describe and explain social and

344

cultural differentiation in the Caribbean and other parts of the Americas where Afro-Americans form a significant population category. One of these models, the African survival approach of Herskovits (1958, 1966) has already been briefly discussed. Mintz's criticism of its substantive shortcomings may be supplemented by R.T. Smith's (1956:228) critical assessment of its methodological limitations for an understand of contemporary Black family organization.

> Writings on New World Negro family organization have tended to concentrate to some extent on the controversy as to whether the form of the New World Negro family is the result of the peculiar conditions obtaining on the plantations during the period of slavery or whether it can be seen as a modified survival of an 'African' family pattern. Equally plausible theories supported by historical evidence have been advanced on either side, and the polemical discussions have brought to light a considerable body of information and have been productive of many profound insights. It would seem, though, that there is a need for synchronic analysis, which attempts to understand the working of the system without any pre-conceptions as to its previous states. There is always a danger that the prior task of sociological analysis may be side-stepped when historical factors are prematurely introduced as 'explanatory' devices.

This evaluation of historical explanation also applies to the "slave-society model," an approach which attributes much of the behavior of contemporary lower-class Afro-Americans to the conditions of slavery (Frazier 1957, 1966). Both models may also be questioned on theoretical grounds. Even if the one or the other is fundamentally correct in attributing the *origin* of much of present-day Black social life and ideology to either slave society or the African heritage, this by itself does not account for the *transfer* or *persistence* of historically-based society and culture, except, perhaps, by reference to general acculturation.

It is for these kinds of reasons that most scholars have long relied on synchronic models of Afro-American behavior and belief. Considerable controversy has surrounded the utility of three of these models for interpreting the form and meaning of distinctively Black social usages.

The Culture of Poverty

St. Vincent meets many of the societal criteria of Oscar Lewis' (1966:21) "culture of poverty"--a cash economy with high unemployment and underemployment and low wages for its unskilled population; a paucity of adequate social and economic benefits for the low-income population; a bilateral kinship system; and a high value placed by the dominant class on ". . . thrift and the accumulation of wealth and property . . . [which] stresses the possibility of upward mobility and explains low economic status as the result of individual personal inadequacy and inferiority." Many of the material and social conditions of those said to belong to the culture of poverty are also present in Leeward Village (see Chapter 5). Still, it has been argued that despite the presence of all these features the beliefs, values, and attitudes associated with the model--fear, despair, fatalism, etc.--do not apply to most poor villagers, and that, on the contrary, members of the village poor have shown a remarkable capacity to react in a multitude of positive and creative ways to the many social and economic adversities facing them. Such an interpretation, however, runs counter to the Vincentian folk view regarding village poverty as well as to scholarly anthropological interpretations of situations resembling the Leeward Village one. Probably the simplest and most parsimonious explanation of the unemployment, underemployment, low wages, absence of savings, shortages of cash, and other signs of economic deprivation among villagers is that suggested by the "temporal orientation" said to characterize those living under the culture of poverty. The use of temporal orientation to explain community poverty would imply that villagers exhibit ". . . a strong present-time orientation with little disposition to defer gratification and plan for the future" (Lewis 1966:22). The relevance of present-time orientation to the behavior of villagers is suggested by several different sources. First, there is the view of villagers themselves that many their fellows are lazy and unambitious. Second, many middle- and upper-class islanders, including some elected officials, state that villagers could do much to improve their lot in life if they would only work harder and quarrel less. Third, there is the anthropological view that Vincentian youths observe a "leisure ethic" as opposed to a "Protestant work ethic" (Hourihan 1973:34), that other Black West Indians are present-oriented (Freilich 1961:964), and that this trait is also found among poor urban Blacks in the United States (Johnson and Sanday 1971:135-137).

Hourihan (1973:29), for example, proposes that the aversion

towards agricultural labor he observed among the island's youth is partly a product of ". . . a leisure ethic which counterpoises the Protestant ethic towards work." This leisure ethic is defined as ". . . the acceptance of leisure in the present as opposed to working and saving for leisure some time in the future" (1973:34). Freilich (1961:964) offers an equally unequivocal interpretation of work attitudes in describing temporal orientation among Black Trinidadian peasants.

> Is it the past, present, or the future that is con-
> sidered most important to the Negro peasant? Using Levi-
> Strauss' terms, the community has a "conscious model"
> (1953:527) for their time orientation and they have a name
> for it, "now-for-now". It is *the present* that is most
> significant, not the past or the future. The present is
> certain and to be enjoyed. Nor should present enjoyment
> be sacrificed for future possible undesirable repercussions
> . . . .
> A man will go out and fête (take pleasure in every
> possible form--dance, drink, sexual play, etc.) with his girl
> friend when both his time and his money might, economi-
> cally, be better spent (in terms of future security and
> income) on his estate. If one inquires about these things a
> very frequent reply is simply: "Now-for-now, man!"

Present-time orientation and the leisure ethic contain the implications that since those who operate under them are unable or unwilling to control their immediate wants or emotions, they are the authors of their own misfortune. In essence, the two notions place the blame for poverty at the feet of the poor themselves.

Several scholars have shown that characterizations such as these are either misinterpretations of temporal orientation among members of different socio-economic strata or lacking in empirical support (see Liebow 1967:29-71; Miller, Riessman, and Seagull 1968; Ryan 1971:112-129; Valentine 1971:209-210). Indeed, the whole concept of the culture of poverty of which present-time orientation is a key ingredient has been severely criticized on theoretical, methodological, and substantive grounds (see Valentine 1968; Lewis *et al* 1967; Leacock 1971).

The Leeward Village situation supports the findings of these other studies. There is little evidence of present-time orientation in the community even though many villagers often expend all their resources on the satisfaction of immediate needs and are indeed reluctant to participate in certain occupations, such as agricultural labor and peasant cultivation. But this has to do with the conditions of the local economy rather than a psychological or ideological predisposition towards leisure or idleness. Both wage-labor and small-scale independent farming, the two main livelihood pursuits, yield such small material benefits that even minimal household support is not guaranteed. The chances of failure in own-account farming owing to ecological, climatic, and market forces are great and the opportunity for full-time employment as an agricultural laborer, even at the low wages offered, is small. Peasant cultivation and estate wage-work also carry low status and prestige. Alternatively, there are many less strenuous local and external economic alternatives to which labor can be put which provide higher rates of economic return and respectability. All these factors are well known to villagers and acted upon accordingly. Rather than lacking future-orientation, villagers generally have a clear perception of what life holds in store for them based both on their own previous failures in agriculture and on observing those who have spent their whole lives bent over a hoe with little to show for their efforts (cf. Liebow 1967:63-71). If, indeed, villagers were obsessed with the present it would be difficult to account for the features associated with the overall local organization of occupations: a preference for secure, high paying, prestigious employment among young people; the reappraisal of occupational attainment among adults so that formerly rejected jobs become socially acceptable; the circumvention among women of the ideals surrounding the sexual division of labor; the complex manner in which the available occupations are combined; and the eagerness of villagers to migrate in such great numbers wherever and whenever they can.

Social Class and Cultural Pluralism

The limitations of the ethnohistorical and culture of poverty approaches have been known for some time and most scholars have rejected them in favor of models which describe Afro-American behavior and belief either from the perspective of class stratification or cultural differentiation. Those who favor one or the other of these two models have been engaged in a lively scholarly debate for many years. Critics of the "social class model" (e.g., Despres 1964; M.G. Smith 1960; Valentine 1972) contend that its applicability to the Afro-American experience is limited since a class analysis ignores the presence of cultural differences between Blacks and non-

Blacks in their respective societies. Those who take issue with the "plural society model" (e.g., Benedict 1970; Despres 1964; R.T. Smith 1961, 1970; Valentine 1972) argue that the model's emphasis on the cultural distinctiveness of New World Blacks distorts the manner in which the societies in which they form either most the population--nearly all of the non-Hispanic Caribbean--or are important minorities--the Spanish-speaking Caribbean, portions of South America, and the United States--are functioning, integrated units based on a society-wide system of shared beliefs, values, and institutions.

To be sure, this very brief sketch of a couple of the criticisms leveled at the two prevailing models of Afro-American socio-cultural differentiation exaggerates both their weaknesses and the distinctions between them. For example, class based differences resulting from the arrangement of a society into a series of ranked, hierarchical strata defined by differential access to power, wealth, and prestige are usually described by life-style or subcultural variability. But stylistic and subcultural distinctiveness is fundamentally different from cultural differentiation (M.G. Smith 1960:769) and underscores that an overarching framework of cultural homogeneity characterizes the society (Tumin 1967:66). In addition, although it is possible to incorporate class-specific style of life or subculture with the notion of inter-class cultural uniformity and societal integration, all too often lower-class Black differentiation has been viewed as evidence of "instability" (Goode 1966), "disorganization" (Blake 1961), or "pathology" (Moynihan 1965). On the other hand, attempts to integrate the plural society model, in which lower-class Blacks are seen as possessing a culture radically different from and incompatible with the way of life practiced by other segments of their societies, with the class-based notion of societal integration have led to the conclusion that the society itself is disorganized.

> I have suggested that Jamaican society is disnomic. This cannot mean that the individual forms of social structure are unbalanced. In fact the contrary is the case. The structure of domestic and family groupings [among the different classes] is itself balanced. But the existence of such types of familial associations in conjunction with poverty and colour create disnomia of the total society. The forms of the family are balanced in themselves, but their existence is symptomatic of disnomia in the society as a whole (Henriques 1953:162).

A major difficulty in trying to determine whether a given society is differentiated by "cultural sections" or "social classes" is that the two models are concerned with different issues and levels of abstraction and therefore define their problem from varying perspectives (Benedict 1970). A class analysis is concerned mainly with society-wide phenomena, particularly its *structure* and the relation between its strata. The plural society model focuses on differences in *culture* between the segments of a society and does not concern itself with structural issues except in the political arena where it defines the plural society as held together by force (e.g., M.G. Smith 1960). Failure to appreciate the different orientations of the two models has undoubtedly been a central factor preventing the social class/plural society debate from reaching a satisfactory conclusion. Recognition that the two models are not necessarily contradictory because they are not asking the same kinds of questions is essential in trying to appreciate the relationship between them.

The Bicultural Model

The social class model correctly points out that in certain societies the different social strata are united by an overarching system of shared beliefs, values, and goals. The model of cultural pluralism is useful insofar as it suggests that in some societies that have been described as class-stratified, the lowest stratum features a distinctive way of life not shared with the other strata. The bicultural model attempts to reconcile these two seemingly contradictory positions by providing a framework which simultaneously describes differentiation in these societies from the perspective of both models. But the bicultural model is more than just a synthesis of class and pluralism. Rather, it is an alternative way of looking at differentiation in class-based societies in which full-blown, lower-class cultural differences are interwoven with a society-wide cultural tradition.

Anthropologists are increasingly recognizing that Afro-Americans are participating in two different cultural traditions, Black culture and an overarching or "mainstream" culture, in many New World societies (Abrahams 1983; Bryce-Laporte 1970; Lieber 1981; Reisman 1970; Rodman 1963, 1971; Valentine 1972; Young 1974). Biculturation is a process whereby those Blacks defined as lower-class by the social class model and carriers of a separate culture by the plural society model are participating in two cultural traditions at the same time. They are both aware of and use the way of life characteristic of the total society and a way of life which is uniquely their own. The plural model is of little help in describing this kind of situation although it focuses on multi-cultural societies, for the model defines each of the constituent cultures as non-overlapping and self-contained. Likewise, the social class model, despite its emphasis on stylistic or subcultural variability, is incapable of describing double cultural competence since inter-class differences are defined as manifestation of cultural homogeneity.

The sources of biculturation among Afro-Americans are as varied as they are complex. Black people have a heritage which includes enslavement, forced migration, protracted servitude, and the destruction or transformation of most pre-slavery lifeways. The consequence has been the production of new behavioral repertoires, values, and beliefs. Some of these are simply duplications or altered variations of those held by most societal members regardless of their class, ethnic, or racial background. Others are reformulated "survivals" of those African elements and complexes which were not destroyed or forgotten during slavery (Herskovits 1958, 1966). Still others are distinctive patterns of action and belief which emerged out of the nature of the relation between Blacks and Whites in the societies of the New World. The key feature of this relation has always been inequality. Its attributes are differential access to power, privilege, property, and prestige on the basis of racial and/or ethnic affiliation. More specifically, the institutions, resources, and social positions which are positively evaluated, actively pursued, or otherwise promise important material or social rewards are not equally available to Black people in most New World societies.

The other sources of biculturation are post-Emancipation socio-economic conditions, contemporary class stratification, ethnic and racial prejudice, and poverty (Blauner 1970). While poverty and racism are intimately linked to the nature of economic differentiation, social placement, and cultural evaluation in class-based societies, the social exclusion and oppression of Black people are only part of the picture of their New World experience. An equally crucial factor has been their exposure to mainstream culture and patterns of behavior in these societies (Valentine 1972). But although they are acutely aware of and are actively encouraged to accept societal beliefs and values, many Blacks have been prevented from actualizing the associated patterns of action because access to them has been severely restricted. The consequence has been the maintenance--in the case of certain identifiable "Africanisms"--and generation--in the case of past and present adaptations to New

World conditions--of distinctive sets of norms, social forms, and institutions.

Double cultural competence among Afro-Americans is acquired in much the same way as mono-cultural facility among non-Blacks. Familiarity with the lifeways of the total society is achieved through the formal education system, through the media, through socialization in the home where mainstream behavioral patterns are informally imparted, and through interaction with members of the dominant sectors of society. Internalization of non-mainstream culture is attained through normal enculturation in which Black, lower-class norms, values, and behavior are offered as socially acceptable and viable alternatives to the societal way of life. An important element of "rediscovery" also occurs through repeated situational adaptations to recurring incentives and constraints.

Biculturation in Leeward Village

Although social organization and cultural life are differentially expressed between upper, middle, and lower class in St. Vincent, the island is not a plural society. This is not to say that there is no discontinuity in behavior and belief between the different strata; only that those differences that do exist--and there are many--are embedded within a larger framework of common goals, interests and understandings. In a small society like St. Vincent where Blacks, Coloreds, and Whites have lived side by side for several hundred years and where other ethnic groups--Caribs, East Indians, *Bajans*, Portuguese, etc.--form a tiny part of the population all social segments are more or less aware of the range of cultural patterns and social forms practiced in the society (cf. Crowley 1957). To be sure, as in all hierachical state-level societies, social and physical barriers and customary constraints limit intense inter-class filiation. But these have not been enough to divide the society into incompatible "cultural sections." All Vincentians are united by an acceptance of the basic tenants of Christianity; by shared ideals of marital and family life; by common educational and occupational aspirations; by collective interests in reggae and calypso music; by agreement on the legitimacy of the political system; by an overlapping comprehension of (if not equal facility in) both standard English and non-standard creole speech; by acceptance of the same societal indices of social placement--race, color, wealth, and 'respectability'--and by a keen interest in national events--elections, carnival, and cricket matches.

Despite the presence of such transcendent interests, understandings, and pursuits, members of any particular stratum will naturally be far more proficient in and dedicated to the features which distinguish it from the others. But habituation and familiarity alone cannot account for differential allegiance to class-based practices and beliefs. Elite and middle strata mores and values are shared by all members of the society and ". . . European tradition is paramount among all classes . . ." (Lowenthal 1972:101). What distinguishes the lower class from the others and fosters the continuity of distinctively lower-class features are the events, processes, and conditions which have been described already in considerable detail: a legacy of over 200 years of enslavement; continuing racial and cultural discrimination; economic underdevelopment; and grossly differential access to livelihood pursuits, food, clothing, shelter, health care, education, power, and prestige. The result is that most poor Vincentians are prevented from acting out middle- and upper-class lifeways. It is this blockage that has been instrumental in generating the various adaptive social forms and values not shared with the rest of the society.

The bicultural orientation of Leeward Villagers in many ways resembles that reported for poor Blacks in the United States.

> Highly effective skills for individual and collective survival have been fashioned from the available bicultural resources. In the face of general economic insecurity, varying combinations of hard work, useful if not prestigeful skills, effective networks of mutual assistance, resourceful techniques of dissimulation and hustling, have vouchsafed not only for subsistence but flashes of luxury here and there. Exclusion from the dominant institutions and marginality with respect to mainstream social processes have been met by constructing alternate or parallel institutions in the Black community . . . and developing distinctively adaptable social forms. . . (Valentine 1972:34).

Although most of the Black aboriginal heritage was destroyed by the conditions of slavery, cultural dualism in Leeward Village is a complex and multi-faceted amalgamation of two historical traditions, British and West African. Rooted in the plantation-based slavery era, lower-class cultural duality continues to be shaped by a rigid system of class stratification which is still party based on color. Differences in culture and opportunities for social and economic advancement are attributable to island social differentiation, because full access to and participation in the institutions characteristic of the upper echelons of society are denied to members of the lower class. Nevertheless, lower-class persons are often required to be aware of and able to manipulate the norms, values, and ways of acting emblematic of the larger society. Wage-labor employment for members of the dominant classes, for example, requires adherence to societal norms of punctuality, work habits, and speech, including prompt and regular attendance on the job, completion of tasks within a circumscribed period of time, and communication in "proper English." Employers are unconcerned that these expectations are either difficult to observe or alien to the traditional work ethic of the Black lower class: a watch is an expensive luxury few poor people can afford; the temporal orientation and work ethic in rural subsistence activities such as farming are governed by natural phenomena (sunrise and sunset, seasonal variations in rainfall, maturation patterns of different cultigens); and Creole is the normal language in the work situation. As well as being required to manifest a degree of competence in mainstream norms, poor Black villagers are also actively and deliberately encouraged to adopt societal patterns of respectable behavior. The clergy, secular members of the village elite, and peers who have converted their unions from *living* to marriage, encourage those "living in sin" to formalize their unions in accordance with the societal ideal of marriage as the only appropriate arena for mating and reproduction.

The resultant dual cultural participation of Leeward Villagers has been discussed or hinted at in a number of different arenas: the distinction between the societal and lower-class-specific systems of social ranking based on an opposition between respectability and reputation; the counterpoising of the local community and the larger society in effigy hangings; the contradiction between occupational aspirations and achievement; the dualism between a societal-jural and local-folk system of land tenure and transmission; the division between a mainstream and lower-class-specific system of kinship nomenclature; the antithesis between ideal and actual parental-roles among both men and women; the distinction between legal, Christian marriage and non-legal conjugal behavior; and the duality between the ideal of a stable nuclear family household and the actual pattern of local household composition and organization.

If the plural society model were an appropriate scheme for depicting behavioral and ideological discontinuity between the village and the external society, then its various "cultural sections" should exhibit non-overlapping, incompatible cultural differences. In particular, poor villagers should subscribe to a radically different way of life than other societal members as far as social differentiation, economic organization, and family life are concerned. In fact, nearly the opposite is the case. Villagers have not abandoned the general social usages and values associated with these institutions but have reformulated or "stretched" them in so that the distinctive variants they have been developed are also acceptable or even desirable. Conversely, these variants are not simply subcultural or stylistic class-based refinements. Reputation seeking behavior, *family land* holding patterns, *effigy hangings*, child minding arrangements, *keeping* patterns, and so on are independent and often contradictory alternatives to the mainstream way of life. A social class model by itself is simply too unrefined to handle the meaning, complexity, subtlety, and viability of the response of villagers to their position within the island system of stratification.

It goes without saying that the bicultural orientation and other adaptations that have been generated among lower-class villagers do not themselves compensate for their poverty. And, of course, many other human groups have shown a strong capacity to adapt in positive and multiple ways to social and economic adversity. What the various coping mechanisms that have been described here do show is the creative manner in which a collection of Black people have sought, either deliberately or through unconscious trial and error, to deal with the adversities associated with enforced migration, the degradation of slavery, the prejudice of racism, and the exploitation of classism in one of the poorest societies in the New World.

References Cited

Abrahams, Roger D.
1970. A Performance-Centred Approach to Gossip. Man (N.S.) 5:290-301.

1983. The Man-of-Words in the West Indies: Performance and the Emergence of Creole Culture. Baltimore: The Johns Hopkins University Press.

Abrahams, Roger D. and Richard Bauman
1971. Sense and Nonsense in St. Vincent: Speech Behavior and Decorum in a Caribbean Community. American Anthropologist 73:762-772.

Abrahams, Roger D. and John F. Szwed, eds.
1975. Discovering Afro-America. Leiden: Brill.

Alland, Alexander, Jr. and Bonnie McCay
1973. The Concept of Adaptation in Biological and Cultural Evolution. *In* Handbook of Social and Cultural Anthropology. John J. Honigman, ed. pp. 143-178. Chicago: Rand McNally.

Alland, Alexander, Jr.
1975. Adaptation. Annual Review of Anthropology 4:59-73.

Anderson, James N.
1973. Ecological Anthropology and Anthropological Ecology. *In* Handbook of Social and Cultural Anthropology. John J. Honigmann, ed. pp. 179-239. Chicago: Rand McNally.

Anderson, Robert M., ed.
1938. The Saint Vincent Handbook. 5th edition. Kingstown, St. Vincent: The Vincentian Press.

356

Arensberg, Conrad M. and Solon T. Kimball
1968. Community Study: Retrospect and Prospect. American Journal of Sociology 73(6):691-705.

Aschenbrenner, Joyce
1975. Lifelines: Black Families in Chicago. New York: Holt, Rinehart and Winston.

Ashcraft, Norman
1966. The Domestic Group in Mahogany, British Honduras. Social and Economic Studies 15(3):266-274.

1968. Some Aspects of Domestic Organization in British Honduras. In The Family in the Caribbean. Stanford N. Gerber, ed. pp. 63-73. Proceedings of the First Conference on the Family in the Caribbean. Rio Piedras, Puerto Rico: Institute of Caribbean Studies, University of Puerto Rico.

Augier, Fitzroy R. et al
1960. The Making of the West Indies. London: Longmans, Green.

Auguelli, John P.
1962. Land Use in Guadeloupe. Geographical Review 52(3): 436-438.

Austin, Diane J.
1983. Culture and Ideology in the English-Speaking Caribbean: A View from Jamaica. American Ethnologist 10(2): 223-240.

Ayearst, Morley
1960. The British West Indies: The Search for Self-Government. London: Allen and Unwin.

Barlett, Peggy F.
1980. Adaptive Strategies in Peasant Agricultural Production. Annual Review of Anthropology 9:545-573.

Barnes, John A.
1961. Physical and Social Kinship. Philosophy of Science 28:296-299.

1972. Social Networks. Addison-Wesley Modular Publications 26:1-29.

Barrow, Christine
1976. Reputation and Ranking in a Barbadian Locality. Social and Economic Studies 25(2):106-121.

Barth, Fredrick
1966a. Anthropological Models and Social Reality. Proceedings of the Royal Society 165:20-34.

1966b. Models of Social Organization. Royal Anthropological Institute of Great Britain and Ireland Occasional Paper No. 23. London.

Bender, Donald R.
1967. A Refinement of the Concept of Household: Families, Co-Residence and Domestic Functions. American Anthropologist 69(5):493-504.

Benedict, Burton
1970. Pluralism and Stratification. *In* Essays in Comparative Social Stratification. Leonard Plotnicov and Arthur Tuden, eds. pp. 29-41. Pittsburgh: University of Pittsburgh Press.

Bennett, John W.
1969. Northern Plainsmen: Adaptive Strategy and Agrarian Life. Chicago: Aldine.

1976. Anticipation, Adaptation, and the Concept of Culture in Anthropology. Science 192(4242): 847-853.

Berleant-Schiller, Riva
1981. Plantation Society and the Caribbean Present. Part I: History, Anthropology and the Plantation. Plantation Society 1(3):387-409.

Berreman, Gerald D.
1972. Race, Class, and Other Invidious Distinctions in Social Stratification. Race 13(4):385-414.

Betley, Brian J.
1976. Stratification and Strategies: A Study of Adaptation and Mobility in a Vincentian Town. Ph.D. Dissertation, Department of Anthropology, University of California at Los Angeles.

358

Blake, Judith
    1961. Family Structure in Jamaica. New York: Glencoe.

Blauner, Robert
    1970. Black Culture: Myth or Reality? *In* Afro-American Anthropology: Contemporary Perspectives. Norman E. Whitten, Jr. and John F. Szwed, eds. pp. 347-356. New York: The Free Press.

Boissevain, Jeremy
    1968. The Place of Non-Groups in the Social Sciences. Man (N.S.) 3(4):546-556.

Bottemanne, C. J.
    1959. Principles of Fisheries Development. Amsterdam: North-Holland.

Braithwaite, Lloyd
    1975. Social Stratification in Trinidad: A Preliminary Analysis. Kingston, Jamaica: Institute of Social and Economic Studies, University of the West Indies.

Brana-Shute, Gary
    1976. Drinking Shops and Social Structure: Some Ideas on Lower-Class West Indian Male Behavior. Urban Anthropology 5(1):53-68.

    1979. On the Corner: Male Social Life in a Paramaribo Creole Neighborhood. Assen, The Netherlands: Van Gorcum.

Brana-Shute, Gary and Rosemary Brana-Shute
    1980. The Unemployed of the Eastern Caribbean: Attitudes and Aspirations. Washington, D. C.: United States International Development Cooperation Agency, Agency for International Development.

Brierley, John S.
    1974. Small Farming in Grenada, West Indies. Manitoba Geographical Studies Number 4. Winnipeg, Manitoba: Department of Geography, University of Manitoba.

Brookes, Dennis
    1969. Who Will Go Back? Race Today 1(5):131-134.

Brown, Susan E.
1977. Household Composition and Variation in a Rural Dominican Village. Journal of Caribbean Family Studies 8(2):257-267.

Bryce-Laporte, Roy S.
1970. Crisis, Contraculture, and Religion Among West Indians in the Panama Canal Zone. *In* Afro-American Anthropology: Contemporary Perspectives. Norman E. Whitten, Jr. and John F. Szwed, eds. pp. 103-118. New York: The Free Press.

Burns, Sir Alan C.
1954. History of the British West Indies. London: Allen and Unwin.

Byrne, Joycelin
1969. Population Growth in St. Vincent. Social and Economic Studies 18:152-188.

Carmichael, A. C.
1833. Domestic Manners and Social Conditions of the White, Coloured, and Negro Population of the West Indies. 2 volumes. London: Whittaker, Treacher.

Census Research Programme
1973. 1970 Population Census of the Commonwealth Caribbean. Volume 4, Part 8. Kingston, Jamaica.

Chernick, Sidney E.
1978. The Commonwealth Caribbean: The Integrative Experience. Baltimore: Johns Hopkins University Press.

Clarke, Edith
1966. My Mother Who Fathered Me: A Study of the Family in Three Selected Communities in Jamaica. 2nd edition. London: Allen and Unwin.

1971. Land Tenure and the Family in Four Selected Communities in Jamaica. *In* Peoples and Cultures of the Caribbean. Michael M. Horowitz, ed. pp. 201-242. Garden City, New York: Natural History Press.

Cohen, Yehudi A.
1954. The Social Organization of a Selected Community in Jamaica. Social and Economic Studies 2(4):104-133.

1961. Patterns of Friendship. In Social Structure and Personality: A Casebook. Yehudi A. Cohen, ed. pp. 351-386. New York: Holt, Rinehart and Winston.

Cohen, Yehudi A., ed.
1971. Man in Adaptation: The Institutional Framework. Chicago: Aldine.

Coke, Thomas
1808. A History of the West Indies, Containing the Natural, Civil, and Ecclesiastical History of Each Island. Liverpool.

Colthurst, John B.
1977. The Colthurst Journal: Journal of a Special Magistrate in the Islands of Barbados and St. Vincent, July 1835-September 1838. Millwood, New York: KTO Press.

Comitas, Lambros
1964. Occupational Multiplicity in Rural Jamaica. Proceedings of the Annual Meeting of the American Ethnological Society, 1963. pp. 41-50. Seattle: University of Washington Press.

Crane, Julia G.
1971. Educated to Emigrate: The Social Organization of Saba. Assen, The Netherlands: Van Gorcum.

Crowley, Daniel J.
1957. Plural and Differential Acculturation in Trinidad. American Anthropologist 59:817-824.

Curtin, Phillip D.
1969. The Atlantic Slave Trade: A Census. Madison: University of Wisconsin Press.

Davenport, William
1968. The Family System of Jamaica. In Marriage, Family, and Residence. Paul Bohannan and John Middleton, eds. pp. 247-284. Garden City, New York: Natural History Press.

Davison, R. B.
1962. West Indian Migrants: Social and Economic Facts of Migration from the West Indies. London: Oxford University Press.

Davy, John
1971. The West Indies Before and Since Slave Emancipation. London: Frank Cass.

Deerr, Noel
1949. The History of Sugar. 2 volumes. London: Chapman and Hall.

Despres, Leo A.
1964. The Implications of Nationalist Politics in British Guiana for the Development of Cultural Theory. American Anthropologist 66:1051-1077.

Dirks, Robert
1972. Networks, Groups and Adaptation in an Afro-Caribbean Community. Man (N.S.) 7(4):565-585.

Doorhan, Isaac
1971. A Pre-Emancipation History of the West Indies. London: Collins.

Duncan, Ebenezer
1970. A Brief History of St. Vincent With Studies in Citizenship. 5th edition. Kingstown, St. Vincent: The Vincentian.

Eastern Caribbean Population Census
1963. Windward Islands Population Census 1960. Port-of-Spain, Trinidad: Central Statistical Office.

Ebanks, G. E., P. M. George, and C. E. Nobbe
1974. Patterns of Sex-Union Formation in Barbados. Canadian Review of Sociology and Anthropology 11(3):230-246.

Edwards, David
1961. An Economic Study of Small Farming in Jamaica. Kingston, Jamaica: Institute of Social and Economic Research, University of the West Indies.

362

Finkel, Herman J.
    1964. Attitudes Towards Land as a Factor in Agricultural Planning in the West Indies. Caribbean Studies 4:49-53.

    1971. Patterns of Land Tenure in the Leeward and Windward Islands and their Relevance to the Problems of Agricultural Development in the West Indies. *In* Peoples and Cultures of the Caribbean. Michael M. Horowitz, ed. pp. 291-304. Garden City, New York: Natural History Press.

Firth, Raymond
    1946. Malay Fishermen: Their Peasant Economy. London: Kegan Paul, Trench, Trubner.

    1951. Elements of Social Organization. London: Watts.

Fitchen, Janet M.
    1962. "Peasantry" as a Social Type. Proceedings of the Annual Meeting of the American Ethnological Society, 1961. pp. 114-119. Seattle: University of Seattle Press.

Foner, Nancy
    1978. Jamaican Farewell: Jamaican Migrants in London. Berkeley: University of California Press.

Foster, George M.
    1961. Interpersonal Relations in Peasant Societies. Human Organization 19:174-184.

    1963. The Dyadic Contract in Tzintzuntzan, II: Patron-Client Relationships. American Anthropologist 65:1280-1294.

    1967. Introduction: What is a Peasant? In Peasant Society: A Reader. Jack M. Potter, May N. Diaz, and George M. Foster, eds. pp. 2-14. Boston: Little, Brown.

Frank, Andre G.
    1969. Latin America: Underdevelopment or Revolution. New York: Monthly Review Press.

Fraser, Thomas M., Jr.
    1975. Class and Changing Bases of Elite Support in St. Vincent, West Indies. Ethnology 14:197-209.

Frazier, E. Franklin
1957. The Negro in the United States. New York: Macmillan.

1960. Introduction. *In* Caribbean Studies: A Symposium. Second Edition. Vera Rubin, ed. pp. v-viii. Seattle: University of Washington Press.

1966. The Negro Family in the United States. Chicago: University of Chicago Press.

Freeman, Gary P.
1982. Caribbean Migration to Britain and France: From Assimilation to Selection. Caribbean Review 11(1):30-33, 61-64.

Freeman, J. D.
1961. On the Concept of the Kindred. Journal of the Royal Anthropological Institute 91:192-220.

Freilich, Morris
1961. Serial Polygyny, Negro Peasants, and Model Analysis. American Anthropologist 63:955-975.

1968. Sex, Secrets, and Systems. *In* The Family in the Caribbean. Proceedings of the First Conference on the Family in the Caribbean. Stanford N. Gerber, ed. pp. 47-62. Rio Piedras, Puerto Rico: Institute of Caribbean Studies, University of Puerto Rico.

Friedman, Jonathan
1974. Marxism, Structuralism and Vulgar Materialism. Man (N.S.) 9(3):444-469.

Frucht, Richard
1968. Emigration, Remittances and Social Change: Aspects of the Social Field of Nevis, West Indies. Anthropologica (N.S.) 10(2):193-208.

1971. A Caribbean Social Type: Neither "Peasant" Nor "Proletarian". *In* Black Society in the New World. Richard Frucht, ed. pp. 98-104. New York: Random House.

Geertz, Clifford
 1959. Form and Variation in Balinese Village Structure. American Anthropologist 61:991-1012.

 1963. Agricultural Involution: Processes of Ecological Change in Indonesia. Berkeley and Los Angeles: University of California Press.

Gibbs, Bernard
 1947. A Plan of Development for the Colony of St. Vincent, Windward Islands, British West Indies. Port-of-Spain, Trinidad: Guardian Commercial Printery.

Goldberg, Richard S.
 1984. The Definition of Household: A Three-Dimensional Approach. Caribbean Studies 4(1):29-36.

Gonzalez, Nancie L. Solien
 1969. Black Carib Household Structure: A Study of Migration and Modernization. Seattle: University of Washington Press.

Gonzalez, Nancie L.
 1984. Rethinking the Consanguineal Household and Matrifocality. Ethnology 23(1):1-12.

Goode, William J.
 1966. Illegitimacy in Caribbean Social Structure. In The Unwed Mother. R. W. Roberts, ed. pp. 42-60. New York: Harper and Row.

Goody, Jack
 1972. Domestic Groups. Addison-Wesley Modular Publications 28:1-32.

Greenfield, Sidney M.
 1961. Socio-Economic Factors and Family Form: A Barbadian Case Study. Social and Economic Studies 10(1):72-85.

 1966. English Rustics in Black Skin: A Study of Modern Family Forms in a Pre-Industrialized Society. New Haven, Connecticut: College and University Press.

Handler, Jerome S.
1973. Some Aspects of Work Organization on Sugar Plantations in Barbados. *In* Work and Family Life: West Indian Perspectives. Lambros Comitas and David Lowenthal, eds. pp. 95-126. Garden City, New York: Anchor Books.

Harold, Cedric and Kenneth John
1966. St. Vincent: A Socio-Political Perspective. Flambeau 6:7-11.

Harris, Marvin
1968. The Rise of Anthropological Theory. New York: Crowell.

Heider, Karl G.
1972. Environment, Subsistence, and Society. Annual Review of Anthropology 1:207-221.

Helm, June
1962. The Ecological Approach in Anthropology. American Journal of Sociology 17:630-639.

Henney, Jeannette H.
1968. Spirit Possession Belief and Trance Behavior in a Religious Group in St. Vincent, British West Indies. Ph.D. Dissertation, Department of Anthropology, Ohio State University.

1980. Sex and Status: Women in St. Vincent. *In* A World of Women: Anthropological Studies of Women in the Societies of the World. Erica Bourguignon, ed. pp. 161-183. New York: Praeger.

Henriques, Fernando
1953. Family and Colour in Jamaica. London: Eyre and Spottiswoode.

Herskovits, Melville J.
1937. Life in a Haitain Valley. New York: Knopf.

1958. The Myth of the Negro Past. Boston: Beacon Press.

366

Herskovits, Melville J.
1966. The New World Negro: Selected Papers in Afroamerican Studies. Bloomington, Indiana: University of Indiana Press.

Herskovits, Melville J. and Frances S. Herskovits
1947. Trinidad Village. New York: Knopf.

Hill, Donald R.
1977. The Impact of Migration on the Metropolitan and Folk Society of Carriacou, Grenada. Anthropological Papers of the American Museum of Natural History 54(2):189-392.

Hillery, George A., Jr.
1955. Definitions of a Community: Areas of Agreement. Rural Sociology 20:111-123.

HMSO
1967. St. Vincent: Reports for the Years 1964 and 1965. London.

Horowitz, Michael M.
1960. A Typology of Rural Community Forms in the Caribbean. Anthropological Quarterly 33(4): 177-187.

1967a. Morne-Paysan: Peasant Village in Martinique. New York: Holt, Rinehart and Winston.

1967b. A Decision Model of Conjugal Patterns in Martinique. Man (N.S.) 2:477-488.

Hourihan John J.
1973. Youth Employment: Stubbs. In Windward Road: Contributions to the Anthropology of St. Vincent. Thomas M. Fraser, Jr., ed. pp. 29-34. Amherst, Massachusetts: Department of Anthropology, University of Massachusetts.

1975. Rule in Hairoun: A Study of the Politics of Power. Ph.D. Dissertation, Department of Anthropology, University of Massachusetts.

Hunter, David E. and Phillip Whitten
1976. The Study of Anthropology. New York: Harper and Row.

John, Kenneth R. V.

1966. Footnotes on Slavery. Flambeau 3:10-14.

1973. St. Vincent: A Political Kaleidoscope. *In* The Aftermath of Sovereignty: West Indian Perspectives. David Lowenthal and Lambros Comitas, eds. pp. 81-91. Garden City, New York: Anchor/Doubleday.

Johnson, Norman J. and Peggy R. Sanday

1971. Subcultural Variations in an Urban Poor Population. American Anthropologist 73:128-143.

Keesing, Roger M.

1976. Cultural Anthropology: A Contemporary Perspective. New York: Holt, Rinehart and Winston.

Kroeber, Alfred L.

1948. Anthropology. New York: Harcourt, Brace and Javanovich.

Kunstadter, Peter

1963. A Survey of the Consanguine or Matrifocal Family. American Anthropologist 65:56-66.

Laguerre, Michel S.

1982. Urban Life in the Caribbean: A Study of a Haitian Urban Community. Cambridge, Massachusetts: Schenkman.

Leacock, Eleanor B., ed.

1971. The Culture of Poverty: A Critique. New York: Simon and Schuster.

Levy, M. J., Jr. and L. A. Fallers

1959. The Family: Some Comparative Considerations. American Anthropologist 61:647-651.

Lewis, Oscar

1961. Some of My Best Friends are Peasants. Human Organization 19:179-180.

1966. The Culture of Poverty. Scientific American 215:19-25.

Lieber, Michael
    1981. Street Life: Afro-American Culture in Urban Trinidad. Cambridge, Massachusetts: Schenkman.

Liebow, Elliot
    1967. Tally's Corner: A Study of Negro Streetcorner Men. Boston: Little, Brown.

Lipton, Michael
    1980. Migration from Rural Areas of Poor Countries: The Impact on Rural Productivity and Income Distribution. World Development 8(1):1-24.

Lowenthal, David
    1961. Caribbean Views of Caribbean Land. Canadian Geographer 5(2):1-9.

    1972. West Indian Societies. London: Oxford University Press.

Lowenthal, David and Lambros Comitas
    1962. Emigration and Depopulation: Some Neglected Aspects of Population Geography. The Geographical Review 52(2):195-210.

Manners, Robert A.
    1960. Methods of Community-Analysis in the Caribbean. In Caribbean Studies: A Symposium. 2nd edition. Vera Rubin, ed. pp. 80-98. Seattle: University of Washington Press.

Manning, Frank E.
    1973. Black Clubs in Bermuda: Ethnography of a Play World. Ithaca, New York: Cornell University Press.

    1974. Nicknames and Number Plates in the British West Indies. Journal of American Folklore 87:123-132.

Marshall, Dawn I.
    1982. The History of Caribbean Migrations: The Case of the West Indies. Caribbean Review 11(1):6-9, 52-53.

Marshall, Woodville K.
1977. Introduction. *In* The Colthurst Journal: Journal of a Special Magistrate in the Islands of Barbados and St. Vincent, July 1835-September 1838. John B. Colthurst. pp. 1-41. Millwood, New York: KTO Press.

Mathieson, William L.
1967. British Slave Emacipation, 1839-1849. New York: Octagon Books.

Mayer, Adrian C.
1966. The Significance of Quasi-Groups in the Study of Complex Societies. *In* The Social Anthropology of Complex Societies. Michael Banton, ed. pp. 97-122. London: Tavistock.

McCary, Charles
1980. Along the Windwards. *In* Isles of the Caribbean. Robert L. Breedan, ed. pp. 88-113. Washington, D.C.: National Geographic Society.

McCoy, Terry L. and Charles H. Wood
1982. Caribbean Workers in the Florida Sugar Cane Industry. Gainsville, Florida: Center for Latin American Studies Occasional Paper No. 2, University of Florida.

Midgett, Douglas K.
1975. West Indian Ethnicity in Great Britain. *In* Migration and Development: Implications for Ethnic Identity and Political Conflict. Helen I. Safa and Brian Du Toit, eds. pp. 57-81. The Hague: Mouton.

Miller, S. M., Frank Reissman, and Arthur A. Seagull
1968. Poverty and Self-Indulgence: A Critique of the Non-Deferred Gratification Pattern. *In* Poverty in America: A Book of Readings. revised edition. Louis A. Ferman, Joyce L. Kornbluh, and Alan Haber, eds. pp. 416- 432. Ann Arbor: University of Michigan Press.

Mintz, Sidney W.
1968. Caribbean Society. International Encyclopedia of the Social Sciences 2:306-319.

370

Mintz, Sidney W.
1970. Foreward. *In* Afro-American Anthropology: Contemporary Perspectives. Norman E. Whitten, Jr. and John F. Szwed, eds. pp. 1-16. New York: The Free Press.

1971. The Caribbean as a Socio-Cultural Area. *In* Peoples and Cultures of the Caribbean: An Anthropological Reader. Michael M. Horowitz, ed. pp. 17-46. Garden City, New York: Natural History Press.

1974. Caribbean Transformations. Chicago: Aldine.

Mintz, Sidney W. and William Davenport, eds.
1961. Caribbean Social Structure. Social and Economic Studies 10(4):380-535.

Moran, Emilio F.
1979. Human Adaptability: An Introduction to Ecological Anthropology. North Scituate, Massachusetts: Duxbury.

Moynihan, Daniel P.
1965. The Negro Family: The Case for National Action. Washington, D.C.: United States Government Printing Office.

Murdock George P.
1965. Social Structure. New York: The Free Press.

Nag, Moni
1971. The Influence of Conjugal Behavior, Migration, and Contraception on Natality in Barbados. *In* Culture and Population. Steven Polgar, ed. pp. 105-123. Cambridge, Massachusetts: Schenkman.

Netting, Robert McC.
1968. Hill Farmers of Nigeria: Cultural Ecology of the Kofyar of the Jos Plateau. Seattle: University of Washington Press.

1971. The Ecological Approach in Cultural Study. Addison-Wesley Modular Publications 6:1-30.

New Democratic Party
1979. Manifesto 1979/80. New York: Aristographics.

O'Loughlin, Carleen
1968. Economic and Political Change in the Leeward and Windward Islands. New Haven, Connecticut: Yale University Press.

Orlove, Benjamin S.
1980. Ecological Anthropology. Annual Review of Anthropology 9:235-273.

Otterbein, Keith F.
1963. The Household Composition of the Andros Islanders. Social and Economic Studies 12:78-83.

1966. The Andros Islanders: A Study of Family Organization in the Bahamas. Lawrence, Kansas: University of Kansas Press.

1970. The Developmental Cycle of the Andros Household: A Diachronic Analysis. American Anthropologist 72:1412-1419.

Paine, Robert
1970. Anthropological Approaches to Friendship. Humanitas 6(2):139-159.

Paul, Max
1983. Black Families in Modern Bermuda. Göttingen, Federal Republic of Germany: Edition Herodot.

Philpott, Stuart B.
1968. Remittance Obligations, Social Networks, and Choice Among Montserratian Migrants in Britain. Man (N.S.) 3: 465-476.

1971. The Implications of Migration for Sending Societies: Some Theoretical Considerations. Proceedings of the Annual Meeting of the American Ethnological Society, 1970. pp. 9-20. University of Washington Press.

1973. West Indian Migration: The Montserrat Case. London: Athlone Press.

Pitt-Rivers, Julian A.
1954. The People of the Sierra. New York: Criterion Books.

Powell, Dorian L.
1982. Network Analysis: A Suggested Model for the Study of Women and the Family in Barbados. *In* Women and the Family. Joycelin Massiah, ed. pp. 131-162. Women in the Caribbean Project. Volume 2. Cave Hill, Barbabos: Institute for Social and Economic Research, University of the West Indies.

Proudfoot, Malcolm J.
1950. Population Movements in the Caribbean. Port-of-Spain, Trinidad: Central Secretariat.

Rappaport, Roy A.
1968. Pigs for the Ancestors. New Haven, Connecticut: Yale University Press.

1977. Ecology, Adaptation and the Ills of Functionalism (Being, Among Other Things, a Response to Jonathan Friedman). Michigan Discussions in Anthropology 2:138-190.

Redfield, Robert
1956. Peasant Society and Culture. Chicago: University of Chicago Press.

Reisman, Karl
1970. Cultural and Linguistic Ambiguity in a West Indian Village. *In* Afro-American Anthropology: Contemporary Perspectives. Norman E. Whitten, Jr. and John F. Szwed, eds. pp. 129-144. New York: The Free Press.

Reubens, Edwin P.
n.d. Migration and Development in the West Indies. Kingston, Jamaica: Institute of Social and Economic Research.

Richardson, Bonham C.
1975. Livelihood in Rural Trinidad in 1900. Annals of the Association of American Geographers 65(2):240-251.

1983. Caribbean Migrants: Environment and Human Survival on St. Kitts and Nevis. Knoxville: University of Tennessee Press.

Roberts, George W.
1955. Emigration from the Island of Barbados. Social and Economic Studies 4:245-288.

Roberts, George W. and Sonja A. Sinclair
1978. Women in Jamaica: Patterns of Reproduction and Family. Millwood, New York: KTO Press.

Rodman, Hyman
1959. On Understanding Lower-Class Behaviour. Social and Economic Studies 8:441-450.

1961. Marital Relationships in a Trinidad Village. Marriage and Family Living 23:166-170.

1963. The Lower-Class Value Stretch. Social Forces 42: 205-215.

1966. Illegitimacy in the Caribbean Social Structure: A Reconsideration. American Sociological Review 31(5):673-683.

1971. Lower-Class Families: The Culture of Poverty in Negro Trinidad. London: Oxford University Press.

Rubenstein, Hymie
1975. The Utilization of Arable Land in an Eastern Caribbean Valley. Canadian Journal of Sociology 1(2):157-167.

1976. Incest, Effigy Hanging, and Biculturation in a West Indian Village. American Ethnologist 3(4):765-781.

1977a. Economic History and Population Movements in an Eastern Caribbean Valley. Ethnohistory 24(1):19-45.

1977b. Diachronic Inference and the Pattern of Lower-Class Afro-Caribbean Marriage. Social and Economic Studies 26(2):202-216.

1980. Conjugal Behaviour and Parental Role Flexibility in an Afro-Caribbean Village. Canadian Review of Sociology and Anthropology 17(4):330-337.

1982a. Return Migration to the English-Speaking Caribbean: Review and Commentary. In Return Migration and Remittances: Developing a Caribbean Perspective. William F. Stinner, Klaus de Albuquerque, and Roy S. Bryce-Laporte, eds. pp. 3-33. Research Institute on Immigration and Ethnic Studies Occasional Paper No. 3. Washington, D.C.: Smithsonian Institution.

Rubenstein, Hymie
    1982b. The Impact of Remittances in the Rural Caribbean: Notes on the Literature. *In* Return Migration and Remittances: Developing a Caribbean Perspective. William F. Stinner, Klaus de Albuquerque, and Roy S. Bryce-Laporte, eds. pp. 237-265. Research Institute on Immigration and Ethnic Studies Occasional Paper No. 3. Washington, D.C.: Smithsonian Institution.

    1983. Caribbean Family and Household Organization: Some Conceptual Clarifications. Journal of Comparative Family Studies 14(3):283-298.

    1984. Occupational Complexity in an Afro-Caribbean Village. Journal of Caribbean Studies 4(1):111-140.

Rubin, Vera and Lambros Comitas, eds.
    1976. Ganja in Jamaica: The Effects of Marijuana Use. Garden City, New York: Anchor Press/Doubleday.

Ryan, William
    1971. Blaming the Victim. New York: Vintage Books.

Sacks, Karen
    1979. Causality and Change on the Upper Nile. American Ethnologist 6(3):437-448.

Sahlins, Marshall D.
    1968. Culture and Environment: The Study of Cultural Ecology. *In* Theory in Anthropology: A Sourcebook. Robert A. Manners and David Kaplan, eds. pp. 367-373. Chicago: Aldine.

Sanford, Margaret
    1974. A Socialization in Ambiguity: Child-Lending in a British West Indian Society. Ethnology 13:393-400.

    1975. To Be Treated Like a Child in the Home: Black Carib Child Lending in a British West Indian Society. *In* Socialization and Communication in Primary Groups. Thomas Williams, ed. pp. 159-181. The Hague: Mouton.

Schlesinger, Benjamin
    1968a. Family Patterns in Jamaica: Review and Commentary. Journal of Marriage and the Family 30(1):136-148.

Schlesinger, Benjamin
  1968b. Family Patterns in the English-Speaking Caribbean. Journal of Marriage and the Family 30(1):149-154.

Service, Elman R.
  1962. Primitive Social Organization. New York: Random House.

Shephard, Charles
  1831. An Historical Account of the Island of St. Vincent. London: Ridgway and Sons.

Shimkin, Demitri B., Edith M. Shimkin, and Dennis A. Frate, eds.
  1978. The Extended Family in Black Societies. The Hague: Mouton.

Slater, Marian K.
  1977. The Caribbean Family: Legitimacy in Martinique. New York: St. Martin's.

Smith, Michael G.
  1955. A Framework for Caribbean Studies. Mona, Jamaica: Extra-Mural Department, University College of the West Indies.

  1956. Community Organization in Rural Jamaica. Social and Economic Studies 5(3):295-312.

  1957. The African Heritage in the Caribbean. In Caribbean Studies: A Symposium. Vera Rubin, ed. pp. 34-46. Seattle: University of Seattle Press.

  1960. Social and Cultural Pluralism. In Social and Cultural Pluralism in the Caribbean. Vera Rubin, ed. Special Publication, Annals of the New York Academy of Sciences 83:763-785.

  1962a. West Indian Family Structure. Seattle: University of Washington Press.

  1962b. Kinship and Community in Carriacou. New Haven, Connecticut: Yale University Press.

  1965a. The Plural Society in the British West Indies. Berkeley: University of California Press.

Smith, Michael G.

1965b. Stratification in Grenada. Berkeley and Los Angeles: University of California Press.

1966. Introduction. *In* My Mother Who Fathered Me: A Study of the Family in Three Selected Communities in Jamaica. 2nd edition. Edith Clarke. pp. i-xliv. London: Allen and Unwin.

Smith, Raymond T.

1956. The Negro Family in British Guiana: Family Structure and Social Status in the Villages. London: Routedge and Kegan Paul.

1960. The Family in the Caribbean. *In* Caribbean Studies: A Symposium. 2nd edition. Vera Rubin, ed. pp. 67-79. Seattle: University of Washington Press.

1961. Review of Social and Cultural Pluralism in the Caribbean. American Anthropologist 63:155-157.

1964. Culture and Social Structure in the Caribbean: Some Recent Work on Family and Kinship Studies. Comparative Studies in Society and History 6(1):24-46.

1970. Social Stratification in the Caribbean. *In* Essays in Comparative Social Stratification. Leonard Plotnicov and Arthur Tuden, eds. pp. 43-76. Pittsburgh: University of Pittsburgh Press.

1973. The Matrifocal Family. The Character of Kinship. Jack Goody, ed. pp. 121-144. Cambridge: Cambridge University Press.

Solien, Nancie L.

1960. Household and Family in the Caribbean: Some Definitions and Concepts. Social and Economic Studies 9(1):101-106.

Spiro, Melford E.

1953. Is the Family Universal? American Anthropologist 56:839-846.

St. Vincent

1871. Saint Vincent Government Gazette. Kingstown, St. Vincent: Government Printing Office.

St. Vincent

1881. Saint Vincent Government Gazette. Kingstown, St. Vincent: Government Printing Office.

1891. Saint Vincent Government Gazette. Kingstown, St. Vincent: Government Printing Office.

1899. Saint Vincent Government Gazette. Kingstown, St. Vincent: Government Printing Office.

1912. St. Vincent Blue Book, 1910-1911. Kingstown, St. Vincent: Government Printing Office.

1963a. Annual Administration Reports of the Colony of Saint Vincent for the Year 1959. Kingstown, St. Vincent: Government Printing Office.

1963b. Annual Report of the Department of Labour for 1956. Kingstown, St. Vincent: Government Printing Office.

1965. Annual Administration Reports of the Colony of Saint Vincent for the Year 1960. Kingstown, St. Vincent: Government Printing Office.

1967a. Annual Administration Reports of the Colony of Saint Vincent for the Year 1963. Kingstown, St. Vincent: Government Printing Office.

1967b. Report on the Postal Department for the Year 1964. Kingstown, St. Vincent: Government Printing Office.

1969. Annual Report of the Royal Saint Vincent Police Force for the Year 1968. Kingstown, St. Vincent: Government Printing Office.

1970. St. Vincent Digest of Statistics for the Year 1970, Number 20. Kingstown, St. Vincent: Statistical Unit.

1976. St. Vincent Digest of Statistics for the Year 1975, Number 25. Kingstown, St. Vincent: Statistical Unit.

St. Vincent
   1979. St. Vincent Digest of Statistics for the Year 1978, Number 28. Kingstown, St. Vincent: Statistical Unit, Ministry of Finance.

   1980. Budget Address. Kingstown, St. Vincent.

   1983. Digest of Statistics for the Year 1981, Number 31. Kingstown, St. Vincent: Statistical Unit, Ministry of Finance, Planning, and Development.

   1984. Digest of Statistics for the Year 1982, Number 32. Kingstown, St. Vincent: Statistical Unit, Ministry of Finance, Planning, and Development.

St. Vincent Labour Party
   1979. Manifesto--General Elections. Kingstown, St. Vincent: Reliance Press.

Stack, Carol B.
   1970. The Kindred of Viola Jackson: Residence and Family Organization of an Urban Black American Family. In Afro-American Anthropology: Contemporary Perspectives. Norman E. Whitten, Jr. and John F. Szwed, eds. pp. 303-312. New York: The Free Press.

   1974. All Our Kin: Strategies for Survival in a Black Community. New York: Harper and Row.

Stampp, Kenneth M.
   1956. The Peculiar Institution: Slavery in the Ante-Bellum South. New York: Vintage.

Starbird, Ethel A.
   1979. St. Vincent, the Grenadines, and Grenada: Taking It as It Comes. National Geographic 156:399-425.

Stavenhagen, Rodolfo
   1975. Social Classes in Agrarian Societies. Garden City, New York: Anchor/Doubleday.

379

Steward, Julian H.
1955. Theory of Culture Change. Urbana, Illinois: University of Illinois Press.

1956. The People of Puerto Rico. Urbana, Illinois: University of Illinois Press.

Thomas-Hope, Elizabeth M.
1978. The Establishment of a Migration Tradition: British West Indian Movements to the Hispanic Caribbean in the Century After Emancipation. In Caribbean Social Relations. Colin G. Clarke, ed. pp. 66-81. Centre for Latin-American Studies Monograph Series No. 8. Liverpool: University of Liverpool.

Todaro, Michael P.
1981. Economic Development in the Third World. 2nd edition. New York: Longman.

Tumin, Melvin M.
1967. Social Stratification: The Forms and Functions of Inequality. Englewood Cliffs, New Jersey: Prentice-Hall.

University of the West Indies Development Mission
1969. The Development Problem in St. Vincent. Kingston, Jamaica: Institute of Social and Economic Research, University of the West Indies.

Valentine, Charles A.
1968. Culture and Poverty: A Critique and Counter-Proposals. Chicago: University of Chicago Press.

1971. The "Culture of Poverty": Its Scientific Significance and its Implications for Action. In The Culture of Poverty: A Critique. Eleanor B. Leacock, ed. pp. 193-225. New York: Simon and Schuster.

1972. Black Studies and Anthropology: Scholarly and Political Interests in Afro-American Culture. Addison-Wesley Modular Publications 15:1-53.

Vanstone, James W.
1974. Athapaskan Adaptations: Hunters and Fishermen of the Subarctic Forest. Chicago: Aldine.

Vayda, Andrew P.
   1975. New Directions in Ecology and Ecological Anthropology.
   Annual Review of Anthropology 4:293-306.

Vayda, Andrew P. and Roy A. Rappaport
   1968. Ecology, Cultural and Noncultural. *In* Introduction to
   Cultural Anthropology. J. A. Clifton, ed. pp. 477-497. Boston:
   Houghton Mifflin.

The Vincentian
   1979. The Way the Votes Were Cast. Kingstown, St. Vincent:
   The Vincentian Press.

Voydanoff, Patricia and Hyman Rodman
   1978. Marital Careers in Trinidad. Journal of Marriage and the
   Family 40(1):157-163.

Wagley, Charles
   1960. Plantation America: A Culture Sphere. *In* Caribbean
   Studies: A Symposium. 2nd edition. Vera Rubin, ed. pp. 3-13.
   Seattle: University of Washington Press.

Weber, Max
   1966. Class, Status and Party. *In* Class, Status, and Power:
   Social Stratification in Comparative Perspective. Reinhard
   Bendix and Seymour M. Lipsett, eds. pp. 21-28. New York: The
   Free Press.

West Indian Census 1946
   1950. Part H. Census of the Windward Islands. Kingston,
   Jamaica: Central Bureau of Statistics.

Whitten, Norman E., Jr.
   1965. Class, Kinship, and Power in an Ecuadorian Town: The
   Negroes of San Lorenzo. Stanford, California: Stanford University Press.

   1967. Adaptation and Adaptability as Processes of Microevolu-
   tionary Change in New World Negro Communities. Unpublished
   paper presented at the Annual Meeting of the American
   Anthropological Association.

Whitten, Norman E., Jr. and John F. Szwed
 1970. Introduction. *In* Afro-American Anthropology: Contemporary Perspectives. Norman E. Whitten, Jr. and John F. Szwed, eds. pp. 23-60. New York: The Free Press.

Whitten, Norman E., Jr. and Alvin W. Wolfe
 1973. Network Analysis. *In* Handbook of Social and Cultural Anthropology. John J. Honigmann, ed. pp. 717-746. Chicago: Rand McNally.

Williams, Eric
 1964. Capitalism and Slavery. London: Andre Deutsch.

 1970. From Columbus to Castro: The History of the Caribbean, 1492-1969. London: Andre Deutsch.

Wilson, Peter J.
 1969. Reputation and Respectability: A Suggestion for Caribbean Ethnology. Man (N.S.) 4:70-84.

 1973. Crab Antics: The Social Anthropology of English-Speaking Negro Societies of the Caribbean. New Haven, Connecticut: Yale University Press.

Wolf, Eric R.
 1955. Types of Latin American Peasantry: A Preliminary Discussion. American Anthropologist 57:452-471.

 1966. Kinship, Friendship, and Patron-Client Relations in Complex Societies. *In* The Social Anthropology of Complex Societies. Michael Banton, ed. pp. 1-22. London: Tavistock.

World Bank
 1979. Current Economic Position and Prospects of St. Vincent. Report Number 2438-CRB. Latin American and Caribbean Regional Office.

 1980. World Tables. 2nd edition. Baltimore: The John Hopkins University Press.

Wright, G.
 1929. Economic Conditions in St. Vincent, B.W.I. Economic Geography 5:236-259.

Yanagisako, Sylvia J.
    1979. Family and Household: The Analysis of Domestic Groups. Annual Review of Anthropology 8:161-205.

Young, Virginia H.
    1974. A Black American Socialization Pattern. American Ethnologist 1:405-413.

Young, Sir William
    1795. An Account of the Black Charaibs in the Island of St. Vincent's With the Charaib Treaty of 1773, and Other Original Documents. London: Sewell, Cornhill and Knight and Triphook.

Index

388

Poverty
causes and consequences 3, 7-8,
333-334
culture of 7, 131-132, 219, 345-
347
in Leeward Village 3, 79, 129-
131
See also St. Vincent, poverty in

Powell, Dorian L. 221, 223
Proudfoot, Malcolm J. 45, 72, 73

Rappaport, Roy A. 4-7
Redfield, Robert 103
Reisman, Karl 2, 343, 349
Replaceability 136, 226-227, 234,
341
Reputation 109-113, 129, 131-132
and sexual behavior 257-259
See also Respectability
Respectability
and occupations 133, 135-136
and sexual behavior 257-259
and stratification 66, 109-110,
125, 127-129, 131,132
See also Reputation
Reubens, Edwin P. 74, 75
Richardson, Bonham C. 25, 44, 72,
73, 76, 193, 198-200, 203, 214,
215, 337
Roberts, George W. 9, 40, 61, 220,
249, 267, 268, 270
Rodman, Hyman 2, 7, 9, 80, 98, 131,
132, 179, 219-221, 223, 226-228-
234, 239, 241, 242, 246, 257,
258, 260, 265, 266, 291, 312,
336, 337, 340, 342, 343, 349
Rubenstein, Hymie 2, 44, 77, 86,
113, 133, 171, 185, 200, 242,
251, 292
Rubin, Vera 220
Ryan, William 346

St. Vincent
agricultural decline 30-31, 47-48
agricultural exports 8, 41, 47-48
and colonialism 13, 26-28, 31
economic decline after Emancipation 40-42, 45
economic dependency 50-51
economy during slavery 28-31
geography 19-22
infrastructure 8
population 19, 28, 39
poverty in 12, 23, 25, 67-69
Sacks, Karen 25, 154, 155
Sahlins, Marshall D. 5, 6
Sanday, Peggy R. 345
Sanford, Margaret 227, 244, 246,
304
Schlesinger, Benjamin 219
Seagull, Arthur A. 346
Service, Elman R. 1, 5, 24, 53,
65-67, 82, 99, 126, 128, 129,
133, 135, 142,145, 149, 151, 159,
199, 214, 326
Sexuality
constraints on 263-265
and economics 261-263
learning about 257, 263
normative status of 265-266
and reputation 257-258
and respectability 258-259
See also Extra-residential mating
Shephard, Charles 19, 26-28, 32, 38,
39, 50, 88, 91, 95
Shimkin, Demitri B. 223, 338
Shimkin, Edith M. 223, 338
Siblingship 248
Sinclair, Sonja A. 9, 220, 249, 267
Slater, Marian K. 9, 55, 80, 220,
221, 266
Slavery
adaptation to 35-38
economic decline during 30-31
family life during 37-39